S0-ADE-983

WITHDRAWN

932 R497e

Rice, Michael, 1928-

Egypt's making

ENTERED FEB 1 6 2005

EGYPT'S MAKING

Michael Rice's bold, original work evokes the fascination and wonder of the most ancient period of Egypt's history, from the origins of the Egyptian state to the end of the Old Kingdom. Combining detailed attention to archaeological evidence with a dynamic and readable narrative, the text covers a vast range of topics. These include

- the origins of the first Egyptians
- the roots of the kingship
- the development of the nation-state
- early cities such as Hierakonpolis, Naqada and Abydos
- the splendours of the Pyramid Age
- the nature and effects of Egypt's contact with Western Asia
- the earliest development of the historic Egyptian personality.

The final chapter draws on Jungian theory, exploring the psychological forces that contributed to Egypt's special character, and which account for her continuing allure up to the present day.

Wholly revised and updated in the light of the many discoveries made since its first publications, *Egypt's Making* is a scholarly yet imaginative approach to this compelling ancient civilization.

Michael Rice has published extensively on Egypt and the Near East, including *Egypt's Legacy* (Routledge pbk 2003), *Who's Who in Ancient Egypt* (Routledge 1999), *The Power of the Bull* (Routledge 1997) and *The Archaeology of the Arabian Gulf* (Routledge 1994). He has established museums throughout the Arabian peninsula states. He was appointed a CMG in 2002 and awarded the Order of Bahrain (1st class) in 2003.

COLUMBIA COLLEGE LIBRARY
600 S. MICHIGAN AVENUE
CHICAGO, IL 60605
WITHDRAWN

EGYPT'S MAKING

The origins of Ancient Egypt 5000–2000 BC

Michael Rice

Second Edition

Routledge
Taylor & Francis Group

LONDON AND NEW YORK

First edition published 1990
Paperback edition first published 1991
Reprinted 1993, 1995

Second edition published 2003
by Routledge

11 New Fetter Lane, London EC4P 4EE

Simultaneously published in the USA and Canada
by Routledge
29 West 35th Street, New York, NY 10001

Routledge is an imprint of the Taylor & Francis Group

© 1990, 1991, 2003 Michael Rice

Typeset in Garamond by Wearset Ltd, Boldon, Tyne and Wear
Printed and bound in Great Britain by The Cromwell Press,
Trowbridge, Wiltshire

All rights reserved. No part of this book may be reprinted or reproduced or
utilized in any form or by any electronic, mechanical, or other means, now
known or hereafter invented, including photocopying and recording, or in any
information storage or retrieval system, without permission in writing from
the publishers.

British Library Cataloguing in Publication Data
A catalogue record for this book is available from the British Library

Library of Congress Cataloging in Publication Data
A catalog record for this book has been requested

ISBN 0-415-26874-5 (hbk)
ISBN 0-415-26875-3 (pbk)

Formative influences in the political and social organization and in the iconography of most ancient Egypt, the appearance of the earliest evidence of the historic Egyptian identity, and the nature and extent of Egypt's contact with southwestern Asia, notably Sumer and Elam, and the lands bordering the Arabian Gulf.

CONTENTS

ILLUSTRATIONS

Figures

Maps

INTRODUCTION TO THE
NEW EDITION

In the years which have passed since *Egypt's Making* was first published (1990) the study of the early periods of Egypt's history has made a number of significant advances. Many of the accepted verities which applied then have now been revised, in some cases drastically; much new information has come to light, demanding the reappraisal of previous, staunchly held convictions.

These considerations led to the conclusion that a revised edition of the book should be undertaken. It has been in print continuously since its first publication and, broadly, seems to have stood the test of time. Its survival has been gratifying, the more so since it was avowedly not put forward as a work with scholarly pretensions.

Books seem sometimes to get themselves written because there is something in the air which makes their production especially timely. I wrote *Egypt's Making* primarily because I was deeply interested in the influences which led to Egypt becoming the first nation-state in the history of the world. At the time there seemed to be little readily accessible information available to the reasonably well-informed but non-professional reader who might wish to acquire it. M.A. Hoffman's brilliant *Egypt before the Pharaohs* went some way towards providing the sort of thing that I wanted; from an earlier generation W.B. Emery's *Archaic Egypt* had for long been virtually the only popular publication in the English language which dealt with Egypt's origins since the seminal series of monographs produced, year in, year out, by the indefatigable William Matthew Flinders Petrie at the turn of the nineteenth century and the early years of the twentieth.

Petrie's excavations remained of fundamental importance, though many of his conclusions were no longer valid, but inevitably such works were dated. Emery's work was particularly significant though some of his conclusions are no longer sustained, but it is the record of a most singular achievement by a scholar who in his time opened up an awareness of an epoch which was otherwise hopelessly obscure. I would not presume to thrust myself into their company (though I knew Emery slightly and he was always invariably kind) but I thought that it would be agreeable and perhaps rewarding to look at the issues involved and to see what I might make of them.

Then there was the particular perspective from which I had come to view Egypt in the course of the several decades of my professional life which has been involved with the archaeology of the Arabian peninsula and the Arabian Gulf, through the establishment of learned journals on the archaeology of the region,[1] the organization of Departments of Antiquities[2] and the creation of museums, thirteen in all, throughout the Arabian peninsular states.[3] This work had made me deeply aware of the importance of recognizing the common or related experience of the cultures of the ancient Near East as a whole. I became especially interested in the evidence of the influence of early western Asiatic cultures, of Sumer and Elam (southern Mesopotamia and south western Iran respectively), on the nascent culture of the Nile Valley.

These and similar themes seemed suddenly to seize the interest of scholars in the field. Books and studies began to appear reviewing the origins of the Egyptian state and, with the arrival of Arabian archaeology as a discrete discipline, a process which had only begun in the 1960s and 1970s and in which I had played a minor part, attention was occasionally focused on the interconnections between Mesopotamia, Elam and early Egypt. My book happened to arrive at the same time and without doubt profited by the coincidence.

The upshot of this process has been, in large part, effectively the rewriting of *Egypt's Making*. I have attempted to bring up to date the contents of the book and to introduce much of the new material which has become available over the interval between its original writing and the publication of this edition. I have been immeasurably helped by the books on this period of Egyptian history which have appeared during the past decade. I have made some reparation for the use which I have made of them in the Acknowledgements which follow these introductory pages.

Perhaps because of the influence of this most benign civilization, Egyptologists tend to be courteous, sympathetic people, on whom the benevolence of the civilization has rubbed off. It cannot always have been easy: for some bizarre reason, which I no more understand now than when I drew attention to the phenomenon in *Egypt's Making*, the study of ancient Egypt does attract some very strange people, all of them with very firmly held opinions of an often peculiar character, on the irrefutable correctness of which they insist vociferously, in ever larger, more densely argued volumes.

Why Egyptology should attract this fringe of committed eccentrics is not clear to me, but it has always been so, at least since the seventeenth century when the Great Pyramid started to feature in the writings of European travellers, many of whom began to weave fantasies about its construction and purpose. It must be very tiresome for professional Egyptologists to be told emphatically and often not very politely, that they have got it all wrong, *it* being the basis of their professional training which they are sternly abjured to throw aside and are roundly condemned for not doing so. Most of the more sophisticated members of the profession seem generally able to rise above the flood of argument which might seem likely to engulf those of lesser calibre. However, some of the smaller fry, perhaps less confident of their own status and reputations, have a tendency to respond like the lesser clergy in the late Middle Ages, faced with heretical opinions. 'Anathema, anathema' they cry, to any who will listen.

It is difficult now to write an overview of the development of Egypt's early civilization and not to notice some of the more sensational issues which have caught the attention of many Egyptophiles and of the producers of the more vividly devised television programmes. That there are many anomalies in the evidence of all great ancient societies, and in none more so than in Egypt, is beyond question. What is less defensible is to seize on an anomaly – signs of degradation of the stone from which the Sphinx is built, the age and purpose of the Giza Pyramids and, one of my own favourites, the puzzling way in which the granite facing stones are overlaid on the Valley Temple of Khafre – and then to pile fantasy upon hypothesis.

Because so many of the lay public and practitioners of other scientific and academic disciplines are now exposed to such a welter of information (of one sort and another) on matters which touch Egyptology it does not serve the study well simply to attempt to brush away any expression of interest, even if it may be judged misguided, without giving it the courtesy of a considered reply. It is not enough to say that all Egyptologists *know* that the Giza pyramids were tombs when clearly a great many people (not, I hasten to say, myself) think otherwise.

But there are two aspects of Egypt's early history which have become increasingly important to me over the years, which are reflected in this revised text. First, there is my unbounded admiration for the *political* sophistication which the founders of the Egyptian state displayed, from the very beginning of their program to create a unified political construct in the Nile Valley. This entailed ensuring the acceptance of a common cultural identity along the length of the Valley, eventually extending from the first cataract to the Mediterranean. It required the creation and acceptance of institutions and systems of social organization from south to north. It demanded a complex bureaucracy and a system of government which in essence would have been recognizable in most developed regions of the world in the first half of the twentieth century. It revealed a sensitive understanding of the balance necessary for all rulers to achieve between coercion, persuasion and reconciliation. Having some modest experience of the ways of government in the Near and Middle East and an abiding interest in the vagaries of politics and politicians, this aspect of Egypt's emergence as a nation-state, often taken for granted requires, I believe, recognition and respect which it is only now achieving.

It has been interesting to observe what appears to have been a shift in the attitudes of scholars – and others – to aspects of the early centuries of Egypt's existence as a nation-state. For a long time there have been a number of unassailable, unarguable truths asserted about such matters as the age of the pyramids and Sphinx and the methods which were used to construct them. Gradually, however, some of the most firmly held opinions have begun to be conditioned as new researches (and new researchers) appear on the Egyptological scene.

One of the most interesting is the gradual replacement of the esoteric explanation of the wonders of Ancient Egypt by a more thorough and, it might be said, often a more objective examination of the physical and material evidence of the construction of the monuments. A product of this process has been an increasing respect for the skills of Egyptian craftsmen in the Early Dynastic period and the early years of the Old Kingdom. To focus on the technology of Ancient Egypt and bring to its study the benefits of modern technology and research is certain to produce answers to some of the questions which baffle Egyptologists and technically-minded observers alike.

An effect of a slightly different slant being brought to a familiar field of study is the question of the extent of the Egyptians' use of stone in their early (i.e. pre-Old Kingdom) architecture. The conventional view has long been that only in the Third Dynasty did the use of stone achieve monumental proportions, signalled by the astonishing splendour and the inherent technology of the Step Pyramid complex. Nothing can detract from the magnificence of that achievement but it is now clear that stone was more generally employed, in the Second Dynasty for example and at Helwan at an even earlier time, in the First Dynasty. These factors and the discovery of monumentally worked stone blocks, set up in an astronomical alignment in the desert far to the south of Egypt and dating from the seventh millennium BC, have demanded a revision of past attitudes and the recognition that Egypt's millennia-long involvement with the crafting of monumental stonework is of far greater antiquity than was originally believed. From this one realization will stem a realignment of many beliefs about the beginnings of the civilization of Ancient Egypt.

This having been said, it must be acknowledged that it would be perverse to write about the monuments on the plateau at Giza and ignore the controversies which have sprung up around them in recent years.[4] Controversy and the pyramids and Sphinx are no strangers to each other; monuments which have attracted so much wonder over the centuries similarly have attracted speculation of all sorts, from considered scientific appraisal to more imaginative, even fervid fancies. In brief, the propositions which have been advanced about the structures and purpose of the Khufu, Khafre and Menkaure pyramids and the other major constructions linked with them, spatially and in likely purpose, may be summarized as follows:

- there is no direct evidence that the three pyramids were built by or for the three kings with whose names they are associated, though a tradition that they were so associated in New Kingdom times at least is witnessed by an inscription of Amenhotep II;
- there is no firm evidence that the pyramid identified with Khufu was intended as his or anyone else's tomb;
- the layout of the three pyramids on the plateau replicate the distribution of the three stars in Orion's Belt in the constellation Orionis and the relationship of these stars to the Milky Way replicates the relationship of the three pyramids to the River Nile;
- the date at which the pyramids were first planned, if not in part built, was greatly earlier than the conventional date of their (final) construction in the second half of the third millennium BC;
- the Sphinx, as noted earlier, appears to display signs of weathering which can only be the result of heavy and persistent rainfall over an extended time-scale, a climatic event which could not have occurred in the past seven thousand years of hyperaridity;
- the Valley Temple associated with the Causeway and pyramid of King Khafre represents a style of building unlike any other in Egypt except 'the Tomb of Osiris', conventionally associated with King Seti I and both should be recognized as originating from a much earlier time.

The principal contention of the proponents of what has come to be called, often disparagingly, 'alternative Egyptology' is that the Giza monuments are relics of a lost civilization, considerably older than the dates conventionally attributed to them.[5] Thus the Sphinx has been accorded a pedigree which, on the estimate of the distinguished geologist who has examined the evidence of weathering, would have its construction dated to 7000–5000 BC, an estimate considered conservative by some, who would set its construction back still further, to c.10500 BC, on the basis of supposed astronomical computations.

Later studies,[6] taking into account that there was heavy and protracted rain in northern Upper Egypt throughout much of the fourth millennium, have proposed that this could explain the degradation visible today in the architecture of the Sphinx. This view would also lend support to the contention that the Sphinx and other of the Giza monuments should be attributed to the Early Dynastic period, thus being dated to several hundred years before their conventional dating, though eschewing the more extravagant dates which have been proposed for them.

The two 'ventilation shafts' of the pyramid traditionally identified with King Khufu are said to be aligned with the constellation of Orion and with ά Canis Major (Sirius), which were associated with Osiris and Isis respectively. Robotic investigation of one of the shafts has revealed a limestone plug with two copper insets, in the upper reaches of the shaft.[7] Further investigation of this phenomenon by the German engineer whose robot-mounted camera made the discovery was forbidden by the Egyptian Supreme Council of Antiquities, until late in 2002. A much heralded breaching of the limestone plug was broadcast to a large international audience, in a television program sponsored by National Geographic.

It was, as most cynical observers had already forecast, an anti-climax of an appropriately monumental order. Behind the plug, once optimistically described as a door, was simply a small, empty space.

The proposal that the three pyramids were aligned with the three stars in Orion's Belt seemed plausible and initially attracted support from orthodox Egyptologists. That terrestrial monuments should mimic the heavenly bodies seemed quite acceptable in the light of the Egyptians' skill in employing stellar alignments to orient large structures like the pyramids themselves as well as their evident enthusiasm for stellar associations in the early centuries of the Dual Kingdom. The general proposition, 'As Above, so Below' was one which had a special appeal to the people of Ancient Egypt. However, subsequent workings of the calculations involved have set doubt on the projections of the relative position of Menkaure, which is out of alignment with its two colleagues and does not align with the star Mintaka (δ Orionis), the third of the stars in Orion's Belt either.[8]

As to the purpose for which the pyramids were built, there is no dispute that those pyramids which are thought to have preceded the supposed date of the construction of the Giza group, Netjerykhet's (in the past, more generally known as Djoser) Step Pyramid and those of his successors and the Maidum pyramid of Sneferu were intended as tombs, as were those of the later kings of the Old and Middle Kingdoms. There is plenty of evidence that in the later periods of history the Egyptians associated the three pyramids with the three kings. This of course proves nothing more than that they did so but the record of the Egyptians' assessment of their own past should never be lightly dismissed.

The Valley Temple of King Khafre, described above, does appear to be architecturally anomalous. The raising of the great monoliths which are part of its internal structure, some of them said to weigh two hundred tons, represents a formidable logistical and engineering task. Whilst the skill of Egyptian engineers is confirmed by the presence of countless great monuments, the question of the manipulation of Khafre's lintels, all two hundred tons of them, requires an explanation. Their presence is one of the genuine mysteries of the Giza plateau. No explanation so far advanced, including the suggestion that the Egyptians were able to lift exceptionally heavy weights by the application of sonics, has been found convincing.

The evidence of the degradation of the limestone underlay of the Valley Temple's exterior walls must be presumed to have taken a significant period of time, which implies that the present granite casing may have been imposed on a long-standing structure which, like the Sphinx, is taken to have been degraded by the action of heavy and consistent rainfall.[9] This does not explain why the under surface of the granite casing was apparently cut and shaped to butt on to the degraded sandstone, rather than the other way about, which would certainly have been easier to achieve.

That there are considerable anomalies in the architecture and likely age of the Giza monuments is indisputable. Giza is not unique in this; there are aspects of the architecture and construction of the great European cathedrals which are still baffling. That such anomalies indicate the intervention of refugees from Atlantis, extraterrestrials from wherever or the existence of a lost high culture from Neolithic times, is much less certain, to express one's doubts no more forcefully.

The search for explanations alternative to accepted scholarship is always rewarding for those who exist happily in the margins of an otherwise unexceptionable discipline and such indulgence will obviously continue. Exasperating though it must be for professionals, it is a perfectly proper activity for those who believe that they have a point of view to express and convictions to defend. Simply to attempt to silence them by ridicule rather than by burning at the stake is unlikely to be any more successful than were past attempts to stamp out heresy. The time must surely be approaching when some sort of international project to examine the anomalous areas should be invoked, if only to define the present extent – or limits – of Egyptology.

That the ancients were capable of extraordinary achievements in remote times is undoubted. Archaeology, though it insists on its essentially scientific basis is fundamentally humanist, concerned to erect the least improbable hypothesis from a multitude of inexactitudes. Egypt is not the only land whose archaeology is as rich in anomalies as it is in treasures of the human spirit; it is simply that there is more of everything there and more of its remains inspire wonder. Yet consider an artefact from another, totally remote and different culture and from a vastly more distant time than any work from Egypt, the Lion-Man of Hohlenstein-Stadel,[10] a site in central Germany, a land whose past could hardly be compared with that of Egypt. The Lion-Man is a superbly carved figure in mammoth ivory, approximately ten inches high, intricate and subtle in craftsmanship and decoration. It has been securely dated, according to its excavators, to *thirty two thousand* years before the present. What sort of culture was abroad in Germany in Aurignacian times which could produce an artefact of this quality? Such a dating and such an artefact makes even a twelve thousand year-old Sphinx seem parvenu. All that is certain is that Egypt is full of wonders and she will continue to astonish, Atlanteans and extraterrestrials notwithstanding.

Revising a book like *Egypt's Making* provides an opportunity to do what all writers long to do; alter, correct, rephrase or otherwise amend what is enshrined in naked print. The new material which I have added is largely drawn from the published reports of scholars, to whose work I am deeply grateful. Readers of the original edition will see that I have excised the Appendix which dealt with the Pharaoh Hound, the putative living descendant of the ancient Egyptian hunting hound. This is because at the time of writing this Preface I am working on a book length study of this intriguing and enigmatic animal. The format of this edition is somewhat different from that of the earlier, in an endeavour to achieve clarity. It falls into two parts; the first containing the primarily historical material, the second more discursive reviews of the Egyptians' interesting preoccupation with the east and with islands, and then the application of some of C.G. Jung's concepts to the understanding of the ancient Egyptian psyche.

At the end of the preface to the first edition I wrote 'Ancient Egypt is at its most compelling in the wonders that it reveals and the directness with which its people – craftsmen as well as kings – can speak to us today. If we listen we may learn, before it is entirely too late'. I see no reason to amend that view.

Michael Rice
Odsey, Cambridgeshire

PREFACE TO THE ORIGINAL EDITION[1]

I began writing this book as a sort of celebration of most ancient Egypt, of the origins of a culture which seems to me to be without precedent or equal. I have no idea why so many people from my native island in the North Atlantic, which is after all pretty remote from the Nile Valley, should feel so profound an attraction to Egypt; but they do and I am one of them. From the first moment I set foot in Egypt, more than twenty-five years ago, I have experienced a sense of belonging which is most peculiar: as far as I am concerned it defies explanation. Certainly I do not look for explanations which depend upon a previous incarnation (very dubious) or the occult (idiotic). But the fact remains...

When finally I came to Egypt I was fortunate. The elements of chance in my professional life brought me to Egypt at a low point in the country's long sequence of history; the optimistic upsurge which had seized the people of Egypt after the revolution of 1952 and the débâcle of the Anglo–French–Israeli collusion of 1956 (one of the most ill-omened events in the politics of the postwar period) had burned itself out. Egypt was then stuck in that dismal morass of half-baked socialism which was the ruination of so many Third World countries in the 1950s and 1960s. A series of diplomatic and military misadventures further isolated the country. Few visitors went there; the great temples and the other sites surviving from the most majestic civilization yet to be assembled on the face of the earth were empty and desolate. But for the very few it was a time of privilege, to be able to wander uninterrupted amongst these splendid monuments, savouring them and finding them ready to reveal themselves to those who were able to give them time – the most precious of commodities in contemplating the past – in generous measure. It was rather like finding oneself transferred to Egypt in the early nineteenth century, when European travellers were few, though without the discomfort.

Of all Egypt's localities the one which to me is the most seductive and the most enduring in its interest is Saqqara, the site of the great burials from the time of the archaic kings and of the unique pyramid complex of the Third Dynasty king, Djoser Netjerikhet. I spent long tranquil hours there alone or with a few companions: it is one of the most magical places on earth. As I wandered through the ruined buildings of Djoser's monument or saw the excavations, conducted by Brian Emery for the Egypt Exploration Society, of the First and Second Dynasty tombs, or 'read' the records of life in the Fifth Dynasty tombs of Ti and Mereruka, I became more and more attracted by these early periods, before the end of the Old Kingdom, when the spirit of ancient Egypt was at its most vital, its most vibrant. From that time onwards my interest came to focus on these earlier periods of Egyptian history, with a commensurate delight in the artefacts produced by Egyptian craftsmen in prehistoric times and in the early formative centuries. These were perhaps the first in the history of the world to be conscious of their craft and to take a proper, professional pride in it.

I have always been interested in origins of things, ideas, or institutions. I am especially interested by the development of our species in the post-Neolithic period, after the tremendous change from living in hunting bands to the beginnings of settled community life. Hence the origin of the city concerns me profoundly, as do the insecurities or aspirations which led men to live within a city's walls.

It may be paradoxical, therefore, that I have chosen to write about Egypt in the fourth and third millennia, when the city became established as a historical phenomenon in the burgeoning societies of the Near East. The paradox lies in the fact that the Egyptians, unlike a number of their neighbours and contemporaries, were not great city builders. But they were the inventors of the most advanced and highly developed pristine society that we know, whose beginnings we may observe and attempt to understand. Their failure to build cities on any scale is indeed part of that story.

I am fascinated by the elegance and assurance of early Egypt, by the sumptuous character of the society which grew out of its simple beginnings, by the sophistication and complexity of the institutions which so swiftly were established within it, and by its innocence. The earliest Egyptians were god-ruled but not god-obsessed; they were, in this regard, as in so many others, fortunate.

I too was fortunate in these years to find many friends in Egypt. I was received with equal cordiality in the high, imperial rooms of the British Embassy and in the houses of small officials in little towns. In one such, on a warm summer night, I heard the watch calling the hours, a lantern carried on his shoulder. It was like the end of the second act of *Die Meistersinger*, but without the tumult.

I travelled up and down the Nile, the first of rivers. Once, I had arranged to meet a boat below the middle Egyptian town of Minia, to sail upstream to the rock tombs of Beni Hasan. I arrived in the little town just before dawn; I was escorted along the river banks just as the sun returned, a god as much as ever he was, through villages to whose inhabitants I must have been as strange a phenomenon as a Martian. We reached the point where a rowing boat was waiting to take me from the west to the east bank, where I would meet the river boat on which I would travel to Beni Hasan. The boatman greeted us; he was a giant, nearly seven feet tall, with flaming red hair, not altogether a common sight in Egypt. His boat was moored a yard or so from the bank; he picked me up, carried me in his arms as he waded in the water and deposited me, with great gentleness, in the boat.[2] He did not speak as we crossed the river, nor when I thanked him and said goodbye; he would take nothing from me, but smiled with a curious tenderness and something like complicity. I think he may have been a mute; I suspect that he had been on that stretch of the river for a very long time.

I have tried to respect the findings of contemporary Egyptological scholarship and not to stray too far into the wilder growths of speculation or interpretation. Clearly, I have felt able to raise issues and to discuss possibilities which perhaps few professional Egyptologists would consider appropriate, since current professional thinking leans towards the austere in scholarship and away from the speculative. But what I have written is rooted in an essentially humanistic ground and does not, I hope, disregard the historical proprieties. However, I must acknowledge that it is idiosyncratic in that it pursues issues which interest me especially and that it does not adhere to a very rigid chronological sequence; rather it follows where my particular interest leads.

Egyptology has become, like many aspects of archaeology, intensely specialized. It has the best part of two centuries of scholarship behind it and few professional Egyptologists nowadays are inclined to take a synoptic view; fewer still to venture into areas outside their own specification.

To the members of another professional group I feel that I must also make some reparation. These are the Jungian psychologists who may well feel that I am imperfectly grounded in their discipline, yet have not hesitated to invoke Jung and my understanding of his ideas in an attempt to throw light upon the development of Egyptian society in its earliest manifestations. Again, if I have offended I can only ask for pardon; my admiration for Jung is boundless and I believe that in his system and in the directions he indicated for the analysis of myth, the collective unconscious, and the character of social groupings, lie the best prospect of understanding the nature of the human psyche in its societal context. I have no doubt, however, that the principles which Jung articulated so generously can be applied to the emergence of a society like Egypt's, with great profit for those who would seek to understand the processes which were at work.

Practitioners of other vocations may, on the other hand, be quite pleased with me and with what I have done. One is a profession to which I belong myself, though nowadays somewhat vicariously: I think I may be said to have pushed back the origins of state propaganda to a very satisfactory antiquity, though perhaps few people will thank me for having done so; heraldry and the designing of all manner of containers equally can be shown to have an ancestry of a very respectable extent. In planning and decision-making in Archaic Egypt, in the interplay of management decision and specialist advice, the processes involved must have been little different from those which now pertain, with the professionals' exasperation with the whimsicality (or worse) of the client no doubt as powerful a factor then as it is today.

I said that this book began as a celebration of most ancient Egypt; it has not entirely ended as that. For many years I have been deeply interested in and concerned with the archaeology of the Arabian Gulf and of the Arabian peninsula. In this connection I have come increasingly to wonder at the possibility of contact between the peoples of these two nearby but very different cultures. As a consequence I have found myself being drawn further and further into a consideration of where these two may have met, in time as well as in location.

An involvement with the archaeology of the Arabian Gulf is in itself no qualification for pontificating about the origins of Pharaonic Egypt. However, as I have said, I have inevitably found myself becoming aware of the many elements of similarity between Egypt in the late predynastic age and the cultures of Sumer in what is today southern Iraq and Elam, in south-western Iran; the latter is particularly relevant. These similarities have long been known and have frequently been reviewed, but I have been impressed, too, by the curious incidence of similarities in form and content of the art of most ancient Egypt and of some of the cultures which flourished in the Gulf in the late third and early second millennia. The hiatus in time, of something approaching a thousand years in some cases, is perplexing.

It seemed to me that it might be rewarding to look again at what is known as the origins of the Egyptian state from the perspective of the eastern extremity of the Arabian peninsula and from the mysterious rectangular sheet of largely shallow water which comprises the Arabian Gulf. On that almost inland sea and on its shores so much of the early history of 'man the dweller in cities' was acted out, so many of the myths which have later influenced the civilized world were given form and substance, and so much of the apparatus of the sort of society which we have come to regard as the normal lot of city-dwelling man was first developed. To look back from the Gulf towards Egypt at the time when both societies were young has proved, indeed, a remarkable vantage point.

Some further consideration of the problems relating to chronology must be given, if only because the various comparisons between Egypt, Mesopotamia, the Gulf, and western Persia which will be made throughout this text depend for their relevance upon their being contemporary, or at least approximately so. Throughout this book I have, in referring to dates, employed what might be termed the 'conventional chronology'. This assumes that the First Dynasty of Egyptian kings began in the thirty-second century BC, probably c. 3180 BC, though many scholars today who accept the conventional framework of Egyptian chronology regard this date as too early, preferring to place the beginning of the First Dynasty at around 2900 BC. It was preceded by some two thousand years of the predynastic period and succeeded by approximately one thousand years of the Archaic period and the Old Kingdom. This generally accepted Egyptological chronology places the collapse of the Old Kingdom following the reign of King Pepi II, at around 2180 BC.

A settled chronology for Egypt is central to the chronological structure of the early historical period in the whole of the ancient Near East. This is why it has always been considered as of such importance; without a secure chronology for Egypt, the history of the early Aegean, the Levant, even of the Mesopotamian cultures, begins to come apart.

The accepted chronology of Egypt is derived from an amalgam of otherwise quite disparate sources. The Egyptians, unhelpfully, had several calendars by which they regulated their years. They were acute observers of the heavenly bodies and were competent, if rather limited, mathematicians. The Egyptian year notionally began with the first appearance of the Dog Star, Sirius, known to the Greeks as Sothis, and to the Egyptians as Sopdet. Its rising was considered by the Egyptians as marking the first day of the first month of the Inundation, the first of the three seasons into which their year was divided.

It is the Greek name for the star which has stuck and the calendar which is inaugurated by the appearance of Sirius is in consequence known as the Sothic calendar. The problem with the Sothic year is that it does not correspond exactly with the solar year, but is shorter than it by approximately six hours. This results in the two years, the Sothic and the solar, gradually slipping apart; the same situation would pertain in the western or Gregorian calendar without the intercalation of a leap year in every four.

The Egyptian year was originally three hundred and sixty days in duration. It was, at some remote time in the past, extended to three hundred and sixty five by the introduction of five extra days but still the six hours' gap remained. As the years went by and became centuries, the calendar became seriously out of alignment, with all the seasons falling at the wrong time of the year, as it were.

The Egyptians were clearly aware of the deficiency of this calendar and quite happily introduced two others which were more accurate. But they kept records of the Sothic cycle, which takes the formidable term of one thousand, four hundred and sixty years to return to its beginning.

Writing in the third century AD the Roman grammarian Censorinus states that the Sothic and the civil New Years coincided in AD 139. With the known factor of one thousand, four hundred and sixty as the length of the Sothic cycle it is possible to extrapolate to set the beginning of earlier cycles in 1317 BC and 2773 BC. Two inscriptions from the New Kingdom and one from the Middle Kingdom give reasonably firm dates for Sothic risings, though not the beginning of the cycle.

The Egyptian bureaucracy, from the earliest times, kept records of the annual inundation of the Nile, associating them with the reigns of the kings. Of such records the inscribed tablet, of which various fragments survive and which is known as the Palermo Stone, is the most important. By a combination of the extension of the Sothic cycles backwards in time and their alignment with the names of the kings and the length of their reigns in the Palermo Stone and other inscriptions, a rough chronological structure begins to emerge.

In addition to the Palermo Stone, king lists from Abydos, Turin, Saqqara and Karnak have provided information about the names of the Kings and some of the important or striking events of their reigns. Such lists, and possibly others now lost, were doubtless available to Manetho, the High Priest of Heliopolis in the reign of Ptolemy II Philadelphus, who reigned from 285 BC to 246 BC. He wrote a history of Egypt, parts of which have survived only in extracts quoted by other authors; these are fragmentary and often corrupt.

Manetho's history was devised in three parts. The first dealt with the time of the gods, the second with those mysterious figures 'the spirits of the dead, the demigods', who were said to have succeeded the gods in the rule of Egypt; the third relates the histories of the mortal kings. It is thus this part which provides the basis for all the records of the kings, published first by followers of Manetho in late antiquity and which still informs all subsequent histories of Egypt.

Clearly Manetho had access to valuable records of the kingship, now lost. He lists thirty dynasties in all, the first beginning with the Unification. Dynasty follows dynasty, neatly but unhistorically; we know that a number of dynasties listed by Manetho as following one upon another were in fact coterminous, or overlapping. In some cases he lists lines of Kings for which there is little or no historical evidence.

Manetho gives, in many cases, estimates for the reign of individual kings and totals for the duration of the dynasties; the two figures do not always tally. It is the attempt to relate Manetho's computations to known historical sequences which has caused many Egyptologists some very difficult and perplexing arithmetical problems.

The crucial date is, of course, the beginning of the First Dynasty. The estimates for this critical event have become later, over the past century or so, in the most remarkable fashion. The range of dates extends from Petrie's estimate of 5546 BC, a figure which no one would support today, through 3500 BC by Hall, 3400 BC by Breasted, down to the more generally accepted range of 3200–3100 BC, promoted by Sewell, Drioton and Vandier, Frankfort, and Hayes, amongst others. Scharff and Moortgat would put the date as late as 2850 BC, nearly *three thousand* years later than Petrie.

Computing the extent of the predynastic period is even more fraught. To some extent, at least, Petrie's sequence dating, in itself a helpful device but one of no absolute chronological value, has made the situation more complex. He assumed that one style in pottery making or design followed *from* another; he assumed, too, that an extended timescale would be required to move from the origins of a form to its elaborated or degenerated successors. In fact, of course, it is impossible to quantify such a sequence, in the sense of applying a timescale to the process. The design of a pot may go through a series of transformations very rapidly; similarly a type like the black-topped vases, originally associated with the Badarians and hence the senior of all Egyptian pottery types, may persist over the centuries, even over millennia.

The fact is that there is really no reliable archaeological evidence to support the accepted dating of the predynastic periods. There is only one stratified predynastic site, and that a very small one, which yields Badarian, Naqada I, and Naqada II levels together; current work at the site of Hierakonpolis, of which much will be said later in this text, may elucidate the sequence further. Most cautious writers on the predynastic periods are careful to issue a caveat and to observe on what fragile and often antique evidence the generally accepted ideas about the predynastic are based. They are right to do so.

Another disconcerting factor is that though most of the material evidence for the predynastic is drawn from excavated or plundered graves, the quantity of graves concerned is really very small when given the apparent spans of time involved and the extent of the settlements. The argument is usually advanced that predynastic cemeteries, like predynastic settlements, were generally sited on the edge of the cultivation and hence have been long since buried beneath the accretions of centuries of occupation and agriculture. There may well be some truth in this but it is disconcerting nonetheless that a great early dynastic site like the one at Helwan, to the south of Cairo, can yield some ten thousand graves of officials and the like whilst there are no comparable burials known from the immediate predecessors of the Helwanites in anything like the same quantity.

It is generally assumed on the basis of the very extensive repertory of pottery and later stone vessel shapes that the predynastic period in Egypt lasted for some two thousand years – from *c.*5000 BC to *c.*3000 BC. Once again, there is no archaeological or historical corroboration for the attribution of such a timescale; it could be five hundred years as easily as two thousand. The problem is compounded by the fact that Egyptian chronology is the control by which the chronologies of the ancient Near East as a whole are formulated. When, for example, a historian observes that Naqada II in Egypt corresponds with the late Uruk in Mesopotamian chronology he really means no more than that it has been agreed that the late Uruk period in Mesopotamia corresponds with Naqada II in Egypt. There are, as yet, simply no absolute standards by which real dates in these early times can be established.

Nor is the evidence of carbon 14 dating altogether conclusive. In any batch of dates obtained from organic materials drawn from the same sources or archaeological horizon there will often be fairly violent discrepancies between the range of one date and another. The archaeologist's tendency when faced with a number of inconsistencies in the materials for which he is trying to secure a date is, perhaps understandably, to dismiss those which do not conform to recognized time-frames as 'aberrant' and to see them as affected by external factors, like changes in the radiation to which they have been exposed, or in some other way infected. Carbon 14 sequences may be useful in determining relative sequences of objects but they are at best of dubious value in computing absolute dates.

There are some disconcerting gaps in the evidence as it stands at present, which may not be evident from the confidence with which some assertions relating to datings are made. These discrepancies tend to be given added support by the discovery of a flourishing mercantile culture in the Arabian Gulf islands and the surrounding coastlands contemporary with the later Old Kingdom, and Akkadian and neo-Sumerian Mesopotamia; this will no doubt focus attention again on the question of chronology. When it was first excavated, the foundation of the great temple complex at Barbar, Bahrain, was dated to the early part of the third millennium. This attribution has now been revised and it is proposed that the first temple was probably built there around the twenty-fourth century BC, not long before the likely end of the Old Kingdom in Egypt. However, as will be seen from the narrative below, there are a number of factors in the context of the Gulf's archaeology – elements of design, artefacts, and architecture – which would either be more acceptable were they attributable to a period earlier in the millennium than appears to be the case or if their parallels in Egypt could be dated to the end of the third millennium rather than to its beginning.

I have tried, wherever possible, to use illustrations which may not be so familiar to readers of books on Egyptology. The inheritance from Egypt is so exceptionally generous that it seemed to me worth rummaging through some of what might appear to be the more neglected storerooms of that inheritance. To the specialist there will be no revelations, but to those whose concern with Egypt is not professional I hope that some, at least, of these objects will bring surprise and delight, as much as they have done to me.

One last point: Egyptologists will detect an echo in the title which I have given to this book. *Egypt's Making* deliberately recalls one of the last books published in his long lifetime by Sir Flinders Petrie, who virtually invented Egyptology. At much the same time I too discovered Egypt through the BBC broadcast of the sounding of the war trumpets of Tutankhamun from the Cairo Museum. As I write this, it is fifty years to the day that the Second World War began in September 1939. So formidable a cluster of anniversaries, great and small, is pleasing, and through the plagiarism of his title I am able to pay some respect to the man who, perhaps more than any other, tried to penetrate the origins of the essential character of the Egyptian state.

At the end of the day, I have had only one aim in writing this book other, obviously, than that of satisfying myself by writing it. It is that I too may direct attention to this magical land, to the less familiar periods of its history, and, in particular, to the origins of its historic institutions. Ancient Egypt is at its most compelling in the wonders which it reveals and the directness with which its people – craftsmen as well as Kings – can speak to us today. If we listen, we may learn, before it is entirely too late.

Michael Rice 1989

ACKNOWLEDGEMENTS

I am especially grateful to the authors of the various studies on the predynastic and Early Dynastic history of Egypt which have appeared in print since the original publication of *Egypt's Making* and which have informed the present volume. The most valuable references which I have used include those of the late Barbara Adams, Dr Renée Friedman, Professor G. Dryer, Dr B. Midant-Reynes, S.J. Siedelman, D. Rohl, Professor F. Wendorf and Professor R. Schild, and Dr T.A.H. Wilkinson. The appropriate references are given in the Bibliography. Naturally, the use which I have made of their work is wholly my responsibility and I hope that I have not misinterpreted or misrepresented any of them too outrageously.

I am delighted to acknowledge the various institutions and individuals who have assisted me in obtaining permission for the inclusion of many of the illustrations which appear here. These include Dr Patricia Spencer and the Committee of the Egypt Exploration Society, Dr Renée Friedman of the Hierakonpolis Expedition. Not for the first time, I have benefited from the advice of Dr Harnet Crawford of the Institute of Archaeology, University College London, on the archaeology of Mesopotamia. Again, any lingering errors or inadequacies in the text are entirely my own.

I am also indebted to Andrew Wheatcroft, the Head of Publishing Studies at Stirling University, who oversaw the original publication of *Egypt's Making*, for his unfailing encouragement and guidance.

I am, as always, much indebted to my friend John Ross whose marvellous photographs of many of the objects herein displayed have added immeasurably to the quality of this edition, as his work did for the earlier edition.

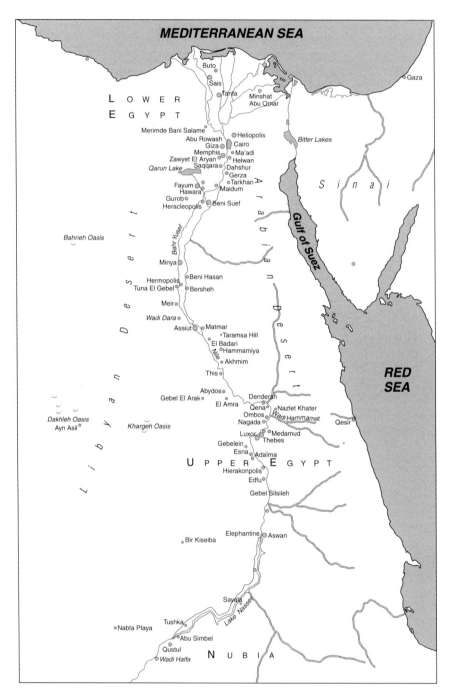

Map 1 Egypt: principal sites mentioned in the text (*c.* 3300–3100 BC)

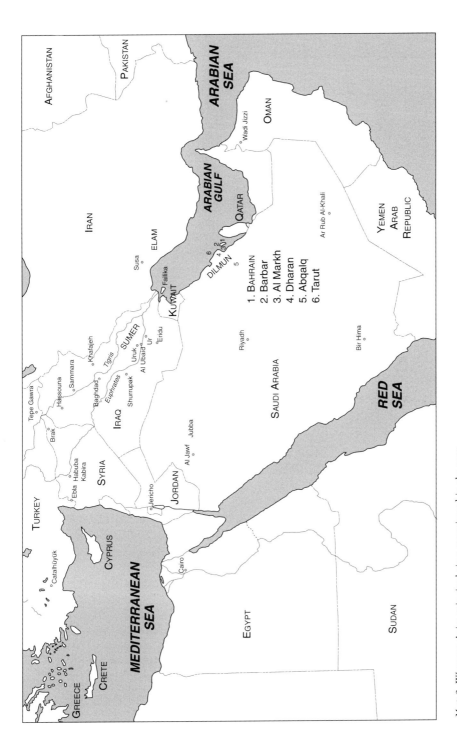

Map 2 Western Asia: principal sites mentioned in the text

1

THE LAND OF EGYPT

There was a time when, in one small strip of the world's land surface, man achieved an almost total equilibrium with his environment and created a society as near perfect as he has so far been able even to conceive. This was the Golden Age, as near as ever man has yet come to experience that fugitive state. Sadly enough for the race of men it ended all too soon, rather more than four thousand years ago.

The time in which this fusion of the marvellous and the real occurred was a magical millennium, a thousand years or so of superb achievement, of an unexampled advancement of the human spirit spanning the closing centuries of the fourth millennium before the present era and continuing through most of the third. In terms of historical time as it would be expressed today, this represents the period from around 3200 BC to c.2200 BC. There has been no other time quite like it in all human history.

The land, of course, is Egypt and the times involved represent what historians categorize as the predynastic and Early Dynastic[1] periods and the Old Kingdom, the time of Egypt's first and finest greatness. The earliest phases represent as distant an epoch as may be found in the study of the emergence of a complex, literate society. Nonetheless we know that the people of that thousand years produced a way of life so powerful and enduring that it lasted, in outward form at least, for more than three thousand years, even surviving several extended interruptions. It continues to this day to exercise a unique fascination and to induce in its observers either a sense of almost fearful wonder or an exuberant borrowing of forms and motifs, often in the most bizarre and inappropriate contexts.

The recollection of Ancient Egypt (or, more accurately, what often stands for Ancient Egypt) has, in a quite extraordinary way, managed to infiltrate itself into so many aspects of the modern world and into the minds of countless individuals living today. But often what later ages have taken to be quintessentially Egyptian are in fact only simulacra, infected by centuries of foreign influence, of the real forms which can only properly be traced in the dawn and springtime of Egyptian civilization. It will be the purpose of this present study to analyze some of these characteristics, to attempt to identify their original forms and to understand the factors which determined the emergence of the historic Egyptian personality in its earliest manifestations. It will be seen that the concept of the archetypes, developed in particular by Carl Gustav Jung (see Chapter 13), seems particularly apt when applied to some of the mighty images which stream out of Egypt in the earliest periods of its existence as a corporate state. There can surely be little doubt that the extraordinary appeal which Egypt has exercised on the modern world (the world, that is, since the Renaissance when ancient Egypt first began really to penetrate European consciousness) is a consequence of this marshalling and unleashing of the archetypes. The unique inheritance which the world draws from most ancient Egypt consists not only of the pyramids and superlative works of art which survive in such extraordinary abundance from the earliest periods onwards, but also of the recognition and the subsequent releasing of the archetypes into the consciousness of men, the consequence of the genius of Egyptian artists and designers who first gave the archetypes their material form.

THE EXPERIENCE OF THE NUMINOUS

Whenever the people of other lands observed Egypt and speculated about the nature of her culture and society, they seem always to have harboured the suspicion that Egypt was in touch (or certainly at some time had been in touch) with powers beyond the confines of the world they knew. Understandably the Egyptians did nothing to diminish the aura of mystery and the numinous quality with which their land seemed to be suffused, as much as it was suffused with the light of the sun which lit the river banks and surrounding deserts with a brilliant radiance. They were not disposed to admit, even to themselves, that the wonders of Egypt and the proximity of the divine were alike the consequence of man's invention. That the invention itself was so superlative that it seemed superhuman does not diminish the essential humanity of the Egyptian achievement, nor, for that matter, does it significantly augment it, for most in Ancient Egypt the sense of the human and the superhuman come very close together, as aspects of the same integral experience.

It is amongst Egypt's most notable characteristics that in all essentials its nature was determined in the earliest days of its existence and that those essentials continued to dominate Egyptian history for her entire lifetime. Egyptian culture very swiftly reached peaks of elegance and sophistication and Egyptian art of technical perfection, which have hardly ever again been equalled. Once Egypt's unique contribution to the management of human societies, the kingship, appeared at the end of the fourth millennium BC Egyptian state institutions rapidly achieved a maturity and effectiveness which allowed the state to endure in the same essential form over the succeeding three millennia.

THE KINGSHIP

These achievements, in virtually every department of the state and of life, resounded down the centuries; they were in large part the work of a succession of extraordinary figures, the earliest rulers of the united land of Egypt, and their immediate colleagues and supporters. Between 3200 BC and 2700 BC they seeded Egypt deep in the fertile soil of the Valley; for another five hundred years what they planted flourished wonderfully. Though the early kings are often shadowy figures, the shadows which they cast on the history of mankind are very great.

The early Egyptians had a particular genius, never remotely approached by any other ancient society, for devising symbols which instantly encapsulate complex and diverse concepts. They are the supreme symbolists; every aspect of their society – art, religion, and the life which revolved around the king – reflects this strange and very individual quality. Kingship was the ultimate Egyptian institution: the king represents the absolute focus of all early Egyptian history. The kingship was personified, in what is surely one of the most inspired images in the entire course of symbolism, as a golden hawk soaring limitlessly high above the world. The hawk is a creature of the sun, infinitely remote, one whose natural habitat is the empyrean, the exalted firmament which lay beyond the Imperishable Stars. Not even the majestic lion nor the raging, dominant bull, though they were both creatures associated with the kingship in early times, quite achieved the breathtaking vision of the falcon of gold as the ultimate icon in which the concept of sovereignty was so perfectly enshrined. The king of Egypt was himself a falcon, the reincarnation of Horus, the falcon-god.

The Egyptians recognized that if a man, with all the too unmistakable evidences of humanity, was to be exalted above all other men and to be given absolute rulership over them, his simple mortality must be thrust down and his mortal nature replaced by something altogether more sublime. Thus came the audacious idea of recognizing the holder of the kingship as himself divine, his divinity confirmed by his assumption of the crowns and regalia which were the marks of the ruler of the Dual Kingdom. It is a neat equation, even if, like the serpent which eats its own tail, the argument strikes the dispassionate observer as notably circular.

The course of Egyptian history produced thirty dynasties of kings according to the compilation of the Hellenistic historian Manetho.[2] We are concerned here with the period which preceded the welding together of the disparate elements which represented the polity of the Valley into the nation-state which was to become Egypt, generally called the predynastic period, and then with only the first six groups of historic kings; of these the first two are the most immediately important, as well as the most tantalizing and obscure. The later dynasties all produced remarkable men but it is the kings of the Early Dynastic period who were the begetters of Egyptian

3

civilization, even in its most luxuriant flowering; it was their immediate successors, the sovereigns of the Old Kingdom, who drew on the benefit of their extraordinary enterprise.

Even so, the kings whose names are recorded as comprising the First Dynasty were not the first kings in Egypt. The origins of the Egyptian kingship, though it is without doubt the most ancient in the world, are lost in the obscurities of the later centuries of the prehistoric period, in the latter part of the fourth millennium BC.[3] It is only with the coming of writing that it is possible to put names to the kings with any sort of assurance. But before this time there are hints of prehistoric chieftains, even of kings who ruled part or all of the land which was to become Egypt. Their names are often matters of conjecture; the material remains associated with their rule are sparse and fragmentary though, as will be seen, sophisticated techniques of excavation and analysis are now revealing more and more about the times in which they lived. We can only glimpse them occasionally through the prehistoric, preliterate miasma; nonetheless, they were the forerunners of the kings of historic times. Their titles, elements of their regalia, customs associated with their roles as the links between the visible and the unseen worlds, were abstracted and adapted by the later kings for their own use and for the augmentation of their own majesty. The various crowns, the crook, the flail, the bull or monkey tail, the lion's and the leopard's pelts, all were once the properties of lesser princes which came to add to the splendour of the universal king who ultimately triumphed over all of them, sovereign and alone.

ART AND INNOVATION

Egyptian craftsmen of the earliest periods produced works of a superlative beauty but they made objects with a truly wonderful technique and an applied and disciplined skill hardly ever equalled anywhere in the world in later centuries. Indeed the Egyptian craftsmen of these periods deserve to be recognized as amongst the supreme master craftsmen of all history. Not for nothing was the High Priest of Ptah, the paramount creative god of Memphis, called the Master of the Master Craftsmen.

In all of these activities, indeed in the entire round of their existence, the Egyptians had but one motivation: it was so evident and fundamental that it never required statement or articulation. They were obsessed in a positive and glorious sense, with life. Their genius was directed towards the celebration of life and its prolongation to eternity. The entire power of the state and those who lived in it, from the divine king to the humblest peasant, was focused on this single purpose, to sustain the life of Egypt. In this exalted enterprise art was required to fulfil a particular responsibility.

At no time was this wholesale identification between what might be called the corporate life of the Egyptian state and its harnessing to the objective of the prolongation of life so significant as during its beginnings. It was, indeed, as if the whole genius of the nascent state was directed towards resolving the dilemma of man's transient existence. It is this objective and the extraordinary quality of the works of art and of architecture which were created to advance it that distinguish the first thousand years of Egyptian history and which mark that time out from the long sequence of centuries which succeeded it. What made this period so very exceptional was the purely innovative quality of early Egyptian achievement, as much in art as in state institutions, probably in ritual also, when virtually everything that is identified with what is customarily called 'Pharaonic civilization' throughout its history was invented. In its first flowering it was pristine and in all essentials untouched by conflicting or confusing external influences. Similar considerations applied to the evolution of the Egyptians' beliefs and intellectual concepts as to the development of the forms of their material culture and of their architecture. The role of kingship, the nature of the gods, the relationship between the gods and their chosen people, the application of architectural forms, and the flowering of Egyptian art and craftsmanship are all to be seen in their purest form and most immediate impact in the first millennium or so of Egypt's national existence.

THE SUMERIANS

In its first flowering, the perfection which Egyptian society achieved can best be apprehended by a parallel consideration of the only other society which can be compared with it in antiquity and, though very different, in achievement. This is the contemporary culture which arose far away to the east of Egypt, in the southern extremity of Mesopotamia, 'the land between the Rivers'. This rich and complex culture is known to history as Sumer and its contemporary, somewhat to the east and south of Sumer, was Elam, the region of Iran which has been called Susiana and Khuzistan. These lands, together with the eastern seaboard of the Arabian peninsula, shared the Arabian Gulf as a common highway.

The Sumerians were the peers of the Egyptians. It was the Sumerians (so far as we know) who invented the wheel, sailing boats, international trade, banking, and the first profoundly influential corpus of epic literature. It was believed that they were the inventors of writing, in advance of Egypt by a few hundred years, but more recent discoveries (see 65) suggest that Egypt was nearly contemporaneous in the development of a sophisticated writing system. What does seem certain is that the Sumerians inaugurated the practice of living in cities, of building monumental religious and state architecture, of creating civil and religious hierarchies and administrations. Their contribution to the modern world is immense, to the extent that without them the world would in no way be what it is today. Less is known of the Elamites, though elements of their culture seem to be derived from Sumer: what is clear however is that they were as intensely visual a people, in terms of the art which they created, as were the Egyptians.

Though the Sumerians were a creative, lively, disputatious people who enjoyed life and the business of living, they had, by comparison with the Egyptians, no sense of special election, no sense of being the favoured children of the gods. When they considered their place in the world they took, generally, a fairly despondent view of it. Their gods were hostile and frequently malignant: at best they might remain indifferent to the affairs of men. Man had, in the Sumerian view, only been created by the higher gods to avoid trouble with the lesser gods, who resented having to carry out disagreeable and laborious tasks while the great gods enjoyed themselves. In consequence a still lesser creature was created, to provide the gods with labourers who were also programmed perpetually to praise them, a curious psychological need which Near Eastern divinities (other than the gods of Egypt, interestingly enough) have always manifested. For such humble reasons was the Sumerian made and there was very little in prospect for him; all that he could hope for, at the best, was to get on with the business of living and to avoid angering a god.

Only one Sumerian god was particularly well-disposed to man: Enki, the Lord of the Abyss, the god of the sweet waters under the earth. Enki is a complex and well-realized phenomenon. He is particularly identified with the earliest days of the Sumerian people; some authorities would see him, indeed, as their original divinity, the most senior of all gods. Enki's name originally meant 'Lord of Earth'; he is the principal figure in the cycle of myths concerned with the Sumerians' concept of their origins and of the arts of civilization. At the centre of these myths lies the mystical and mysterious land of Dilmun, the prototype of the terrestrial paradise. Indeed, perhaps surprisingly, it is the Sumerian legend of the Paradise Land and not the Egyptian which has underlain this universal myth. Sumerian myths are the first to describe that place of primeval innocence and joy, which has informed the beliefs of Judaism, Christianity, and Islam, which to a substantial extent are the inheritors of the Sumerian mythologues and those of their successors, the Akkadians and Babylonians. The Egyptians did not look back to times past as ideal, for they knew that their existence, the perpetual 'now' of the Valley, could not be bettered. They believed that eternity would be represented by the glories of the land of Egypt, written large and sustained for ever. However, it will be seen that they may have preserved the memory (or perhaps simply sustained the same archetypal concept) of a far distant land to the east, an island which they identified with the Rising Sun, as the Land of Light and the place of the origins of their world order (see Chapter 11).

The men of the earliest societies of Egypt and, to a somewhat lesser degree, of Sumer were participating in an extraordinary experiment. They were the first to live in highly organized, highly structured societies, which were hierarchic and, in the case of Egypt, profoundly autocratic. These societies were far removed from the relatively simple communities which descended from the Stone Age. The societies of Egypt and Sumer were the first in which a developed and pervasive culture, extending over a considerable area and persisting through time, became the decisive mechanism of an extended community and its essential, dynamic force. Other societies had experienced random aspects of the growth of institutions or the harnessing of technique comparable with the experience of the society which was to be created beside the Nile or, in different degree, in the cities of Sumer: at Çatalhüyük,[4] for example, or at Jericho,[5] where early attempts at formulating a sophisticated *civilization* (in the sense that the word implies a relationship with an urban system) were abandoned. An even more extraordinary and almost unbelievably early experiment in the domestication of plants and animals carried out in the far southern Egyptian deserts, substantially before 10000 BC, likewise came eventually to nothing.

THE PRISTINE SOCIETY

The experience of the Egyptians at the end of the fourth millennium and for much of the third was of life in an essentially pristine society, one of the very few occasions in the history of humankind when that term could be used with confidence. It must be insisted that *pristine* does not imply *primitive*: quite the opposite, in Egypt's case. The Egyptians' world really was new: after the millennia-long Stone Age Egyptian man woke to a splendid dawn. From the evidence of his art he saw himself as part of a universal order, of the totality of nature, presided over by the immanent god himself. From this perfection of order came that assurance, a calm acceptance of oneness with the divine and with the works of the divine, which is the peculiar mark of Egyptian society at this time. In later times, from the Fourth Dynasty onwards, portraits of individuals show them, tranquil and poised, with their eyes fixed on some distant vision; sometimes the expression is so rapt as to be almost ecstatic.

The sense of assurance and security which the god-ordained and directed nature of Egyptian society induced was the product of Egypt's physical topography. By the will of gods she was protected on all sides from incursion, largely also from contamination, by less fortunate or more envious peoples. After the late predynastic flow of influences from the east which, it will be seen, stimulated rather than confused him, the Egyptian was able to cultivate in peaceful certainty his responses to the world around him. Although a member of one of the most resourceful, creative and richly developed societies known to man he was not dependent on a vast library of received impressions flowing into him from outside himself. Such pressures as there were came from a wholly Egyptian environment, were benevolent and in no way alien to him. Nothing that happened outside the Valley affected him; this could, of course, be said of many peoples in many different times and places but all those who lived after the first half of the third millennium were, willy-nilly, increasingly influenced by the aspirations, inventions, or ambitions of others. For the Egyptian in the early centuries, this was simply not so; he lived alone within his own world, with his own kind. He could, as it were, listen to the sound of the world turning and, listening, learn from the sound of its motion. No other influence pervaded the supremely tranquil environment in which he was so securely lodged.

The Egyptians valued order above most other qualities. Order and truth were one and their preservation was the highest good. The king, it was said, ruled in truth; to sustain the truth and order of the universe was the most solemn charge to which even a king of Egypt might aspire. To know what is true, to be able to define and order the world so that it conforms with its own essential nature, requires an absolute assurance on the part of whoever may set out upon such a task. The certainty that they were not as other men, that their land was different from all other lands and that they alone had certain and unimpeded access to the highest order of divinity, was deeply engrained in the Egyptian consciousness from the very earliest days. Partly this was the consequence, no doubt, of being ruled by an immanent divinity, of knowing that God was a near neighbour, perpetually guiding the universe of which Egypt was, quite clearly, the centre. The Egyptians had a sense of being peculiarly fortunate, singled out by a high and benevolent destiny. They did not proclaim their sense of selection with the strident assertiveness of the much later Hebrews or with the rather icy arrogance of the Chinese (who simply doubted the actual humanity of the rest of mankind, despite some appearances to the contrary), and certainly not with the often implacable cruelty of Christian apologists. The Egyptians, with a tranquil assurance which can sometimes be exasperating, merely *knew* that they were the favoured children of the gods. They did not need to proselytize – that would have been futile – or to demand recognition for their distinctiveness, for that would have been irrelevant. Nothing could dent the certainty of their fortune or the security which it induced.

Nothing, that is, until after a thousand years the Golden Age which was early Egypt disintegrated in near-anarchy and confusion. But this time was distant and mercifully unknown to the creators of the Egyptian state. They could see, for the evidence was all about them, how favoured was their land. But, in a land which was to become a byword for antiquity and the unchanging harmony of life, man was a comparative latecomer. Before man came the Valley was the preserve of a rich and diverse fauna which flourished throughout the millennia, until the climate began significantly to change, probably in the sixth millennium BC.

THE RIVER

Egypt's landscape is determined, even in the desert areas, by the presence of the river. Distantly it may be seen glinting suddenly as the sun strikes it through a gap in the hills: close to, it surges or flows imperceptibly, depending on the course through which it runs. No one stretch of the river is quite the same as another: at one moment it may be bound by high limestone rocks, at the next it will open out until it seems as though the traveller is sailing on a boundless lake. At one point the desert will run menacingly down to the river's edge; then, the river turns and the land is fertile, full of small villages and the shouts of children. No representation of Eden is so telling as the banks of the Nile in the richly cultivated areas where the grass, cropped by patient donkeys, runs right to the water's edge.

A prodigality of adjectives, of scale, quantity and drama, has been expended recklessly on descriptions of the Nile. All are vain: the Nile is, simply, itself, unique. It is, of course, very much more than a river; the Egyptians knew it to be the prototype of all streams. As it races or meanders, depending upon its mood and the nature of the landscape through which it flows, it draws into itself all the elements of nature: earth, air, and sky. It is one of the earthly manifestations of the sun in splendour, capturing the sun's rays so that they are spun out across the Two Lands of which it is the one unifying and eternal connection. The Nile is the real, eternal king of Egypt; is Egypt.

The Nile is the first and greatest of all rivers. To the Egyptians it was, simply, The River; all other rivers were counterfeit, pretenders never wholly to be trusted. Some rivers of which they had knowledge were to the Egyptian mind demonstrably perverse; of these the Tigris and Euphrates in neighbouring Sumer were the most reprehensible for they flowed from north to south whereas the Nile had made it evident for all to see that a proper river should only flow from south to north. The rivers of Mesopotamia were thus flowing upside down, wholly frivolous and irresponsible riverine behaviour indeed, to the Egyptian way of thinking. This fact merely went to confirm the Egyptian view of foreigners and of everything to do with them.

That Herodotus' observation about the Nile has become a cliché employed by every writer who comments on the Egyptian landscape does not diminish its essential truth: 'the Nile is the gift of Osiris, but Egypt is the gift of the Nile'. The Nile is the most paradoxical of rivers for it flows imperturbably through a great desert, its waters rich with life rushing through a landscape that is mostly barren and scoured, typical desert terrain.

Egypt is unchanging in beauty and in the ways of its people; it is like no other land. Nowhere does the contrast between rich cultivation and the parched aridity of the desert strike more forcefully. The river, when it returned at the time of the inundation to renew the land, was until very recent times greeted joyfully as a beloved god, come back to assuage the pain of his people and to bring comfort and prosperity to them. To this day the river is a living creature for the country people and it gives life to the eternal quality of the land so that there is continuity between 'now' and 'then'; desert and sky, the land and the river, birds, animals, and men are brought into a perfect synthesis and express, as nowhere else on earth, the unity and perfection of all life and all creation. The miracle of birth, the cycle of the seasons, the fusion of earth and sky are accomplished in Egypt as they seem hardly to be anywhere else on earth; the gods always seem very close, even today.

The inundation was always magical to the Egyptians, a testimony to the covenant between them and the gods and a guarantee of the gods' concern for the people of the land of Egypt. From the time of Akhenaten, the Eighteenth Dynasty religious zealot, a eulogy survives which praises God and expressed the pious and complacent thought that God had, with singular compassion, placed a Nile in the sky to provide the flood for those who could not enjoy the benefit of the rich deposits which the Nile's waters left on the banks and marshlands which bounded it.

This was the particular miracle which the Nile delivered every year, unless the whim of the gods or the failure of the proper observances interrupted it. The river rose in the summer, the water spread across the banks and fields, filling the canals and allowing the farmers to distribute it even to distant cultivable areas. The earth was black and fertile: blackness was so much a part of the image of Egypt that it was called *Kemi*, the black land. Then, with what seemed extraordinary swiftness, the land was green, giving with abundance and sustaining a large, contented, and well-fed population. To paraphrase Dr Pangloss, all was undoubtedly for the best in the best of all possible lands.

To say that the Nile is Egypt is no more than to express a simple, self-evident truth. The Nile bears Egypt in its flood and over the millennia has laid down and then made fertile by its inundation the black earth from which Egypt is made. To the eye of Horus, floating in the sky high above the land of which he was the divine patron, protector, and, in a sense, the embodiment, Egypt is a slender strip of cultivation, two narrow banks divided by the river.

The Nile pours through the Valley which it has made for itself, on its journey from the remote Ethiopian highlands, far beyond the southern confines of Egypt, to the broad, reed-infested waters of the Delta, where it debouches into the Mediterranean, through its several mouths. In length the river journeys some four thousand miles; this was the torrent which was required to bring to fruition the most remarkable manifestation of social creativity yet achieved.

So profoundly ingrained in the Egyptian consciousness was the presence of the Nile that it even determined elements in the Egyptian vocabulary. Thus 'north' signified 'to go down stream' whereas 'south' meant 'to go up stream'. 'Right' and 'left' were equated with 'east' and 'west', the orientation being determined by standing on the river's bank and facing in the direction of its flow. 'South' also meant 'face' whereas 'north' seems to have been identified with the back of the head. Everything was oriented to the river and to its flow northwards to the sea.

For the whole extent of human history until the present day and from far into the period before man came both to harness and to glorify the Valley, the melting of the snows in the Ethiopian highlands precipitated the Nile's paradoxical inundation, for the flood reached Egypt during the harshest, most deadly months of summer. This fact alone, the mysterious rising of the river's waters when everywhere and everything around its banks was desiccated and in a state of profound exhaustion (like Osiris the Dead God before his revival) gave an uncanny, supernatural quality to the river and the life which it demonstrated, so clearly independent of and, in a sense peculiarly mysterious, superior to the life of the land around it.

At the time of the inundation the waters flooded back over the land, drawn to areas distant from the river by canals and by the immemorial device, the *shaduf*, the comfortingly repetitive creaking of this ancient device was always one of the sounds most evocative of the Egyptian countryside. The water was rich in life and revived the dead land; soon the whole land would be green.

The Nile is a huge, perpetually moving road, the supreme conveyor of historic experience: it is also a stupendous theatre. Not only was the longest of all recorded histories played out along its banks, with actors and settings of colossal proportions, it was ever capable of remarkable *coups de theatre*, of wonderful effects of light and drama: such effects it can still produce, with the splendid prodigality of an Edwardian actor-manager.

CLIMATE AND ECOLOGY

The climatology of deserts and their origin and growth are coming increasingly to be understood. That there have been frequent relatively short-term fluctuations in precipitation and humidity in regions which are now wholly desert is clear, though these should not encourage a picture of lush, verdant landscapes teeming with animals where now there are only rock- or sand-strewn wastes. Even a very small variation in precipitation or mean temperature can permit a significantly larger faunal or human population to become rooted in a particular region. The establishment of a larger community with the introduction of animal species which may cause further depredation or, conversely, the planting of trees and crops which can, for a time at least, arrest it, are factors which promote or control the spread of deserts. However, there is little doubt that where human communities flourish the greatest agent for their spread is man himself, though he is assisted enthusiastically by the goat, one of the earliest of his domesticates.

Twelve thousand years ago, when settlement began in the Near East, very marked and remarkable phenomena began to appear. Away to the east in the valley watered by the twin rivers of Mesopotamia, men were putting down roots (literally as well as metaphorically) by starting and maintaining small settlements which were to become the first farming villages. In sites to the north of what is today Iraq and in northern Iran and parts of Syria, increasing sedentation led to the realization that cereals could be cultivated and, later, that animals, corralled or herded, could be managed to the benefit of populations growing increasingly numerous as a consequence of precisely these factors of sedentary existence and the controlled management of the resources which were to hand. The first of the animals to be domesticated was, almost certainly, the dog. It may be questioned which domesticated which, the dog or the man but, in any event, the dog had long been the loyal companion of the hunting bands to which these little settlements were the successors and which was to become a familiar and affectionately regarded companion wherever humans congregated. The integration of the dog into the company of humans probably long predates the change to sedentary living.

In North and Central Africa different sets of circumstances developed which determined the way in which human societies evolved there.[6] The Sahara had supported large herds of wild cattle which had been exploited by bands of hunters since the end of the last glaciation, _c._ twelve thousand years ago. The Ice Age did not extend to North Africa but the general moderation of the climate over much of the northern hemisphere also affected the northern reaches of Africa. By the beginning of the sixth millennium, _c._ 5000 BC, the western Sahara was inhabited by communities which still followed the wild cattle and had begun to domesticate animals which were managed in herds. The moderation of the climate had provided for an increase in precipitation and for the formation of large bodies of standing water, which provided the one resource vital to the survival of wild cattle, which could not manage for more than three days without access to plentiful quantities of water. Conditions in the Sahara must generally have been very agreeable at this time. Gradually, however, the climate changed again and the process of desiccation set in; this led ultimately to the conditions of extreme aridity which have characterized the region over the past four thousand years.

The people who lived in the Sahara were remarkable in one particular respect, the production of one of the great artistic traditions of the late Stone Age.[7] The paintings of the animals with which they shared the pasture lands, the vivid scenes of the hunt and, occasionally, the creation of strange and often menacing creatures of fantasy are, by any standards, of the highest quality of rupestral art. As their lands desiccated the Saharan people migrated eastwards, towards the Valley of the Nile. These migrants were one of the founding stocks of what became the population of Egypt.

Until the beginning of the sixth millennium BC the Nile Valley was relatively unpopulated, except by the animals for which it must have been paradisial as it must also have been for the hunters who occasionally preyed on them. The change in climatic conditions which triggered the migrations had effects over large parts of the Near East and other migrant communities moved into the Valley, from the south, from whence hunters had long followed the wild herds northwards from the East African savanna and from the north, through the route which in historic times was to be known as 'The Way of Horus', by means of which the legendary 'Followers of Horus' came into Egypt. They were revered by the Egyptians in historic times as providing one of the crucial contributions to the unique culture which was to be seeded in the Valley and which was, in a remarkably short time, to become the majestic civilization of the world's first nation-state. Other migrants came from the east, entering the Valley via the Wadi Hammamat, the Eastern desert. All of these groups coalesced to form the historic population of Egypt.

THE EGYPTIAN DESERTS

As the Nile cut its way deeper and deeper down through lime- and sandstone platforms, the descent of man and his ancestors (in a quite literal sense) may be traced, for at the top is located the earliest evidence of hominid occupation whilst on the Valley floor the most recent inhabitants have left their traces.

Although most scholarly attention has, naturally enough, focused on the development of the culture which arose in the Nile Valley, the deserts of Egypt were also of great importance in determining the historic character of the Dual Kingdom. Indeed, archaic humans had established themselves in the several oases of the western desert long before the arrival of modern humans. There are five major oases in the western desert which were inhabited in ancient times and continue to be so. One of these, Qanun, is the location of the only surviving lake in Egypt.

Two of the most important desert sites archaeologically are Nabta Playa[8] in southwest Egypt, north of the Sudanese border and the Dakhleh oasis,[9] to the northwest of Nabta. Some of the earliest migrants into proto-Egypt settled at Nabta. The playas are the surface residue of standing bodies of water which settled in depressions in the western desert; the sources of water attracted the 'new people' who migrated northward encouraged by the climatic changes in the post-Epipalaeolithic period. Nabta, which is a large, kidney-shaped basin, approximately ten km by seven km, became habitable by reason of a shift in the African monsoon which markedly increased the level of ground water and enabled wells to be viable virtually year-round. Excavation has shown a remarkable picture of people living in quite large communities in the Middle and Late Neolithic periods. That they were living in the deep desert did not prevent them from becoming the first people in Egypt to create large megalithic monuments; indeed, Egypt's immense tradition of monumental stone architecture and much of its deepest held customs and beliefs owe their origins to the early inhabitants of the deserts. This remarkable phenomenon will be examined further in the next chapter.

When, for the first time, prospective settlers from the west found their way to the Nile and at last arrested their journey towards the east, they found a veritable wonderland waiting for them. Along the river banks vegetation grew lushly, concealing the ready game. The river and its lagoons were abundant with fish whilst on the plains, in the wider parts of the Valley, lion, giraffe, even elephant lived out their lives with lesser beasts in a splendid and harmonious ecology. In historical times Egypt achieved a well-balanced, largely agricultural economy augmented by the management of its natural resources; its eventual development can only be understood in terms of an agricultural continuity having its existence on the scale of a nation, for the first time in history. Agriculture, hunting, fishing, and the raising of breed herds all contributed to the prosperity of the Valley. All that the first inhabitants had to do, seemingly, was to harness the resources which lay before them. Typically, however, the gifts which the gods had given were overexploited; but that was to come later. In the beginning abundance and a relatively temperate climate combined to produce a situation of unrivalled potential in which to lay down the foundations of a unique human experiment.

The climate in the Nile Valley was marginally more benign in predynastic times than it was during the early historic periods. In the fourth millennium the seasonal rains which activated the wadis, the otherwise dried-up watercourses in the deserts of southern Upper Egypt and lower Nubia, were more considerable than they were in the later third millennium. There is actually some documentary evidence, in the form of the records of the Nile flood levels inscribed on the Palermo Stone, one of the most important third millennium records of the history of the early kings extant.[10] This chronicles the principal events of the reigns of the kings of the earliest dynasties, albeit often fragmentarily and obscurely. The records, however, show that the levels of the floods decreased during the First Dynasty: the mean level of the flood during the early years of the dynasty was greater by nearly a metre than during the Second to Fifth Dynasties.

ARABIA

Far away to the east, across the breadth of the intervening deserts leading to the shores of the Arabian Gulf, the expanse of relatively shallow water which divides Arabia from Iran, there is also evidence of a significant volatility of climate at this time and during the centuries leading to it.[11] The levels of the Gulf have oscillated fairly violently over the past seventeen thousand years;[12] for example, the island of Bahrain, now lying in a bay some twenty miles from the Saudi Arabian mainland, was only separated from Arabia about nine thousand years ago; until that time it was a dome in the eastern

Arabian desert. Between six and five thousand years ago, one of the sites in Bahrain which has yielded pottery of the Ubaid people (the predecessors and presumed ancestors of the Samerians) was a small, offshore atoll, Al-Markh,[13] then lying about a mile away from the principal Bahrain island of which it is now a part. Whilst obviously quite different factors and influences would be at work to affect radical changes in the sea levels in the Gulf and in the annual flood of the River Nile, the coincidence in time of the marked variations which have been described indicate the extent of climatic change in relatively recent times in two parts of the world which otherwise would seem to share many climatic characteristics.

The Arabian deserts are part of the band which stretches from the Atlantic to the western shore of the Arabian Gulf, whose inhabitants shared a regime similar to that experienced by the pastoralists of the Sahara. In the Arabian peninsula, large herds of wild cattle also flourished, the quarry of bands of indigenous hunters who left considerable evidence of their presence on the rocks of what is now the northern and western regions of the Arabian desert. On most of the available rock surfaces in the north and west of the peninsula they left carvings and engravings of the herds and the hunters who followed them. It has been demonstrated that the process of the desiccation of Arabia can be traced from the north, around the area in which the towns of Jubba and Al-Jawf now stand, in which, in comparable conditions to those which prevailed in the Sahara, there were large bodies of standing water, the result of increased precipitation and a rise in the water table,[14] a situation very similar to that which pertained in southern Egypt. Gradually, as the climate became more arid the movement of the hunters and the herds can be traced moving southwards down the peninsula until around 2000 BC they disappear into the northern limits of Ar Rub al-Khali, the vast sand sea of the Empty Quarter. Until about six thousand years ago there were brackish lakes running in from the Gulf along the edge of Ar Rub al-Khali, where there were large game animals, such as hippopotamus, preyed on by Neolithic hunters who produced some remarkably fine stone tools.[15] The fact that the Nile generally followed a higher course than it does today or than it did during dynastic times probably means that many late predynastic settlements, including perhaps some comparable with major centres like Hierakonpolis and Naqada (two cities which will be seen to be of great importance in the late predynastic period) now lie buried beneath the silt laid down by the inundation.

THE ANIMALS AND THE HUNT

Even in times long after their first entry to it, when they had hunted to extinction or driven away the beasts which were once its undisturbed lords, the Egyptians living in the Valley never lost that sense of wonder at the magnificence surrounding them which they must have sensed when first they looked down on the river and the rich and fertile lands which enclosed it. This sense of wonder accounted for at least two of the most distinctive characteristics of the Egyptian psyche in later, historic times: the belief that the gods had specially favoured Egypt by providing the Valley with an abundance of nature's resources, and a sense of oneness with the animals with which they shared it. This identity with animals is manifested in the personification of even the greatest gods in the form of animals and the reverence which was paid to them, as well as in the ability, amounting frequently to genius, to delineate and to portray animals and their lives generally with an absolute accuracy of observation. This is done, moreover, with no hint of patronage, but rather with abundant delight.

Hunting, combined with the probably imperceptible but nonetheless telling desiccation which occurred at the beginning of the historic period in Egypt, led to the reduction, ultimately to the elimination, of whole species from the upper reaches of the Valley. Between the end of the First Dynasty and the beginning of the Fourth (a period of little more than five hundred years) elephant, rhinoceros, giraffe, and the gerenuk gazelle disappeared from the lands north of Aswan. During this time, too, they disappear from the pictorial records in tombs of the chase, which reveal with commendable accuracy the environment and ecology of Egypt at the beginning of her history. Some animals survived, however, despite the odds laid against them by man and climate. Various antelope maintained their herd levels surprisingly well, amongst these was the oryx which, although its numbers declined from its relative density in predynastic times, clung on in the coastal desert lands. This pattern was repeated in Arabia; but then, the oryx is a survival from the Pliopleistocene and as such it has presumably learned much about adaptation.

EGYPTOLOGY AND THE STUDY OF EGYPTIAN ORIGINS

As an academic discipline Egyptology is now more than two hundred years old. It is the oldest of all branches of scientific archaeology; it has greatly affected the character of archaeology as a whole and as a practice which exercises a dramatic appeal to all sorts and conditions of men. But the search for the origins of Egypt and of the unique political system which it developed started not as one might imagine at the beginning of the study of its past, but relatively late. Though enormous advances had been made in all respects in the uncovering of the ancient world during the nineteenth century, and though Egypt was the focus of both learned and romantic interest, virtually nothing was known of the earliest dynasties until late in the century. The names of the kings who made up the founding dynasties were known, often in a wildly corrupt form, from Manetho's lists but no material evidence of their existence had been found. Then the French began a series of excavations at Abydos, which throughout Egyptian history was one of the most sacred of her religious centres.

The excavations, if such they could be called, were a disaster. Directed by Emile Amélineau, a Coptologist by training, in the closing years of the nineteenth century, they were concerned simply with the acquisition of objects for museums and collectors; they were unscientific and, to put it no more forcefully, unscrupulous. There were accusations that objects were destroyed if they appeared to duplicate others, to increase the value of those which remained. The sites themselves were pillaged and no thought was given to the excavations' proper recording or to the protection of the sites involved.

The main site that Amélineau excavated comprised a group of large structures, one of which he confidently pronounced to be the tomb of Osiris, the god to whom Abydos was sacred; he produced a skull which he announced was that of the god himself. He departed from Abydos, leaving the site in ruins and the reputation of French Egyptology, which, by the devoted work of French scholars since the days when Napoleon first opened Egypt to the world deserved to be of the very highest standing, gravely diminished.

Flinders Petrie

By a fortunate chance a young Englishman, William Matthew Flinders Petrie,[16] applied to re-excavate the site. He was granted permission and began on a career which was to span the next fifty years and more, during which time he would virtually lay down the outlines of the entire history of Pharaonic Egypt.

Before Petrie's work at Abydos and later at other sites in Upper Egypt, virtually nothing was known about the origins of the Egyptian state nor of the first kings who constituted the united country's rulers and the true progenitors of its extraordinary culture. He cleared the pits left so disastrously by Amélineau and, by the expenditure of immense patience and labour, pieced together what he presented as virtually the entire chronology of the kings of the First Dynasty, to the extent that his views still dominate much Egyptological thought to this day. To make so extraordinary a discovery was typical of Petrie. He went on to find similar structures as that which the French abandoned, all dated to the first two dynasties, which evidently represented the burial places of the men and women who had created Egypt, though they may not always have been the tombs of kings.

Saqqara

Later, from the mid-1930s to the 1950s, Petrie was followed by another British archaeologist, W.B. Emery, who excavated a whole series of similar structures on the escarpment at Saqqara.[17] These too were burial monuments of the time of the early kings; they are amongst the most remarkable buildings to be preserved from high antiquity and their excavator thought they were the places of royal burial and, hence, that the tombs at Abydos were not.

Saqqara, a few miles south of the Giza plateau, had been recognized as early as 1912 as a site of great importance when it was excavated first by early Egyptologists such as Mariette and Maspero. Later, it was extensively dug by Quibell and then by Firth.[18] The French, working on the site since the 1930s, have achieved the reconstruction of one of the greatest monuments of human genius, the Step Pyramid complex of King Netjerykhet;[19] both Petrie's excavations of the archaic Royal Tombs at Abydos[20] and Emery's at Saqqara have been handsomely published.[21] Emery's volumes, in particular, are notable for the exceptionally fine drawings and reconstructions with which he, a draughtsman by training and one of a very high order, enriched his reports. Although great sites are legion in Egypt, rich in architectural remains and redolent of a majestic past, Saqqara is in the view of many the most numinous site in all Egypt, the place where the sense of the sacred is palpable and the achievement of the Egyptian people in creating a civilization like no other, is all around the visitor.

Dating the prehistoric periods

Petrie was responsible for laying down many of the foundations which underlie Egyptology to this day. Recognizing the difficulty (in his day, the virtual impossibility) of establishing an absolute chronology for preliterate, prehistoric periods, he devised the 'sequence dating' of predynastic pottery. Though now largely superseded, this system was for a long time a valuable technique by which, by tracing the development (sometimes a theoretical one) of one type of pottery from another and hence establishing a sequence of styles, Petrie believed he was able to give a general structure to the prehistoric past which had not previously been attempted.

He established the three (he would have said four) principal southern predynastic cultures known, from the locations in which they were first recognized, as the Badarian, Amratian, and Gerzean civilizations; the last two are now usually identified as Naqada I and Naqada II, whilst a third Naqada level has been added, representing the period immediately before the unification and the foundation of the kingship, which is sometimes referred to as 'Dynasty 0'.[22]

Petrie's publications of the tombs of the early kings and their supporters and of the prehistoric periods alerted the scholarly world to a whole new dimension of history. He also brought out, in the immense stream of publications for which he was responsible, books on the slate or schist palettes which are so significant a category of late predynastic artefact,[23] as well as works on scarabs, tools, and many which described excavated sites with important predynastic and archaic components.

Hierakonpolis

Other workers in the field did, however, add to the catalogue of reports dealing with these formative centuries and the sites from which the evidence was drawn. Amongst these one of the most important was Hierakonpolis, which was probably the ancient capital of one of the contending princes who sought to unify the Two Lands; however, the publication of the excavations carried out in 1897–8 by Quibell and Green[24] was less extensive than scholars of today would have wished, though laudable attempts have recently been made to disinter the material still concealed in the notes and drawings of the site's early excavation.[25]

Hierakonpolis was largely overlooked by Egyptology until quite recent times. Over the past three decades however very dramatic discoveries have been made there which have transformed our understanding of the processes which led to the emergence of the Egyptian state. These will be considered further in Chapter 5.

THE HISTORIOGRAPHY OF ANCIENT EGYPT

In more than a century and a quarter since Petrie started working, or the nearly seventy years since Emery commenced his excavations at Saqqara, much significant work has into the early periods been undertaken but, by comparison with the attention given to other later periods of Egyptian history, it has been relatively slight, until recent times. Reisner, the distinguished American Egyptologist, carried out his magisterial review of the development of the Egyptian tomb from predynastic times to the appearance of the pyramids,[26] the period with which this book is principally concerned. Similarly Lauer, the French Egyptologist who worked at the site for many years, did spectacular work in restoring the Netjerykhet Complex at Saqqara and in so doing revealed its incomparable quality.[27] But the fact remains that this, the most crucial part of Egyptian history, was for too long dependent on researches whose origins are almost lost in the mists of archaeological beginnings.

The nature of Egyptian society in this period, though it is so remote in time from our own, is nonetheless deeply relevant, in the same way as the society developing in the east, in Sumer, is relevant. For the first time men, in both locations, were undertaking large-scale projects in what is effectively social engineering. At the same time, and most particularly in Egypt, they were evolving a series of symbols, forms, and institutions which, because they endured so remarkably well are still pertinent and potent today. The line which connects our world with theirs is direct and unbroken; they are a profoundly important element in our cultural ancestry. To understand them a little is to add greatly to the understanding of ourselves.

2

THE ROOTS OF THE EGYPTIAN STATE

Egyptian society did not spring fully ordered and organized instantly into being: the point must still be made, for both the appearance and the reality are so extraordinary. In a matter of a few short centuries the Egyptian kingdom was devised and formulated, to endure in all its essential characteristics for three thousand years, the longest lasting of all complex human societies. Egypt's social sophistication was profound at a time when all the world, except for Sumer, was locked in a benighted barbarism which in all its essentials had been unchanged for thousands of generations, since indeed, Palaeolithic times; if Egyptian society did not in fact emerge fully developed, an observer might be forgiven for thinking that it did, so far removed was it from any sort of human experience up to that time.

Egypt's emergence as a true nation-state is well charted. Her roots lay deep in the earth of the Valley on which her splendid temples, palaces, and tombs were to be built; but she was also profoundly African, by no means wholly impervious to foreign influence in the earliest times, though the character and extent of that influence is much debated still.

The procession of the dynasties into which Egyptian history is divided falls, broadly, into two parts, the predynastic and dynastic periods, and thereafter into a diversity of subdivisions of often bewildering complexity and number. At this point, however, we are concerned with that period which is termed the 'predynastic', that is to say, the time from somewhat before 5000 BC, when distinct communities can first be seen emerging, first in the deserts, then on the banks of the Nile. This process began long before the supposed unification of the state, which is conventionally dated as taking place during the early years of the thirty-second century before the present era. The predynastic period, therefore, deals with the time to c. 3200 BC.

THE DUAL KINGDOM

Just as Egyptian history is divided, arbitrarily but with considerable convenience, into these two broad divisions, so too there were always two Egypts.

The king was Lord of the *Two Lands*;[1] everything about Egypt was expressed as a duality. Though Egypt was unified in the course of the first centuries of royal rule she always maintained the notion of two kingdoms, Upper and Lower Egypt, south and north, which the king alone sustained in perpetual equilibrium and whose balance or pivot, the point at which the two kingdoms were said to meet, was somewhere near Memphis, just south of Cairo, the modern capital city.

It is quite remarkable how this quality of the two Egypts is evident throughout the long march of Egyptian history. It is not merely a poetic concept, not simply the elegant encapsulation of two topographical and historical diversities bound together in a common political destiny. The difference between them is never reconciled; like the concepts of 'left' and 'right' they are eternally opposed, whilst eternally joined. Only the king is common to each and, as Dual King and, more important still divine master of each, he brings them into union.

The southern kingdom, Upper Egypt, was always recognized as the more dominant of the two regions. It was from the south that the most enduring influences in Egyptian society came and without doubt most of its greatest leaders were southerners too. Throughout her long history Egypt constantly needed to return to the south to refresh herself and to restore her institutions, when the weight of years or of external pressures bore too heavily upon her.

Whilst there is abundant evidence for the presence of predynastic principalities in the south which were clearly kingdoms in embryo, there is no real archaeological evidence at all to suggest that a kingdom existed in the north in predynastic times. Until very recent times there has not been anything like a comparable degree of excavation of predynastic sites in northern Egypt as there has been in the south, little indeed though that has been. The fact that much of the Delta was incapable of being excavated because of the rise in the water table prevented work comparable to that carried out on Upper Egyptian sites. Recently, however, a series of excavations at Buto using advanced techniques capable of dealing with conditions such as those which prevail in the Delta, has revealed evidence of the character of the area in the late predynastic period.[2]

Whatever rudimentary political structures existed in the Valley during the fourth millennium were concentrated in the south. This fact will have been of crucial importance when a family of southern princes appears to have determined on the unification of the Valley. Long before this point, however, many of the indigenous elements which were evident in Egypt in historical times were already of immense antiquity. Some of them may be traced back to the Epipalaeolithic at the end of the Stone Age and to the profoundly important traditions laid down in late Neolithic times, notably in the southern deserts.

THE FIRST EGYPTIANS

The earliest examples of the use of stone monumentally at Nabta, one of the most important of the desert sites which have been studied increasingly in recent years, date to *c.*7000 BC. This is long before any comparable constructions of worked slabs and blocks of stone can be detected in any other ancient context. But more extraordinary still is the evidence that these early inhabitants of the western desert aligned their stone constructions to the cardinal points and to the solstices; the constructions which they left behind them have been described as 'calendar circles'.[3] Thus these early settlers were true pioneers, for thousands of years later the builders of the pyramids at Giza also established the extraordinary precision of their constructions by aligning with the constellations and by studying the movements of the planets and stars.[4]

Near the calendar circles were found stone covered burials of cattle from the same time.[5] This alone shows how profoundly deeply rooted were the cattle cults of historic Egypt. Indeed, it might be said that the cattle cults and particularly the worship of the bull represent the oldest form of 'religion' to survive in Egypt. The king's identification as a great wild bull and the multitude of gods in bovine form represent a great diapason which echoes throughout the whole of Egyptian history, from the very earliest days to its latest manifestation.

The people of Nabta moved north and eastwards, towards the Valley, as the region desiccated, the consequence of another shift in the African monsoon at the beginning of the fourth millennium and it was they who were responsible for the beginnings of Egypt's long and wonderful preoccupation with monumental stone architecture. They also contributed to the mélange of peoples who were responsible for the social diversity and complexity which typifies early Egypt leading, at the end of the fourth millennium, to the appearance of the kingship. It is clear from this evidence that the deserts played a crucial role, one that was at least as important in the formulation of the historic Egyptian personality, as did the more populous Nile Valley. It is to the people of the deserts that Egypt in historic times was indebted for the original initiatives which led at last to the flowering of the remarkable civilization that it became.

One singular conclusion that the archaeologists working in this area have arrived at in investigating sites in the far south of the country is that the tradition of pottery-making is vastly older in Egypt than had previously been recognized.[6] Pottery has been recovered from Egyptian sites dating to the ninth millennium, far earlier than the first pottery yielding sites in south west Asia, which were always believed to have been anterior to any examples from Egypt. The pottery in the southern Sahara is found in association with hunter-fisher communities which settled on the shores of permanent lakes rich in fish and large game like hippopotamus. Their experience was to be mirrored in Arabian sites many millennia later.

22

To the northwest of the Nabta Playa is Bir Kiseba,[7] another of the important early desert settlements which was especially identified with the hunters who followed the herds of wild cattle from further south in Africa. At Tushka,[8] on the Nile north of Abu Simbel, a remarkable discovery was made of the burials of two humans whose graves were surmounted by the bucrania of wild bulls. Nearby were burials of cattle and the whole area was clearly of ritual or cultic importance. The Tushka burials have been dated to 14,500 years before the present.

The practice of marking graves with bucrania is well known throughout antiquity but Bir Kiseiba is vastly more ancient than any other example known. It demonstrates the length of the relationship between humans and cattle and how enduring was the cultic aspect of that relationship. Nearly ten thousand years after the Tushka bucrania burials the bucrania of wild bulls, more than three hundred of them, were mounted around the mastaba of high-status burials at Saqqara and in the Third Dynasty, c.2650 BC in the great funerary complex built for King Netjerykhet a wild bull's skull was ceremonially interred in a stone-lined chamber in the southern court of the Step Pyramid enclosure (see Chapter 7).

Dakhleh too was inhabited from 7000 BC, its early inhabitants, like those of Nabta, being drawn from the early waves of migrants who eventually contributed their genes to the founder stocks of the historic Egyptian people. Later, in Neolithic times, the inhabitants built large hut circles and were responsible for a rich repertoire of rock art. In the Old Kingdom they built a large temple and a palace for the governor of the district at Ayn Asil.[9] Dakhleh lies some four hundred kilometres due west of Thebes. It maintained contact with the Valley throughout the Old Kingdom period, though evidence of activity in the Early Dynastic period is relatively slight.

Remarkable though these early communities are, they are not the oldest evidence of modern humans in Egypt. The earliest burial found in the Valley is of a child at Taramsa Hill, near the Ptolemaic temple of Hathor at Dendera; the burial is dated to c.55,000 years before the present.[10] At Nazlet Khater, near Tahta, the burial of a man has been dated to c.30,000 years before the present.[11] They are presently the oldest known, fully modern humans to be found in Egypt.

The presence of these communities, the calendar circles and the cattle burials all indicate that the communities were already moving towards an ordered social structure, perhaps with some form of hierarchy and evidently with individuals who practiced special occupations and others who directed the communal efforts in respect of them. It might be said that the whole fabric of later historic Egypt might be seen by the evidence from these remote settlements.

PREDYNASTIC CULTURES – EL BADARI

Around 5000 BC the earliest Egyptian villages appear. The communities which they formed were small no more at best than a few hundred people living together in flimsy huts, close enough to the river to share in its benefits but generally settling themselves on little hillocks or raised ground, sensibly enough, to avoid the flood when it came.

Each of the three principal predynastic cultures identified in Upper Egypt was to leave some definitive impress on the historical period. The first is that identified with the site of the village of El Badari, on the east bank of the Nile, further to the north than its two successors, the earlier named for the site at El Amra (Naqada I), the later for El-Gerza (Naqada II), with Naqada III immediately preceding the unification and the First Dynasty.

The Badarian people were farmers and knew of the cultivation of crops and the management of herds; it is not clear whence their civilization came or from where they themselves originated. They seem to have been fisher folk and evidently kept an access to the Red Sea open, as shells from its shores were used for their adornment. More particularly, they seem to have had contact to some quite substantial degree with western Asia, for the sheep and goats they bred are considered to be of a south-western Asiatic strain. However, it is now apparent that spasmodic, selective herding of animals had been conducted in Egypt from very early times, from long before the first permanent settlements were established in the Valley.

The Badarians appear to have lived in tents or in shelters made of skins. Their domestic economy, in addition to the evidence of animal domestication, must have been quite advanced as they made bread, traces of which have been found in their burials. The probability is that the harvesting and grinding of wild grains and cereals was practiced at a very early date. When they encountered the western Asiatic breeds of ovicaprids and later cattle, which were hardier and better suited to life in the Valley, the Badarians began to adopt them as their own. The circumstances in which that encounter happened are not known however.

Like the Sumerians, who wore woollen kilts or skirts made of sheepskin, the Badarians dressed in animal skins. This has suggested that they may have come from a cooler climate where such clothing would not have been so inappropriate as it must have been for a people living in climatic conditions such as those which prevailed in Egypt although, admittedly, the climate was somewhat more benign than it became later. The Badarians thus seem to be responsible for the first suggestion of Egypt's contact with lands to the east of the Nile Valley, at virtually the earliest period possible. Though they were living, in all probability, barely above subsistence level, they did have the leisure and the ability to develop crafts and skills from which the mighty Egyptian culture of the dynastic future was to stem. Already they seem to have developed a degree of trade with other peoples, including perhaps the importation of wood from the Syrian coast. They had established religious cults, a somewhat higher proportion of female figurines amongst their grave goods suggesting a faith more goddess-oriented than that which prevailed in Egypt in later times, when male gods tend to predominate. The figures are often very graceful, both men and women represented as dancers, their hands raised above their heads, a gesture which may also be in imitation of the horns of cattle; one of the most significant connections of the population of predynastic Egypt is with the cattle people of the Valley and these little figurines are an early manifestation of it. However, though the female figurines are notable, the Badarians produced impressive representations of cloaked and bearded males, in ivory and clay. They also manufactured a very striking range of combs in ivory; the shape of these is distinctly African and is like the combs used even today by Africans and those of African descent.

The Badarians were remarkably skilled for a people who must be presumed to have moved from something like a Neolithic society to a sedentary state. They carved in bone and, in all probability, in wood; their carvings have a notable power. But the most notable of all their products is their pottery.

Badarian pottery is highly distinctive. The style was retained by potters over many generations, even after the Badarian culture had been subsumed into that of its successors. The most frequently encountered Badarian pots are fired to a bright red or brown finish, often with the tops of the vessels burned black, the result it is believed of the pot being inverted in the ashes of the kiln. The fabric of the pots is remarkable; more remarkable still is that the earliest of them are often the finest in the quality of their fabrication. The walls of early Badarian vessels are fired to a hardness which approaches that of metal and they are often eggshell-thin. It is not known how the Badarians acquired the knowledge of the techniques of firing their kilns to the high temperatures required to produce such wares, or how they controlled their firing. Even in their earliest products, Egyptian craftsmen showed skills of a quite exceptional and very demanding order.

It is remarkable that across the intervening Arabian deserts the contemporaries of the Badarians in Egypt, the early Ubaid potters of southern Iraq, also made pottery of the same exceptionally fine quality. This phenomenon, so unlikely in any event and doubly so with two apparently quite disparate peoples living relatively far from each other, is one of the most puzzling of the early, more or less simultaneous, developments of Egypt and of Sumer. A similar observation, marking a decline from the earlier to the later, may also be made of the exceptionally beautiful wares from Hassouna and Sammara in northern Iraq. They are the earliest of all Near Eastern pottery forms and the quality of the earliest is superlative.

The Badarian is essentially a southern culture; however, it is preceded in the north by peoples identified with two important sites in Lower Egypt. Of these the early inhabitants of the Fayum, the area of the great lake always to be celebrated throughout Egyptian history as perhaps the richest source of game for the hunt, left no traces of structures behind them. They may have been seasonal visitors to the area, like the people far away to the east in Arabia and the Gulf who camped on the East Arabian shore and lakeside sites and left behind them the fragmentary evidence of pottery of the type produced by the 'pre-Sumerian' Ubaid people in southern Mesopotamia.

Domestication – sheep and goats

The strains of domesticated goats and sheep which were known to the earliest settlers in the Nile Valley are thought to be of western Asiatic origin. The implications of this suggestion are formidable: that a people with sufficient knowledge of the principles of selection and breeding to import particular strains of animals from a foreign region into the Valley were already present in Egypt or had access to the new societies establishing themselves there. It may not be without significance that on some predynastic pots, goats, sheep and sometimes even bovines are shown standing in boats,[12] as though this was a deliberate attempt to preserve the memory of their journey, from wherever they came, to the Valley. Again, it is likely that these representations may have some cultic or ritual significance.

The domestication of sheep and goats in Naqada II society is well attested. The strain of sheep generally to be found in Egypt at this time is a screw-horned, hairy variety which had largely died out by Middle Kingdom times. The strain is also known in early Mesopotamia and it seems likely that it was introduced from there to Egypt. The goats which had been domesticated at least since Naqada I times are, on the evidence of their horns, similar to strains which were to be found in contemporary Palestine.

Domestication – bovines

The exercise of human controls over the immense herds of wild cattle which roamed the ancient world, occurred relatively late, certainly after the domestication of sheep and goats. The sheer scale of the herds meant that would have been little risk in a competent hunter detaching immature or ageing animals from the herd. It was only as humans became increasingly sedentary that the demand for regular supplies of protein brought about the corralling of selected animals and the eventual controlled breeding of bovines for this purpose.

The introduction of cattle into Egypt was principally, no doubt, up the eastern approaches to the Valley from further south in Africa. The cult of the bull was to be of immense importance in Early Dynastic Egypt: the king was identified throughout all of Egyptian history as a divine bull.[13] It is possible, to judge by certain similarities in the two instances, that aspects of the bull-cult were derived from the most elaborately developed centre of the cult in antiquity, at Catalhüyük on the Konya plain in Anatolia.[14] This remarkable site was the first great centre for the cult of the bull which has been identified archaeologically, in which the aurochs, the huge wild bull, is associated with a Great Goddess figure. The ritual or cultic significance of cattle, particularly of the bull, long antedated domestication. Wild bull skulls and horns are found in very early architectural contexts in Iran and Syria.[15]

The bull in Egypt is an important cult animal in the earliest times in which it is possible to speak of a burgeoning society ancestral to that of historic Egypt, even before this time in the case of the burials at Tushka. The hunting of cattle in the predynastic period is well-attested and is a dominating theme in rock engravings in the Upper Egyptian deserts, with many scenes of bulls being lassoed and hunted with dogs. There were substantial domestic herds extant in the fifth millennium, in the early Neolithic period in Northern Egypt and at Badari in the south.[16]

Throughout the Early Dynastic period cattle are depicted in many contexts and their management represented a major concern of the great landowners and the temples, the latter requiring a constant supply of animals for sacrifice. The significance of the wild bull can be appreciated by the fact that the king was identified with the aurochs throughout Egyptian history.[17]

Domestication – canids

From the earliest times the Egyptians seem to have reserved a particular place, both in their society and in their hearts, for the genus *Canidae*. Kings, great officers of state, and later, nobles and lesser men and women chose to be associated in close and affectionate relationship with dogs. It has been suggested that the founder population which formed the basis of the historic Egyptian community was the product of migrations of peoples seeking more amenable conditions in which to live their lives after the deterioration of the climates of the North African littoral and the increasing aridity of the Arabian desert. With these migrants came their dogs; the herders and hunters of the Sahara depicted dogs frequently in the scenes which they incised or painted on the rocky overhangs in which they habitually sheltered.

Four hunting hounds appear on an important early predynastic object, a pottery dish once in the Russian Golenishchef collection,[18] on which the four dogs are shown with their handler, who holds them on leashes. The dogs are clearly ancestral to the 'classic' Egyptian hunting hound of dynastic times, known as *tjesm*.[19] This is the alert, aristocratic, prick-eared hound which appears on countless Old Kingdom reliefs and which survived as a distinct and cosseted breed throughout Egyptian history. Its days of greatest favour, however, were during the centuries of the Old Kingdom. It is remarkable that dogs were being specifically managed at this early time; the earliest archaeological evidence of the domestication of the dog in Egypt comes from even earlier, from Merimde Bani Salame.

Dogs were given affectionate names by their human companions and were provided with burials which were intended to secure their survival in the Afterlife as reliably as the funerary customs of their masters would provide, that both dog and human would be together for ever.

The domestication of the dog probably occurred many times, in many different locations. It has been argued that it happened first in very remote times and that the history of dogs and humans are inextricably bound together.[20] It is surely one of the most extraordinary aspects of early Egyptian society that, in the midst of creating the first nation-state, forming institutions of great complexity, eventually building the most enduring monuments in world history, uniquely amongst ancient societies the Egyptians brought the dog into a close association with them, making them part of their daily lives, in an enduring and affectionate companionship.

MERIMDE BANI SALAME

A large and well-developed northern site has been identified at Merimde, dating from the fifth millennium;[21] its earliest level has been attributed to c.4800 BC, thus making it contemporary with early Badarian in the south. The site is approximately 180,000 square metres in extent, and thus represents a major settlement. Some evidence of trade with Palestine, with the people of the Sinai peninsula and even perhaps with more distant eastern peoples, has been detected here. Among the goods found is a particular type of weapon, the pear-shaped mace which later played an important part in Egyptian history. This type of mace seems to have originated in Mesopotamia and Susa and it was replaced by the disc-shaped mace which is more typically Egyptian.

As communities began to coalesce in the Valley, a process which began in the early sixth millennium BC, the first evidences of structured societies may be discerned. Three of the earliest, which reveal influences from south western Asia, are recorded here.

MA'ADI

At Ma'adi (today a suburb of Cairo) another major northern predynastic settlement has been identified. It seems to have owed its origins to an early manifestation of the trade in copper, considerable quantities of which have been found there, the source of which was probably located on the Sinai peninsula. Large quantities of Palestinian pottery have been recovered from sites at Ma'adi and indicate a sustained and flourishing relationship in pre-dynastic times.

One of the singularities of the Ma'adi cemeteries of this period, which are very extensive, is the burial of dogs and gazelles in their own graves. At El Omari, near Ma'adi, one grave revealed a skeleton holding a staff, perhaps part of the primitive regalia of a person with some authority in the community.[22]

BUTO

The excavations at the Delta site of Buto have opened up a new chapter in the study of early Egypt and of the Delta in the late predynastic period.[23] Buto was always regarded as the capital of Lower Egypt in antiquity, the northern compliment to Hierakonpolis in the south, one of the most influential centres in the process which led to the creation of the Egyptian kingship and the eventual unification of the Valley. The predynastic population of Buto shared in the important northern culture which is identified with Ma'adi, where it was first recognized.

The earliest level at Buto is contemporary with Naqada I in the mid-fourth millennium. Buto I shows connections with the Canaanite culture of southern Palestine: pottery from Buto shows parallels with that found at Nahal Mismar near the Dead Sea, the site of the discovery of a substantial hoard of finely made copper objects of advanced manufacture and design. The pottery at Buto is made from local clay, employing Canaanite forms. This indicated that Canaanite potters were present in Buto at the time, working alongside their Egyptian counterparts.[24] Buto II ends with late Naqada II and at this point influences from Upper Egypt become widespread in the north and indeed, throughout the whole Valley.

Some parallels have been suggested[25] with a group of clay objects of unknown function, which are very similar to clay cones of late Uruk manufacture which were used to decorate the walls and columns of temples there. Initially it was thought that these might indicate the presence of travellers from Uruk, probably merchants residing in Buto and importing some of their own goods and customs, but this view is now discarded. Since their discovery at Buto similar 'cones' or as they tend now to be called, 'nails' have been found on a number of Early Dynastic locations, including Hierakonpo-lis.[26] Whilst their purpose is still unclear the fact that they were not confined to Buto has diminished the possibility of the connection with Uruk architectural forms. However, the fact remains that their only known parallels are to be found on Mesopotamian sites, thus suggesting another addition to the growing list of Mesopotamian elements or inspirations to be found on early Egyptian sites.

NAQADA I

Around the beginning of the fourth millennium the Badarian culture in the south gave way to the first of those identified with the site of the ancient settlement of Naqada, an archaeological horizon which once was more generally called the Amratian period, after its original find-site of El-Amra in northern Upper Egypt. Naqada was the location of one of the most important centres of population traditionally associated with the followers of the god Set, who was particularly identified with the people of the south. The Naqada I people were almost certainly the direct descendants of the earlier settlers and their culture really represents a more advanced phase of the Badarian. They quickly developed a relatively high material culture, based on the greatly increased potential that they realized through the improved domestication of animals. Gradually during this period the old reliance on hunting diminished and the prosperity which came from improved farming techniques led to a substantial increase in population.

The Naqada I people built reed boats and began the historic river traffic that was to be the means, for as long as Egypt remained a nation, of ensuring the country's unity and political control. They ornamented their pottery with designs of animals and brought the ancient craft of stone-flaking to a high degree of skill; ivory, presumably traded up from the south, from the obscure regions of Africa, was employed, as with the Badarians, for making combs, but now also for knife-hilts and vases, while gold took its place amongst the precious substances with which the craftsman began to familiarize himself. Copper too was used for the first time, hammered cold and shaped into pins and harpoon heads.

Draughtsmanship, ever one of the glories of Egyptian art (though still relatively unappreciated for its high quality) appeared, at first tentatively, in the drawings of boats, animals, and rudimentary landscapes which decorated the pottery. Textiles, too, were decorated and one example survives from Gebelein which shows the remarkable standards which the Egyptians achieved, even at this early period: one in particular depicts a fisherman casting his nets in the Nile and is a vivid naturalistic work.[27] A loom is shown on a Naqada I dish, demonstrating that craftsmanship technique and the equipment that powered it were already respected.

Naqada I pottery is, like the products of the Badarian potters, very distinctive; one of the most common forms is a red fabric scored with designs and then filled with a white decorative finish. A wide variety of designs was thus produced, showing animals and the hunt, fishermen, boats, and scenes of what appears to be ritual dancing, with the dancers again holding their arms above their heads.

The pottery is well made, its forms often seeming to imitate other materials. Basket shapes obviously replicate woven products; of the others, a wide-mouthed vessel like an inverted bell is particularly memorable. Naqada I pottery is diverse and varied; already the Egyptian craftsman is delighting in the exploitation of form and the special relationship which, throughout Egyptian history but particularly in the earliest periods, persisted between the craftsman and the materials which he used. To an extent which is unparalleled in other early cultures the Egyptian craftsman appears always to be wrestling, vigorously and joyfully, with the materials he employs, testing them and seeking to establish how far he can assert his mastery over them. This extraordinary unity of the craftsman with his materials, which was to be one of the marks of the Egyptian artist ever afterwards, appears for the first time in the Naqada I period.

Naqada I pottery reveals some evidence of western Asiatic influence on what had already become basic Egyptian forms. There are similarities with some of the designs developed in south-western Asia, notably in Susa,[28] but some authorities would see them only as general design concepts typical of societies at this stage of development. The origin of the cultures of south western Asia are, in many ways, as elusive as those of Egypt. The pottery of Naqada I is approximately contemporary with late Ubaid ware which marks the end of the sequence which proceeds the appearance of the people who can definitely be identified as Sumerians; strictly, the Sumerians can only be so identified by their language, the earliest written evidence for which appears somewhat before 3000 BC. Unlike the Badarians, who buried their dead away from their settlements, the Naqada I people kept their dead close by, suggesting that there was at least some cultural differences between the two groups, or else the acceptance by the later group of some practices unknown to their predecessors.

There is a concentration of important Naqada I sites along the river between Naqada and Abydos, the region from which the most creative forces in Egypt were always to spring. Naqada itself was a centre of the people who honoured the great and enigmatic god Set as their supreme deity; their capital was called Nubt, literally 'the town of gold'. Like its counterpart Hierakonpolis, 'the city of the Falcon', identified with Horus and called Nekhen in antiquity, it was a flourishing settlement in Naqada I times.

The Naqada I people seem to have had some curious practices for which there is no evidence of continuation in dynastic times. It has been suggested that they were headhunters, from the number of severed skulls found in their graves; however, this could as likely be the evidence of the dismembering or disarticulation of skeletons practiced by various early communities. The character of life in Egypt at this time must have been tribal and communal from various representations it seems their warriors wore feathers in their hair, rather like their contemporaries in Susa and the Sahara. Other than the bow and arrow and the spear, the Naqada I people's most typical weapon was the disc-shaped mace which was eventually superseded by the pear-shaped mace, which is of south-western Asian origin.

The Egyptians hated the darkness and the cold: the sun was a generous and beloved divinity. In the same mood, gaiety and the love of life are always close to the surface of even the humblest Egyptian art. Animals were a source of delight to the Naqada I people and many early works convey the sense of wonder and happiness which their observation and that of all the natural world induced. The domesticated species, of course, figure largely in the work of predynastic artists but even the great beasts, lion and hippopotamus for example, could be treated with friendly license. The hippopotamus was a creature to be feared by the river folk and in later times it often personified the malign forces of the underworld. But in predynastic times a potter could produce a wide-necked vessel around the rim of which marches solemnly a procession of little hippopotami, moulded expertly. But one of them, evidently bored with the regularity of their progress, turns aside, to peer hopefully over the edge of the bowl, a touch of humour which, because it changes the rhythm of the work as a whole but gives point to it, is near to genius. To break the regularity of a line of animals by giving one a particular individuality became a favoured device of artists throughout the Old Kingdom.

The hippopotamus never ceased to amuse the Egyptians, as well as to frighten them. They were fascinated by its massive shape and its anthropomorphic character, with the expression of its massive features and crafty little eyes the very caricature of humanity. One of the finest carvings, in alabaster, of the period probably just around the time of the unification or perhaps a short while before it, is of a hippo, massive and four-square but with a curiously cheerful, even complacent, expression on its face. It is of a monumental quality which anticipates later, larger works.[29]

NAQADA II

The second of the southern predynastic cultures identified with Naqada now appears, in the form of the second Naqada horizon. In fact, the Naqada II or Gerzean phase presents a natural succession from its immediate predecessor, with the important difference that it was responsive to a much more powerful and, it would appear, more sustained alien influence than either of those which it followed. The Naqada II period is marked by dynamic changes in Egypt, when these foreign influences seem especially to have heightened the native Egyptian genius and to have produced a galvanic series of new advances in the Valley's society. At much the same time the appearance in southern Iraq of the Sumerians in their role of city-builders initiated the long course of Mesopotamian history by changing the established character of the earlier, modest villages and little settlements into social and political structures considerably more formidable in scale. It should however be emphasized that such foreign influences in Egypt that can be identified at this time are essentially peripheral to the strong and distinctly Egyptian persona which is already very much in evidence, throughout parts of the deserts which could support habitation and throughout the Valley.

The Naqada II phase is crucial to the formation of the dynastic state. The settlements which were apparent in the Naqada I phase now grow considerably, in the case of Naqada, Hierakonpolis, This\Abydos and other, less important centres which became, to all intents and purposes, cities. An engaging model of a town wall from this period shows two little watchmen peering apprehensively over the top of it, on the look-out, presumably, for marauders.[30] One of the problems of living in cities was early on found to be their capacity for exciting the envy and the predatory instincts of peoples living outside their walls.

All forms of manufactured goods proliferate: stone vessel carving becomes an industry which was to be one of the glories of Egyptian art for the next half millennium. Pottery takes on a form quite different from that which characterized the first Naqada period; made in an attractive pale brown to pinkish fabric it is decorated with a brilliant repertory of drawings and designs applied in paint before firing. Some of these are abstract, others repeat the repertory of ships, animals, and hunting introduced in Naqada I. The earliest Naqada II pottery seems to be influenced by foreign forms: vessels supplied with filter spouts and triangular lug handles look like imitations of wares produced by the Uruk potters of Mesopotamia.[31] By this time, c.3400 BC, Uruk pottery production had spread widely from its home in southern Mesopotamia; it has been assumed that the Uruk-style wares (but not Uruk pottery itself) that inspired the Egyptian potters reached Upper Egypt by land routes through Palestine, suggested by the discoveries at Buto. However, a trans-Arabian route is equally feasible; a westward route across the northern deserts, from the head of the Arabian Gulf westwards, had long existed.

The Naqada II people seem to have been much impressed by boats. Whether this implies that they were originally from a region where water transport was even more important than it was in Egypt, is not certain; it may simply have been a sensible response to their proximity to the river. But an extraordinary number of their productions, painted on pottery and carved in or on slate and schist, represent boats. Clearly these are often sacred vessels and as such were the ancestors of the sacred barques in which Egyptian divinities, like their Sumerian counterparts, were accustomed to travel. The representations of boats from this period often contain enigmatic passengers, often in threes and frequently represented with feathers in their hair; many are presented with extraordinary elegance and a highly developed sense of form, showing figures leaping from the boats almost balletically. They are, demonstrably, works of art of high accomplishment.

The Naqada II preoccupation with boats, which probably included seagoing craft as suggested by the representations on the rock walls of the Upper Egyptian deserts and wadis, including the Wadi Hammamat which links the Nile Valley with the Red Sea, indicates at least the possibility of the

Valley people having maintained quite far reaching trade routes and relations with foreigners who came from distant lands. At this time, too, considerable specialization in the work of the craftsmen becomes apparent,
when contact with south-west Asia appears to be most active.

Precious metals now begin to be used with some frequency in Upper
Egypt. Gold and silver were both accessible to the Valley people though the
silver that they used particularly was in fact a 'white gold', a natural
amalgam of the two metals found in its native state. The prodigality with
which gold in particular is used at this time indicates a marked upturn in
the taste of the Egyptian clients who commissioned the vessels and artefacts
on which it was used and in their ability to recompense the artists and
craftsmen who produced them, as well as being able to maintain the mining
expeditions necessary to obtain the ore. Mining became one of the principal
industries of Egypt in Naqada II times, with expeditions to Nubia for stone
(also a source of gold) and to the turquoise mines of Sinai.

CONTACT WITH SOUTH-WEST ASIA

Whether there was *direct* contact between the Egyptians of the late predynastic period and the people of south-western Asia of the late Ubaid, Uruk,
and Jemdet Nasr periods is not clear and what is still more obscure is the
reason that prompted the contact between them. The solution which envis-
ages the south-western Asian people (it is hardly right yet to call them
either Sumerians or Elamites) becoming aware of the Nile Valley as a source
of gold, is attractive. After all the Valley was rich in gold, but how the easterners might have acquired the knowledge of it is another matter; the Sumerians did however sustain long exchange routes and knew of the supplies of
copper which were available in Oman.

It is possible that if there were traders in touch with the Delta, as seems
most likely, they may have encountered reports of the mineral riches of
southern Egypt. The theory of the Mesopotamians' search for gold having
brought them into contact with the Valley people also proposes an influx of
specialists and craftsmen into Egypt drawn there by the reports of the riches
of the little independent 'courts' which, it is clear, were established in
various of the predynastic centres of population such as This (the location of
which is uncertain but probably lies in the region of Abydos), Naqada and
Hierakonpolis. The names of the lesser rulers who actually preceded the
kings of Egypt, rather than those of the 'demi-gods' of the national myth,
have been found recorded on the rocks of southern Upper Egypt; unfortu-
nately many are judged indecipherable. It was in all probability as a result of
the search for gold that these 'princes' sought to control the trade routes and
the access to its sources from their various strongholds. It would have been
to their courts that the gold-hungry easterners made their way.

EGYPT AND SUMER COMPARED

In considering the possibility of contacts between the people of the Nile Valley and the Mesopotamians there is an important distinction to be made between the impact of this post-Neolithic phase, with which we are dealing, on the peoples of the two regions. In Sumer the whole pattern of the society underwent a radical and permanent change as the city came to predominate as the characteristic Sumerian social institution. In Egypt the shift from the Badarian and Naqada I cultures and the impact of the foreign influences, whilst they produced real effects and marked changes, were more important in inspiring a rapid development of the unique Egyptian personality which was to establish itself over the next few hundred years.

This autochthonous personality remained as the essential form of the society for as long as the society lasted. Considered in another way, the Naqada II phase is an intermission (though an intensely creative one) between the late Neolithic stages of the Valley society's development and the coming of the great dynasts who were to unite the Two Lands into the Dual Kingdom and thus create the historic Egyptian state.

In historic times the Egyptians were always deeply resentful of any incursions by foreigners into their land; they resisted them vigorously, though with varied success. However, in those early years the influence from the east seems to have been more benign and hence more acceptable; at least it does not appear to have been resisted and, in so far as it touched off some important elements in Egypt's development, seems to have been of quite a different quality from the barbarous onslaughts of the largely savage tribes, whom the Egyptians in later times identified dismissively as the 'sand dwellers', originating in the north and east.

The apparently common factors which manifest themselves in Egypt and Sumer around this time are too many not to warrant some speculation about the possibility of their common, or at least their related, origin. A comparative examination of the two peoples is appropriate by reason of their close geographical proximity and the fact that they emerged at roughly the same time in their historic form.

A glance at the map will show that Egypt and Sumer are not really far distant from each other, though they are separated by formidable desert barriers which stretch eastwards from the Nile to the western borders of Sumer, with the Red Sea dividing most of Egypt from Arabia; seen from space the proximity of the two lands is even more telling. By early historic times there was a caravan route running north-eastwards out of Egypt, skirting Sinai and climbing up the coastline of the eastern Mediterranean, where it linked with other routes from the Sumerian cities which ran into the Middle Euphrates region to sites such as Habuba Kabira across western Iraq into Jordan and Syria. Even in historic times this route was hazardous, the caravans being preyed on equally by ferocious nomads and the guardians of the cities which straddled the routes; then, if those dangers were surmounted, they survived only at the mercy of the desert, which, though it may have been marginally less dreadful than it is today, would have produced problems of the logistics of survival of immense difficulty for such early travellers. As there is no evidence for the domestication of the camel until long after this time, to speak even of 'caravans' in the earliest period is really anachronistic; if pack animals were employed at all they were probably the fractious and argumentative ass and the onegar. The land routes could hardly have been the most efficient or the most generally used until long after the period with which we are concerned.

Yet contact was established very early on between the predynastic Egyptians and the Mesopotamians, seemingly in sufficient depth for the later people to have left unmistakable material evidence of their influence on Egypt. The evidence, scanty and often unrelated though it is, makes it clear that the influences at work ran from Sumer or Elam to Egypt and not, apparently, in the opposite direction, at least until very much later. It seems likely that the contacts began early in the fourth millennium and continued until the two civilizations reached the point where each assumed its distinctive historical character at the end of the millennium and the beginning of the third.

That the two societies, Egypt and Sumer, developed along parallel but wholly disparate lines is a matter of history and would be explained by the entirely different environment which was to be found in Mesopotamia and in Egypt. For centuries Egypt was insulated from any pressure of other peoples which the Egyptians themselves could not easily contain; the majestic flow of the god-congested Nile, once its power was harnessed, provided the means for a standard of living which confirmed the Egyptians in their view that they were the favoured children of the gods, living in an ideal world.

The control of water supplies was obviously of profound importance to both people. Both cultures developed alongside powerfully flowing rivers. Of all ancient technical achievements, after the discovery of the methods of crop cultivation and herd management, unquestionably the most important was the recognition that the inundations of the great rivers could be harnessed and the land around them made fertile by the controlled distribution of water. That the control of the rivers' flood was a major preoccupation of the state in Egypt as well as in Sumer is evident from the archaic representations of the earliest kings engaged in the ritual cutting of canals.

According to their own traditions, the Egyptians were from the earliest times so expert in the practice of irrigation that Narmer himself, the supposed unifier of the Two Kingdoms, displaying a positively heroic enthusiasm for hydraulic engineering, is said to have diverted the course of the Nile to found his capital city at Memphis, near the borders of Upper and Lower Egypt. Certainly in historic times major river works were constantly undertaken by the central as well as by the provincial administrations of Egypt.

The discovery of many of the techniques of this branch of engineering by a river people could have been as the result of an empirical process of accident, observation, and experiment. But the fact that both the Egyptians and the Sumerians developed irrigation programs so early and thus made possible the extraordinary advances of their societies, more or less simultaneously, makes the possibility of yet another area of contact and exchange of ideas between them seem more likely than chance or the uncertainties of simultaneous invention.

It is particularly at this point, as the Naqada II horizon appears in the latter part of the fourth millennium, that men who were either Sumerians or who knew Sumer well entered the Nile Valley and contributed to the foundation of the most wholly monolithic political society known until perhaps the present day. In this characteristic, incidentally, Egypt was very different from Sumer, for the political structure which developed in the valley of the Twin Rivers was characterized by a multitude of little city states, constantly struggling for a short-lived hegemony, one above the rest. Never, whilst Sumerian culture flourished, was a lasting empire established over the little cities, except at the very end of their existence in the Ur III period, *c.* 2020 BC which, it will be seen, was a time of general upheaval in much of the Near East. With the collapse of the so-called 'Neo-Sumerian' empire, with its capital at Ur, the Sumerians disappear from history, their language retained only as a liturgical medium.[32] It was only when the influence of semitic-speaking peoples began to predominate at the end of the third millennium, coming in from the deserts which surrounded Sumer, that one interest was able to assert itself over all the others, exemplified by the creation of the empire of Sargon the Great.

THE WADI HAMMAMAT

About 130 miles south of the extreme tip of the Sinai peninsula, on the western shore of the Red Sea, lies the Egyptian port of Qesir. It is backed by the harsh, often snow-capped Red Sea mountains, the home of eagles, ibex, and gazelle, which yield only a bare existence to their nomadic inhabitants. The mountains are cut with *wadis*, ancient dried-up water courses, the paths of rivers which have long since ceased to flow but which still when the early summer comes, rush with water from the snow-laden heights. It is a strange and, even for Egypt, a paradoxical region, in a land crackling with paradox.

One of the largest of these dead river beds is the Wadi Hammamat which runs through the mountains due west of Qesir. Throughout Egypt's history the wadi was a great trading route with the caravans moving to and from the sea coast and the Nile Valley cities, strung out along the river which here makes an enormous bend and runs, first eastwards and then turns back westwards, ultimately to resume its flow to the Mediterranean.

The mountains are rich in many prized stones including schist, which from the earliest times was used for making the cosmetic palettes which were a feature of early Egyptian ways of life and death. Gold is also found here, that metal which the Egyptians used with such abundance and delight.

The Wadi Hammamat forms a natural corridor through the eastern desert which links the river and the sea, with little more than a hundred miles between them. It is significant that all the principal archaeological evidence which indicates contact with Mesopotamia and western Asia is found in the predynastic and Early Dynastic sites which are concentrated along this stretch of the Nile. From Hierakonpolis in the south to El Badari in the north is a distance of only about 130 miles. On many artefacts of the late predynastic period, such as the hilts of ceremonial knives, on ceremonial maces, palettes and painted pottery, boats of an apparently Mesopotamian type with notably high prows and sterns have been identified; they are abundantly included in the carvings and drawings incised on the rock walls of the wadi. Clearly the boat was an important and even perhaps a sacred object to the people who inscribed so many representations of it on the walls of the wadi. If some travellers at least made the long haul from the Arabian Gulf, far away to the east, to Egypt they may well have thought the fact worth recording, the more so if the boat itself was invested with some sort of sacred character. Several of the representations show a large black ship with a huge sail, which seems to have been especially significant to those who recorded it.

From the headlands in the north, where the lagoons, canals, and rivers of what is now southern Iraq made movement by boat the natural means of transport for the early settlers in southern Mesopotamia, the Sumerians set out in search of trade. Hugging the western (Arabian) coast they would have landed at the several islands which were the most important components of the economy of the ancient Arabian Gulf. From these island Bahrain, though largely unpopulated in the early third millennium, was fertile with plentiful supplies of fresh water Tarut and, further south Umm an-Nar, they would have been able to take on water and provisions; the prevailing winds would have sped them on their journey. Then for six months of the year the voyage westwards from the mouth of the Gulf, beyond the Straits of Hormuz, would have been facilitated by currents which would have driven sailing craft rapidly along the south Arabian coast.

In the context of possible contacts with Egypt by the Sumerians and Elamites it is important to remember that the culture which flourished in the Arabian Gulf, even in its earliest manifestations in the Ubaid period, was a mercantile, seagoing culture, its people avid for trade. It is entirely possible that their enthusiasm for profit took them all the way across (or around) Arabia to the Valley. It may be argued that so substantial a voyage, around the Arabian peninsula, in extent amounting to some four thousand nautical miles, would have been far beyond the capacity or the confidence of early seamen. However, man has not changed so much since the end of the Neolithic period that the people of that time would not have found it as impossible to resist the challenge of pushing on beyond each day's horizon as their successors would today.

3

THE PURSUIT OF THE DIVINE

Egyptian artists, craftsmen – call them what you will – who were employed on the building of tombs and palaces, on the decoration of their interiors, the making of their furnishings, the design and management of their structures, were all engaged in processes which are recognizable today and to which are attributed specific designations. It is certainly true that their motivation may be qualitatively different from their modern successors, closer to the medieval craftsman who only was seen to have produced a sublime work of art in the eyes of subsequent generations. Yet the kings, queens and great nobles of Egypt, even in its earliest days, cosseted and honoured men of talent who produced those artefacts which today are hailed as great works of art. It may be that the argument of their motivation is futile; it is by their works that we may judge them.

Whether, amongst the migrants who drifted into the Valley in the early centuries of the processes which ultimately provided the basis of the population of historic Egypt, there were those who possessed such skills, we cannot know, though the evidence of the people who manipulated and set into position the megaliths with such astronomical precision at Nabta in the deserts in the far south must be remembered. There must also have been some from the western Sahara who knew of the traditions of rock paintings which are so improbable and so splendid a legacy from these artistically talented cattle-herders, whose work was once thought to be inspired by Egyptian original until it was realized that they dated from a thousand years before the foundation of the Egyptian state.[1] However it may have been; much of Egypt's enduring celebrity is the consequence of the work of those who practiced their skills in material and enduring form.

That the earliest extensive repertory of the work of hunters seeking to express some innate yearning or merely to fill an idle hour, is to be found inscribed, pecked, or engraved on countless rock surfaces is not without significance. The rock surfaces of the Egyptian deserts, particularly the eastern desert, provided a limitless canvas, the exploitation of which clearly proved irresistible to the herdsman or his companions, as it did in the Sahara or in the wastes of western Arabia.

The Egyptian was entirely at home in working with living rock faces, from the beginning of the fourth millennium BC, at the latest. The rock art of the ancient Near East is the most extensive and certainly the most informative documentary source surviving of the life of the people of the hunting bands in their transition from the ancient transhumant to a more settled way of life. Rock drawings reveal much about hunting, ritual, the dance, costume, and the way of life of the desert people who produced them and the fauna with which they shared their lives.

In Egypt the densest distribution of rock drawings is in the south, reaching down into Nubia. The great eastern desert wadi system, centred on the Wadi Hammamat and its tributaries, is exceptionally richly provided with elaborate and often highly skillful representations of men, animals, boats, and formal inscriptions from at least the late fourth millennium (perhaps earlier still) down to Roman and later times. It is particularly in the southern eastern desert regions that the drawings which supposedly mark the progress of shipborne travellers from Mesopotamia are to be found, which will be described further below.

The drawings (they are more strictly-speaking engravings) are generally incised or pecked onto the relatively smooth and often friable surface of the rocks which border the desert tracks, or on the shaded overhangs of outcrops which have always provided shelter during the fiercest heat of the day. Low hills are sometimes favoured; often a remote chasm or defile will be selected as the site of an outpouring of creative endeavour, in such cases giving the area the character of a sanctuary or sacred place. The work ranges from the simple doodlings of untalented individuals, through erotic representations of occasionally quite inventive versatility, to productions of a high, startling artistic quality. The quite exceptional quantity of drawings in the Sahara, Egypt and Arabia, executed over many millennia, suggests nothing so much as a significant population of artists dedicated to the exercise of their art; they are not to be dismissed as merely the products of desert ennui, a filling in of the empty hours of a drowsy, sun-drenched afternoon. The rock-art of all these regions is the product of the unconscious, seeking expression and release.

The scenes which appear on the Egyptian rock surfaces reveal many elements of continuity between the late Neolithic period, to which the early works belong and the long sequence of royal rule which was to follow them. Although Egyptian rock art shares traditions with both the Sahara and Arabia even at its earliest it is recognizably Egyptian, powerful and assured in technique and content. Egyptian rock art is of vital importance in providing insights into a society which was preliterate, of which they are the only surviving record.

The rock art of ancient Egypt is so extensive a documentary phenomenon, especially in the deserts of the south east of the country that it was soon identified by Egyptologists as demanding study. In his early exploration of the southern parts of the Valley, Petrie compiled records of the principal graphic themes that he encountered. Other travellers followed him, Arthur Weigall[2] before the First World War and, perhaps the best known of all the recorders of Egyptian rock-art, Hans Winkler, published immediately before the outbreak of the Second World War in two handsome volumes.[3] The sites which he described, illustrated by many admirable photographs, are situated between Qena and Aswan, a region which is particularly rich in rock art sites.

Winkler believed that he could detect various categories of the work of the differing groups who inhabited the regions he examined or who passed through them. To one of these he gave the name 'Eastern Invaders', immigrants whom he identified especially by the representations of boats of a type which he recognized as Mesopotamian.

Winkler's work drew attention to the frequency with which large sailing craft and rowing craft were depicted in remote desert locations, often far from the river. Initially, Egyptological opinion found it difficult to account for this occurrence and it was an appreciable time before scholarly consideration came to be given to what was, certainly, a puzzling phenomenon.

It is possible that some of the scenes engraved on the rock walls may have a ritual significance. The animal cults which are so powerful a part of later Egyptian ritual and belief obviously had their origins here and there are some scenes which seem to represent sacrifices in the course of the hunt or in preparation for it.

The publication of Winkler's volumes was followed quite speedily by that of a British scholar, J.H. Dunbar, who surveyed sites in Lower Nubia[4] in the 1920s and 1930s. He was particularly interested in the depictions of the dogs which accompanied the hunters and he makes the observation that the dog is absent from those scenes in which elephant appear. He suggested that this may be because the elephant had already withdrawn from this part of the Valley before the dog arrived.[5] This is inherently improbable however, and it will be seen to be unlikely in the light of evidence recovered from Hierakonpolis (see 85 below). A important survey was carried out in the 1970s by Gerald Fuchs in the region of the Wadi Barramiyya, close to a major trading route which in ancient times led to the gold mines which supplied much of that precious metal for the temples and palaces.[6] Amongst the many arresting images which he recorded was a falcon, in the position adopted by the Horus falcon surmounting the *serekh*, the sacred heraldic device adopted by the First Dynasty kings.[7]

In recent years, another well focused series of expeditions to the eastern desert, under the style 'The Followers of Horus' (led by David Rohl) have revisited some of Winkler's sites and reviewed his work.[8] Many of the sites have been lost over the intervening sixty years and more; the expeditions have, however, identified others, several of which are of particular

Figure 3.1 The rock drawings of southern Upper Egypt are often of great complexity and
vivacity. They show many episodes of contact with high-prowed boats, frequently
with large numbers of oarsmen and featuring tall, warrior or divine figures with
high plumed headdresses. Such boats are customarily described as 'Mesopotamian'.

One of the most celebrated rock drawings, from Wadi Abu Markab el-Nes,
which was first identified by Hans Winkler before the Second World War. The
two towering figures in the high-prowed boat and their smaller companions have
excited much speculation over the years. The tall figures may be divine. To the
right another figure, with an elaborate headdress, appears to be holding a rope
attached to the boat in which the dominant figures stand.

importance. The region in which the rock-art is located was somewhat more
benign climatically in the predynastic period and would have been able to
support both animal and human life. It was good hunting country, hence
the concentration of rock art in what is now a particularly desolate region.
One image recorded by this expedition at Wadi Mineh (North) is of a boat
of 'Mesopotamian type' with a falcon standing in the prow of the vessel.[9]
This image, like that recorded by Fuchs, is of considerable significance for it
is obviously suggestive of the badge of the prince who was to claim the sovereignty of the Valley and whose symbol was the falcon. What a Horus
falcon was doing standing on the prow of a Mesopotamian vessel, is another
matter entirely.

Many of the sites which Winkler found which picture the high-prowed
Mesopotamian-type boats also include mysterious standing figures, generally
of superhuman scale, sometimes nude, sometimes wearing what appear to
be short tunics or long caftan-like robes. Frequently they have plumes or

43

Figure 3.2 A remarkable carving on a rock face in the Wadi Adab, which appears to represent an ancient Mesopotamian solar symbol, an attribute of the god Uttu who, in later times, was recognised as the sun-god of the Sumerians.

The half-disc in the crescent at the top of the engraving is known in Mesopotamia in the late fourth millennium. It is a pictograph, the form of epigraphy which preceded Sumerian cuneiform; it represents the word 'sun'.

Taken with the Falcon, the symbol of the Egyptian divine kingship depicted on the prow of a 'Mesopotamian' vessel, found in Wadi Mineh (South) it suggests a notable Mesopotamian contact with southern Upper Egypt in late predynastic times.

feathers in their hair; by their size, markedly greater than their presumably human companions they are variously described as 'chiefs' or divine beings. In one scene, in the Wadi Barramiyya, two of these enigmatic figures, wearing double plumes, stand beside a high-prowed boat, a horned animal, and hunting dogs, attended by a small hunter with a single plume or feather in his hair.[10]

A particularly important concentration of rock art is to be found in western Arabia. It is very widespread; some of it is also extremely early, with the representations of large, standing warriors, for example, having been dated to the fifth millennium BC.[11] The Arabian rock carvings provide evid-

Figure 3.3 A very large ship, with a central cabin or shrine, with many oarsmen indicated by
the vertical lines on the boat's deck. One large figure, wearing a high-plumed
headdress points forward; it is suggested by the Eastern Desert Survey Report that
this gesture signifies 'Westwards'. Wadi el-Barramiya.

Source: all references are from D. Rohl (ed.) *The Followers of Horus Eastern Desert Survey Report Volume
One* (ISIS 2000) and the photographs are by D. Rohl, by whose permission they are reproduced
here.

ence of the desiccation of the peninsula and the effect which this had on the
previously abundant herds of wild cattle on which the hunters preyed.

Many of the themes found repeatedly in the work of Egyptian rock artists
are present in that of their contemporaries in southwestern and western
Arabia, in Iran and later in Oman, though in the case of the Iranian
examples such correspondences tend to be found in glyptic art and in the
decoration of pottery rather than in rock drawings. These common themes
include the warrior with a feathered headdress, the buckler with handles
projecting from its ends, the lyre, the bucranium (very widespread, in all
forms), and a dagger with a lunate pommel, which is also found in Egypt
during the First Dynasty.

In the plastic arts, Egyptian potters and vase makers excelled early in the
history of settled communities in the Valley. Reference has already been
made to the pottery of the earliest cultures in the southern Valley and
though pottery-making was always one of the subtlest of Egyptian crafts,
stone was the medium with which the craftsman came to feel most assured
and in which his genius in the early centuries was most richly demonstrated.
Egypt is exceptionally well-provided with fine stone of all colours and com-
positions, ranging from soft, almost plastic stones like the chlorites, to the
hardest diorites and granites. All of these were used in predynastic times but
the finest stone vessels appear in the First Dynasty. These are the outstanding products of all Egyptian craftsmanship in the making of small artefacts;
for technical skill and sheer mastery of form their work in stone is unparalleled. There was a long tradition of working in stone, which had its roots in
Upper Egypt.

Figure 3.4 That boats were of great symbolic importance to the earliest inhabitants of Upper
Egypt is shown by this predynastic model of a man lying in a foetal position in a
coracle-like vessel, surely one of the most poignant images from this early period,
conveying a deep sense of desolation. As was probably the case here, the boat was
frequently used to represent the transit of the dead to the Afterlife. Naqada I,
probably from Middle Egypt.

Source: Rijksmuseum van Oudheden, Leiden. 71962/12.1

From the earliest times the Egyptian artist demonstrated a characteristic
which was wholly typical, the ability to produce works with the immediacy
and impact of a sketch, in plastic materials, or even in those less tractable. A
little figure lying in the bottom of a pottery boat, a form of coracle, conveys
a poignant sense of isolation, even of desolation, is a simple work of great
power. It is said to come from the early predynastic period, but is quite
without precedent in Egypt.[12] It suggests the mythical perception of the
boat as the means of transit between the worlds, of the living and the dead, a
convention which endured in Egypt for many centuries, which will be
encountered in many forms. Some Old Kingdom reliefs, though they are

carved in stone, have this same quality, to a quite remarkable extent, of instant recognition as this little model.

In Old Kingdom times, the owners of the great tombs took pleasure in surrounding themselves with scenes which recalled the crafts and skills of the workers on their estates. A pair of swinging weights, the management of which must have demanded considerable skill, provided the power source for the cutting of stone vessels. All vases made in this way show signs of drilling, unless the regular rings left by the drills have been pared away. What is difficult to understand however, is how the craftsmen were able to exert regular pressure *under* the shoulders of a narrow-mouthed bowl or how they were able to cut away, with perfect regularity, the interior of a bowl made from a friable substance such as schist or greywacke. The point has been made before that the walls of many Egyptian vessels are so fine and so regular that no deviation from a perfect circle can be detected in their shape, nor is any variation in the often exceptional thinness of the vessel's walls to be found.

Egyptian stone vessels of the early periods come in an immense variety of shapes and sizes, ranging from tiny cosmetic jars to large pots for the preservation of oil, wine, or grain. The best are exquisitely proportioned and some of the most sumptuous, presumably those destined for royal use or for presentation to the king or the gods, are decorated with gold; this custom is particularly associated with the late predynastic period and the First Dynasty, though King Khasekhemwy in the Second Dynasty also had vessels mounted with gold fittings; the embellishment of these vessels might be thought to have become a trifle precious. The gold ornamentation imitates the cloth that might have been placed over the vessel's mouth and the strings that tied it on.

Sometimes the early masons and workers in stone display an exuberance quite un-Egyptian in the marrying of one stone with another, often with effects which are not altogether fortunate. An example of this practice is a stone cup or goblet from the early First Dynasty Queen Herneith's Saqqara tomb (S 3057).[13] Its body is made from a dark and elegant schist, mounted on a foot made of a particularly vibrant pink stone. This form of the goblet was to survive until later in the dynasty although such later examples seem generally to have been made sometimes in copper, but when stone is used, schist for example, or a fine brecciated limestone, the form looks altogether happier.

BOAT GRAVES

An enthusiasm for boats was held by Sumerians and Egyptians alike, not only because they were the most convenient means of transport in their river-based societies, but because they were invested with a mystical significance which transcended their purely functional role. The presence of a boat model in a grave at Eridu,[14] dating from pre-Sumerian times (Ubaid IV, contemporary with Pate Naqada I) was thought to be the first evidence for the invention of sailing boats capable of being launched on the waters of the Arabian Gulf, as well as on Sumer's rivers and lagoons. What may be the earliest boat model yet discovered was recently (2000) excavated from es-Sabiyeh on the northern coast of Kuwait; this has been dated to Ubaid II\III, c. 4000 BC.[15]

The Egyptians were also buried with boats, which range in size from the small pottery examples found in predynastic graves to gigantic rivercraft, the evidence of which has been found, for example, in the burial complexes of the Early Dynastic kings as well as in the pyramids of Khufu (Cheops) in the Fourth Dynasty, and Senwosret in the Twelfth. The oldest Egyptian representation of a boat, however, is probably very much earlier, from Naqada I times.

Boats were buried with the kings of the First Dynasty. Great nobles too were provided with boats; at one grave, a large mastaba at Saqqara (S3503), dated to the reign of King Aha, a boat was buried beside the mastaba, with a model of a noble's estate of the period.[16] In later Old Kingdom Egypt the

Figure 3.5 A large, mud-brick built *mastaba* tomb (S3357), from the reign of the first king of the First Dynasty, Aha, has a ship burial and a model of a country estate beside it, complete with farm buildings and pens for livestock.

Source: from W.B. Emery, *Great Tombs of the First Dynasty* vol. II: pls LVII, LVIII, LIX. Reproduced by courtesy of the Egypt Exploration Society.

dead king is promised a place of honour in the barge of Re, where he may assist in the Sun God's daily voyage across the heavens. In Mesopotamia, too, sailing seems to have been one of the pastimes of the divinities. The Sumerian gods used boats to visit each other, sailing along the canals which linked the cities. Thus Enki visited Inanna, sailing in his boat, *The Ibex of the Absu*, along the canals; in this, his progress is echoed by the great Egyptian god Ptah who visited the goddess Hathor by boat. Enki and Ptah share a number of characteristics, apart from their mutual enthusiasm for sailing.

Ships of the type portrayed on the Wadi Hammamat walls, on countless pots and other objects, are to be found in many early Mesopotamian and Elamite or Susian media. They are represented widely for example on late fourth/early third millennium cylinder seals found in large numbers on western Asiatic sites whose use persisted throughout most of the third millennium. They are represented, too, on the round stamp seals of the Arabian Gulf, which are dated to the end of the third millennium and the beginning of the second.

THREE FIGURES

The extraordinary number of representations of boats, in drawings, engravings on rocks, in two-and three-dimensional models, would suggest a positive armada of ships, certainly a remarkable degree of marine activity. There can be little doubt that boats and their occupants also had a ritual significance, though what that significance might have been is obscure. Many of the most compelling representations show three figures in a boat, often a type of skiff; this constant repetition of the boat with three occupants is too frequent not to be especially significant. A sizeable vessel with a striped awning amidships is shown with its three occupants distributed one in the stern and two sitting in the powerfully curved prow. A black basalt amulet from Gebelein shows three schematically depicted passengers, seated side by side, in a vessel which has animal heads fore and aft.[17] In the Egyptian Museum, Cairo, is a decorated knife hilt which shows three figures once again, with an ideogram representing water denoting that they, too, are on board ship.[18] The three hold hands (another common device) and one holds up a sort of stylized weapon or fan.

The theme of 'three standing figures' is one of considerable power in Early Dynastic times. The repetition of the group of three figures in predynastic Egypt, in Sumer of the same period, in early Elam, and from later times in the Arabian Gulf, is one of the more intriguing phenomena in ancient iconography, and the recurrence of motifs which endure in their significance and associations is remarkable.

This phenomenon of the three figures in association, either as a family – father, mother, son – or a trinity or triad, is immensely ancient. Jung recognized 'the Divine Triad' as one of the most ancient of the archetypes;[19] in Egypt it is particularly to be found in the late predynastic period and in the First Dynasty. An example of the triad, which seems to recall much earlier Egyptian originals (which may, of course, themselves be drawn from western Asiatic precedents), is a stamp seal from Failaka in the Bay of Kuwait, which shows three figures standing in a boat with the smallest (to the right) apparently leaping out of it, grasping a curved object.[20] This figure seems to be nude, whilst the other, larger standing figures, one of whom holds a bow, appear to be wearing long robes. However, this seal cannot be dated later than the early second millennium, whereas the Egyptian example, with which it has notable similarities, is taken to be at least a thousand years older.

Although the Sumerians and the Egyptians were contemporaries, flourishing at a time when they alone in all the world were laying down systems for the management and *mores* of complex societies, there is a profound difference the way in which they tried to express and to apply something approaching reason to the apprehension of supernatural powers in their lives. In the case of both peoples the involvement of the divine powers affected the management of the state as much as it elicited unforeseeable consequences of their concern for the affairs of humans. The Egyptian kingship is a divine institution; in Sumer the ruler was the delegate of the divine, for whilst Egyptian kings lived on equal terms with the gods, early Sumerian rulers, 'great men' as they were more modestly called, were always, theoretically at least, stewards of a divine master. Each Sumerian city, its temples, fields, even the people themselves, were the property of the god to whom the city belonged.

There is little similarity, equally, between the way the Egyptians and the Sumerians visualized and personified their gods. Sumerian divinities were essentially human in appearance, and their attributes and their behaviour were merely the characteristics of humankind written large. The Egyptian gods were a great deal more complex and diverse.

It appears that the earliest divinities were abstractions, represented by objects which had acquired a special sanctity. The most ancient sign for 'god', *netjer* is abstract; it is thought that it represents 'a staff bound with cloth'.[21] It is a fetish, an object which, for whatever reason, is perceived to have acquired a particular and numinous character. Fetishes of this sort were evidently adopted as the totems or standards of some of the early clans into which the predynastic people seem to have divided themselves. The standards can be seen being borne before the earliest kings on the schist palettes and ceremonial maceheads of the late predynastic period.

The next category of divine beings from the various Egyptian colleges of deities was that which revealed the gods in human form. Many of these are known from the First Dynasty; Re, Ptah, Atum, Isis and Neith. Much later Osiris appeared; all these are shown as human, albeit with divine attributes. In later times, though the custom may reach back to the earliest days, the

Figure 3.6 This enigmatic statuette from El Amra, carved in schist and dating from the Naqada I period, is remarkable both for its disturbing suggestion of menace and for the shape of the figure's hood, which is very reminiscent of the high crown of Upper Egypt, though evidence for its existence only appears at a much later date. It has been suggested that the figure represents a shaman or magically-endowed individual.

Source: photograph John G. Ross. Musée de Saint-Germain-en-Laye 77705 Q.

gods took shapes in which human figures were shown surmounted by animal heads, thus neatly conflating two of the categories of divinity. The priests and other officiants in the temple ceremonies wore masks under which they impersonated the gods attendant upon the king.

The anthropomorphic gods were represented as the predecessors of the king on the throne of Egypt. These were Ptah, Re, Shu, Geb, Osiris, Set, and Horus. Then came Thoth and Maat; these concluded the divine or semi-divine dynasties, the reigns of whose kings were of astronomical length. After the gods came the demi-gods, the 'Spirits of the Dead' (as they were evocatively called) who were the 'Followers of Horus'. These seem to have been the chiefs or kings who were the immediate predecessors of the First Dynasty. The dynasties of historic time then began and the number of gods proliferated as those who were identified with particular districts gradually assumed more and more significance. Thus Min, represented as an ithyphallic, one-armed man, was the patron of that region of the Wadi Hammamat through which Mesopotamian influences supposedly entered Egypt, and there is some evidence that his worship was associated with a fish cult, though this was not sustained.

The third aspect of Egyptian god-making turned to investing certain animal forms with the prerogatives of divinity. The slate palettes, which are amongst the earliest graphic representations to survive, provide much of the evidence of this practice: setting aside for a moment the occasional monsters which appear amongst the predynastic fauna – scorpions, lions, bulls, the ubiquitous falcon, the ibex, gazelle, hounds are all shown as personifications of the gods, assisting the king in putting down his enemies or in conducting the rituals of the state. Men needed the power of animals; even the early kings, in the later predynastic period and the First Dynasty, called themselves by animal names: Scorpion, Catfish, Fighting Hawk, Serpent are four of the best known. An early palette, now in the collection of the Manchester Museum, shows a man wearing an ostrich mask, evidently hunting the birds which are shown in line at the head of the palette.[22] The artist has contrived, with remarkable skill, to suggest considerable menace in the representation of the birds whose heads actually look like masks themselves.

It may be that the animal-headed divinities of Egypt owe their existence to the effects of some form of shamanism. There is no direct or specific evidence of shamanistic practices in predynastic Egypt. It would nonetheless be surprising if such practices were wholly absent from the society which flourished in Egypt at this time, which has many characteristics of the ancient hunting communities in which shamanism has always been a powerful conduit for contact with the spirit world, or with the human unconscious; a distinction which depends mainly on taste. A peculiarly sinister hooded figure, carved in schist is said to come from the important Naqada site of El Amra. A tall, standing man, wrapped in a totally enveloping cloak, wears a diamond-shaped cowl, the crown of which is surmounted by a ball; two blank, staring eye sockets are set into the hood, emphasizing the sense of menace which the figure conveys.[23] The hood is remarkably similar in outline to the White Crown of Upper Egypt, the first actual evidence of which comes from many centuries later.

The El Amra figure is unique in form though there are other, bearded male figurines known from the same period. There is no indication of the figure's status but if a representation of a shaman were to be sought from a predynastic Egyptian context, it would be an impressive candidate.

The ancient Egyptians knew of narcotics and probably of hallucinogens; the conflation of animal and human is typical of shamanistic societies, with the shaman returning from deep trance ('communing with the ancestors' or with 'the gods'), and recording his visions received whilst he was transported.[24] At the deepest state of trance it has been suggested that the subject will see visions of the animal which is of special importance to the people, especially if they are hunters.[25]

The greatest compendium of shamanistic visions available to the modern world is to be found amongst groups such as the Kung San of the Kalahari[26] and some of the Australian aboriginal peoples. The painted caves of south western Europe also reveal evidence of paintings produced under the effect of hallucinogens or recalled from trance. In Egypt there are many representations of the soul's journey after death; an especially powerful image is that of a human-headed bird flying down a tomb corridor or flight of descending steps. These scenes come generally from context later in Egypt's history than those discussed here but they express a typical metaphor of the journey to the underworld, a form which is known from many widely dispersed cultures. By contrast, one of the most familiar literary allusions to the king's journey to the Afterlife is the description of him 'flying up' to join the company of the gods. These scenes appear frequently in tomb decorations and funerary equipment and are typical recreations of shamans' experiences (in other cultures) in the trance state.

It must remain uncertain whether Egypt employed psychedelic techniques in their temple rituals and ceremonies; it is however beyond doubt that they depicted situations which, in other cultures, would be cited as revealing psychedelic experiences and probably Altered States of Consciousness (ASCs). It is not wholly unthinkable that the Egyptian practice of conflating human and animal physiology in their representations of the presence of divine or supernatural entities may have derived from the exploitation of hallucinogens or have been the product of trance-induced visions.

THE 'TWO LORDS'

Egyptian legend always retained what was represented as the recollection of a conflict between south and north, Upper and Lower Egypt, before the Unification, even in mythical times. Later this became codified into a cycle of myth in which what may have been the battles in the Valley are echoed by a series of clashes in a celestial dimension between Horus, later the house god of the kings, and Set, the god of Naqada and Ombos, a cult centre near the Nile access of the Wadi Hammamat. In Ptolemaic and Roman times, more than three thousand years after the time of the unification, the dispute between the gods was still raging.

The conflict between the gods was represented as the mirror image of the struggle for the rule of Egypt. In the earliest form of the legends, the elaborate series of spells and incantations carved on the interior walls of the pyramids of some of the Sixth Dynasty Kings which from internal evidence are known to descend from a much earlier tradition, Egypt is divided, north and south, into 'the portion of Horus' and 'the portion of Set'. It has been suggested that before the unification, which came about on the initiative of southern princes, the north had overcome the south. It now appears however that the terms 'south and 'north' may be relative and that they originally applied to, and achieved their special significance, to the geographical position in the Valley of the sacred cities which competed for the kingship in late predynastic times (see Chapter 4).

Horus

It has been proposed, from the days of the earliest chroniclers of Egypt, that Horus, the young falcon god, was in fact an alien and that he originated in Arabia. This alien nature of the falcon is suggested in the Edfu inscriptions which are thought to descend from very ancient originals. It has also been suggested that his name means 'the distant one', recalling perhaps his origins far away from the Valley, though equally it could evoke the figure of the falcon flying high above the desert seeking its prey.

An anomaly of the cult of Horus is that the Egyptians do not seem to have employed the hawk as a hunting bird. This is its role *par excellence* in Arabia and it is surprising that neither Horus nor any of the other hawk and falcon gods of Egypt is ever represented as a hunter. It seems unlikely that they had any particular reservation about so representing him: after all, the hound, which is particularly identified with the god Set, is often shown as the companion of man at the chase.

The 'Hunters' Palette', a predynastic artefact of great celebrity and significance, has been recognized as containing many elements which may identify the hunters depicted as west Arabians. Clothing, hairstyles, and weapons are virtually identical with those shown on rock carvings in western Arabia.[27] It is not impossible that Horus was a divinity of these people; this palette will be considered further for the information which it provides on the customs and symbolism employed in the period around the emergence of the kingship.

Horus was Osiris' son, incarnate eternally in the living king just as the dead king was identified with Osiris; one of the oldest and certainly the most august of the royal titles of the king proclaims him as the living Horus. Horus fought with Set to avenge his father's death, to rule over Egypt in his place, and to carry on his work of bringing the benefits of civilization to the people. A late myth survives which purports to descend from remote times; it relates how Horus drove back foreign invaders whence they came, beyond the Red Sea into Asia.

Other of the great gods were sometimes thought of by the Egyptians themselves as originating outside Egypt. Some were Libyan; several came from Syria and the north, particularly in the later periods. Diodorus reports a tradition, admittedly a very late one, that Osiris and Isis, the immortal brother and sister of later Egyptian myth, were Arabian in origin.

Set

The most enigmatic of all the gods of Egypt was Set, 'Lord of Ombos', a divinity who represents the chaotic and anarchic principles in nature but who also stood for the projection of the people of the south, the personification of the strain from which the initiatives for the union of Egypt proceeded. Set is one of the profound archetypal figures, who haunts all societies, in all times.[28] He is ambivalent and unpredictable; his actions are often masked, obscure, and misleading. He is the Trickster, the archetype who teaches men that they must never depend upon appearances but must look for the reality behind appearance. He is the storm, which brings relief in desert lands: but he is also the desert. He is the swift hound, the faithful companion of the chase but also a malevolent, ambiguous creature compounded of mythical as well as real elements.[29] He is a figure of infinite complexity, who changes his shape at will, glimpsed for a moment and then gone.

Set was always acknowledged as one of the great, primeval entities who emerged from the collective unconscious of the Egyptian people, probably in the earliest periods of their occupation of the Valley. He was the perpetual counterpoint to Horus and like him was also closely associated with the king, who was said to reconcile the two gods within his person.[30]

In the earliest times, when Set was a storm divinity and for southern Egypt at least he was one of the most powerful of the gods, perhaps the greatest of all. He was, incidentally, the patron divinity of the house to which Rameses the Great belonged, whose father, Seti I, was named for the god.[31] Evidently the rulers of the Nineteenth Dynasty did not associate Set with evil.

OSIRIS

Osiris is one of the great gods but a relatively late arrival in the Egyptian pantheon. Although he is mentioned in the Pyramid Texts he came to prominence only in the late Old Kingdom when he replaced the ancient canine divinity, Khentiamentiu, whose equally ancient temple he inherited; he is invariably shown in human form, 'sorrowful of face' (which is often painted green) and wrapped in the cerements of a mummy. He was the most beloved of all the gods and was thought of as a kingly and just divinity, merciful and comforting, who would reward the justified after death. The legend of his dismemberment by Set is sometimes cited as evidence of his original role as a fertility king who was sacrificed and the various parts of his body ploughed into the ground to ensure its fruitfulness. It once was thought that this discouraging African custom was the fate of kings of Egypt in predynastic times but the legends of Osiris' dismemberment, given his late appearance in Egypt, can hardly be taken as evidence of this practice in Egypt, in the absence of any more substantial testimony of which, indeed, there is none whatsoever.

Some authorities have proposed that Osiris originated in western Asia and entered Egypt from the same Red Sea entry as those who brought the Mesopotamian and Elamite influences into Egypt, until he reached his eventual cult centre, at Abydos in northern Upper Egypt. If the theory of Osiris' western Asiatic origins is at all feasible then Osiris might be identified with that god who was eventually best known as Dumuzi (or, in the Semitic form, Tammuz), the Sumerian divinity who brought the arts of husbandry and agriculture to the black-headed folk and then was killed and descended to the underworld. The parallels between the two gods include Isis searching for her husband Osiris after his murder, like the goddess Innana who descended to the Sumerian underworld seeking the dead Dumuzi. Osiris is to be identified with the western Asiatic divinity, Asar,[32] and that his worship may be more evidence of western Asiatic penetration into Egypt; Asar is his name in Egyptian, Osiris being the Greek form of it. However, chronology would appear to be against this suggestion, for Osiris' comparatively late achievement of prominence in Egypt is long after the stream of western Asiatic influences seems to have dried up.

THE CANINE GODS

The Egyptians loved dogs and treated them in ways which recall immediately the most besotted dog lover raised dogs to the level of divinity, as they did other animals. Of the canine divinities Anubis is perhaps the oldest, certainly the most celebrated. But he was not the only one nor, originally perhaps, the most important.

Osiris, who became so influential in later Old Kingdom times and onward, in fact succeeded to the place and worship of an ancient canine divinity of Abydos, an Upper Egyptian god of the dead, Khentiamentiu. The most important of the primeval canine dogs was without doubt Wepwawet, a god of graveyards who was particularly identified with the person of the king. Wepwawet was the 'Opener of the Ways'; he was the Egyptian *psychopompos*. He was one of the protagonists of the early dynasts in his role of 'guide of the gods': he was portrayed, like Khentiamentiu, as a dog *couchant*. Although in later times he was somewhat eclipsed by Anubis, in the early periods he was very powerful. Wepwawet was especially identified with king, in life and in death. He was the king's guide and he led the procession of the divinities of Egypt when they attended the king on the great occasions of state.

Wepwawet was described by the Greeks as a wolf but the wolf is not indigenous to Egypt. However, in some ancient rituals, long before the

Greeks existed Wepwawet is associated in the state processions of which he is the leader with officers who wore wolf-pelts and this suggests that there may have been some remote, wolfish connotation.[33] It may be that the cult of Wepwawet was brought into Egypt in very early times by settlers from a region where wolves were known and, seeing the jackal, a familiar sight near all human habitations in Egypt as elsewhere, mistook the jackal for the wolf.

The handsome, slender hunting dog, with prick-ears, a long muzzle, and a tail which curls round over its back, is familiar from many Old Kingdom contexts in particular; the word used to describe it *tjesm* probably simply means 'hound'. Often it is shown sitting beneath its owner's chair, alert and watchful or at the chase; often like its master, it is named. This elegant hound has a claim not only to be recognized as the superb Anubis but also as the more equivocal animal of Set. The hunting dog was possibly a cross between the gentle eyed wandering desert dogs and the small Egyptian jackals. The Egyptians represented the jackal quite distinctively, emphasizing its thick bushy tail and rounded ears.

The actual descent of the hunting hound, the dog called *tjesm* by the Egyptians, is complex, its history beyond the scope of this present work. Whilst most zoological opinion believes that all domesticated dogs are descended from tamed wolves, some commentators have suggested that at some time, early on in the settlement of the Valley or even before it, the *tjesm* may have had an infusion of Golden Jackal genes in its ancestry. The probability is that the Egyptians themselves were not over-concerned with the distinction between the various species of canid, but merely celebrated their nature in all canine forms.

THE LEGEND OF OANNES

There is a parallel in Sumerian lands to the Egyptian legend of the spirits attendant upon a divine innovator like that associated with Horus, in the form of the Babylonian Oannes legend. This was written down by the priest Berossus writing in Babylon in the third century BC, at much the same time that his Egyptian colleague Manetho was writing his still more celebrated history. Berossus relates that a strange creature, half man, half fish, came swimming up the Arabian Gulf, attended by other monsters, and taught the arts of civilization to the people who were to be the Sumerians.[34] The monsters which attended him were the *apkallu*.

In Sumerian legend Enki had his beginnings in the ocean. Whilst the coincidence would certainly not warrant too elaborate a hypothesis being built upon it, the Egyptians, too, had a version of their creation myths in which the self-begotten Atum, the elder god of the theology evolved by the sun priests of Heliopolis, emerges from the waters of chaos on the 'primeval island'.

The concept of the magical island was a powerful one for the Egyptians; the primeval island was also often thought of as a mountain or hill rising out of the waters (see Chapter 11). The pyramid was also a development of a similar concept and symbolized both the mountain of creation and the sunlight, streaming down from heaven. The idea behind the Mesopotamian ziggurat is similar in that it, too, is the sacred mountain, but there is otherwise no connection between them although the stepped pyramids of Egypt, like the great one built for King Netjerykhet at Saqqara, inevitably recall something of the Sumerians' towering terraced structures. The ziggurat, however, did not really develop its full significance in Sumer until long after the age of the pyramids in Egypt and it was never a royal tomb; although temples on platforms were known in the fourth millennium, the earliest stepped structure dates from the middle of the third. Nonetheless, the concept of the Holy Mountain as the place of origins was present in Sumerian[35] religious belief from early times.

PTAH

The 'divine emerging island' is associated with the creation myths and the greatest of the Egyptian creator gods was Ptah of Memphis. He bears many of the qualities of the amiable Enki of Eridu in Sumer. Ptah was, like Enki, the 'Lord of Earth'; it was said of him 'all gods, all men, cattle, creeping things, everything that lives is Ptah'. He was hailed as Lord of Destiny, Lord of Truth, Master of Fate. He was amongst the most enduring and the most sympathetic of all the gods; in the Memphite theology, developed by Ptah's priests, it was even suggested that *all* Egypt's gods were actually manifestations of Ptah. He is invariably represented in human form, though mummified. He is always shown wearing a tight-fitting cap, a form of headgear quite unique amongst Egyptian divinities. The meaning of his name is unknown: 'Opener', 'Sculptor', and 'Engraver' have been suggested, the latter two being appropriate for so great an artificer god.

Ptah was also identified with an immensely ancient divinity associated with the very beginnings of the world, named Tanen. Sometimes Ptah *was* Tanen; as Ta-Tanen he was identified as the land of Egypt, 'the land named in the great name of Ta-Tanen'. In this context, Egypt is 'the Risen Land', the land that initiated the world's creation. Ptah-Ta-Tanen is 'the Lord of Years'.

In the tendentious area of ancient philosophy another interesting similarity may be detected between Egypt and Sumer, if only, as with the others, mistily. Both groups of gods, Sumerian and Egyptian, bequeathed to their peoples a set of precepts and a concept of order underlying the universal creation. The Sumerians believed that Inanna brought from her father, in this case represented as Enlil, the Lord of the Gods, the fundamental requirements of human life and civilization, immutable manifestations of the divine will which were at the root of Sumerian society. These divinely inspired concepts were called *me* and included the kingship and the divine, truth, law, rejoicing, the crafts, and a host of others. To the Sumerian these meant civilization, the difference between man's state and the brute creation. They accepted them as the means by which the gods governed their people.

MA'AT

The key to the Egyptian world was represented by the concept *ma'at*, a term which is elusive and which, like the Sumerian *me* resists precise translation. *Ma'at* is order, balance, the harmony of the universe, a disciplined weighing of many elements in a coherent whole; *ma'at* is also truth, for truth and order, in cosmic or universal terms, must be identical. Ma'at is represented in the hieroglyphic dictionary by the most charming of all glyphs,[36] a girl with a single feather in her hair ♪. Again, as in the majestic image of the golden falcon identifying the divine, ever-living king, the representation of truth by this exquisite child is an inspiration of poetic genius. One of the most beautiful of the Egyptian creation myths has the Creator initiating the whole process of creation by lifting *Ma'at* to his lips, and kissing her. From that tender and graceful act the entire cycle of existence unfolds and the universe is born. Even the gods and the king himself were subject to *ma'at*, just as Wotan in Norse myth cannot gainsay Fate. It has been suggested that the observation of the stars, in which the Egyptians were most skilled, gave rise to the idea of *ma'at*, the perfect embodiment of order being represented by the perpetual round of the never-setting circumpolar stars which exercised a profoundly important role in the early royal cults, at the beginning of dynastic times before the assertion of the supremacy of the sun.

ARCHITECTURE AND THE SEREKH

In two other areas there is little doubt that Egypt took from Sumer ideas of profound importance and lasting significance. These were methods of architecture apparently wholly un-Egyptian, and the art of writing.

The most common building material in Sumer was baked mud brick, though some stone was used by the Sumerians in their early days in the foundations of one important temple, the White Temple at Uruk.[37] This appears to be earlier than the use of stone in Egypt but, presumably because of the difficulty of obtaining supplies of good stone, the Sumerians did not persist with its use.

It is interesting to speculate on the means by which the Sumerians came to their discovery of sources of fine stones, which they used primarily for statuary and decoration, for the land they occupied was virtually bereft of any that could be quarried and used for architectural purposes. They were always cautious in its use, for it was scarce and its general supply depended upon importation from lands far distant from their own. It may be that they discovered the technique outside their own land, or were introduced to it themselves by some other people; as they were migrants into the inhospitable land which they were to occupy it is possible that they originated in a land rich in stone. The Sumerians built in mud brick and, despite the gloomy prognosis of some of their writings which emphasized the impermanence of the works of man, many of their buildings have survived to this age, ravaged but not destroyed by the intervening centuries.

Mesopotamian architecture was to be the inspiration of one of the most important borrowings that the Egyptians made. This was an acquisition which came to symbolize one of the most exalted of their sacred institutions, the Divine Kingship. It is in the representation of the names and titles of the early kings that this most striking and least expected evidence of Mesopotamian influence may be detected. This is the more remarkable when it is remembered with what sanctity a man's name, let alone a king's, was invested in Egypt. The reason for this view is simple: the notion is that a man's name is full of power; if this is true of all men it must be infinitely more so for the king who was also god. The king was king by right as the Incarnate Horus who succeeded his dead father, Osiris; because he was Horus, he was king. In the earliest times he assumed a Horus name; this name proclaimed the king's divinity and its peculiar and sacred, indeed unique nature, was revealed by the form of its presentation. The often simple hieroglyphs which expressed the king's name, and which are the earliest examples in Egypt of true writing, are enclosed in a rectangular architectural abstraction, known to archaeology as the *serekh*, on which a majestic falcon perches, at once protective and proclamatory. This is the Horus who said 'I am Horus the Great Falcon on the ramparts of the House of Him of the Hidden Name',[38] the herald of the unknown god, himself a god. Thus, from the earliest times the worship of the king is also linked, symbolically, with that of the mysterious, unknown, and formless one god who, some authorities (but by no means all) have contended, lay behind all the plethora of national and local divinities. The falcon perches above the king's name, endowing it with sanctity and protecting it from the king's enemies.

But the *serekh* is more than a convenient perch on which Horus may settle. It appears to represent the front of a fortified palace of the late fourth millennium, with its narrow gateway, floral tracery above the gates, clerestories, and recessed buttresses. This last feature in particular reveals its origins: buttresses of the identical form are known from the exterior walls of Sumerian buildings and on Elamite seals several hundred years before they appear in Egypt. In the second half of the fourth millennium, post-3500 BC, this very distinctive form of building design began to appear in the Sumerian cities, notably in Uruk. The White Temple at Uruk is probably the best example of this treatment of the exterior walls.[39]

Recessed buttressing is apparent in the platforms on which the temples were built which eventually evolved into the ziggurats, so typical of Sumerian cities in their full flowering. The alternating recesses and projections produce a pleasing and striking effect, the more so in the brilliant sunlight, characteristic both of Sumer and Egypt, which emphasizes their shape with deep shadow. Several seal impressions from the Jemdet Nasr period, roughly contemporary with the end of Naqada II, show high-walled, fortified palace buildings with recessed buttresses and other details which are repeated on Egyptian buildings of a time only shortly later.[40]

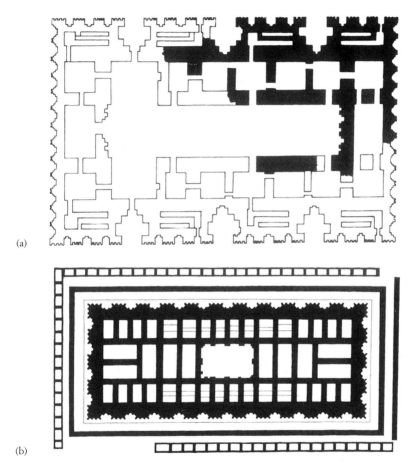

Figure 3.7.1 An evident borrowing from Western Asia in the late fourth millennium is the architectural feature common to all the great *mastaba* tombs of the nobles and high officials of the First Dynasty, the recessed panelling which articulates the exterior walls of the tombs. Like the *serekh*, this seems to be derived from southern Mesopotamia, in this case from the walls of a fourth millennium temple in Uruk.

Sources: (a) Plan of the White Temple at Uruk; (b) Plan of a First Dynasty tomb from W.B. Emery, *Great Tombs of the First Dynasty*, vol. II. Reproduced by courtesy of the Egypt Exploration Society.

Figure 3.7.2 This view of the First Dynasty mastabas under excavation at Saqqara.
Source: photograph John G. Ross.

Whilst the Sumerians relied on brick for their buildings, the Egyptians, as soon as they were able, took to the use of stone as naturally as a child models in clay. But in the early centuries, in the most important buildings of which they could conceive – the eternal residences of the gods who ruled them, living or dead and their principal assistants – they employed a material wholly identified with a distant and alien people and built in baked mud brick.

How distant and alien such people were is, of course, the nub of the question. It is surely very odd that the Egyptians should have chosen to identify their kings with the *serekh* in life and the recessed panel facades of their tombs in death, and in doing so, building in a material less suited to their purpose than that which lay easily to their hands.

Recessed buttressed buildings served two other, associated purposes, both in that mortuary sphere to which the Egyptian paid so much attention. First, the burial places of the First and Second Dynasty kings and their great nobles, at Abydos, Saqqara and other royal cemeteries, are built in the form of earthly palaces, their interiors painted and decorated to simulate the hangings and furnishings which they would have contained in life: some even contain bathrooms and lavatories, for the convenience of the dead. The exteriors are fretted with buttresses which, since they bear no practical, architectural purpose, are clearly decorative or symbolic.

The second, later use to which the form was put, as late as the end of the Old Kingdom at least, was in the shape of the great sarcophagi which were made to contain the mummified remains of the kings and great princes, several hundred years after the *serekh's* first appearance. These represented the *serekh* in three dimensions and again are representations of the palaces in which the 'Great Ones' passed their days. They are a miniaturization of the mastaba. The coffins of Middle Kingdom nobles still retain elements of the design.

Though the *serekh's* origins are to be found in the temple buildings of Sumer and in the seals of Elam, this does not explain why the rulers of what was to become Egypt should have chosen it as their badge. Why an architectural form should have had this profound importance to them is wholly obscure; perhaps the shape of the *serekh* or the sound of the word which expressed it conveyed some other nuance or significance which is lost to us.

Eventually, probably during the Third Dynasty, the *serekh* began to be replaced by the unequivocally Egyptian *cartouche*, a carefully plaited and knotted coil of rope which contained the royal names down to the end of Egypt's history. Perhaps the *serekh*, which means, literally, the 'proclaimer', was ultimately thought to be too alien a form; it did, however, continue to be used in certain contexts whenever the designers of a temple's interior wished, for example, to demonstrate the antiquity of a particular motif or the long span of the worship of a particular divinity. That it was dropped from general currency, however, is a rare example of an Egyptian decision to

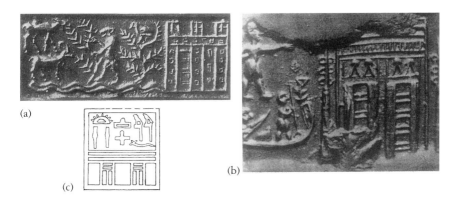

(a)

(c)

(b)

Figure 3.8 The *serekh,* the heraldic device which proclaims the most sacred name of the King of Egypt in his capacity as god, is derived apparently from Western Asiatic seal impressions of the late fourth millennium (a and b). The serekh illustrated (c) here is that of King Djet of the early First Dynasty.

Sources: (a), (b) Western Asiatic sealings; (c) *serekh* of King Djet.

change something which had become established in use; for this decision, too, there must have been a reason. But to the early kings the *serekh* was of such symbolic potency that, alien or not to Egypt, they chose it to enclose and protect their most sacred names, the names indeed by which they were proclaimed true kings. The *serekhs* of the early kings are known from the many seal impressions and inscriptions which have been recovered from their reigns. They are amongst the most austere and elegant heraldic designs ever produced. One of these is that which proclaims the Horus name of King Djet. His name means 'Serpent' and a serpent hangs in the sky above the buttressed and battlemented castle walls.

THE REED SHRINES

Although the Egyptians created some of the most magnificent architecture that the world has seen, like the Sumerians they never lost their respect for their earliest form of structure, the simple mud and reed hut which, in various forms, was the original shrine, temple, palace, or family house. Throughout their history they venerated in particular the national shrines of Upper and Lower Egypt, which appear to have been made of reeds. The pavilion of the great *Heb-Sed* festival, the jubilee in which the youth and potency of the king were renewed, was also a simple wooden or reed structure. In this aspect such structures closely parallel the reed shrines of the Sumerian divinities. Enki, for example, is frequently portrayed sitting in his reed house, and when he sought to save man from Enlil's wrath at the time of the Flood he whispered his message not directly to Ziusudra, the king who was the prototype of Noah, but to the walls of that king's reed house in Shuruppak.[41] Perhaps it is not surprising that two river peoples should make use in their earliest days of the material that was most readily to their hands: but the symbolic significance of the primitive reed hut was patently strong and highly emotive for both of them, a coincidence less easy to explain without the possibility of the religious identification pursued by both peoples having originated in the same place. Even in their latest temples, immense edifices built entirely in stone, colossal and portentous, the Egyptians recreated the reed shrine in monumental stone as the holiest place in the temple, often locating it deep in the darkened interior where it could be reached only by the highest ranks of the priesthood and the king himself.

WRITING

It has long been accepted that the Sumerians were the first society in the history of the world to develop a permanent system of recording ideas, narrative, speech and quantities. The medium of such records was, first, a pictographic form of epigraphy where symbols, drawn mainly from life, were used to represent both the object depicted and a subjective idea drawn from it, either alone or in combination with another symbol. Gradually, the script was refined, going through a series of adaptations until it was finally synthesized into the form known as 'cuneiform', the wedge-shaped characters which provided the script for Sumerian scribes and their Akkadian and Old Babylonian successors.

It was always believed that the earliest examples of Egyptian epigraphy were to be found painted or incised on pottery vessels of the late predynastic period, thus dating from several hundred years after the earliest pictographic texts of southern Mesopotamia. Examples of what are clearly early hieroglyphs, dating to c.3300 BC, have been found at Abydos,[42] thus closing the gap appreciably between the Mesopotamian and Nile Valley forms of writing. The discovery of these early Egyptian hieroglyphs which has brought about at least the partial revision of the chronology of the history of writing will be considered in the next chapter.

Many of the characters which made up the Egyptian hieroglyphs of the dynastic periods had their origins far back into predynastic times. Some of the symbols which the Egyptians adopted may have been in use as early as the beginning of the fourth millennium.[43] Egyptian epigraphy is much connected with the welling-up of deep-seated images and forms from the unconscious itself, cloaked in symbolic form. But the impulse to formulate these profound symbols into a system which could express concepts or sounds and hence provide the basis of a system of written records is a step which probably did require external stimulus. Such stimulus, it must at present be assumed, came from some sort of contact with, or awareness of, the development of systems of writing in Mesopotamia.

Writing in Mesopotamia began as a process of recording the treasure, represented by herds, goods and slaves, of the temples which in the fourth millennium were the dominant institutions in the polity of Sumer. In Egypt the earliest of what may be called 'documents' since they carry texts or inscriptions, are ceremonial or votive objects associated with the kings, palettes or large mace-heads for example or ivory labels which seem to record the important events of a reign or devices which identify royal property. However, in predynastic times the large pots which were used to store grain, oil, or wine, were marked with signs which may be ancestral to more developed later forms of writing. As in Sumer much of the impetus for Egyptian writing came from the demands of accountancy and the need to maintain accurate and immediately reliable records.

By the beginning of the Early Dynastic period the distinctive Egyptian script was in full and confident use and as with their borrowings of Sumerian architectural forms, the Egyptians quickly transmuted the idea of writing into their own distinctive epigraphy. It would surely be stretching coincidence too far to postulate independent invention of so complex a concept in such close historical and geographical proximity, at the same time in two such substantially different environments.

Structurally there are similarities between some aspects of Sumerian and Egyptian epigraphy. Most of these similarities are to do with the relationship of sounds to the form of the signs: but some authorities have postulated that some Egyptian words are in fact of Sumerian origin. These include the words for hoe, spade, plough, corn, beer, and carpenter; significantly, these all seem to be related to crafts, to the making of things. Other authorities would take a much more cautious view and would doubt whether there was any actual borrowing; in the case of the word for 'plough' however, which in Egyptian is *mr*, there seems to be little doubt that the word was taken from the Sumerian vocabulary.[44] Both peoples also employed determinatives in their writing, to indicate the meaning of a sign which might have several applications or meanings in different contexts.

Of special interest, particularly in the light of subsequent history when the Sumerians' cuneiform became the common form of writing throughout the Middle East for more than two thousand years, is the question why, assuming always that they did in fact know them, the Egyptians so rapidly decided that the Sumerian pictographs (the form from which cuneiform developed) were unsuited or inappropriate to their needs. Seemingly, having grasped the idea of writing in principle, they immediately returned to Egypt and began to set down what they wanted to say through the medium of what later generations have come to call hieroglyphs, a term which reveals the sacred character with which they were invested. However pictographs, in the sense of the representation of an object which signify what it represented, were retained as determinatives, which elucidate the meaning of a hieroglyphic group.

The Sumerians themselves early discarded their pictographs as inadequate and successive stages of the cuneiform script evolved, until it reached its final development towards the middle of the second millennium by which time the Sumerians themselves had disappeared. The Egyptians, who firmly believed that nothing of theirs could ever really be improved upon, never abandoned their hieroglyphs, though they adapted and refined them over the centuries. In later periods they did produce two forms of what, by comparison with the monumental hieroglyphs, was cursive: these were respectively *hieratic* and, later, *demotic*, which were generally used in other than monumental or ritual inscriptions, though a notable use of demotic appears in the inscriptions of the Rosetta stone. But to the very end of Egypt's history the people of the Valley kept loyally to their hieroglyphs. The Greeks' astonishment at the extraordinary repertory of characters, symbols and pictures which they saw, gleaming and redolent of mystery, on the temple walls at the very end of the long course of Egypt's history, is perpetuated in the word which they employed to describe what they believed must be 'sacred signs', as they gazed with wonder at the remains of Egypt's greatness.

SEALS AND SEALING

In one other sphere of the minor arts in Egypt, one which is associated conceptually with writing, there appears to be another definite piece of evidence of contact between the Egyptians and people from the east. This involves the Nile Valley peoples' use of seals, a practice which, at the time it appears in Egypt, was particularly highly developed in Mesopotamia and Elam.

Seals have a very long and distinguished ancestry. The oldest form of the seal is the stamp which impresses a design on clay or other receptive material. It has been suggested that some of the earliest seals of this form, from the Anatolian settlements on the Konya plain such as Catalhüyük, may have been used to impress designs on textiles or on the bodies of their users, in the manner of tattoos.[45]

The seal developed principally as a means of identifying property or certifying the identity of a party to an agreement, in what were largely illiterate communities. The Sumerians and the Elamites developed the seal to a considerable art form. They pioneered a variant on the stamp seal by inventing the cylinder seal which could be rolled out on damp clay and which made a larger, more complex design and one which would permit considerable ingenuity in its execution.

At around the time of the unification, corresponding to the Jemdet Nasr period in Mesopotamia, cylinder seals appear in Egypt for the first time; it is probable that they were employed in the furtherance of trade. Several have been found in graves, presumably of travellers from the east, probably traders. There are reported to be only four certain imports of cylinder seals, the remainder of the seventeen which have been identified, having been locally produced imitations.[46] As the Egyptian seal-makers did not generally understand Sumerian cuneiform, many of the locally made seals are epigraphically gibberish.

It is probably not without significance that the Old Kingdom word for 'noble', which is transliterated as *sahu*, means literally one to whom the king has granted the privilege of carrying a seal.[47] As in the case of the *serekh* it seems surprising that a high rank in the emerging Egyptian state is identified with a completely alien concept. The hieroglyph group denoting 'a seal' is itself sealed with the determinative 𒀭[48].

Later the Egyptians abandoned the cylinder and developed their own distinctive seal form, the scaraboid seal, but this was well into the future. Unlike the Egyptians, the Sumerians were formidable travellers, of necessity as much as by choice. The Egyptians saw little point in moving from their Valley where everything had been ordered for their good; the Sumerians always looked beyond the immediate horizon to other, perhaps more generous lands than those in which they had settled. It is certainly possible, as suggested earlier, that they reached Egypt in the course of their travels.

It must be emphasized that, contrary to a view once widely held, there is no unequivocal evidence of a mass or 'horde' invasion of Egypt by easterners, immediately before the First Dynasty, though the influence of Mesopotamia is surely indisputable. In the event, it is clear that the antecedents of dynastic Egypt can be discerned as far back as the sixth millennium. Contact with foreigners clearly stimulated the native Egyptian genius in the early periods, but that genius was essentially autochthonous. The origins of the 'dynastic race' so long sought by Petrie and other scholars of earlier days, are clearly to be found in Egypt, principally in its southern reaches. From this point onwards the history of Egypt is the history of a man-made institution, the Egyptian kingship.

OTHER MESOPOTAMIAN INFLUENCES

Western Asiatic influences may be detected in the minor arts in Egypt, at the time of the unification, or immediately before it. These may suggest the actual presence of craftsmen from the east or at least a substantial degree of penetration by their ideas, more than might be expected as consequence, for example, of the exchange of goods or their acquisition through the medium of a third party. Amongst these are the appearance of strange saurian creatures with heavy bodies and long necks on which are carried feline heads, depicted on cylinder seals from Mesopotamia and Elam at the end of the

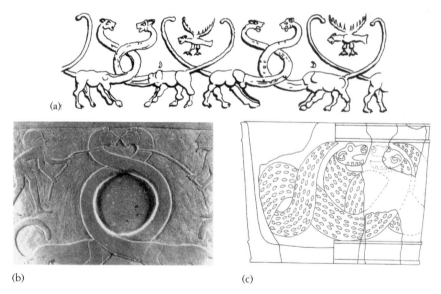

Figure 3.9 Fantastic and composite animals are a feature of late predynastic Egypt and of contemporary Near Eastern cultures. Here, confronted 'serpopards', long-necked creatures with feline heads come (a) from the Narmer Palette, (b) from a Western Asiatic sealing and, later, (c) from early third millennium eastern Arabia, where the creatures have transmuted to feline-headed serpents.

fourth millennium and on some of the decorated palettes produced in Egypt. On the handles of combs and knives from Egypt lines of animals are represented which also are echoed in western Asiatic art, particularly in seal-making. Mesopotamian seals themselves were reproduced in Egypt and here it is possible to speculate that their makers were Egyptians since the designs are clearly based on Mesopotamian originals, though often misunderstood or misinterpreted; in some cases the craftsman has tried to reproduce an inscription without understanding it and has in consequence produced gibberish.

'THE OPENING OF THE MOUTH'

In addition to the Mesopotamian symbols associated with the Egyptian kingship; the strange confronted monsters, the White Crown, cylinder seals of Mesopotamian type found in Egyptian tombs, architectural correspondences such as recessed panelling, the serekh and the pear-shaped maceheads which replaced the disc-shaped Egyptian ones, there may be one other, very distinctive parallel between the cultures of Egypt and Sumer. This involves the ritual in Egypt known as 'The Opening of the Mouth'.

This ceremony was of crucial importance in 'awakening to life' a mummified corpse or a funerary statue. By touching the subject's lips with a ritual object, latterly an adze, the power of speech and hence of consciousness returned. There are countless representations of the ceremony being conducted by the funerary priests; it was accompanied by the sacrifice of a bull, the foreleg of which was amputated and, still flexing with what seemed to be the life-force, was also held to the lips of the mummy or statue.

Attention has been drawn[49] to the similarity of the Egyptian ceremony and a Mesopotamian ritual, intended to give life to a statue. In this case, there appears to be an association with childbirth; there are similarities between the accoutrements of the Egyptian goddess Meskhent and the ancient Sumerian goddess Ninhursag,[50] both of whom have responsibilities in overseeing childbirth.

The earliest textual references to the Sumerian ceremony are dated to the Ur III period (c. 2050 BC), thus, in Egyptian chronology at the threshold of the Middle Kingdom and also, effectively, at the end of Sumer as a distinct entity in Mesopotamia. However the author of the study concerned believes that it may be far older, dating back to times when there were 'links of some sort with the Egyptian Naqada II culture'.[51] The similarities between two such elaborate rituals and the complex and even fanciful concepts behind them are remarkable and can hardly be the consequence of independent or parallel invention; the ideas underlying both ceremonies are simply too distinct. As the scholar responsible for the study remarks 'The use of the "opening of the mouth" in the statue rituals of these two cultures may thus be part of a larger complex of shared metaphors'.[52]

4

THE ROYAL POWER CENTRES

The influences which were abroad in the millennia which followed the end of the last Ice Age were powerful indeed and were to change fundamentally the patterns of human existence; the world had never known their like before. The switch from the old stable ways of the hunter-gatherers, to whom the world was a place wholly predictable, which made few demands on its people that they could not very easily satisfy, had been traumatic; quite suddenly the herds began to decline, game grew scarcer, populations increased, wider territories had to be ranged and hostile groups, anxious for their own survival, were encountered. The world began to be unforeseeable and, hence and probably for the first time, frightening.

The reaction of some of the groups which survived (and most probably did, one way or another) had been to produce a quantum evolutionary leap and change their relationship with their environment, as certainly as if they had become aquatic creatures or learned to fly; they became settled and invented the cultivation of cereals and, later, the domestication of animals. This remarkable creative response, which when it happened probably seemed as obvious and inevitable as do all good ideas, happened in many places and at many times. However, nowhere has it been studied more thoroughly than in the Near East and nowhere is the evidence more generously available. Egypt too displays some of the features of the later phases of this revolutionary process, though to a lesser extent than some of the lands to the north.

THE CITY

So abrupt a transition, experienced over a very few thousand years, brought with it a deep sense of insecurity. This is especially evident in the lives of the earliest villagers and it is one of the most significant factors in the development of the curious human practice of living in cities. Cities first appeared several thousand years after the process of sedentation began, at the very beginning of the sixth millennium BC (*c.*5000 BC) in southern

Mesopotamia. They developed over the centuries, initially as 'central places', serving the needs for defence and communal activity. The latter was often directed towards procedures for survival, like the neutralizing by rituals of invisible forces generally thought to be either malignant or, if properly placated, capable of altering for the better an otherwise discouraging destiny. Eventually they proliferated into a number of small independent communities. Simply living together in close, permanent and inescapable proximity introduced tensions hitherto quite unknown.

Cities were to be of great significance in the development and maintenance of early trade routes, hence of the spreading of different cultures and the promotion of extended communications. Systems of exchange were an early discovery of *Homo sapiens sapiens* and many cities and owed their foundation to the need to have central places for exchange, collection and distribution, later no doubt of manufacture. This is especially true of the early cities of Mesopotamia and the Levant. Later, the first Egyptian cities probably owe their existence to the need of catering to this imperative, particularly to the control of trade routes and of access to high-value resources. Urban settlements were, however, a somewhat un-Egyptian construct and the city never really became a dominant element of the society which arose in the Nile Valley, possibly because trade itself never assumed a significance comparable with that which it had in other areas of the ancient Near East. It is probably not without significance that as Mesopotamian influence attenuates, around the middle of the First Dynasty, so the city in Egypt declines in importance, to a level from which it was never really to recover, at least until the New Kingdom in the mid-second millennium BC.

Most of the outward forms of the political management even of contemporary societies derive from, or at least have the origins of many of their characteristics, in this time. One vital element, common to the embryonic societies of both Egypt and Mesopotamia, was the pressing need for a strong, central, unifying belief, the product of a motivation similar to that which produced the proto-city. In Sumer this need seems to have been manifested in permanent architectural forms of great proportions which dominated the living space of the cities and of a powerful, all-pervasive priesthood, whose professional interests rose above the individual needs of the city states into which, early on, Sumer had fractured. Egypt followed a comparable but somewhat different course.

THE ELITE OF EGYPT AND SUMER

In Egypt the need for a focus for belief and unity came to be realized around the person of the divine ruler. The Egyptians responded in similar terms as their Sumerian contemporaries when faced with the social pressures arising from sudden population growth. They devised a solution involving, the development of élites and hierarchies which came to personify, as it were, the stability of the society. Only in detail did they differ; in Sumer the priesthood was first of all the repository of power in the emerging city states which represented its polity, to be replaced eventually by 'Great Men', who were originally perhaps war-band leaders, who later became permanent fixtures in the society. In Egypt they adopted the far more inspired concept of the divine king.

The powerful urge to create which seems to have seized Egypt in the early years of her unified existence demanded spectacular outlets and responses. Three outstanding achievements must be set to Egypt's account at this time which represent an extraordinary level of creative accomplishment: these are the institution of the divine kingship, the concept of the unified political state and the construction of monumental funerary architecture, a process which culminated in the pyramid. Each of these is a supreme achievement in its own sphere, the first in philosophical concept, the second in the management of society and the third in the making of an artefact, the pyramid that draws to itself a perfection of form and function which is breathtaking. It will be seen that the pyramid is the culmination of the process and encapsulates both the kingship and the state.

Although it is unfashionable to advance such views today there can be little doubt that Egypt's astonishingly rapid development in its early centuries was the result of the emergence of a powerful, united and supremely well-focused élite. The persuasion – or coercion – of the presumably disparate polities in the Valley which still survived after the assertion of supreme power by the princes who achieved the unification, must have demanded the application of a dedicated, like-minded and well-organized cadre of able men, ready to accept and to execute a common but highly sophisticated policy across a still largely Neolithic countryside.

These would have included close relations of the newly elevated king and his immediate supporters. If there were other 'princedoms' in the Valley at the beginning of the third millennium BC, it is most likely that some individuals, the younger men amongst them perhaps, would have elected to join the star which was rising from This, one of the early centres of trade, cult and power.

The members of this élite group must have been specifically recruited for the crucial task of welding the disparate elements of the Valley society into a homogenous whole. It is possible that the group included women, for queens were important and visible figures in the First Dynasty and women enjoyed a respected place in the society. The members of the group must have expected substantial rewards. From the very earliest days, in the reigns of Narmer and of Aha for example, great brick-built tombs were prepared and equipped to provide for the needs of their owners throughout eternity. The tombs were stocked with riches, many of which testify to extensive international contact and already to a taste which is sumptuous and prodigal.

Later, the bureaucracy of Egypt was to be one of the striking components of the society. High officers bore titles which clearly were of great antiquity, going back at least to the beginnings of the First Dynasty and, in some cases, being derived from the structures which the various 'courts' of the pre-unification rulers maintained.

For the first two hundred years of Egypt's history, when the kings of the Thinite line ruled, the aristocracy maintained their positions and status. Later, in the Second Dynasty, men of evident talent beyond the immediate circle of the king began to appear, whilst in the Third Dynasty the great officers of state owed their places to the king directly and not alone to the dispensation of aristocratic privilege.

HIERAKONPOLIS AND URUK

Hazard and the vagaries of archaeology may be responsible for what otherwise appears to be the fortunate chance which has made two directly comparable, seminal sites of the earliest period available for study, one in Egypt, the other in Sumer. They are Hierakonpolis, the City of the Falcon and probably the first capital of Upper Egypt, and Uruk in the south-west of Sumer, immortalized as the city from which Gilgamesh its king, initially accompanied by his doomed friend Enkidu, set out on his quest to overcome evil in the person of Humbaba and then to search for the flower of renewed youth. As a consequence of his journey and the death of his friend he found, instead, understanding. He was a contemporary, approximately, of King Netjerykhet of the Third Dynasty.

Both sites are especially interesting as being amongst the first of cities. The populations of both seem to have undergone, in the latter part of the fourth millennium (around 3200 BC), a particular demographic syndrome graphically categorized as 'streaming-in'. This denotes a specific phenomenon whereby – and for reasons which are far from clear – large bands of people migrated from a more or less permanent life in the countryside beyond the walls, into the city. This development has been studied particularly in the case of Uruk;[1] it has been suggested that one of the factors in the 'streaming-in' to Uruk was the migration to Sumer of a significant number of people, perhaps moving up from eastern Arabia and the Arabian Gulf. Uruk emerged as a major centre of population in the middle of the fourth millennium, some few hundred years, therefore, before the Egyptian unification.

Though it seems almost inconceivable that at such an early period two locations as far distant from each other could have been in contact, the evidence that such was indeed the case is strongly suggestive. If such contact was made and sustained, its existence must be seen as another tribute to the power of the élites which were emerging at this time. The most compelling argument for Hierakonpolis' connection with its Mesopotamian counterpart is the architecture of the city, quite apart from the fact that it was the only place in the Valley at this time which could, in any real sense, be thus described.

THREE PREDYNASTIC CENTRES

In Hierakonpolis a similar process to that which Uruk underwent seems to have taken place, at about the same time. The population in the vicinity of Hierakonpolis appears to have risen sharply in late predynastic times; it has been estimated that at least five thousand people lived there and contermi-nously there is a notable increase in people moving into the Valley as a whole, marking perhaps the final dissolution of the old hunting way of life in exchange for the settled and, in the case of Egypt, for the abundant life of the Valley. But the situation in Egypt, typified by what was happening in Hierakonpolis, was very different from that which prevailed in Sumer. There, the land was dotted with small settlements all with the pretension to the status of city. In Egypt there emerged three important centres, proto-cities, each with a specifically sacred character, which were to compete for political dominance in the Valley. Of these, Hierakonpolis was the most powerful and the most abounding in prestige; the second was the city of This, which was probably located in the region of Abydos and like Naqada all three were ancient and of considerable standing. All lay in the southern half of the Valley; they seemed to be moving along ultimately converging lines of development and ambition which were to converge at the end of the fourth millennium BC. They were not entirely unique; Buto in the Delta, as we have already seen, was also a substantial and important trading centre. In the far south, at Qustal in Nubia,[2] there was a remarkable embryonic state exhibiting many of the characteristics which were to be associated with the Egyptian kingship. But the three southern Egyptian cities were in a differ-ent category of historic importance for it was as a result of their parallel development and their eventual confrontation that the Egyptian state emerged.

Each of these centres exhibited similar characteristics; each was ruled by a dynasty of hereditary chieftains who already possessed some of the attributes of the fully developed kingship when it finally emerged. Each was more populous than other contemporary settlements, each contained examples of monumental architecture, including funerary monuments, each ruler main-tained a court from which the later state bureaucracy was to develop, each maintained contact with peoples within and beyond the Valley, importing high quality artefacts and merchandise for the gratification of the rulers, the embellishment of the court and the furnishing of the temples of the gods. Each ruled a significant area of the Valley and maintained a not inconsider-able state.

From north to south in the Valley these centres of power and influence were Naqada, This\Abydos and Nekhen, the ancient name of Hierakonpolis. Much of the evidence of the status of the élite in each centre is derived from their tombs. In terms of their influence on the development of the political culture of the Valley, the three centres' contributions were uneven. Unusually, certainly in later experience, cultural influences spread before political influence or military conquest. By about 3200 BC the presence of late Naqada II forms in pottery and other artefacts can be found over most of the Valley, even in the Delta in the north which, up to that point, had otherwise maintained something of its own relatively simple character.

Naqada

In Naqada itself, in ancient times called Nubt, 'the town of gold' which was the centre of the cult of the god Set, large brick-built tombs were present in early Naqada II, c.3500 BC. The town controlled the route to the eastern desert and its ruler became rich and powerful by the manipulation of the minerals which were to be found in the desert and of the traders who sought access to their source. There is little doubt that at one time the ruler of Naqada was paramount over the others; however, for reasons which are not known Naqada lost its status, though it was always to maintain its prestige as one of the founts of the kingship.

This/Abydos

To the south and east of Naqada was Abydos. It is thought that This, the centre from which the ultimately victorious line of kings came was nearby Abydos, which had been important since predynastic times. The royal stronghold at This is thought to be buried under the modern town of Girga but the kings of the First Dynasty, from Aha onwards, chose Abydos as the location for their funerary monuments. All the First Dynasty kings and two of the Second were buried there and Abydos retained its sacred character throughout Egypt's existence. Its principal divinity was the canine god, Khentiamentiu. He had an important temple dedicated to him which flourished until late in the Old Kingdom. Then he was usurped by Osiris, and not especially important divinity of the locality who may have been known in predynastic times. He was to be wholly identified with Abydos in later times, though he was only to become significant at the end of the Old Kingdom.

Abydos had been the place of burial of the local élite since the days of Naqada I, in the first half of the fourth millennium. Whilst Abydos was the ancient burial place of the rulers of this part of the Valley it was not their political stronghold, which was situated at This. The earliest settlement levels at Abydos date from Naqada III and in the last stages of the predynastic period the largest grave of the time found in the Valley designated U-j by its excavators,[3] was clearly the tomb of a high status individual who, on the evidence of the quality of the foreign imports found in the grave, including pottery from Palestine, was probably the ruler of much of the land to the north.

Tomb U-j is perhaps the most important predynastic royal tomb yet discovered but it is not the only one to show evidence of what was probably the development of chieftaincy. From one of the graves in the same cemetery comes a particularly telling artefact, a crook-sceptre,[4] indicating that one of what was to be the most familiar items in the royal regalia together with the flail throughout dynastic times, had a very long ancestry. Also recovered from the tomb were one hundred and fifty small ivory labels, with pictographs which have identifiable phonetic values and are thus the earliest evidence of writing, dating to c.3350 BC, yet found in the Nile Valley.[5] The tomb has been attributed[6] to a King Scorpion, not the owner of the famous mace from Hierakonpolis, but an earlier ruler of the same name.

In the political upheavals which evidently characterized this period, it seems that Naqada was the first of these centres to lose its status as a candidate to provide the future rulers of the Unified Valley. It was, and remained, an important centre for its tutelary divinity, Set, who was the counterpart of the patron god of the kingship, Horus. Its ruling family was evidently considered to be of special status for King Narmer, perhaps the last predynastic ruler of the Valley who came from This, married Neithhotep who was buried at Naqada and so may have come from there. Perhaps she was the heiress of the princes of Naqada and by marrying her Narmer acquired the lands which they had ruled. In any event, Neithhotep is generally considered to be the mother of Aha, the undoubted first king of the First Dynasty of Egypt and the heir of the princes of This. From this time onwards Abydos was to be identified with the victorious dynasty.

For it was This which eventually seized the prize of the control of the unified Valley, its princes being acknowledged (perhaps with occasional reservations) as Divine Kings, rulers of the cosmos, no less. Why Hierakonpolis lost to This is not known; the principality had contributed much to the development of the concept of the sacred monarchy and it was always to be revered even by the successful dynasts as a place of particular holiness and special significance to the kingship. But, at the end of the day, it was the princes of This, not those of Hierakonpolis, who wore the crowns. On the Narmer palette, the most enduring icon of this momentous series of events (even if it were produced generations after the events it relates) the king is shown wearing the two crowns, of Upper and Lower Egypt, attended by the standards of those princes who, it may be presumed, supported his claim. One of these standards displays 'The Animal of Set', a canid, or as some would have it, a composite or mythical creature, which symbolized the ancient god of the desert and the southlands, a fact which may be significant.

Hierakonpolis

The princes of Hierakonpolis may well have had the best claim to the hegemony of the Valley. The ruler of Hierakonpolis was possibly the king known as Scorpion who is celebrated on the large votive macehead from Nekhen on which he is depicted carrying out the ceremonies on the opening of an irrigation channel. It is also possible that, like his counterpart at Naqada, he did not have an heir to succeed him, though he is attended by a young man who holds the pannier into which the earth that the king brakes will be held, a duty often performed by the royal heir.

There is no archaeological evidence of warfare between the presumed contenders: another scene on Narmer's palette has been interpreted as the king celebrating a triumph over enemies in the Delta, but it is probably unwise to presume that the palettes, which are ceremonial and votive objects, necessarily depict historical events literally. On the other hand, there are other examples which show what appear to be armed engagements in the Valley, in some cases featuring animals prominently which may be symbolic of the chieftains of different clans when they are attacking fortified cities.

The elimination of Naqada from the race may have had significant long-term consequences for Egypt's future. Naqada was the home of Set, who was probably the principal god of the south in predynastic times. Set and Horus were always portrayed in association, perpetual counterparts, warring but paradoxically united. It may be that Set's acquisition of an ambiguous reputation in later times was a consequence of his stronghold having lost in its attempt to secure sovereignty over the Valley.

That Hierakonpolis was considered especially venerable, reflected by its enduring prestige and that it possessed an already distinct metropolitan character, is demonstrated by a singular feature of its defensive architecture: its great gateway. Both as a defensive structure and as a piece of urban grandification, the gateway of Hierakonpolis demonstrates those same niches and recessed and buttressed panelled walls which later became so evident and powerful a symbol as the *serekh* in which the king's Horus name was presented.

Hierakonpolis lies 113 kms north of Aswan and approximately 650 kms south of Cairo. It is remarkable enough in being a real and unequivocal city. As we have seen, the city was not an institution which really was a natural product of the Nile Valley: the essentially agricultural nature of the society and its dependence on a widely dispersed peasantry, representing the broad base of an enduring hierarchy culminating in the court which flourished wherever the divine king chose to station himself, militated against the growth of cities in the early centuries. But Hierakonpolis, located opposite the modern site of El Kab, was an exception – and a most notable one.

In the fourth millennium it was a large and prosperous settlement, surrounded by a substantial defensive wall and, later, embellished with its high, niched ceremonial gateway. No other city in Egypt of its time could be compared with it: only, far away in Mesopotamia, lay the city of Uruk which, most improbably, bears such close similarities that it is tempting to describe one as the 'twin' of the other.

THE ARCHITECTURE OF HIERAKONPOLIS

Hierakonpolis' wall was huge; it is no less than 9.5 metres thick in places, a really colossal structure. It consisted of a double skin of mud brick, with a void between them.[7] Inside the city was an enclosed temple area; this is unusual for an Egyptian city at any period, for the temple or temples were built on acknowledged sacred sites, but the rest of the city; houses, work-shops, palaces for the nobles, grew up around them in cheerful and random confusion. In Sumerian cities, even from the earliest times, matters were ordered somewhat differently. The temple occupied a specific area which was immemorially sacred; it was marked off from the rest of the city by a *temenos*, a walled area which protected it from the incursions of other, secular build-ings. This is what also appears in Hierakonpolis, though the wall which now stands is Thutmosid in date (mid-second millennium BC) but the temple area is walled round, cut off from the rest of the city, like the practice in Sumerian cities of the time.

Inside the temple area, first excavated in the 1890s and then virtually left untouched until very recent times, was found one of the most remarkable caches of objects ever recorded from an ancient Egyptian site – and certainly the most important works of art associated with the Early Dynastic period ever to be found in one place. The Narmer Palette, the Narmer and Scorpion mace-heads, a magnificent seated red pottery lion, the statues of King Khasehem (Khasekhemwy) and the great gold falcon head which, though is dated to the Sixth Dynasty (thus significantly later than the other artefacts cited here) typifies Hierakonpolis more, perhaps, than any other, were all recovered from the temple zone. A remarkable concentration of maceheads, practical weapons as well as monumental votive objects, was so notable that it has led some commentators to propose that the collection represented some form of ceremonial deposit.[8]

The Temple Oval

Hierakonpolis reveals one very remarkable architectural parallel between an Egyptian structure and what seems to be a definite Mesopotamian example. This is the construction in the Early Dynastic temple known as the 'Temple Oval', possibly dating to the First Dynasty. From the centuries immediately preceding the definite appearance of the Sumerians in what is now southern Iraq (the periods which are identified with Uruk and Jemdet Nasr and are contemporary in Egypt with late Naqada I and Naqada II) there are several

(a)

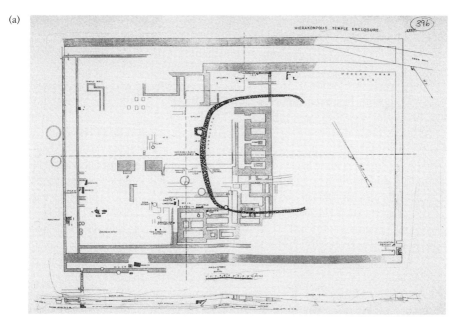

(b)

Figure 4.1 In the late fourth millennium Hierakonpolis, one of the centres of nascent royal power in Upper Egypt, the temple area is bounded by a revetment (a) which is identical in plan and evident purpose to similar structures in Sumer, notably the Temple Oval at Khafaje (b) whilst others are known at Tepe Gawra and Al-Ubaid. A thousand years later, a similar oval structure was built in the great temple at Barbar on the north coast of Bahrain (see pl. 36).

Sources: (a) From J.E. Quibell and F.W. Green *Hierakonpolis I* (1899): pl. LXXII. Reproduced by courtesy of University College London; (b) The Temple Oval at Khafaje, Iraq, first building complex, from *The Temple Oval at Khafaje*, Chicago, 1934. Reproduced by permission of the Oriental Institute of Chicago.

examples of Temple Ovals, oval or semi-circular walled structures or revetments which contain virgin sand; on these mounds, clearly intended as ritually pure places, the earliest shrines identifiable in the town concerned were raised.

Such ovals are known from Khafajae, Al-Ubaid, and Tepe Gawra; recently another has been reported from Tel Brak.[9] There is also an intriguing and very puzzling example of a Temple Oval in the great Temple complex at Barbar on the main Bahrain island, in the middle of the Arabian Gulf.[10] But, disconcertingly, that example would appear to be nearly a thousand years later in date than the similar structure which appears at Hierakonpolis and some five hundred years later than the Mesopotamian ovals. The temple oval at Barbar on the north shore, is identical to the other two except that it has a flight of steps leading down to a sacred well, fed by a perpetual spring, which has suggested to some that the temple itself may have been dedicated to Enki, the Sumerian god of the subterranean waters.

At Hierakonpolis the oval enclosing wall is referred to in the excavators' reports as a 'revetment of rough stones which retained the earth upon which the temple was built. The revetment ran round in a curved or almost circular form'.[11] This is a very fair description of the Oval at Barbar also, except that there the stone revetment is finely shaped, but it must be remembered that it dates from nearly a millennium after the Hierakonpolis oval, But, in any event, there is nothing even remotely like it in the whole of Egypt.

The presence of this apparently Mesopotamian structure in the Upper reaches of the Nile Valley at Hierakonpolis at this time is hardly less remarkable. It is yet another enigma amongst the apparent connections which seem so strangely to link the two most important lands in the ancient world at this formative time.

Another, more equivocal feature at Hierakonpolis which recalls Mesopotamian precedents was the ceramic nails, referred to in Chapter 2. When these were first identified at Buto they were thought to indicate the presence of Uruk-type structures, on the basis of similar nails or 'cones' being used in Uruk to decorate late fourth millennium buildings, introduced by the migrant Uruk potters who do appear to have been present in Buto at the end of the millennium. This is now discounted, though the pottery parallels remain.[12]

The crafts in Hierakonpolis

There appears to have been something of a cult of the oversized in Hierakonpolis; perhaps the taste for the gigantic and monumental in scale so often manifested by the later kings of Egypt had its origins here, in what in effect became a shrine to the archaic kingship. Certainly the huge maces, matched by immense flint knives, nearly a metre long, suggest that in some of the rituals exceptionally large objects were considered appropriate as offerings.

(a)

(b)

Figure 4.2 Hierakonpolis revealed other evidences of apparent contact with Western Asia in the form of ivory plaques (a) carved with representations of birds which are identical to steatite (chlorite) carvings from Tarut (b) in eastern Saudi Arabia and seal impressions from south western Iran.

Sources: (a) Reproduced by courtesy of University College London; (b) The National Museum, Riyadh, Saudi Arabia.

Evidence has also been found of large scale sculpture at Hierakonpolis from the mid-predynastic period.[13]

Hierakonpolis seems to have been the centre of a flourishing ivory carving craft.[14] Many ivory objects, including seals, human and animal figurines, vessels, wands, carved and ornamented plaques, and inlays for furniture, as well as large quantities of ivory fragments for which no immediate purpose can be identified, have been recovered from the excavations of this most important of early Egyptian centres.

Much of the ivory, notably the plaques, is carved with a vigour and a sort of emphatic naïveté which is somewhat un-Egyptian: the ivories' iconography and the techniques of the making of the objects fabricated from it are strongly reminiscent of the carving of the chlorite vessels and inlays which are so notable a part of the art of Elam and Sumer at the end of the fourth millennium and the beginning of the third. The elephant ivory from which many of the Hierakonpolis examples are carved is relatively malleable and soft to carve, unlike the less frequently employed hippopotamus ivory. In this respect it would have seemed a reasonable alternative to chlorite, and one with its own obvious attractions, to any craftsman familiar with that relatively soft stone. However, hippopotamus ivory is used and the point should not be laboured, therefore. The hippopotamus, so often portrayed in the art of the period, was relatively common in Upper Egypt at this time, though later the species disappeared from the river's upper reaches, the consequence of over-hunting.

Amongst the many animal subjects represented by the Hierakonpolis ivories are baboons, dogs, and, in considerable quantity, scorpions. The scorpion, not at first sight the most engaging of creatures, had a powerful appeal apparently to the Hierakonpolitans, one of whose chiefs evidently adopted it as his own name and glyph. It also had an important significance to the people of Elam and the Gulf, in the latter case up to a thousand years later, witnessed by the frequent appearance of scorpions in the design of the Gulf seals.[15]

The Hierakonpolis ivory carvings provide what is perhaps the most remarkable evidence in the minor arts of the transfer of a technique familiar in Elam to an Egyptian context. One of the ivories from the Hierakonpolis hoard, recovered early in the century but now cleaned and polished, displays an identical treatment of the plumage of several of the birds, which are its most notable motif, with that of the plumage of an 'Imdugud' bird – a lion-headed eagle – represented in a piece of chlorite (or steatite) carving from a site on the tiny island of Tarut in eastern Saudi Arabia.[16] In the first half of the third millennium this was to be one of the most important centres of the Dilmun culture, which was located in Bahrain.

In both cases the plumage of the birds (a mythical one in the Arabian example) is indicated by vigorously incised herringbone or chevron patterns. So similar is the treatment of the two that it is impossible to believe that mere copying or, less likely still, chance, has produced the effect in the Hierakonpolis ivory; much more likely is it that the piece was either made by an easterner or by an Egyptian craftsman who had been trained by (or at the very least, exposed to) those who knew Elamite techniques well.

The birds on the Hierakonpolis ivories are carved in high relief; the material is hippopotamus tusk. The chlorite carvings from Saudi Arabia are in much lower relief. The Hierakonpolis carving also depicts large felines. Their bodies are spotted, with the surface incised to suggest the pattern of the animals' coat. In this the treatment is like that on other Saudi Arabian chlorite pieces from the same site as the Imdugud-bird carving, though the technique used is not so precisely similar as in the treatment of the birds' plumage. One of the most frequent representations on the chlorite carvings is of confronted felines, a theme familiar in Egypt and, less common in the Valley, of confronted snakes.[17]

The correspondences between the Hierakonpolis ivories and the Tarut chlorite pieces are striking. In the period immediately following the unification, in the early First Dynasty, ivory seems to have been used less and schist, a material closely related to chlorite, came to be used on an increasing scale for vessels, as much as for the cosmetic palettes for which it had always been popular. Schist is, however, a good deal more friable than chlorite and it may be that Egyptian craftsmen took a while to perfect their technique of cutting it into bowls and goblets. They never used the more manageable chlorites on the scale that the Mesopotamians did, and by the middle of the First Dynasty were producing schist bowls of remarkable technical precision.

There is another curious survival from Hierakonpolis, almost as baffling as the Temple Oval. Several cylinder seals, typical products of Sumer and Elam whose use was diffused to Egypt, have been recovered from the city; they depict lines of captives, their arms pinioned behind them, being led away by their captors, to whatever fate awaits them. But all the captives are dwarves, little men (they seem to be adults, as they are bearded) with notably angry expressions.[18] Dwarves were a familiar phenomenon in Old Kingdom Egypt where they often were of high rank and held important offices in the state. Several were buried in the First Dynasty graves of sacrificed retainers at Abydos and Saqqara: they were present in the households of the kings and nobles and were familiars of the great. What they are doing in such numbers in Hierakonpolis and what the possible implications of their arrest may be, are intriguing questions but, like so many others arising from this most ancient and most enigmatic of Egyptian cities, at present beyond speculation.

Excavations at Hierakonpolis

Excavations at Hierakonpolis are currently directed by American and British scholars. They have continued to confirm – if confirmation were needed – how very exceptional a place it is; indeed, although the word is overworked, it bids very fair to be considered as unique in all Egypt. By the middle of the fourth millennium BC Hierakonpolis was a large and thriving city, the first settlement along the Nile which can be so described. It extended over two miles along the flood plain; the land was rich and fertile, supporting a population which, in microcosm, was an abstraction of the population of Egypt at its height. Early housing for the people is one of the aspects of the society in Hierakonpolis, examples of which, remarkably, have survived over these five thousand and more years. The American expedition in its early years found a house of Naqada I period.[19] In more recent years a potter's house was excavated; it had been burned to the ground, a catastrophe which evidently occurred as a result of an accident in the kiln which fired the potter's productions. A change of wind must have set fire to his house, which was close to his workplace. The excavators believe that the potter, perhaps wisely, rebuilt his house in stone.[20]

Pottery making was an important trade in Hierakonpolis; indeed it was altogether a major industrial centre. Brewing was another of its occupations: a large-scale installation of pottery vats was found on the north side of the town and its output would have contributed both to Hierakonpolis' wealth and, no doubt, to the cheerful demeanour of its inhabitants.

Figure 4.3 The temple in Hierakonpolis is the oldest known in Egypt, thus far discovered. It has been carefully reconstructed from its excavated remains by the Hierakonpolis Expedition. A solitary pole in the courtyard displayed an image of the prevailing divinity, in this case the Divine Falcon, Horus, the patron of the Egyptian kingship. Sacrifices to the god were made in the courtyard, which was surrounded by workshops for the craftsmen who supplied the king and the court with objects of high prestige.

Source: from Davies, V. and Friedmann, R. (1999) 'Egypt', reproduced by courtesy of S4C International.

The site also produced evidence of Egypt's oldest surviving temple, an appropriate discovery for a city which was so bound up with the cult of the Divine Kingship. The remains display the essential historic architectural form which was to remain constant through all of Egypt's history.[21] A large oval courtyard contained an image of the god and round its perimeter were workshops in which craftsmen, the ancestors of all those who made the material culture of Egypt so exceptional, practiced their trades, for the greater glory of the gods and of the earthly incarnation present in the city, if indeed a divine ruler was already recognized.

In the early days of the Americans' work at Hierakonpolis one of the most important archaeological locations to be recognized was part of the predynastic cemetery, designated Area HK 6.[22] When work was resumed in the centre of the cemetery, the first grave excavated dating to early Naqada I, yielded a human burial, accompanied by the remains of dogs. The Egyptian affection for dogs, one of the distinct and recurring marks of their culture throughout history, is thus already demonstrated here. The area around the grave (Tomb 13) and its neighbours produced the remains of at least seven domesticated dogs and with them two young males with whom, it must be assumed, the dogs had been buried.[23] The adjacent tomb contained the remains of a wholly unexpected companion (or, more likely perhaps, the object of the chase) for the grave's inhabitants, a juvenile African elephant, which had been buried intact.[24]

The evidence of rock-art from southern Upper Egypt suggests that the elephant was only present in those regions of the Valley in which the Egyptians had established themselves early in the fourth millennium. The young elephant at Hierakonpolis (and others whose remains have been found at the site) were presumably among the later survivals of the herds before they and the other large animals withdrew to the extreme southern reaches of the Valley, in Upper Nubia. It was over-hunting and the increasing aridity of the climate which drove the larger game further to the south. The two young males and the dogs were perhaps hunters; the whole assemblage may be thought to be some sort of event associated with hunting.

Fragments of two pottery masks were also recovered from the site; thus far, they are without precedent. They have pierced eyeholes, an opening for the mouth and depressions for the nostrils. In the view of the excavators details of the faces represented were comparable with those of figurines of the Naqada II and Naqada III periods.[25] One of the masks was humanoid, the other feline.[26]

Masks were always to be important in Egyptian rituals, as they were in many ancient cultures. By adopting them, the priest or other participant in the temple ceremonies could suppress his own personality and thus is ready to be united with the god. In the later periods there is little doubt that the priests, when impersonating the gods in the great ceremonies in the temples

Figure 4.4 Masks were an essential component in many of the rites conducted in Egyptian temples in historic times, worn by priests impersonating the gods whom they served. An early example of the use of masks comes from Hierakonpolis, in the form of this remarkable pottery face-mask. Naqada I period.

Source: reproduced by permission of the Hierakonpolis Expedition.

and around the king, assumed masks appropriate to the divinity they represented.

The importance of the finds at Hierakonpolis – and doubtless there will be many more – is that they show how deeply rooted the society in Valley really was, even before the formal acknowledgement of the kingship. Whilst the coming of the kings and the subsequent movement northwards up the Valley to a location more central to the two parts of the Dual Kingdom meant a withdrawal from Hierakonpolis and a consequent decline in its relative importance, it was always regarded as a source of the distinctive culture which gave historic Egypt its particular quality.

From the earlier excavations at Hierakonpolis the most arresting discovery which was made, in the fields below the ancient walls of Nekhen, is what seems to be an exceptionally early burial ground of the indigenous élite, the 'Great Ones' of Hierakonpolis.[27] The burial area which has been excavated was important in the early Naqada I period (*c.*3700–3500 BC), a range which has been confirmed by carbon 14 analysis, and again at the beginning of the First Dynasty, *c.*3200–3100 BC. It is from the earlier phase of this time-bracket that the celebrated painted tomb, Tomb 100, which was found – and lost – at the end of the last century descends; however that tomb still remains a unique example, its decorated walls unparalleled.

The group of burials at Hierakonpolis included one which seems to be ancestral to the later stream of royal burials, in a way similar to Tomb 100. This is Tomb 1 in Locality 6[28] in which a sunken pit was surrounded by triple-coursed mud-brick walls, with wooden planks overlaying it. The walls of the pit were plastered, and it was surmounted by a replica of a temple or palace, made from wooden posts, surrounded by a wooden fence. It is really not difficult in this structure to see the ancestor, no matter how simple, of the later *mastaba* tombs of the First Dynasty, the great funerary palaces of the Abydos area, and even the supreme funerary complex built for King Netjerykhet at Saqqara many hundreds of years later still.

Other graves in the complex produced material evidence which illuminates the nascent character of the Egyptian state at this period, and confirms the importance of what was happening at Hierakonpolis in bringing it to birth. A macehead of Naqada I shape and the fragments of others suggest that this was a symbol of authority in the earliest times and that the Hierakonpolis élite (it is too early to call them 'kings' or even chiefs) did not condescend to be parted from them in death, thus anticipating the colossal quantities of ceremonial possessions which were to be extracted from later economies and buried with their successors.

A burial (no. 123) in area HK 43 was of two young men, one of whom was seriously malformed; both appeared to have had their throats slashed.[29] Another burial (24) also revealed a similar cause of death for its occupant. A woman's skeleton showed marks of severe battering to the skull.[30]

These burials and their evidence of severe, violent and purposeful trauma, must prompt the question whether human sacrifice or ritual slaughter, the first of which is well attested in the First Dynasty, was also a custom in much earlier times. The evidence at Hierakonpolis, which is closely paralleled by similar burials at the near-contemporary site of Adaïma (see 90 below), suggests that it was so.

There were also animal cemeteries, or at least what seem to be the ritual burials of animals at Hierakonpolis, thus giving a further example of the great antiquity of the animal cults which were always to be such a feature of Egyptian belief. Dogs, baboons, bulls, and goats were buried there and, in one case (Tomb 7), what seems to be a sort of family burial of cattle – bull, cow, and calf[31] suggesting both the beginnings of the divine family triads which were also always an aspect the Egyptian view of their gods and also the exceptional importance of cattle in the Egyptian view of the world. Indeed, many elements in the evidence from Hierakonpolis seem to point to the people being deeply rooted in the traditions of the Nilotic cattle herders, whose contribution to the ancient Egyptian culture has long been recognized. The Nilotic peoples surviving today in the remote reaches of the Valley and its peripheral areas are probably the living survivors of identical traditions.

By early First Dynasty times the ruler of Hierakonpolis was evidently important enough – and susceptible to influence from far away to the east – to build himself a palace with a handsome niched facade. Hierakonpolis was fortified in the late predynastic period, suggesting that the city's élite was already experiencing some questioning of its right to rule or at least of threats to its prosperity. The great wall which was built around the city in the early Old Kingdom may well be the successor of earlier fortifications.

Near the grave fields a small group of rock carvings was identified, which perpetuate the themes so well known from those in the eastern desert. These include boats and those from Hierakonpolis have a large upright structure amidships, of the type which is usually described as a shrine or cabin; however it has also been seen as a forerunner of the later Egyptian sarcophagus. In one case the boat, bearing a shrine or sarcophagus amidships, is surmounted by the figure of a bull;[32] it is suggested that the intention was to express a royal burial by depicting the principal figure in the story as a bull, one of the manifestations of the king of Egypt.

The prows of the boats are surmounted with the heads of animals, probably the ibex and the gazelle, in the manner of other Egyptian examples and of boats in Sumer and Elam of much the same period. A drawing of a wounded giraffe, a particularly striking representation, is also included amongst the subjects drawn on the rocks.

As we have seen the population of Hierakonpolis in predynastic times was probably not above five thousand. This would mean that virtually everyone in the community would be known to everyone else, at least by sight. It would also produce conditions in which, in a period of exceptional change with creative activity being sustained at a high level, the impact of a charismatic leader – or a group of leaders – would be very great, with stories about their prowess being magnified by repetition and embroidery until they assumed the character of legend.

Whilst the 'Main Deposit', found in the temple area at Hierakonpolis by Quibell and Green who excavated there between 1897 and 1900,[33] contains some of the most important material from Early Dynastic Egypt, it also represents a problem in the chronology of the earliest periods. Since the Hierakonpolis material is regarded as amongst the most crucial in establishing the character and quality of life in the earliest days of the unified kingship, the consideration is an important one.

At some time during the Old Kingdom period the temple at Hierakonpolis was rebuilt and many of the most important objects were collected together and placed in a cache which formed the 'Main Deposit', found by

the excavators. The treasures of the 'Main Deposit' were of immense importance: probably no other cache of objects, even including the contents of
Tutankhamun's tomb, matches them for their aesthetic and historical value.
Other deposits and caches were found on the site: the objects in them range
in time from the late predynastic to the late Old Kingdom.

Petrie was convinced that the Hierakonpolis material was, in effect, *all*
predynastic and based much of his thinking about the chronology of the earliest periods, especially the late predynastic, on this assumption. It is,
however, only an assumption, though virtually all of the chronology of
Egypt, down to about 2000 BC, depends upon it. Many of the objects in the
'Main Deposit' are now seen as later in origin than the late predynastic to
which Petrie allocated them. Though the implications of this redating are
profound, it does not diminish the importance nor the superlative quality of
the objects themselves.

Tomb 100

At some point in the predynastic history of Egypt chieftains first emerged.
By late in the Naqada II period (*c.*3300 BC) a handsome grave at Hierakonpolis, the most important centre of southern predynastic government at the
time, shows a degree of furnishing and design not previously encountered in
the Valley. This, the celebrated Tomb 100, is one of the crucial pieces of
evidence in the evolution of Egyptian political, perhaps also of religious,
structures.

Tomb 100 was a large pit with a primitive superstructure, and, more
important and so far uniquely, with plastered and painted walls; unhappily
it is long since destroyed. It was discovered in 1898.[34] The scenes painted on
its walls are of hunting and the mastery of animals, fights between small
groups of men, a sacrifice, and several boats including a very un-Egyptian,
unmistakably Mesopotamian vessel.

The Hierakonpolis tomb shows that certain individuals were already distinguished from their contemporaries, even in death; indeed the long succession of Egyptian royal tombs seems to have its beginning here. It makes
clear, also, how very ancient the tradition of mural painting was, which was
destined to be one of the glories of Egyptian art.

From the time before the accession of the first kings Tomb 100 was for
long the most elaborate known, lying in a cemetery of rich burials. Certain
brick-built structures had been attributed to the last predynastic kings but
without real assurance until the excavations of a group of large predynastic
tombs at Abydos by the German Archaeological Expedition. That attributed
to the first King Scorpion is now recognized as the largest tomb in the
Valley from predynastic times.

Adaïma

An early site in southern Upper Egypt, Adaïma, possesses characteristics reminiscent of early Hierakonpolis but with important differences and particularities of its own. First identified by the French Egyptologist Henri de Morgan at the end of the nineteenth century Adaïma is currently being excavated by another French team, working under the aegis of Institut Française Archéologique Orientale. Its discoveries have been singular.

Adaïma lies a few miles to the south of Esna, on the edge of the cultivable lands on the west bank of the Nile. It has an extensive cemetery, dating from Naqada I. It was always believed that there was no evidence of human sacrifice in predynastic times but this view has had to be reviewed in the light of the Adaïma excavations. The settlement was a substantial one covering an area of some thirty-five hectares and it flourished in the late Naqada I–early Naqada II period, in the middle of the fourth millennium and then again a little later in Naqada III immediately prior to the First Dynasty. Some of the graves produced gruesome evidence of what looked like deliberate killings.[35] Some of the dead had had their throats cut; in other cases corpses had been mutilated and one of the dead had been beheaded. An adolescent corpse had one of its arms sliced off. Half of a new born baby was found in another grave and a clay coffin contained the cut-up genitalia of an individual, along with the individual himself.[36] Animal burials were also found, including the intact skeleton of a dog, wrapped in a mat.[37]

A new area of the cemetery complex has been excavated producing a large number of intact child burials 'in an exceptional state of preservation'.[38] A rich yield of one hundred and ten Naqada pots was recovered as well as ivory, shell and palettes. The children were all aged between six months and twelve years.

THE LAPIS LAZULI TRADE

A delight in exotic materials seems to characterize this period of Egyptian history, when the craftsmen of the little communities and their masters sought more and more unusual stones or more sumptuous metals to produce richer and more splendid objects. These in turn became the reason why merchants and the chiefs of other, more distant or less well-endowed communities came to cities like Hierakonpolis and so contributed to the rise, ultimately, of the family which ruled there.

Gold and hippopotamus ivory, both products of the Valley, were such materials. But others, like elephant ivory, shells from the coasts of the Red Sea and even of the Arabian Gulf postulate longer routes for contact and exchange. The most remarkable of such long-distance routes was that which

(a)   (b)

Figure 4.5 Lapis Lazuli was highly valued in late predynastic times and appears frequently in
objects associated with the emerging 'royal' courts in Upper Egypt. Lapis came
principally from Badakhshan in northern Pakistan and was traded across the
immense distance separating the mines from the Nile Valley.

(a) A female figurine which, it has been suggested, may have been made in the
Arabian Gulf and exported to Hierakonpolis, where it was found and (b) a small
figurine of an old man wrapped in a cloak (also a favourite Egyptian motif from
Old Kingdom and later times) from Tarut in eastern Saudi Arabia.

Sources: (a) The Ashmolean Museum, Oxford; (b) The National Museum, Riyadh, Saudi Arabia.

brought one of the most sought after, richest, and most splendid of all
materials – gold not excepted – the fine stone known as lapis lazuli.

Lapis is, literally, one of the touchstones of sophisticated early civilizations. It was to be found in large quantities in the cities of Sumer whose
people valued it highly. It is also known from Iranian sites of the late fourth
and early third millennia; it is found extensively in Egypt, around the time
traditionally ascribed to the unification.

The most notable element in the story of lapis, apart from its beauty
when it is recovered in its finest state, a marvellous, living, royal blue stone,
is its place of origin. The sources for lapis have been carefully studied;[39] it is
customarily asserted that the Badakhshan province of Afghanistan is the

only source from which the stone derives. In fact there are three other places which can produce stone of something of the same characteristics as Badakhshan but they are either too distant or inferior in the quality of the stone they yield to merit serious consideration as the source of the exceptionally fine stones which found their way to the early Sumerian and Egyptian palaces and shrines. Quetta on the Pakistan-Afghanistan border has been identified as another source and there are mines in the Pamir mountains.[40]

The Badakhshan mines are located in the far north-east of Afghanistan, in the region of the Hindu Kush. It is a remote, rough and inhospitable country; the mines are to be found in the Kerano-Munjan Valley. They are some one thousand five hundred miles distant from the nearest point in Mesopotamia, away to the north and west. To reach Egypt the stone would need to travel still further, either traded on by land through the Arabo-Syrian deserts into Palestine and down the coast, or, in this case far more likely, by land down into south-western Persia, then by sea down the Arabian Gulf and onwards, either round the peninsula to the Red Sea shores of Egypt or across the peninsula by a land route, given the somewhat more benign climatic conditions which prevailed in Arabia until about 2000 BC. In either event it is a formidable journey, yet it is clear that in the crucial period around the end of the predynastic period, into the early decade of the First Dynasty, the route must often have been travelled.

Lapis appears in Egypt in graves dated to the early Naqada II period, late in the fourth millennium, often in association with foreign, specifically Mesopotamian elements. It is often found in context with gold or gold-mounted objects and generally and not altogether surprisingly seems to be identified with richer burials, suggesting that its acquisition was a perquisite of the developing élite in the communities which were beginning to demonstrate a formal hierarchic status in the Valley.

Lapis continues to be found in Egyptian funerary contexts up to the end of the reign of King Djet in the mid-First Dynasty; then, abruptly, it stops. It is not known in Egypt again until the Fourth Dynasty some five hundred years later; for the remainder of the First Dynasty after Djet, and in the Second and Third Dynasties, no evidence of its import is to be found. That it was apparently not available during the luxurious and magnificent Third Dynasty is particularly telling.

All the great late predynastic sites have yielded examples of lapis, in the form of beads, jewellery, decorative pieces and inlays. One of the most notable pieces, a standing naked female figure, hands clasped before her in a posture which is more typically Mesopotamian than Egyptian, is really characteristic of neither provenance. It comes from Hierakonpolis. It has been suggested that it might have been made in the region of the Arabian Gulf and exported to Egypt.[41]

Whilst it is virtually impossible to find an exact parallel to this Hierakonpolis figurine in the production of Egyptian artists there is a most remarkable similarity between it and another, smaller lapis figure from eastern Saudi Arabia. This has been ascribed to a date early in the third millennium BC; it comes from the region of Tarut at that time an important trading centre for the Dilmun culture.

The Tarut figure is of an old man, wrapped in a cloak,[42] a subject which, a little curiously, is more popular in the art of early Egypt than it is in comparable times in Sumer or Elam. The stone is more skilfully worked than the Hierakonpolis piece but there is little doubt of their affinity. The treatment of the bold, deep-cut eye sockets is similar in both cases, as is the notable air of tension in both figures. It is difficult not to believe that they both come from the same, or a closely related, tradition.

5

THE DUAL KINGS

The foundation of the unified Egyptian state under the First Dynasty of kings was arguably the single most important *political* event of the past fifty centuries, anywhere in the world. It marked the beginning of the end of a world which, with relatively minor variations, had endured since Lower Palaeolithic times, a million years or so earlier. Then the ancestors of modern humans and later fully modern *Homo sapiens sapiens* lived in small communities, bound by common loyalties, with a simple system of community management which, by Neolithic times, probably operated consciously by consensus. A new world began with the recognition of the kingship in Egypt, the emergence of elites and the subsequent creation of the nation-state, of which the king was represented as the divinely-endowed ruler, supported by a highly organized and effective bureaucracy, with the means to organize large-scale projects which both required substantial resources and also stimulated their development. Thus was changed, fundamentally and for all time, the management of human societies. In the future the spoils would go to those societies which adopted the type of structure which the Egyptians first conceived – we still live with the results of that initiative, for better or for worse, to the present day.

To be able to observe, however dimly, the processes by which the first sophisticated political construct in the history of the world evolved, is a very remarkable privilege. It all happened so long ago, in terms of human experience, that the extraordinary nature of the event may not at first be fully apprehended. Yet nothing like the process has ever quite been experienced since that time.

Although the civilization of ancient Egypt was notably benign during its first millennium of its existence it has to be said that the political system devised by the first kings and their ministers is unmistakably totalitarian. A governing ideology imposed over the entire country required an all-pervasive system of control, a cult of personality on the grandest scale, demonstrations of military force and an energetic propaganda machine showing what happened to dissidents or enemies of the state and the consequent coercion of rebels and perceived enemies, a powerful administrating bureaucracy, the construction of monumental buildings to demonstrate the enduring power of the state, are all features of a dominant political system determined on the unquestioned continuation of its power. Other lands have emulated Egypt in this aspect of the management of complex societies but in no other land did the system – a several thousand year duality – survive as it did in Egypt.

In recent years the processes by which the kingship emerged in the Nile Valley have become somewhat clearer than earlier analyses allowed. It is true that the principal elements of the Egyptian civilization appeared with exceptional rapidity and were swiftly formalized into a system which endured over the longest time that has been given to any man-made institution, but there is a marked caesura between the predynastic centuries and the beginnings of royal rule. Nonetheless, at the end of the fourth millennium BC the Egypt of historic times developed seamlessly from the experience of all those groups which had streamed into the Valley and which formed the root-stock of what was to constitute the indigenous Egyptian population.

The official myth, which was always sustained by Egypt throughout its history, was that there were originally two kingdoms, of the south and the north respectively, Upper and Lower Egypt. The idea of the Dual Kingdom always appealed greatly to the emerging Egyptian consciousness as giving evidence of the most exalted example of what constituted virtually a national obsession, the expression of all the most important characteristics of the society – divinity, beliefs, customs, the very order of the universe – as being bounded by a duality: for the one there was always the other, in king, gods nature and the ways of men.

Egyptology, however uneasily, tended to accept this myth of origins (without acknowledging it as such) as it developed in the Valley and to seek for material evidence of the existence of Menes, the mythical Unifier, who was conflated with Narmer and was thought to be the most convincing candidate for the first king who actually brought about the combining of the two kingdoms. Generally he seems to have been so regarded by the Egyptians themselves, although Aha, probably his son, was credited as the first king of the First Dynasty. Now it is recognized that the political realities of that crucial time were more complex – and certainly more convincing – as the first recorded example of practical, opportunistic politics and its rewards.

The closing years of the late predynastic period, now generally expressed as Naqada III,[1] flowed, imperceptibly no doubt to those who lived through them, into the first years of the Dual Monarchy. The actual division is marked by the coronation, if so formal a ceremony occurred at such an early time in the history of the kingship, of Narmer as the first king of the Two Lands united; given that he is frequently portrayed wearing one or other crown, it is a fair assumption that an actual crowning took place. It will hardly have seemed however, as if the last day of the predynastic age was ending, to be followed by the first day of the First Dynasty, though it was a new dawn indeed, in the world's first fully structured kingdom.

It is at this point that the person and the office of the king become vital. For most of the next thousand years he was to dominate the scene over which he now towers, the most powerful and majestic potentate yet conceived by man and the unpredictable processes of history. From this time onwards the records surviving from Egypt demonstrate the extraordinary splendour and the complex and carefully managed rituals which surrounded and contained the life of the king. The corporate life of Egypt came more and more to be expressed in powerful dramatic presentations designed to connect living Egypt with the unseen world of the ancestors and the gods. One of the most compelling achievements which can be set to the account of those who managed the round of great ceremonies is their apparent recognition of the significance and cathartic effect of role-playing. No other people of comparable antiquity seems either to have developed this understanding to the extent that the Egyptians did, with elaborate, complex, and highly organized ceremonies in which the principal participants impersonated gods and ancient powers, or to have formalized such role-playing sequences so exactly, setting them down as ritual dialogues of considerable dramatic and literary quality. This faculty was developed to the highest degree in the ceremonies and rituals connected with the king, who now begins to assume his own superhuman role in the unfolding Egyptian drama.

In the ceremonies enacted at the court in the presence and with the participation of the king, or in the principal temples throughout the Two Lands, the king and his assistants assumed the roles of the great gods and their attendants; in effect they became those powers whose goodwill was vital to the life, prosperity, and health of Egypt. They actually took on the personae of the powers by wearing masks and elaborate costumes, by means of which the presence and involvement of the divinities themselves could be channelled.

But there is something more here than the origins of drama, though the elaborate ceremonies, with the participation of a great concourse of players, with music, dance, dramatic effects, and the generous use of aromatics making the delicate air of Egypt heavy with the scent of incense, would have delighted the directors of the most extravagant theatrical productions. The sacred dramas were used to propitiate or to overcome the powers of chaos which the Egyptians believed could threaten the prosperity of the king and hence of Egypt; by acting out the collective apprehensions of the society, they sought to make them capable of being confronted and thus kept in bounds.

Assisting the king in his performance of these ritual dramas were the great officers of state who impersonated the district or *nome* gods and cosmic divinities who attended the Supreme God, whoever he might for the occasion be thought to be: Ra, Ptah, or Atum for example. The chief priests would take the parts of the divinity who they served, attended by the clouds of assistant priests and acolytes drawn from the temples' extensive staffs, servitors and retainers.

It is not clear whether women participated in the more general cere-monies: no doubt they had their own rituals in which perhaps the Queen or the Queen Mother (as is still the case in some West African societies) took the principal role. The probability is however that they did take part on the larger state occasions when women closest to the king would have played the goddesses who were members of the Egyptian companies of divinities. In later times ladies of high rank held offices in various of the temples; some were no doubt full-time officiants whilst others were perhaps the equivalents of those medieval ladies who held honorary or lay positions in the great abbeys or cathedral foundations. There does not seem to be any tradition of boys or young men impersonating female roles, though both boys and young girls had an important function as dancers.

Several of the dramas of most ancient Egypt survive. One of them is the 'Conflict of Horus and Set', the ritualized version of the mythical struggle between the opposing dualities which made up Egypt's historical person-ality. The very fact that this conflict is conventionalized into the form of a drama with carefully presented dialogue and action is very remarkable. 'The Mystery Play of the Succession',[2] is a work of great antiquity for it is known from the First Dynasty. Its *dramatis personae* included a mysterious group of characters called 'The Spirit Seekers' who disappear after the First Dynasty.

THE CORONATION

The surviving descriptions of the coronation ceremonies of the king of Egypt come from times later than the period with which this book is principally concerned, but it is likely that, even in the earliest times, he was required to play through numerous complex rituals designed to signify his assumption of the sovereignty over Egypt and all its attributes. At one point he ran a course around what was in effect a microcosm of Egypt, an area marked out in the temple court where the ceremony took place; he also enacted all the roles involved in his assumption of the kingship of the Two Lands, playing one part in the north of the complex, one in the south. The coronation formula was expressed in highly poetic terms: 'The Rising of the King of Upper Egypt, the Rising of the King of Lower Egypt, the Union of the Two Lands, the Procession around the Wall'.[3] From this it is clear that the king is visualized as the sun or, perhaps more likely in the earliest times, a star.

The coronation of a king of Egypt would, in many particulars, have been very much like those which have marked the induction of kings in many societies across the world and in many times. However, since no earlier kings are known than Egypt's it must be assumed that such rituals were invented for or by them. Two are perhaps the most familiar and symbolic of all: the crowning and the enthronement.

The importance of the two crowns in Egypt was very great. They were particularly vital expressions of the Two Lands which each symbolized. When first one and then the other was placed on the king's head, that part of his being from which issued the divine commands or, as the Egyptians put it, 'Authoritative Utterance', it was something more than simple symbolism.

The king was always crowned twice, on each occasion in the national shrine relating to the particular kingdom, either of the south or the north, of Upper or of Lower Egypt. The shrines were immensely ancient, descending certainly from remote predynastic times. Then they were presumably magical places in which the chieftains who preceded the kings invoked the power of the hidden gods. The shrines were called, respectively, *per-nesu*, the shrine of Lower Egypt, and *per-ur*, that of Upper Egypt. They survived throughout Egyptian history and were always incorporated into the structure of stone-built temples, where they usually became the holy heart of the temple itself. The shrine of Upper Egypt appears to be animal in shape and inspiration.

The solemn appearance of the king on public occasions was identified with the first glorious manifestation of sunrise; the concept of the sun in splendour is thus, in another conceit of remarkable poetic insight, associated with the rising of the king. The same word is used to describe both sunrise and the king's appearance: the verb is written in the form of a hieroglyph ⌒[4] which denotes the sun rising over the Primeval Hill or the Divine Emerging Island in which the first acts of creation took place. The king is thus identified with the very beginning of creation, graphically as well as verbally and philosophically.

The act of 'appearance' of the king is perhaps the most important ritual in the coronation ceremonies. He appeared before the kingdoms' protective divinities and the representatives of the lands of Egypt, wearing his crowns, the two individual crowns of north and south and the combined crown, the *pschent*, which he wore as Dual King. The importance of crown-wearing is not peculiar to the kings of Egypt. Early English kings held crown-wearings where they appeared at different parts of their kingdom, wearing the crown to assert their sovereignty and ensure the loyalty and obedience of their people.

At the coronation, after the appearance and the crowning, an act of profound magical importance was the enthronement. The throne was described as the 'mother of the king'; it was, probably later, personified as the goddess Isis, sister and wife of Osiris. By possessing the Queen the king's title to the Two Lands was made absolute. As he mounted the seven steps to the throne, constructed in the form of a hieroglyph ⌂[5] which again denoted the Primeval Hill and took his seat on it he became, as it were, infused with the Kingship, from contact with powers with which the throne was charged. The power of the throne still persists in Africa, in, for example, the stool of

Figure 5.1 The duality of the King of Egypt is succinctly expressed in this sealing from the First Dynasty of the king simultaneously enthroned as King of Upper and of Lower Egypt, his regalia identical except for the two crowns. The king is attended in each manifestation by the god Wepwawet, striding on his standard before the king; the king's placenta is prominent before the figure of the god.

Source: from W.M.F. Petrie, *Royal Tombs* vol. II pl. XV.108. Reproduced by courtesy of the Egypt Exploration Society.

the Asantahene, the king of the Ashanti people. Whilst the Asantahene rarely if ever sits on the stool it is the most sacred piece of the royal equipment for it contains the 'soul' of the entire people. Again, even the sovereigns of England, generally speaking not a very magically endowed class, these crowned seated above a magically charged stone.

The coronation of the king of Egypt marked, on each occasion, a new beginning. Time was itself renewed; the Egyptians counted time from the coronation of each king, to the infinite confusion of later generations of historians. In Egypt, as interestingly enough it was in Mesopotamia, the coronation was postponed until a new cycle of nature began. Charming ancient ceremonies took place at the coronation, such as the releasing of flocks of birds into the air, which carried the happy news of the king's accession to all the creatures of the earth, who thus could share in the universal renewal of life.

One of the greatest occasions for the fusing of solemn ritual, magic, pageantry and the drama into one splendid unity was the *Heb-Sed*, the jubilee which the kings celebrated every thirty years, sometimes more frequently. The origins of the *Heb-Sed* are lost; some commentators have seen the ceremony as a play-acting substitute for the ritual sacrifice of the king which they believed took place when his physical powers began to wane. Whether or not this is the case (and there is no actual evidence) it would seem that the king at the *Heb-Sed* underwent a ritual 'death' and then was resurrected, once more youthful and recharged and so capable of guiding

(a)   (b)

(c)

Figure 5.2 Whilst the suggestion of any large-scale invasion or armed incursion into late predynastic Egypt by bands from Western Asia is generally discounted, it is nonetheless to be noted that (a) the characteristic disc-shaped Egyptian macehead of
Naqada I times was abruptly replaced by (b) a bulbous, pear-shaped mace, borne
by the rulers of Hierakonpolis in late predynastic times, which continued to form
part of the royal regalia thereafter. A pear-shaped macehead (c) was recovered from
Tarut, a site in eastern Saudi Arabia, dating to early in the Third Millennium.

Sources: (a), (b) author; (c) The National Museum, Riyadh, Saudi Arabia.

which are displayed symbols or icons later identified with the particular districts into which Egypt was divided. Two of these are Set animals, the hound which identified the god, showing that at this time the Set tribes of the south were already supporters of the royal clan; others represent falcons, a jackal, the thunderbolt of Min, and one possibly representing the mountains. It is significant perhaps that more standards are shown supporting Scorpion than is the case with the slightly later Narmer palette, on which only four standards are displayed.

Before the splendid figure of the king, who wears the high White Crown of Upper Egypt, are two most important ideograms. The first is a Scorpion which is considered by most authorities to represent the king's name. It is uncertain how it would have been pronounced; on the evidence of later times perhaps *Selkh*, *Sekhen*, or something like it. The second is a rosette or star, which is only used to identify the kings at this period. In Sumer a rosette or star indicated a divinity; perhaps in this scene the hand of an immigrant Sumerian scribe or craftsman can be detected.

It is not known where Scorpion's capital was located though the probability is that it was Hierakonpolis.[7] At the time of the unification the two great predynastic centres of Hierakonpolis and Naqada seem to decline in power, at least to the extent that they cease to be royal capitals, though not otherwise in prestige. They still retain their powerful quality as the residences of the two great gods, Horus the Falcon and Set the Hound – or whatever was the nature of the animal sacred to him, whilst some indeed have seen a composite, mythical animal. In any event, the canine inspiration for the animal seems hardly to be in dispute.

THE DUAL KING

The nature of the Egyptian kingship, though it is the oldest such institution on earth, is extremely complex. The titles of the king reveal something of this complexity and of the careful policy of consolidation and conciliation which the early kings practiced, with eventual total and distinguished success. In all cases in matters which touched their sacred and royal character they adopted symbolisms which were attributed to the two parts of the double realm.

Throughout Egyptian history the king bore five 'Great Names' from the time of his accession. The first and most prestigious of the names the king of Egypt bore was his Horus name. This he assumed at his coronation: it was full of power for by its assumption he became not only king of Egypt but also the incarnate god, whose name preceded his own. Two of his other titles were established during the First Dynasty; of these the *nesu-bit*, is depicted hieroglyphically by two ideograms, the sedge, growing plentifully in the waterways of Upper Egypt, and the bee, symbolizing the northern lands.

At some time there may have been a Sedge King and a Bee King (there was a temple consecrated to the northern goddess Neith, 'The House of the Bee'), though nothing survives to confirm this. They would have been chieftains of the congeries of tribes which assembled under their standards; the king of the united Egypt assumed their titles to himself and so demonstrated his paramountcy over the Two Lands. Ever afterwards the *nesu-bit* name of Sedge and Bee was to be understood as 'King of Upper and Lower Egypt'. It was introduced during the reign of King Den, the third king of the First Dynasty, counting from Narmer.

The second title, which demonstrated the new line of kings' concern to conciliate their subjects of the two disparate regions of the Valley is the *nebty* name. This was first proclaimed in the reign of King Anedjib, the fifth king of the founding dynasty and is altogether a more cogent and impressive symbol for the supreme power of the god who was also king of Egypt. It linked the two tutelary goddesses of the kingdoms, hitherto to be assumed to have been in opposition. They are respectively Nekhbet, the Vulture of the South, and Uadjet, the rearing Cobra of the North. In the titulary of the kings they perch upon two baskets; they are read as 'He of (belonging to) the Two Ladies', hence the transliteration 'Lord of the Two Lands'. Always, thereafter, the two goddesses were the special protectors and familiars of the king and were always in attendance on him. Nekhbet was always to be seen hovering behind or above the king, her great wings spread around his head: she would even extend the power of her protective presence to his possessions or of those most favoured by him. Uadjet, in some ways a more dangerous divinity, was bound around the head of the king or around his crown (in later times at least) where, rearing up, with her hood spread malevolently, she would release a blast of furious energy to destroy the king's enemies. Both goddesses are powerful and dramatic symbols which, when they are combined, are most formidable.

The combination of these two dominant and hitherto contending goddesses was a subtle act of political judgment. It was also characteristic of many of the actions of the founders of the kingdom who exercised a sublime and sensitive tact when, coming down river as conquerors from the south, they needed, whenever possible, to subdue the northern part of their prospective dominions and its protagonists by peaceable means, as much at least as by force. That Egypt continued virtually at all times throughout its immense history to be unified (despite the perpetual paradox of the existence of the two kingdoms), except for those interludes which themselves came to be anathematized as unholy exceptions to a rule of nature, was a tribute to the genius of the founders of the state.

Later, in the Old Kingdom, the title 'Golden Horus' was added to the titulary and, in the Fifth Dynasty, the final accolade, *Sa Ra*, 'Son of Ra'. In Egypt the idea of the king as god is indistinguishable from the role of art as propaganda. It was an audacious concept to elevate a man, no matter how much endowed with genius or accustomed to the dispensation of power, to the level of the godhead. If it was not to be rapidly exposed as absurd (the god with a bad head cold, a bilious god, the god defecating) this literal apotheosis had to be absolute and uncompromising: from the time of the Scorpion at least the king was depicted as a superhuman figure, towering over mortals, utterly splendid and awesome. In the promotion of the king in this role, an essentially political conception and not a religious one, art in all its forms had a decisive function to discharge.

Unity was not achieved only through political means, however; the king's authority had to be asserted quickly and with devastating effect. Two documents from the end of the predynastic period testify to this process; both are amongst the most celebrated and the most important of Egyptian artefacts. Both, too, contribute their evidence to the debate on the nature and extent of foreign influences in Egypt in the Naqada II period, from which they derive, or from the years immediately following it.

The palettes

The great votive palette of King Narmer represents a type of artefact peculiar to Egypt and of considerable significance in the early periods; it was recovered from the 'Main Deposit' at Hierakonpolis. Such palettes, generally made of schist, a grey-green, friable stone often of great beauty, range from small utilitarian plates for grinding kohl, the dark-green eyeshadow much favoured by Egyptians, which were customarily included in the kits supplied to the dead and placed in the tomb, to a monumental piece like Narmer's Palette, which was elaborately carved and, from its exceptional size was evidently a dedicatory offering. It was presumably laid up in the Falcon capital as an act of piety by the followers of the victorious king, though it may not actually be a product of his lifetime.

When this type of artefact was first identified in Egypt in the last century archaeologists believed that these 'slates', as they were often called, were Mesopotamian in origin. The mistake is understandable since they often contain many Mesopotamian design elements; the earlier types have a density of action and detail that is only comparable with the cheerful confusion of the elements of some of the early Elamite and later Arabian Gulf seals. Examples of these palettes with a much more richly endowed field of design than is usual with Egyptian artists are the Hunters Palette[8] and the Exotic Animals (or 'Two Dogs') palette[9] from Hierakonpolis.

This last artefact is a very remarkable production. The entire surface, except for the kohl-grinding area, is filled with animals, some of a very strange appearance. Dominating both sides are two great canids, probably jackals. A good cross-section of the larger fauna of Egypt is represented but the strangest, most mysterious figure is that of a dog-or jackal-headed creature, reared up on its hind legs, playing a sort of flute. (Did Orpheus have

Figure 5.3 This limestone head of a ruler has been described as a portrait of King Narmer; it does bear some resemblance to Narmer depicted on the famous palette ascribed to him.

Source: reproduced by courtesy of University College London.

his origins in predynastic Hierakonpolis or is this some masked, musical Master of the Beasts? Perhaps it is the enigmatic god Set who pipes who knows what strange melodies to the whirling animals (and monsters) which attend him).

The palettes are, however, uniquely and peculiarly Egyptian, though they do begin to appear in quantities at the time of what may have been maximum Mesopotamian penetration. They may have originated from some sort of Mesopotamian precedent or workmanship, but the genius of the Egyptian artificers quickly made the palettes one of the most distinctive of early Egyptian artefacts.

The earliest palettes and those which continued to be used by the simpler people are generally rectangular in shape, made particularly elegant by the grinding surface being bounded by two or three narrow, incised lines cut on the stone. This gives even these everyday objects a grace which is formidable. Marvellous representations are there of the chase; others, as we have seen, record royal occasions. Once again it is chastening to observe the techniques employed: the skill required in cutting away the surface and then grinding it and polishing it to the final state is very considerable.

The schist palettes represent a sort of rudimentary sculpture, requiring considerable skill in the making. After the time of King Khasekhemwy, one of the most influential in the Early Dynastic period, sculpture in the round advanced very rapidly. That stone was beginning more and more frequently to be used in architecture is shown by the granite employed in the construction of a monumental doorway in what was probably Khasekhemwy's palace in Hierakonpolis. It is a splendid if somewhat sinister piece of carving; used as the base for the massive door hinge it shows an Asiatic captive sprawled on the ground, his face twisted in a rictus of hate and rejection.

Narmer's Palette is the largest and most handsome of the votive palettes to survive.[10] The Temple of the Falcon at Hierakonpolis, where it was found, was one of the principal centres of the family cults of the founding kings, the meeting place for the followers of the Falcon and for the rites which they practiced there, from predynastic times. The palette is intact. It carries elaborate designs on both sides and seems to be intended to commemorate Narmer's ascendancy over the Two Lands; in that context, it is one of the most important historical documents from remote antiquity as well as being one of the first products of a royal or state propaganda machine. It is designed, with considerable subtlety, to emphasize the king's sovereignty over both Upper and Lower Egypt. The symbolism of the events depicted on the palette are convincing interpretations of the process of the unification of the Valley, or at least the early stages of it.

On the obverse the king is portrayed as ruler of the southern kingdom. He wears the high White Crown which was always distinctive of Upper Egypt, just as the curious, inverted, saucepan-like object served as the Red Crown of Lower Egypt immemorially. The king is attended by his sandal-bearer, a high dignitary, perhaps his son, who is identified by a rosette, the divine or royal emblem. Narmer is shown in the act of striking a kneeling captive, probably one of the defeated princes of the north, whilst above, Horus himself brings to the king six thousand captives from the marshes. The representations are surmounted by two Hathor heads (showing how ancient was the worship of the goddess in that form) and the king's name, its syllables made up of the crude glyphs for chisel and catfish, its unlikely compound. Already the royal name is contained within the palace-facade *serekh*: this will now always be firmly associated with the princes responsible for the unification.

On the reverse the designs are more complex. Here, surmounted by the Hathor heads and the royal name in its palace-façade enclosure, the king walks solemnly forward, wearing the Red Crown of the northern kingdom and carrying his war mace. Behind him walks the same boyish sandal-bearer; another high courtier carries what looks like a bolas, a device used from the remotest times in hunting to bring down the larger game; it may, on the other hand, be a rope for hobbling animals, which came to represent the hieroglyph 'tt'. The king and his two attendants have symbols or devices, the ancestors of hieroglyphs, before them. The king's we know; the sandal-bearer, who before was marked by a seven-petalled rosette, now seems to be identified by a throwing stick and a six-petalled rosette whilst his colleague who, unlike him, is shaven headed (perhaps because he is a child) wears a full and heavy wig, and is marked by another version of the object he carries in his hand, suspended above an inverted closed semi-circle.

Before the royal party, scaled down in much the same proportion to the king's two attendants as they are to him, are four little figures carrying standards on which are displayed the symbols associated throughout Egyptian history with certain of the nomes or districts of the Two Lands. Of the standards which the four little standard bearers carry two are falcons, one is associated with Wepwawet, the dog or jackal tutelary divinity of Asiyut, and the fourth is probably the sign of the Royal Placenta, one of the most potent symbols associated intimately with the king.

The Royal Placenta

The cult of the Royal Placenta is one of the more curious aspects of the Egyptians' reverence for the king as incarnate god. It is of immense antiquity, for the cult was well established by the late predynastic period. By the time of the unification the placenta had assumed the status of one of the gods of Egypt and was thus carried as a standard before the king.

The placenta is the membrane adhering to the walls of the womb in which the embryo is contained. At birth the placenta is discharged and forms what is popularly known as the 'afterbirth'. When it is depicted on the royal standard it retains the elliptical shape it might be supposed to have when it contained the embryo, lying in wait to be born.

For the early Egyptians the placenta was evidently invested with exceptional power. The king's placenta was carefully retained and protected throughout his lifetime; on the evidence of examples in the tombs of lesser figures in the state, it was probably buried with him. If it were to be damaged or destroyed, appalling disaster would result. No other part of the royal anatomy seems to have warranted the same care and reverence as did the placenta. Not even the royal prepuce was accorded comparable honour. In any case, circumcision does not seem generally to have been practiced in the early centuries, to judge by the evidence of a number of men represented uncircumcized in statues and reliefs. Only the placenta was raised to the status of a divinity.

The reason for the placenta's exceptional status is not difficult to find. Because of its uniquely intimate connection with the living body of the god-king, protecting him from the moment of conception, growing with him in the womb and, in a very real sense, giving him life, it was conceived of as another emanation of the king himself. The placenta was thus a form of twin, the witness of the king's *alter ego*, which, at his birth, was born into the realm of the gods. As his twin it coexisted eternally with the king and so the king himself was, at the instant of his birth, two indivisible entities, demonstrating once again one of the most basic and enduring canons of the belief of the Egyptians, which manifested itself in the perpetually reiterated theme of duality. The king was the link between the world of the gods and the world of men, existing eternally and equally in both. All his titles were dualized; he was, in this sense, his own twin.

In the earliest periods the king's procession was led by the canine god, Wepwawet, 'Opener of the Ways'. He guided the king both in the exercise of his royal functions and in war. On the standard on which Wepwawet is borne before the king a curious, balloon-like object stands before him. This is thought to represent the royal placenta which thus, under Wepwawet's protection, is carried with honour in the king's state appearances.

The cult of the placenta is to be seen at its highest manifestation in the earliest periods of which there are documentary records surviving. As the long process of Egyptian history unfolded the role of the placenta gradually diminished, though it certainly never entirely disappeared. Even in later times the royal placenta was still accorded an honoured place in the company of the king, though probably only the wisest and most astute of seers would have been able to account for its presence in the king's entourage at all.

The standards borne before the king probably represent the chiefs who supported Narmer in his bid to unify the Two Kingdoms. They are leading the king to ten headless bodies, lying on their backs with their severed heads between their feet. Above them Horus stands before what may be his archaic shrine, made of reeds. Behind him is a high-prowed ship, again of that type which is frequently described as 'Mesopotamian'. This, and the scenes portrayed on the Jebel el Arak knife handle described below, may be the most explicit recognition of the assistance given by Mesopotamians to the victorious princes when they started out on their program of unification.

On the reverse, the design is dominated by representations of fantastic quadrupeds with the bodies of lions and huge arching necks on which are balanced feline heads. These confront each other, held on leashes by two attendants or handlers of somewhat un-Egyptian appearance. The circular area which they make by the twining of their necks is probably where the kohl would have been ground, if these particular palettes had ever been used for so mundane a purpose.

The motif of confronted long-necked, feline-headed monsters is familiar in the iconography of late-fourth–early-third-millennium western Asiatic designs, particularly those employed in Mesopotamian and Elamite cylinder seals.[11] The device of two serpopards which entwined necks is especially typical of Elamite designs, perhaps the source of much of the western Asiatic influence in Egypt, around the time of the unification. It appears first in Egypt in the Hierakonpolis Tomb 100; it disappears after the First Dynasty. Confronted feline heads are also found amongst the chlorite carvings of the Arabian Gulf in the early third millennium.[12]

A third register completes the reverse side of the Narmer Palette. A great bull, no doubt a manifestation of the king himself or of one of his principal allies, is 'hacking down' the walls of a fortified city, with its huge curving horns. A naked man, presumably the prince or the governor of the city, lies prostrate beneath its hoofs.

The symbolism of the early palettes is very complex. Most of the examples which survive have animals as their most important protagonists and only the Narmer Palette and those known as the Hunters and the Battlefield palettes particularly emphasize humans. The Bull and the Lion are important elements in several of them, though the king seems still to be portrayed either in his own form or in the form of a falcon. This marked disappearance from the iconography of royal monuments in the First Dynasty of the Bull and Lion possibly marks their elimination from the politics of Egypt at this still formative period of the unification. Thus, the argument goes, the Bull Prince and the Lion Prince, once powerful chiefs allied to the Falcon Prince, were excluded from power and the animals which symbolized them were largely dropped from the heraldic catalogue. It is an intriguing suggestion for which there is not the slightest real evidence.

The Narmer Palette is rich in that symbolism which was to persist throughout Egyptian history: only the serpopards eventually disappear. No part of the palette is more potent than those elements which relate to the king and which deal with his power. This indeed was the unique importance of the king, that he subsumed in his own person the entire land of Egypt and everything in it. His overwhelming sovereignty is nowhere better represented than in the royal crowns, the two most important of which Narmer is himself shown as wearing.

The crowns

The king of Egypt, it might be said, had a crown for every occasion. Their variety is considerable but the two shown on the palette were of special power, the high White Crown of Upper Egypt and the Red Crown of Lower Egypt. Although it is not an infallible principle, gods of Upper Egypt like Set tend generally to wear the White Crown whilst the gods of the northern kingdom, like Neith (actually a goddess), wear the Red.

In a dazzling feat of synthesis an archaic designer of genius, retained by the king some time after the unification, came up with a brilliant stroke of propaganda, to combine the two crowns into one. This became a telling and highly evocative symbol of the union; its name signifies 'the Two Powerful Ones', the goddesses of the Two Kingdoms. It was first employed during the reign of King Den, when many of the most notable aspects of the royal administration were first formulated.

In consequence of their particularly intimate connection with the person of the king, both in a physical sense and because they were first among the

Figure 5.4 The Two Crowns, of Upper and Lower Egypt, were themselves divine. The Red
Crown of Lower Egypt is the earlier known, a sherd of Naqada I pottery bearing a
representation of it dating from the mid-fourth millennium; it was also regarded
as the more holy. It is probable that it was originally associated with the rulers of
Naqada and that its Lower Egyptian (northern) attribution was a consequence of
Naqada lying to the north of the eventually victorious city of This/Abydos in the
struggle for the dominance of the Valley.

Source: reproduced by courtesy of the Ashmolean Museum, Oxford.

more obvious manifestations of his claim to the sovereignty, the crowns
represented one of the most enduring elements in the Egyptian belief in the
immutability of the world. The crowns were evidence of the special care
which the gods had of the people of the Valley and their warrant for Egypt's
eternity. Even when the collapse came at the end of the Old Kingdom the
crowns endured.

The crowns, not surprisingly, were themselves divine. They were
members, in the early periods, of the personal retinue of divinities which

attended the king; their role was the protection of the king and the destruction of his enemies. Special chapels were built for the housing of the crowns, so sacred were they.

The earliest Egyptian representation of the White Crown of the south, is on the Narmer palette. The earliest representation of the Red Crown, traditionally identified with the northern Kingdom is much earlier and is moulded on a pottery sherd recovered from a southern site, Naqada, and quite firmly dated to the Naqada I period, in the middle of the fourth millennium, c.3500 BC.[13] Although Upper Egypt was usually regarded as the senior partner in the Dual Monarchy, the Red Crown of Lower Egypt was considered the more holy. This may be because of its greater antiquity; it may also be that the White Crown was derived, as seems possible, from a Western Asiatic prototype and the Red Crown was regarded as superior by reason of its authentic Egyptian origin. The Western Asiatic precedent for the White Crown is to be found on a late fourth millennium cylinder seal from Susa. Figures wearing such crowns seem to be participating in some sort of revel or orgy. In another the White Crown is worn, apparently, by two monkeys.[14]

The dualism of the two crowns may reflect another interpretation of reality, the more so since the antiquity of the Red Crown inevitably calls again into question the reality or otherwise of the northern kingdom and whether it really existed at all, at any rate in terms of a political entity which represented the Delta region. Perhaps 'the north' meant that part of the Valley below the Falcon's domains; the Red Crown may therefore have been part of the regalia of another southern prince whose lands with his capital at Naqada, were absorbed by the conquering family of princes from still further south. When it was decided, for political reasons, to identify a northern kingdom to mirror the southern one, once the unification was securely under way, it would be entirely possible that the crown from downstream would be adopted as a northern symbol. But this is speculation, nothing more; the decision to use the Red Crown to 'balance', as it were, the White, may have been yet another coup by the royal propagandists. What is certain, however, is that the Red Crown always came first in precedence, always enjoying a more exalted reputation than its white peer, despite the latter's identification with the south and the origins of the kingship.

The hero dominating lions

One of the most familiar of the motifs from western Asia that crept into Egyptian design at this time is that of the heroic figure wrestling with wild animals, a thoroughly un-Egyptian concept but one which is associated with the countless representations of Gilgamesh in later Mesopotamian times, though Gilgamesh himself reigned in Uruk within the historic period, c.2650 BC. This same motif is dramatically recorded in the Hierakonpolis

Tomb 100 painting and on a strikingly beautiful ceremonial dagger found at Jebel el Arak in Upper Egypt, a site at the point where the Wadi Hammamat, the dry-course route from the Red Sea, reaches the Nile Valley.

The Jebel el Arak knife[15] is a remarkable survival because, apart from the documentary significance of its decoration, it is itself an outstanding example of two great ancient technologies. The handle of the dagger is beautifully carved in ivory with an assurance and mastery which requires its maker to have been an artist of high achievement and secure tradition. The figures are carved naturalistically, set into their ground with sensitivity and with no suggestion of the 'primitive'. The blade, on the other hand, is the culmination of the old Stone Age technique of stone flaking, here brought to a degree of precision and elegance which is quite exceptional. The result is exquisite, a 'ripple-flaked' blade of a translucent fineness as far removed from the rough hand-axes of Palaeolithic times from whose tradition it descends, as is the Saqqara complex of King Netjerykhet from the mud-walled hut of the prehistoric chief to whom the knife may have been an object of justifiable pride.

On one face of the dagger's handle is represented a tall and majestic figure, his head turbaned like a Sumerian, wearing a long flowing robe of a type which is familiar from Elam; no Egyptian of the time, as far as we know, would have been seen alive or dead in such a costume. He has been identified[16] as a very early manifestation of the god Anhur, the patron of the city of This, whose rulers ultimately took the crowns. Whoever he is, the protagonist, with a curiously complacent expression on his face, grasps a lion in either hand as he stands on a rock, often the site of appearance of Mesopotamian divinities, as we know from many similar representations on seals and stone carvings. Two dogs, of a massive, distinctly un-Egyptian breed, gaze at him fondly as he subdues the two great felines. The turbaned, robed, and bearded figure is also known from Sumerian contexts of the earliest periods – late fourth, early third millennia – in three-dimensional form. Another Egyptian example is a partially preserved figure wearing a long Asiatic type of robe recorded on the 'Two Gazelle' palette, where he appears to be leading forward a bound captive.[17] If the identification with Anhur is correct the knife-hilt may be considered as recording an incident in the rise of This to ultimate supremacy in the Valley.

The lions have attracted considerable interest since the discovery of the knife at the end of nineteenth century, for they are clearly a pair of the massive, powerfully built and heavily-maned Asiatic lions, quite different from the African lion which was once native to Egypt. Their presence on the knife's hilt has suggested to some that it is the work of a craftsman to whom the Asiatic lion was more familiar than the African and that therefore the knife's design must be considered another of the many borrowings from Asiatic or Mesopotamian iconography and that it commemorates incidents which attended the ultimate seizure of power over the Valley by the princes of This, epitomized by a Thinite divinity and a pair of lions which were distinctly alien to the fauna of the Nile Valley. With the ships of 'Mesopotamian' type which are also illustrated on the hilt, the knife's iconography is strongly suggestive of something more than a merely incidental Mesopotamian borrowing.

On the other side of the handle of the Jebel el Arak knife a scene of exceptional historical interest is depicted, for it seems to show the people of the Nile Valley in battle with seaborne opponents whose high-prowed ships, some bearing standards which look like the crescent of Sin-Nanna the Sumerian moon god, suggest that they may have come from Mesopotamia. Naked but for penis sheaths the contenders are locked together in a battle, real or symbolic, which must in either event have seemed important enough for the Egyptians to record it as they did.

THE FIRST DYNASTY

Whilst the unification of Egypt used traditionally to be ascribed to Narmer, it is now generally accepted that he probably *reunified* the Two Lands, restoring the work of an earlier prince of his house, whose name is no longer known. This original unification may have taken place between one hundred and one hundred and fifty years before Narmer's time. It is clear that there were rulers prior to the First Dynasty who controlled all or a substantial part of the Valley. Inscriptions of these shadowy kings have been recovered from sites including Abydos, one of the most important centres of the early kingship. These include Iry-Hor (though his existence has been questioned)[18] and Ka.

At Kafr Tarkhan, a site south of Cairo, inscriptions have been assigned to an otherwise unknown king, the Horus Crocodile.[19] It is possible that he was reigning in northern Upper Egypt at the same time as the early Thinite kings at Abydos. It has already been noted that there is a possibility that there were two late predynastic kings whose names are rendered 'Scorpion'. The king who appears on the large ceremonial macehead from Hierakonpolis, opening an irrigation channel, is well-attested; the recent German excavations at Abydos have produced a grave which may have been attributed to another 'Scorpion' dating to earlier times, c. 3300 BC.[20]

Some of the First Dynasty royal names seem to represent symbolic creatures related perhaps to the special group or society to which the king belonged. Thus Narmer is 'Catfish-Chisel'; 'The Falcon Catfish-Chisel' is more or less what his name and title mean, and its peculiar character is not diminished by the knowledge that in later times the catfish came to signify an abomination. The situation becomes still more confused when it is recalled that fish were often execrated as the enemies of Horus and his father Osiris, since one of them, the oxyrhynchus, was thoughtless enough to consume the penis of Osiris when his body was cut into pieces and scattered throughout Egypt by Set. In certain rituals, in later times, fish were trampled under foot to signify their fate as Horus's enemies. In the First Dynasty, however, this does not apply; many representations of fish survive and there were fish cults celebrated in the temples. A number of ivory fish were recovered from Narmer's supposed tomb; other representations, particularly in the form of schist palettes, also survive in considerable quantity, but only during the First Dynasty.

Narmer is said to have reigned for sixty-four years, the term attributed to him by Manetho which is not intrinsically improbable. This means that he must have assumed the throne as a very young man, the veritable Horus, vigorous and youthful. His 'portraits' show him as a mature man, stately and confident. He is a slender, obviously not tall (though convention makes him tower above his contemporaries), fine-boned, bearded, altogether rather an elegant figure. Invariably, he is shown crowned and dressed in the complex royal regalia: lion tail, Hathor bedecked apron and sandals, these last sometimes carried by a young attendant, perhaps his son or some favoured courtier.

A striking survival from the early First Dynasty is a small ivory figure of an unknown king, now in the British Museum.[21] Though tiny it is powerful and vigorously carved. It depicts the king wearing the Upper Egyptian crown, hunched in his *Heb-Sed* cloak worn at the time of the Jubilee ceremonies. His cloak is richly embroidered.

A more equivocal portrait, however, traditionally attributed to the first king of united Egypt, exists in the Petrie Collection in University College, London.[22] This limestone head, from Abydos, is a disturbing piece; the king (or god, for it has been suggested that it is from a statue of the ithyphallic Min) has a distinctly epicene and decadent look about it, not at all like the clear-cut figure who appears on the great palette. However, the rather long upper lip and wide-set eyes do strongly recall the portrait of Narmer on his great palette and of the young attendant, perhaps the king's heir, who is portrayed with him.

MASTABAS AND FUNERARY PALACES

A very large proportion of the material evidence which survives from ancient Egypt and which provides most of what is known about the life of the people of the Two Lands at all periods throughout its history is supplied by the contents of the tombs in which they caused themselves to be buried, in the forlorn belief that their remains would thus be preserved for all eternity. This contribution of the tomb furnishers to history applies particularly in the time of the early dynasties when tomb building, always one of Egypt's most prosperous industries, first assumed real importance.

The monumental tombs of the First Dynasty are, by any standards, very remarkable buildings. They are amongst the earliest examples of monumental architecture, of any form anywhere in the world, with the exception of Sumer where religious buildings of prodigious scale had been erected in the cities since early in the fourth millennium and, more modest in construction and design, in the late fifth.

The building of great funerary monuments is the most immediate and obvious change in matter anywhere else. The first to be identified, other than that so disastrously savaged by Amélineau, was found at Naqada, the city of the god Set, by Jacques De Morgan in 1896. A little later Petrie began his series of historic excavations at Abydos where a number of these great tombs were excavated and described by him. He had little doubt that they were the tombs of the kings and he published them as such.[23] So matters remained until excavations of comparable structures were carried out on the immense mortuary site at Saqqara, overlooking the ancient capital Memphis, built at 'the balance of the Two Lands'. From the mid-1930s W.B. Emery excavated a series of huge mud-brick rectangular buildings on the escarpment of Saqqara which, as he worked through them, he became convinced were the actual tombs of the kings; indeed he was able to attribute each huge building with firm assurance to every king of the First Dynasty, bar one.[24]

But where, Egyptologists asked themselves, did this leave the monuments at Abydos, particularly as no actual burials had been found in any of them, a disconcerting absence of material evidence? Originally Emery had ascribed the first Saqqara tomb which he excavated to a high official of the First Dynasty, Hemaka, whose sealings were found inside the monument.[25] But then doubts arose, for it was questioned whether divine kings would have willingly accepted the idea of their courtiers, no matter how great, being buried in tombs apparently far more imposing than their own.

A solution to the problem of what now appeared to be two sets of royal tombs, in only one of which, in the nature of things, could the king actually have been buried, was then proposed. Because of their superior size it was decided that the Saqqara tombs were the actual places of burial, a view which was strengthened by the fact that evidence for actual burials had been found in several of them whereas this was not the case in Abydos. It was therefore concluded that, with the Egyptian enthusiasm for dualism, for expressing everything in terms of related or paired opposites, the Abydos 'tombs' must have been cenotaphs, which the king's spirit would have been considered to have occupied. The two monuments thus reiterated the idea of the dual kingship, with the monuments reflecting the royal duality of the king of Upper and Lower Egypt.

Subsequently another factor emerged which changed the view of the situation once again. The monuments at Abydos are strung out along an area known as the Umm al-Qa'ab; beyond the town and behind a temple dedicated to the very ancient canine god Khentiamentiu (the forerunner of Osiris) the remains of a very large structure with panelled and buttressed walls has been identified. This is one of some of the most remarkable of all archaic survivals in Egypt, once frequently called the 'Castle of Khasekhemwy', but now more usually known by its Arabic name, Shunet ez-Zebib; another is located at Hierakonpolis. Both of these date from the end of the Second Dynasty. These are colossal, towering structures built of mud brick, now sombre and menacing in their ruin, but once gleaming brilliantly white.

It seems likely that the First and Second Dynasty kings built these huge structures as 'funerary palaces' (as they have been well-named) and located them close to their tombs, which are themselves comparatively modest, representing only a part of an enormous complex. They contained magazines, shrines, and, perhaps, dummy buildings like those which later graced the Netjerykhet complex at Saqqara and earlier, the 'model estate' in the great Saqqara tomb 3357, attributed to the reign of King Aha.[26] The courts were probably the locations of important religious ceremonies or commemorations.

It has been suggested that these buildings were dwellings for the spirit of the king, attended by the spirits of the courtiers, artisans, women, and even dogs, all of whom were sacrificed in various quantities throughout the First Dynasty. The buildings were almost certainly replicas of the palaces in which the kings lived; their walls rose at least thirty feet and in their day must have been magnificent and imposing structures.

There are notable and curious differences between the two types of funerary monument, in their differing locations. The substructures were not dissimilar but their superstructures were quite different. In some cases the monuments at Saqqara appeared to contain a small tumulus or burial mound inside the tomb, encased in brick. Sometimes this casing was stepped, leading some authorities to see here the origin of the Stepped Pyramid of the Third Dynasty. In Abydos and indeed in most important predynastic burials a tumulus was built up over the burial pit. Thus was the archaic tumulus mound incorporated even in the most extravagant tombs.

Other than their size the most notable feature about the buildings in both locations (and the others at Naqada, Abu Rowash, Tarkhan, and Giza which can be compared with them) is the repetitive design of recessed panelling and buttressing on their facades. This, it is generally agreed, is borrowed from the facades of temple buildings at Uruk in Sumer, from the end of the fourth millennium, when the unification of Egypt was achieved; indeed, the tombs at Saqqara are altogether very reasonable replicas of the plans of pre-Sumerian temples, a circumstance that could hardly be the consequence of chance.

It can only be a matter for wonder that at so very early a date there were men in Egypt capable of designing buildings of this size and of this complexity, supervising the construction processes involved, and carrying out the interior designs and furnishings. It is difficult to see how they acquired their skills, other than by contact with the only people of the time who did have experience of large-scale architectural projects, the Sumerians who had a tradition of sophisticated architecture reaching back for nearly a thousand years before the formal unification of Egypt.

What Sumerian architects would have been doing in Egypt is another matter. It can hardly be that travelling merchants brought with them the idea, for example, of recessed temple façades, persuaded the local Egyptian chiefs (with whom it is presumed they had commercial relations) to adopt them as the façade decorations of their palaces, subsequently of their tombs and, simultaneously, as the most important element in the royal badge, the *serekh*. The fact, too, that there are so many of these great monuments suggests a matter of royal policy firmly applied and not the casual borrowing of a random idea from a distant and alien culture.

The precision with which the great tombs are built is as striking as the scale on which they were planned and executed; with other examples of early Egyptian craftsmanship there seems to be little tentative about even the earliest monuments, rather the buildings and the materials from which they are constructed are handled with a vigorous assurance and élan. Development of technique and of architectural form can indeed be observed throughout the First and Second Dynasties but these are again always redolent of an assured tradition. The interiors, honeycombed with magazines and store-rooms, were richly decorated, gleaming with gold leaf and filled with the opulent products of armies of artificers. The exterior walls, recessed and buttressed in the tradition apparently inherited from Uruk centuries before, were painted white. Interestingly, the recessed buttressing itself is more complex in design in the earlier part of the dynasty. The lavishness with which every detail of the tombs' decoration was executed is breathtaking; in addition to the pilasters covered in gold leaf, and there were rich paintings on the walls, imitating the interiors of the palaces. Some of the tombs had their interior walls whitewashed also, and coloured paint was applied to the surface, recalling the painting of the Hierakonpolis Tomb 100.

It is unrewarding to look to the native Egyptian domestic architectural traditions of the fourth millennium for any understanding of the remarkable revolution in form and design which is represented by the royal funerary monuments of the First Dynasty. Something is known of the houses for the living in both the Naqada I and Naqada II periods. In the first, the huts which the people constructed were flimsy affairs, little more than 'hides'; in Naqada II times more extensive building techniques were acquired and quite substantial structures came to be built, to judge from the models of houses which have been recovered from sites of the period. Nothing is known of palatial buildings – if such existed – or temples, other than the little reed or wicker shrines which represent the cult centres of the north and south.

THE ROYAL SUCCESSION

Recent excavations by the German Archaeological Institute at Abydos have thrown considerable light on the early kingship and the sequence of the kings of the First Dynasty. A clay sealing found in a tomb attributed to King Den[27] has been restored and gives the sequence of kings from Narmer, followed by Aha, Djer, Djet, Den. Another sequence completes the sequence adding Anedjib, Semerkhet and Qa'a, from whose tomb the sealing was recovered.[28] The names of the kings are preceded by the figure of the canine god, Wepwawet in his role as leader of the royal procession and Opener of the Ways. In addition, there was a queen, Merneith, who was probably the mother of King Den, who may have acted as regent before he was of an age to assume the responsibilities of government.

The German expedition's work at Abydos has already added greatly to the knowledge of the characters involved and the internal politics of the late predynastic period and the First Dynasty. From the clearing of the important large tomb, designated U.j, which is ascribed to Naqada II, c. 3250 BC, the sealings found in it suggest that it was the grave of a King Scorpion, not the Scorpion of the celebrated macehead from Hierakonpolis, but another of the same name from at least a century earlier.[29]

The graves of the First Dynasty kings have been re-excavated, with important results. The tomb of King Den, the fourth king of the dynasty, has been handsomely restored. Objects from the tomb of King Djet had apparently been excavated during the Middle Kingdom and laid out in the forecourt, where they were found. For whatever reason, it appears that they were covered over and, presumably, forgotten. They included seal impressions, arrow heads, gaming pieces, ceramics and a copper spiral from a model Red Crown.[30]

King Aha

Although King Aha, now recognized as the first king of the First Dynasty, proclaimed his martial qualities in his name which means 'Fighter', he seems to have been a notable conciliator, the reconciler of opposing factions. He ruled long and wisely. He was a great builder, always one of the proudest activities of a King of Egypt. He honoured in particular the creator god, the supreme craftsman, Ptah of Memphis: it seems that Ptah was particularly linked with the Thinite house. So enduring was Aha's memory that Manetho recorded that the Egyptians maintained that from him (or rather from the king in Manetho's list who is identified with Aha) they learned to worship the gods and to live together in a civilized manner. It is recorded that he died in the sixty-third year of his reign, from injuries which he received in a hippopotamus hunt.

Two features mark the tomb at Saqqara which is attributed to his reign[31] from others in the same place; on one side was laid out a small model estate, showing farm buildings, granaries, and other agricultural structures, to remind the owner of the tomb no doubt of the pleasures of the Egyptian countryside and to ensure him an adequate supply of produce for eternity. Close by was the first of what was to become a long line of an enduring aspect of Egyptian funerary practices, the burial of a boat for a king or great prince, to enable him to travel to the eternal realms, beyond the imperishable, ever-circling stars. The boat burial of Aha's reign is the earliest surviving example of this practice.

Aha's name is written with a falcon grasping a mace, with a pear-shaped head; this ideogram is supported by a shield. The macehead may stand for the new weapon with which the Falcon and his followers imposed their will on the people of the Valley. His name appears on a faience plaque, early evidence of one of the most long-lasting Egyptian crafts.

King Djer

Djer's reign marks the further consolidation of Thinite rule over the Valley; if later legend is to be believed it was a time when the sciences flourished, for Djer was commemorated, far into Egyptian history, as a great physician. It is curious that a ruler of such superlative power as the king of Egypt should be remembered as practicing a calling that was certainly not so highly regarded in antiquity as it is today. However, Djer's writings on anatomy and the treatment of diseases were said still to be in circulation in late antiquity, nearly three thousand years after his lifetime. One of his prescriptions, incidentally, was said to be for strengthening the hair, suggesting that incipient baldness was a concern to the people of Egypt five thousand years ago, as much as it is to modern man. It is perhaps not without significance that what has been hailed as the oldest surviving toupee was found in a predynastic burial at Hierakonpolis.[32]

One of the few documents to survive from the early First Dynasty, and which comes from Djer's reign, casts a more equivocal light on the king's reputation as a healer, at least if the general interpretation of one part of it is correct. The document in question is an ivory label from Saqqara.[33] It is in three registers and seems to depict some important state or religious ceremony. A proud hawk, surmounting the *serekh* on which the king's name is blazoned, stands at the end of the first register. Towards him advance little figures carrying offerings, including a ladder, whilst a mummy or perhaps a statue follows it. Other bearers bring a fish, a bird, and a great ceremonial spear to the falcon: at the end of the register however, a more sinister scene seems to be enacted. Two figures face each other and one seems to be plunging a knife into the other's breast; he holds ready a vessel, of a typically elegant First Dynasty form, in which, presumably, he will catch his victim's blood.

Figure 5.5 This wooden label shows what appears to be a scene of human sacrifice or ritual
murder, which is being enacted in the upper right-hand corner of the first register.
A bound and kneeling captive is about to receive a knife-thrust, whilst his
assailant holds a beaker in which presumably the captive's blood will be caught.
The issue of human sacrifice in the First Dynasty is difficult to reconcile with the
Egyptians' generally benign commitment to the prolongation of life, rather than
its arbitrary, even if ceremonial termination.

Source: the Egyptian Museum, Cairo. Photograph John G. Ross.

It seems certain that what is shown here is a rite of human sacrifice; there
are other similar representations of the same ritual. There is little doubt that
the passive figure in this strange and rather chilling little drama is a victim,
for his arms appear to be drawn back in the manner which always represents
a pinioned prisoner in Egyptian iconography. The ladder which appears in
the first register was an important and probably a primitive element in
Egyptian ritual; it conveyed the rather obvious idea of the king mounting to
the stars. The spear, too, was an immensely ancient component in the cults
associated with the early kingship and with the mythology attending the
origins of the Egyptian state.[34]

The reign of Djer was remarkable for the rapid advance of all the arts of
civilization. By a singular chance a cache of jewels was found by Petrie in
the king's tomb at Abydos still adorning a human arm, wrapped in linen,
which had been cut from the mummified body and thrust into a cranny in

121

the tomb's walls.[35] A rich hoard of copper vessels, tools, and weapons was found in a monument from Djer's reign at Saqqara, together with a superb gold-handled knife, evidence of the sumptuousness of the accoutrements of the king's ministers and the opulence of his court.

More retainers were despatched on the king's death. These, fortunate or unfortunate according to the point of view taken of their selection to join their royal master, included Bekh, whose name was inscribed on two copper axes and also on an ivory label, where it was associated with the king's name, suggesting that he may have enjoyed some special status. Another of Djer's retainers apparently sacrificed was Kahotep; he too had his name inscribed on a copper axe, a very distinctive artefact cast with side-lugs, a form which Petrie believed did not otherwise appear in Egypt until several hundred years later.[36]

The burials of retainers or, as Petrie would have it, of 'courtiers' around Djer's tomb are vividly illustrated in Petrie's report. In one case at least the photograph of a burial is alarming, apparently showing the occupant of the tomb struggling to climb out of it. It is usually asserted that the victims of this custom went willingly to their deaths or were drugged before burial. This comforting view does not appear to apply to the occupant of Grave no. 537, who seems to be desperately attempting to climb out of his tomb.[37]

King Djet

The next to assume the thrones of the Dual Kingdom was the Serpent King Djet or Uadji, whose name commemorates the great serpent goddess of the south. Djet's reign marks another high point in the early First Dynasty. After more than a century of the rule of the Thinite house, life in the Valley had developed at an unprecedented degree, in affluence and in the assurance which affluence brings. The power of the kings is increasingly manifest in the splendour of their possessions and the richness of the establishments which they maintained. During the central years of the First Dynasty crafts such as carpentry, joinery, carving, and inlay, advanced rapidly, becoming very skilled and sophisticated.

The tomb at Saqqara which is attributed to Djet's reign is colossal, measuring 56 by 24 metres.[38] The central chamber in which the occupant's body, in all probability, lay or which was to be visited by his *Ka* is particularly remarkable, for the room was originally panelled in wood, inlaid with strips of gold plating. It is one example of the Saqqara monuments which seemed to warrant Emery's attribution of royal burials to them – or at least renders that attribution still more understandable. The tomb was probably built for a high official, Sekhemka.

Around the great building was a low platform on which were mounted an astonishing display of some three hundred bulls' heads modelled in clay with the actual horns set into place.[39] This practice is not unique to Djet's

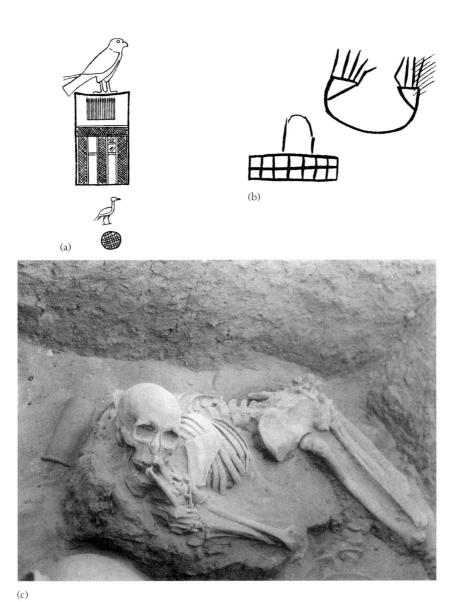

(a)

(b)

(c)

Figure 5.6 Many of the royal and noble tombs of the First Dynasty are surrounded by the graves of retainers, evidently sacrificed on the death of the owner of the tomb and destined to accompany him to the Afterlife. The names of those so destined were set up over their graves; here (a) Bekh and (b) Ka-Hotep. Most of the inhabitants of the graves seem to be lying tranquilly, as if accepting their fate or having gone to it drugged. However, a macabre example of a candidate for sacrifice trying to escape his fate is shown here (c), apparently struggling to rise out of his grave.

Source: W.M.F. Petrie *Tombs of the Courtiers and Oxyrhykos* (1925): (a) pl. III.461; (b) pl. III. 8; (c) pl. XIV.537. Reproduced by courtesy of University College London.

reign, though his tomb is the first known to demonstrate it; another example is the tomb of Queen Herneith, perhaps a consort of King Djer, who was buried in the reign following Djet's. The *mastabas* which display bulls' heads in this way seem to connect these early kings with the great bull cults which were so much a part of the emerging culture of post-Neolithic societies.

Bull cults were important in Egypt, especially in the early periods,[40] where the bull is a primary royal symbol. The bull was regarded as the herald of the gods; the animal was particularly associated with the ithyphallic god Min, who was also identified with the bee, a creature which was part of the mystical persona of the king. The king always bore the title 'Bull of his Mother' but the royal iconography generally did not portray the king with 'bullish' attributes in later centuries; bulls in fact are particularly associated with the First Dynasty. The most accomplished and impressive representation of the king as bull is undoubtedly the fragment of a slate or schist palette which shows a royal bull goring his fallen enemy.[41] The carving is exceptionally fine, technically of a very high standard; the stone

Figure 5.7 The exteriors of two of the massive mastaba tombs at North Saqqara are decorated with an array of the modelled skulls of the aurochs, *bos primigenius*, as many as three hundred pairs of bulls' horns having been set into the clay models of the skulls.

Source: from W.B. Emery, *Great Tombs of the First Dynasty*, vol. II: pl. VII b. Reproduced by courtesy of the Egypt Exploration Society.

has a wonderful plasticity and the animal's body is beautifully rendered. The carving has a curious dream-like quality about it, almost a suggestion, though it is paradoxical, of slow motion with the great bull's head slightly turned towards the spectator, being presented as if it were engaged in some ritual act.

Bulls were associated with the planets and constellations, from very early times both in Egypt and in Sumer as well as in Elam and later in other parts of the ancient world. Earlier still, bulls had been portrayed on the painted walls of the shrines at some of the earliest of all 'towns', at Çatalhüyük on the Konya plain in Southern Anatolia.[42] The 'bucranium', the bull's skull or its head in outline, which appears painted on Egyptian pottery of the early period, is an immensely ancient design, appearing in a highly stylized form on the earliest Near Eastern pottery, from northern Iraq, at sites like Hassouna and Sammara; in Egypt the bucranium seems from early times to have been associated with the cow-headed goddess Hathor. In the third millennium the bull was a powerful symbol in Elam and, later, in the Gulf, where the island of Failaka seems particularly to have been a centre of bull cults.[43] Later still, of course, the Cretans were to raise the running of the bulls to the level of a national pastime.

An exceptional example of the perfected austerity of form and design which is characteristic of Djet's reign survives in the form of a large memorial stela, one of two originally set up outside his tomb at Abydos. This magnificent memorial of the king and of his reign is expressed by the rearing serpent, suspended in the sky above the battlements of the fortified palace whose facade forms the *serekh* in which the king's name is written. Djet's stela demonstrates its restraint, exceptional refinement, and an understanding of form which is not to be repeated by artists of other nationalities until the coming of the Greeks, two thousand five hundred years later. Even then, the Greeks hardly ever achieved the monumental simplicity that the unknown master of the stela of King Djet produced with such divine assurance. It is one of the masterpieces of Egyptian art.[44]

It is not clear how the Egyptians managed so early on and with such little experience on which to draw, to demonstrate that most rare and exalted ability in design, to refine and reduce a design to its bare and simple essentials and in doing so produce works of art which transcend mere greatness. Yet the chaste elegance of an art reduced to exquisite proportion, as, for example, that which the potters of the later Song Dynasty in China achieved, is demonstrated by Egyptian artists thousands of years before their Chinese counterparts. The Egyptian craftsmen were working at the beginning of their tradition and not after many centuries of innovation, rejection and experiment.

The finest works of art of the period display a distinctive blend of austerity and elegance which is almost arrogant in its demand to be recognized on its own terms: it is an art which is wholly aristocratic, produced by members of an elite for the most exalted members of society, both human and divine. It is moving and quite extraordinary to see Egyptian artists so very early on reducing their works to their essential components of mass and form. Once the experimental forms, exotic and eccentric as they often are, either become adopted into the canon or disappear, artists and craftsmen of genius in the Early Dynastic period seem already capable of stripping out all inessential elements in a design and retaining only those which express its deepest character.

Everything associated with the king was of the finest quality. Carving, not only on the scale of the stela, but even in minor pieces such as those used in the games which were frequently put into the tombs of the noble dead, now achieved great elegance and precision. The reign of Djet was an early example of those times when all the influences seem to conspire to produce high art and the evidence of life striding forward to excel; Egypt was to experience many such times, more often perhaps than any other nation. Like his predecessor, Djet recorded a campaign as 'the smiting of the easterners'.

Djet had his servants buried in both his monuments at Abydos and at Saqqara. It was said that a great famine took place during his reign and that he built a pyramid at a location now identified with Saqqara. No pyramid is known to survive from so early a period, however; the first pyramid, the Step Pyramid of King Netjerykhet, dates from the beginning of the Third Dynasty.

Queen Merneith

After Djet's reign, the sovereignty of Egypt seem to have been assumed by a woman. Merneith compounded her name with the great goddess of the north. Her northern affiliations may have contributed to the Thinite family's policy of conciliating Lower Egypt, as their dynastic succession became more and more established as each royal generation passed.

Women were important in Early Dynastic Egypt. The queens were called 'She who unites the Two Lands', recalling by this title perhaps the event early in the dynasty when a southern prince possibly married the heiress of the north and so brought the two kingdoms into association. The queen was also 'She who sees Horus and Seth' as though to her was reserved the privilege of the actual manifestation of the two perpetually counter-balanced gods, joined only in the divine person of the king.

To find a queen ruling apparently with all the power accorded to a king of Egypt is, at this early time, mildly surprising, though the generally high status of women in early Egypt should be recalled and the probability is that she was acting as regent for her son, the future King Den. The Egyptian traditions stated that it was only decided that a woman could occupy the throne when the Second Dynasty was well advanced, but there is no doubt that Merneith was buried with the solemnity accorded to a king: her tomb at Abydos and that associated with her reign at Saqqara (S3503) are of con-

siderable grandeur. The Saqqara monument was memorable for the subsidiary burials of menials and artisans who were, willy-nilly, obliged to
accompany the inhabitants of the tomb to oblivion or the promise of eternal
life. The burials included a maker of pots, a painter supplied with his pig-
ments and the reeds whose crushed ends constituted his brushes, a shipmas-
ter, indeed an entire household of upper servants.[45]

King Den

Den, or Dewen, also known as Udimu, became king in his own right after
the period in which Merneith had held the regency. His reign is marked in
particular by advances in all the arts and the prosperity of Egypt, whose
beginnings were evident in Djet's reign, came to its full flowering. The royal
administration developed considerably during this reign; the king, ruling
through his chosen assistants, the most powerful of whom were probably
members of his family (though this was not invariably the case in First
Dynasty times), extended his control over the whole Valley.

Den's reign was one of the longest and most influential in the First
Dynasty, remarkable for the advances which the state made in the quality of
the accoutrements of the kingship and of the men who were the king's principal adjutants. One of these, Ankh-Ka bore the title 'Chancellor', even at so
early a period. He was also one of the first to be recorded as a provincial governor, indicating how ancient was the administrative structure which
ensured the security and prosperity of the Dual Kingdom.

Another of the leading figures of Den's reign was Hemaka, who was
buried in a large mastaba tomb at Saqqara,[46] from which was recovered a
beautiful steatite disc, inlaid with scenes of hounds pursuing a gazelle. His
tomb also yielded the oldest roll of papyrus to survive in Egypt; sadly, it was
blank but it suggests that the practice of writing was already widespread.
Den was the first king of Egypt to adopt the title conventionally transliterated as 'he of the sedge and the bee', rendered as 'King of Upper and Lower
Egypt' and now, more concisely 'Dual King'.

He led campaigns against marauding tribes on the frontiers, to ensure
that such barbarians would not disturb his kingdoms. He seems to have
been a considerable warrior in addition to his other qualities. He conducted
relations with his foreign neighbours; in particular contact between Egypt
and Syria-Palestine seem to have been close at this time.

In another scene, this time on an alabaster palette from a monument at
Saqqara,[47] he is shown in what was to become the immemorial gesture of a
king of Egypt dealing with those who set themselves or their people against
his authority. Though the picture, an effective piece of propaganda no doubt
calculated to discourage any other stirrings of rebellion, is damaged, it is
probable that Djer is wielding a pear-shaped mace, the weapon which was
always to be represented in such scenes. One record from the reign of Djer

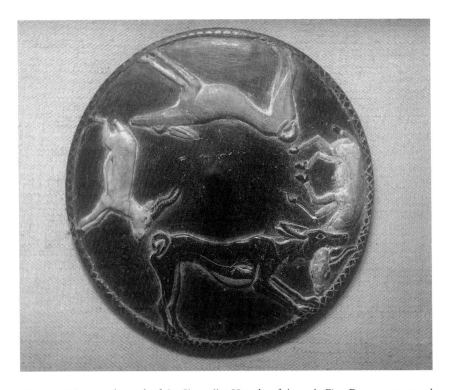

Figure 5.8 The *mastaba* tomb of the Chancellor Hemaka of the early First Dynasty, excavated at Saqqara, produced this exquisite inlaid steatite disc, probably originally intended as a gaming piece. The *tjesm* hunting hounds pursue their quarry for all eternity.

Source: photograph John G. Ross. From W.B. Emery, *Excavations at Saqqara: The Tomb of Hemaka* (Cairo 1938) Frontispiece.

speaks of 'the year of the smiting of the land of Setjet', the land to the east of Egypt which is usually taken to mean western Asia.

Chance and the unusual incompetence of the robbers who plundered the monument at Saqqara dated to Den's reign preserved an immense cache of objects, many of them of spectacular quality.[48] Weapons, tools, an enormous variety of stone vessels, including examples in rock crystal, alabaster, and schist, were preserved. So too were the games which would help the occupants of the tomb to while away eternity. The lid of the box which contained the king's gold seal was also preserved, a witness to the sophistication of the royal government at this time and to the exceptional quality of the work of the artists and craftsmen whom Den evidently considerably encouraged.

Den was long remembered by the Egyptian people and records purporting to descend from his reign were quoted in the New Kingdom, including a prescription which was included in the Ebers medical papyrus, for Den, too, was renowned as a physician. One of the medical studies thought to descend from this time dealt, in a remarkably objective manner, with the nature and treatment of fractures. It was during his reign that the double crown was said to have been adopted for the first time. It seems also that during this king's reign all evidence of the Mesopotamian connection ceased and from this time onwards Egyptian forms exclude alien influences until the end of the Old Kingdom.

Queen Herneith was buried in a great tomb at Saqqara (S3507) during Den's reign.[49] She was a survivor from Djer's reign and was buried with many fine objects, but without the usual holocaust of servants. The burial chamber still contained the remains of a large wooden sarcophagus and the scattered bones of its one-time occupant. Her tomb, like Djet's, was supported by lines of outward-facing modelled bull-heads.

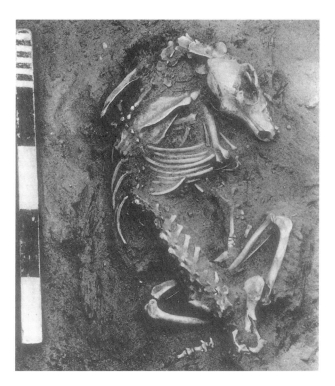

Figure 5.9 An apparent exception to the practice of sacrificing servants on the death of a 'Great One' of the First Dynasty was the burial of Queen Herneith, early in the dynasty. Though she was buried in a large and magnificent tomb she was joined there only by her dog, a *tjesm* hunting hound, laid across the tomb's threshold, to guard his or her mistress.

Source: photograph by courtesy of the *Illustrated London News* Picture Library.

The fact that she was buried without any retainers at all is very striking. Her lonely distinction is emphasized by the fact that only her dog accompanied her on her last, dark journey. It was laid across the threshold of her tomb, to guard its mistress through eternity. It is a curiously touching survival; the dog appears to be of that most ancient of all breeds, the prick-eared, long-skulled hunting hound, for long centuries the companion of the Great Ones of Egypt. It was described by Emery, who excavated the tomb, as 'of a breed akin to the saluki'.[50] However, there is no doubt that it was an Egyptian hound, an early example of the breed which the Egyptians called *tjesm*. Queen Herneith is the first named dog-lover known to history.

King Anedjib

After Den came Anedjib, according to the list of kings. Manetho maintains that son followed father throughout the First Dynasty but Anedjib seems to be the first king accorded by later authorities with sovereignty over the entire Two Lands, suggesting that up to his reign the Thinite assumption of the kingship was still disputed by some interests. Anedjib, however, is named as the first king of the united Egypt in the Saqqara king list, but he was usurped (or at least his monuments were desecrated) by his successor Semerkhet, which suggests that the dynasty was not wholly secure and that there was some residual resistance to them still abroad.

Anedjib introduces a new style into the titulary of the kingship. He adopted the title 'The Two Ladies', thus honouring the goddesses Uadji and Nekhbet, who were the tutelary divinities of the south and north and the particular guardians of the kings. He is thus really the first 'Dual King' of Egypt. His acknowledgement of the power of the two goddesses suggests that he was concerned to fuse the interests of the two great rival gods. Anedjib's reign marks a notable falling off in standards compared with the prosperity of his predecessors, a falling off demonstrated by the relatively modest size of his tomb when compared with those of Den, Djet and certainly of the dog-loving Queen Herneith. However though his Abydos monument is relatively small he could afford to install sixty-four retainers in subsidiary graves around it.

The design of the tomb (S3038) at Saqqara[51] attributed to his reign is very remarkable, for within the superstructure of a familiar *mastaba* format there was found hidden what is in effect a buried, miniature stepped pyramid. This was entirely unexpected when it was discovered though it is known now not to be unique; Queen Herneith's tomb has the same feature though, in her case, in what is clearly a more primitive form. It has been suggested (not altogether convincingly, though the concept is quite Egyptian) that the combination of the two forms of tomb represents the stepped mound or tumulus of the south contained within the rectangular panelled structure of the north. There is certainly nothing to suggest that the panelled structure is northern; after all it was chosen by a southern line of princes to contain their royal names in the form of the *serekh*. The Saqqara monument has been attributed to a high official serving the king, Nebetka. A feature new to Egyptian funerary architecture was a bucranium buried in part of the tomb's superstructure.[52]

In any event, the stepped structure finally conquered, bursting out of its concealment magnificently in the burial monument of King Netjerykhet, several hundred years later. Then the Step Pyramid swallows the *mastaba* which was the original form of the tomb conceived by Imhotep, Netjerykhet's architect.

King Semerkhet

The First Dynasty was now moving towards its end. King Semerkhet, the fifth of the line ruled, it seems, only for nine years; the sole funerary monument to have been found which might be attributed to him is at Abydos.[53] Manetho recorded that in his reign 'a very great calamity' befell Egypt: Manetho does not describe it, but it has been suggested that Semerkhet was a usurper, with only a dubious claim to the kingship.

King Qa'a

He was followed by the last king of the dynasty, Qa'a, who reigned, according to Manetho, for twenty-six years. There are several monuments at Saqqara associated with his reign; some are particularly impressive and of great size.[54] The interior walls of this imposing building were found to be painted imitating, it is thought, the gaily coloured matting which hung upon the walls of the royal palaces.

Qa'a is thought to have celebrated two Heb-Sed festivals, suggesting that his reign may have been quite long. It has been suggested that on the death of Qa'a there was a period of dynastic upheaval. There are two shadowy kings listed from this time, Ba, whose name is known from only one inscription, and Sneferka, which may have been an alternative Horus name adopted by Qa'a.[55] The presence of the sealings of the first king of the Second Dynasty, Hotepsekhemwy, in Qa'a's tomb may indicate that he conducted his predecessor's funerary rites and the transition was peaceful.

Qa'a's tomb at Umm al-Qaab, at Abydos, has been excavated by the German Archaeological Expedition. From it were recovered the fragments of one of the king's seals which, when restored, confirmed the sequence of the kings of the First Dynasty, from Narmer to Qa'a.

6

THE LEGACY OF THE FOUNDER
KINGS

All the royal mastabas at Saqqara and the funerary palaces at Abydos are surrounded by the subsidiary burials of servants and lesser figures in the court. No one can speculate with any hope of certainty about the attitude of those Egyptians who were obliged to go down into the grave with the great men or women whom they served. With rare exceptions, such as that cited in the previous chapter, little trace has been found of resistance amongst these subsidiary dead, no general signs of dreadful struggles as was evident, centuries later, in the mass graves at Kerma, far to the south (in what was, for the average Egyptian, deepest Africa), nor the chilling if faintly farcical episode of one of the women in the drama of the death pit at Ur in Sumer, who seems to have been a little late for her own funeral and who slipped in after her companions, to join the ranks of those about to die. The Egyptians were buried in orderly tombs, neatly laid out with appropriate offerings; presumably they had administered to them some sort of tranquillizing drug or swift-acting poison, to carry them out of this world into the promise of the next or, more brutally, clubbed into insensibility. The argument which most scholars advance to account for what appears to be the placid acceptance of premature death is that by this means only would they expect to achieve immortality, as part of the retinue of the eternal king, as at this time there was no belief in the general application of eternal life beyond the king and his immediate entourage. It is as good an explanation as any.

Though they brought an entirely unprecedented degree of civilization and prosperity to Egypt there is undoubtedly a sense of strangeness which surrounds the reputation of the kings of the First Dynasty. Whilst there is clearly a progression from a relatively simple chieftaincy demonstrated by the predynastic kings, to a high and fully articulated monarchy, the actual transition is marked with considerable suddenness. To those accustomed to the splendour of the kings of Egypt as their image has descended to the modern world, there is something disconcerting about the customs and rituals which attend the kings of the First Dynasty. Although much of the immemorial legacy of Egypt descended from their times and many of the attributes associated with the kingship were laid down in their reigns, there is an uneasy quality about their occupancy of the thrones. Even their origins are mysterious.

They were honoured greatly by later generations as the founders of the kingship and of the unified kingdoms, but their memories seem also to have been feared. At some time after the end of the dynasty all the tombs in which the kings and high officials were buried, on the escarpment at North Saqqara looking down on Memphis, at Abydos and at Helwan, were destroyed in immense conflagrations. The fires were intense and the destruction of the houses of these great dead was without doubt deliberate. Somehow the customary explanation, of dynastic upheavals and the vindictiveness of their political opponents, seems inadequate for so violent a manifestation of rejection carried out with such ruthless determination over the whole country.

HUMAN SACRIFICE

One reason for the somewhat equivocal reputation which the First Dynasty seems to have enjoyed in the minds of the later generations could be associated with the cults of ritual death, reflected in the funerary practices of the dynasty. The Egyptians were obsessed, as no other people has ever been, with life and its perpetuation. All their beliefs centred on the need to extend life beyond the frontiers of death. To this end also was directed their love of and identification with the living world they saw around them. In apparent contradiction of this principle there are the companies of retainers that the kings of the First Dynasty took with them, who were sacrificed and buried with their royal master or sometimes mistress.

There is something cruelly matter-of-fact about the neat rows (their very neatness is disturbing) of subsidiary burials which surround most of the great burials at Saqqara and many at Abydos and other royal centres. There is no doubt that these interments took place at the same time as the principal was laid in his tomb; the same mound usually covers them all.

Sometimes the occupants of the subsidiary graves were courtiers, harem women or undifferentiated attendants of the king. In some cases they were craftsmen and specialists who might continue to provide their master with their services eternally. The degree of specialization of craft and trade indicated by the inhabitants of the subsidiary graves in the Royal Tombs suggests an incipient class structure or emergent hierarchical society in Egypt, even in the earliest times. The king of Egypt was god; hence, all others must have been equal in his sight. However, it is evident that hierarchies existed, perhaps even in predynastic Egypt, as witnessed by the differing relative sizes of the attendants on the maces of King Scorpion and King Narmer and the palette of the latter. The status of the craftsmen, singled out for the particular honours of ritual death in the service of their master or mistress, suggests the existence of an elite, other than the nobility or the upper class of official.

133

Throughout Egyptian history and particularly in the early periods there was a developing class of middle-rank people, who occupied an increasingly important place in the fabric of the state and who often penetrated its highest courses. Binding all these influences together was the king. A later description of the majesty of the king of Egypt would have applied even more in the days of the First Dynasty. It ran 'He is a god by whose dealings one lives, the father and mother of all men, alone, by himself, without an equal'.[1]

The practice of the immolation of servants was discontinued at the end of the First Dynasty and was allowed to fall into disuse; it was in any case, a most un-Egyptian custom, in conflict with their notions of the integrity of life. But it is wholly in character that ever afterwards a well-founded Egyptian, royal or simple, went on his last great journey attended by quantities of little servant figurines, in wood, faience, pottery, stone, or metal, which would serve as his 'answerers' and undertake any disagreeable or distasteful tasks which he might be called upon to discharge, during his progress to the light of perpetual life.

There is only very tenuous evidence for the practice of the ritual killing of servants *before* the First Dynasty: occasional examples have been suspected at Adäima[2] however and evidently at Hierakonpolis (see 87 above). The custom seems particular to the princes of This; certainly, it was adopted by them and their close colleagues on a generous scale. What prompted it is beyond speculation; if we knew more of the ancestry of the Thinite kings we might be able to determine why they followed this barbarous practice, to judge it by subjective standards.

HELWAN

The prosperity which the unification brought to Egypt and in particular to the northern part of Upper Egypt where Memphis the capital was situated is nowhere demonstrated more dramatically than at the site of Ma'sara and Ezbet el-Wadi, near Helwan. There upwards of ten thousand graves have been excavated;[3] they are the burial places of officials and others of what might be called the upper bureaucracy who must have provided much of the administrative class of the capital area. Some of the people buried there were no doubt nobles, close to the king and probably his familiars, but none of them seems to have been a royal personage. The quantity of pottery and of personal possessions buried at Helwan was prodigious; for a society to be able to extract at such an early date so much of its material wealth from circulation, generation by generation, displays a remarkable degree of confidence in the kingdoms' economic future. It must also have been good news for the artists and craftsmen who, also generation by generation, would have been required to replace the wealth of what had become, to a substantial degree, a grave-oriented society.

Amongst the graves at Helwan are examples of the burials of dogs and donkeys;[4] as these do not seem to be the subject of cult or religious observance, it may be that they were family pets, since the Egyptians always kept animals about them, as members of their households. The burial grounds at Helwan are of great importance for what they reveal about the quality of life enjoyed by relatively modest people, the officials, courtiers, and those who served the court, during the first flowering of the kingship in Egypt. It must be presumed that the dead buried at Helwan served their royal masters at Memphis which was then in the first phase of its existence as the capital of the Dual Kingdom, and at the great religious centres nearby. These would have included Heliopolis which, even in the very early period, and probably in predynastic times as well, was established as the centre of the cult of the sun, a cult which was only to assume a national status later in the Old Kingdom.

The Helwan graves range from extensive and complex structures comparable with those at Saqqara to relatively modest interments. They were excavated principally in the 1940s and 1950s.[5] They are of great importance in assessing the character of life in Egypt during the early centuries, both because of the quality of the objects and architecture which they contain and because their evidence makes necessary the reversal of a number of otherwise long-held ideas about early Egyptian religious belief and funerary practice. The First Dynasty custom of burying boats close to elite tombs appears at Helwan also.

Some doubt has been cast on the original dating of the Helwan tombs. There is evidence that as early as the Epi-Palaeolithic period burials the area was occupied and again in Neolithic times.[6] Many are clearly Early Dynastic; others, however, date from as late as the Third Dynasty when many of the architectural techniques which would seem remarkable in an Early Dynastic context have become almost commonplace. However, the interest of Helwan lies in the fact that it is principally a cemetery of the non-noble. As such it shows both the development of tomb-building, reaching down, at a relatively early date into the middle ranks of society and the comparative luxury of the goods with which such people were able to surround themselves in death as in life.

Thus, some of the tombs revealed at Helwan (also at sites such as Abydos and Saqqara) show that already First Dynasty Egyptian architects were confident in the use of stone for walls, ceilings, and staircases. At Helwan nine of the tombs excavated used limestone extensively in their construction;[7] however, it must be remembered that this is a tiny percentage of the total excavated. It is frequently asserted that the earliest use of stone was in the late Second Dynasty but quite apart from the revetment of Hierakonpolis, the First Dynasty tombs at Helwan (as well as some of the larger, contemporary tombs at Saqqara) demonstrate that this is not so. Some of the blocks used for the wall and floor the burial chambers are huge,[8] suggesting that they are already the products of a long-established and assured tradition.

Helwan has also provided evidence of the advanced nature of the textile industry in First Dynasty Egypt. Wool was used widely, in particular for making the cloaks in which early dynastic men are often portrayed. Linen, too, of exceptional delicacy, equalling the most exquisitely fine, gossamer-like fabrics the like of which have only been made in modern times, was also produced.[9] Such fabrics were evidently available on a generous scale and presumably, were made industrially by skilled craftsmen working either on the great magnates' estates (as is attested from somewhat later times) or, as was probably the case for the fabrics used by the rather less exalted occupants of some of the Helwan graves, produced by craftsmen working on their own account, in workshops like those which existed for the production of stone vessels and pottery containers. An endearing characteristic of the burials at Helwan is that a relatively high proportion of the graves, when compared for example with the contemporary but rather grander tombs at Saqqara and Abydos, contained objects which had been broken during the time of their use and then, thriftily, repaired. In the case both of pottery and of stone vessels this was done by drilling holes in the vessel and its broken part and then binding them together, either with copper wire or with cord.

Most of the Helwan tombs seem to have been destroyed by fire, in conflagrations like those which were destroyed in the First Dynasty tombs at other sites. It is really very strange that this wholesale posthumous destruction was evidently practiced across the land of Egypt, not only of the tombs of the kings and the Great Ones but also of the relatively modest inhabitants of the tombs of Helwan.

Helwan is a pleasant place, some 20 km south of the modern capital of Cairo. It is celebrated today for its medicinal waters and its less salubrious steel plants. Something must have drawn the First Dynasty Egyptians there, to populate such considerable tomb fields. Whatever it was, that impulsion is lost, but the existence of the large numbers of tombs with their substantial architecture and their rich furnishings, calls for a reassessment of another of the long-held beliefs about religious ideas in Early Dynastic Egypt, namely that the prospects of eternal life were first reserved exclusively for the king, then for his closest attendants, and only later for members of the court.

Many of the dead of Helwan, like those of even earlier, predynastic burials, seem to have been laid in a foetal position, as though anticipating rebirth. Whilst nothing could diminish the king's claim to divinity, in this life as much as in the life after death, it appears that his subjects, or at least those who were buried at Helwan, had quite considerable expectations of immortality.

A study of the architecture of the Helwan tombs has concluded that the use of stone in their construction indicates a high level of building skills available in this region of northern Upper Egypt in the First and Second Dynasties.[10] The ability to manipulate stone, it is suggested, may have contributed to the remarkable achievements of the builders of the monuments at Giza. More controversially, it has been cited in another study as possible evidence for an Early Dynastic date for the building of several of the Giza monuments, including the Great Sphinx.[11]

THE KINGSHIP AND THE NATION-STATE

The invention of the kingship is one of the most enduring of all Egyptian achievements, one with universal significance, from whose forms all successive great kingdoms in the Near East (and perhaps others more distant still) if they did not draw their inspiration certainly demonstrated the same solution in their response to similar social and psychological imperatives. Few, if any of them, however, achieved any semblance of the majesty which the Egyptian kings seem so easily to have assumed.

If human ingenuity or ambition were to set out consciously to create such an institution as the kingship, the Nile Valley would have been amongst the least suitable locations which it would have been possible to choose on which to launch it. The narrow river banks, with the occasional wide expanse of cultivation drawn out and extended over a length quite disproportionate, with the occasional, widely dispersed oasis, would surely seem to be the least favoured ground for such an epoch-making innovation, the invention of the first nation-state in the history of the world.

That the king and his followers even conceived of uniting all the Nile Valley is the measure of the Thinite princes' ambition. The differences between Upper and Lower Egypt, south and north, in custom, culture, beliefs and rituals were profound; this is demonstrated by the fact that throughout Egyptian history such differences were insisted upon and it was only the king that provided the link between them: he alone was Dual King. The extent of this achievement in welding the entire Valley into one state can be measured, paradoxically, by the fact that the Egyptians maintained the fiction of the separate identities of the two kingdoms throughout the long sweep of Egyptian history. The union of the Two Lands was really an unnatural construct which at various times throughout Egypt's history, when the central kingship faltered, for example, or when the threat of foreign invasion became a reality, came apart at the seams and the Valley fragmented into small principalities centred on the administrative districts into which both Egypts were divided. Yet, despite this tendency to fracture, the vision of the early kings was so powerful and enduring that always an heroic figure, usually and most significantly from the south, would emerge to impose once again the ancient Thinite concept of the united lands.

The partners of the Thinite prince, who was presumably a young man as the first king of the dynasty is said to have reigned for sixty-four years, were important chieftains like himself, to judge by their standards which he was evidently proud to depict being borne before him on various of the documents which survive from his time; however, he seems to have been accepted as being supreme over them or quickly made himself so. Whether the paramountcy was by some ancient right attached to the eponym of the Falcon clan or whether it became his as the consequence of some irresistible charisma that he possessed, the Falcon he was and the united Egypt which he was to create was, *par excellence*, the Falcon's land. At least one of his peers, the Lord of Ombos, possibly the eponym of the federation of southern clans which honoured the swift hound as its symbol, must have nurtured some reservations about the Falcon's claims to the sovereignty. But the dissension which the ancient affront to the status of the Set tribes was eventually to precipitate was, for the moment, in the future.

On a day probably in the first quarter of the thirty-second century (*c.* 3180 BC) the Falcon prince set out on his annexation of the land to the north of his patrimony, accompanied, as the stories afterwards told, by the Spirits of the Dead, the demi-gods who were to be immortalized as the Companions or Followers of Horus. Thus the royal propagandists skilfully suggested that he was attended not only by the living 'Great Ones' of Egypt but also by a ghostly retinue of heroic figures from the ancient past. An appeal to what was evidently a powerful myth by the prince and his advisors suggests how well they understood their people and those whom they sought to absorb by identifying his advance to the northern kingdom with the shades of long-dead chieftains, whose legends evidently were still current and still capable of exciting a loyal response from the people.

After the years of spasmodic and, it must be presumed, frequently localized rebellion the strong central government of the kings eventually produced a deep and largely a lasting peace throughout the Valley. The Two Lands were, as a consequence of the Valley's topography, wholly secure and easily capable of efficient defence. To east and west ranged the great deserts. The route through the mountains to the east could be policed with relative ease. To the west the seemingly limitless Libyan desert provided its mantle of protection to the Valley.

CONTROL OF THE SOUTH – NUBIA

To the south only the area below the cataract could provide entry to the barbarous hordes from Africa; the gates to Egypt could be closed against them by the expedient of building guard forts in the gorges of the Valley and, from time to time, by sending punitive expeditions to put down the Nubians and others welling up from Africa, if they seemed minded to intrude upon the Valley's tranquillity.

Egypt's relations with Nubia, and indeed with all of black Africa to the south, have only in recent years been reappraised. Historians have tended to assume that the African south was significant to Egypt only as a source of labour, soldiers, precious metals, ivory and rare woods. What was not appreciated until more recent research was the high cultural level achieved by the Nubians from an early date; to what extent their culture was derived from Egypt or to what extent Egypt drew into itself influences from Africa is still disputed.

Some spectacularly rich burials of the late predynastic period have been found in Nubian sites. At Sayala, Nubian chiefs were buried with a fine panoply of imports and very rich objects: copper axes, ingots of copper, chisels, two enormous bird shaped palettes, and two monumental sceptres with gold batons.[12] The maceheads which top the sceptres are pear-shaped and on one of the batons was depicted a series of animals, magnificently engraved. This was a superlative object and would have been a prized possession in the Treasury of an Egyptian king; in fact hardly anything quite so fine has been recovered from Egypt of the same period. Sadly this majestic object disappeared from the Cairo Museum soon after its discovery in the early years of this century.

Qustul

At Qustul a group of graves has been excavated which, from the luxury of their contents, prompted their excavator to describe them as the burial places of Kings of the Nubian A Group, people who were contemporaries of the Egyptians of the late predynastic and Early Dynastic periods.[13] Certainly the contents of the Qustul tombs are very fine: some of them show an elaboration of design and concept which is remarkable for what has hitherto been regarded at best as an outlying province of Egyptian culture, in the latter part of the fourth millennium. A richly decorated incense burner depicts a personage, wearing what appears to be the White Crown of Upper Egypt, seated in an Egyptian style boat. With him is a bull and two dogs of the *tjesm* strain.[14]

There is evidence of the familiar preoccupation with boats at Qustul, as there is on the rock walls of the many lower Nubian sites which are decorated with rock drawings. Whether or not the graves are of kings, the peers of their colleagues to the north, there is little doubt that the Nubian chiefs of the late fourth millennium were able to sustain an extensive trade with their contemporaries in Egypt proper. Trade was evidently active and considerable; during the early dynastic period, however, relations between Egypt and Nubia seem to have declined and the A Group Nubians disappear by the Third Dynasty. It may be suspected that the kings of Egypt, who frequently record punitive expeditions to Nubia even in the earliest times, were responsible for the destruction of what might have become a rival to their power.

Elephantine

The policy of closing the southern gates of Upper Egypt at the First Cataract at Aswan contributed to the early development of Elephantine Island, as an emplacement to prevent marauders from the south entering the Valley. The island was first occupied in Naqada II times, when it was fortified.[15] The region which it controlled was important to the Egyptians by reason of the colourful crystalline limestone rocks which could be extracted from its vicinity and which were greatly favoured by Egyptian architects and their clients of all periods.[16]

The First Dynasty kings were concerned to define and protect Egypt's international boundaries, another notable political innovation. This belief in the integrity of Egypt is reflected in the lack of external territorial ambition demonstrated by the rulers until the second millennium when, like the rest of the Near East, Egypt began to harbour imperial ambitions. But such ambitions were essentially alien to the Egyptian mentality and Elephantine and other frontier strongholds in the south were designed to preserve inviolate Egypt's essential identity.

The north-east

In the northern extremity of Lower Egypt, the defensive situation was complex. There it was necessary to keep watch on the long Mediterranean shoreline, though throughout most of the third millennium no other power was really capable of mounting a substantial seaborne invasion against Egypt. Only the corridor to the north-east, reaching up to Sinai, through Gaza to the Levantine coast, and, further east still, across the northern Arabian deserts, presented real hazards. From these regions and especially from Sinai as from the eastern deserts of Egypt itself, there constantly flowed tribesmen from the unsettled Semitic-speaking groups who moved around this vast and inhospitable region. They preyed upon the outposts of the Egyptian state whenever they sensed they could get away with the seizure of herds, cattle, or goods. Constantly the king set out to destroy them and as constantly the nomads vanished, withdrawing to their own uncharted wilderness.

The terms which the Egyptians used to describe their eastern neighbours are various, often offensive, and frequently confusing. The term which is usually rendered as 'Asiatics' is *Aamu* and implies people coming from the east. It seems probable that first and foremost amongst the people so described were the nomadic inhabitants of Egypt's own eastern deserts, whom the Valley people always feared and disliked. The term was also used to include the peoples of Sinai, notably in the south, who shared, particularly in the late fourth and early third millennia in the general culture prevailing in southern Palestine and also, to a degree which cannot yet be fully assessed, in the cultures of ancient north-western Arabia.

Arabia

It is a matter of speculation to what extent the early Egyptians were aware of or had any real contact with the tribes who lived in the western part of the Arabian peninsula. The peoples who lived to the west of Sumer, the barbarous, illiterate, and savage tribes (in the Sumerians' minds at least) who inhabited the Syrian and Arabian deserts, were generally called *Martu*. They were the ancestors of the *Amuru* who ranged across much of the northern, central, and eastern Arabian deserts, moving through the oases over immense distances.

Archaeological research in south-western Arabia has revealed contact with Egypt at the end of the third millennium[17] but, so far, little before it. However, some contact is suggested at a much earlier period by the iconographic similarities between the hunters depicted on the 'Hunters' Palette' and on western Arabian rock carvings at Bi'r Hima, which is surprisingly far to the south of the peninsula.

Connections with Sinai and Palestine have been suggested from the plentiful implementation of Syrian and Palestinian pottery in the late predynastic and Early Dynastic periods and a study of one particular detail in the design of Narmer's Palette.[18] This is a curious feature which has been identified as a 'desert kite', an enigmatic structure which is certainly found in the Sinai and in the Palestinian deserts but which is also typical of the northern Arabian desert. The 'kites', long lines of stones which have been interpreted as the remains of corrals or traps for animals, are thought to date from as early as the end of the fourth millennium. In Arabia, particularly in the north-west, structures of this sort and also rather larger ones which sometimes even assume almost monumental proportions, seem to be associated with early copper-working regions.

THE PEACEABLE KINGDOM

For nearly a thousand years even the potential conduit of danger represented by the 'Asiatics' was kept securely closed. Peace reigned as securely in the Valley as the king reigned in Memphis. Nothing obtruded to disturb the peaceful development of Egypt, nothing clouded the tranquil progression of day following day, king succeeding king, with apparently only occasional contention in the succession.

By the time of the Old Kingdom, from the Third to the Sixth Dynasties, (*c.*2868–*c.*2181 BC), the effect of these long and tranquil centuries on the psychology of the early Egyptians may be imagined; it can also be appreciated in the reliefs of ordinary life carved on the tombs of nobles and court functionaries and in the literature of the time. The Egyptians developed a profound sense of certainty, of the order of the world and of their place in it.

They could no doubt believe that, living in the secure, tranquil, richly endowed land that was theirs, was an existence ordained by a beneficent providence and that, as it had been, so would that life always be. The conservatism which is so often described as one of the most innate characteristics of Egyptian culture comes from this time, laid upon the profound conservatism of the peasant, no matter where he lives.

At this time, from the latter part of the fourth millennium, through the early phase of the dynastic period at the beginning of the third, the vast preponderance of the Egyptian population was engaged in simple agriculture. The population has been estimated, variously, at between one and two million people,[19] though the estimate depends largely on guesswork and is probably much too high. They lived, in the main, in small village communities scattered over the Valley floor and, as they became increasingly habitable, in the marshlands of the Delta. Their lives would not have been harsh or unduly arduous: the river and the land were generous and sustained the people relatively comfortably. For the vast majority life would have gone on its tranquil progress, uncomplicated by contact with the court, the Great Ones, or the king.

The Egyptians from the earliest recorded times sustained a lively interest in two other human corporate pastimes, which, typically, they invested with their own particular qualities. These were games playing, particularly board games, and organized sports. In most tombs, from the First Dynasty onwards at least, are to be found a variety of board games. Many of these have animals as the counters: dogs, gazelles, jackals, lions, and bulls all have their turn in different games. The games, so far as it is possible to reconstruct them, are dependent on the throwing of sticks or other equivalents of dice to effect progressive moves. That they were so frequently placed amongst the funerary equipment of a well-appointed Egyptian setting out on his last journey to the west, suggests that they may also have had some ritual significance. However, as the affluent dead of the early dynasties filled their graves with all manner of evidence of their earthly wealth (in the certain belief that they *could* take it with them) this point need not be argued too exhaustively.

So much of the evidence for the ancient way of life in Egypt comes from tombs that it is difficult to reconstruct what the buildings of the living were like. However, there are occasional glimpses of architecture other than the funerary, from contemporary and later references, for in such matters the Egyptians were conservative, preferring to retain forms over immensely long periods, even if sometimes they were effectively disguised like the mound within the pyramid or the wattle shrine, built in stone in the heart of the later temples.

THE TEMPLES OF EARLY EGYPT

Very little can be said with certainty about the earliest temples to be built in Egypt, or of the ceremonies which were practiced in them. The names of some temples of the First Dynasty may be known from the inscriptions on ivory labels on which temple structures appear to be depicted; from these representations the buildings would seem to be flimsy and unpretentious, as might be expected, probably made from reeds or light timber. The large structure at Hierakonpolis may have been an anticipation of the soaring, majestic temples which were to be associated with Egypt throughout its later history, but these had to wait for their introduction in the Third Dynasty and until the Fourth for their most splendid manifestations in the Valley of the mortuary temples associated with the pyramids, a tradition which was continued, though in somewhat different form, into the Fifth.

Despite Herodotus' remark, admittedly made at least two and a half millennia after this time, that the Egyptians were the most religious people in the world, it is more likely that the timeless, unchanging, tranquil, and essentially integrated life in the Valley in the early centuries of a united Egypt was precisely the consequence of an absence of specifically religious commitment or involvement. Religion, even in the special sense that the word must be used in early Egypt, was the business of the king and his immediate colleagues; at least this would be the case in respect of national cults. These had as their focus and indeed their whole point and purpose, the person of the king as intermediary between Egypt and the gods.

Local and tribal (or even perhaps clan) cults were a different matter. Each part of Egypt had its complement of greater and lesser divinities; there were, too, the primordial forces of nature like the storm, which were to be propitiated. The preoccupation of the theologians advancing for example, one system of philosophy concerning the origin of Egypt (and hence of the cosmos) against another, Memphis *contra* Heliopolis as it might be, would have touched the Egyptian in the fields or on the river bank not at all. Only much later, as one of the marks of decay in the Egyptian state, did the priesthoods which emerged in part as the result of the sort of mild ancestor worship to which the cult of the king eventually led, begin to require a formal power base, rooted in the temples.

Like the manoeuvrings of the Christian orders in the later Middle Ages, they sought to advance the worldly interests of one group above another. The rise of ritual and the power of the temples were signs of the beginning of the end for pristine Egypt. The joyful life of the countryside, broadcast so vividly in the reliefs of so many Old Kingdom tombs but drawing on a tradition greatly older, was replaced by solemn processions of gods with their mortal and immortal attendants.

THE SECOND DYNASTY

King Hotepsekhemwy

It is not certain that there was an actual dynastic disruption following the death of Qa'a, the last king of the First Dynasty, and the reign of the next king, though Manetho shows a new dynasty beginning.[20] That king is Hotepsekhemwy who is acknowledged as the first of the Second Dynasty; his line is, however, still identified as Thinite and it may well be that the kings of this dynasty were related to those of the First Dynasty. His name means 'The Two Powers are at Peace', which has been taken to suggest that an earlier dissension between the protagonists of Horus and those of Set, had been resolved. Hotepsekhemwy conducted the funerary ceremonies of his predecessor, which suggests that there was no real break between the First and Second Dynasties. It is possible that Hotepsekhemwy's tomb and that of his successor, Raneb, may lie under part of the subterranean chambers of the Step Pyramid, to be built in the next dynasty.[21]

The first kings of the Second Dynasty are obscure figures and little is known of their reigns. We can only presume that the period of their sovereignty was marked by a continuation of that same unrest that marked the final years of the First Dynasty kings. It cannot be certain that the Second Dynasty actually followed the First; they may, in part at least, have been contemporary, ruling different parts of the Valley simultaneously.[22]

King Raneb

Hotepsekhemwy was followed on the throne by Raneb, whose name is the first in Egyptian history to introduce the name of the Sun-god Ra. Raneb's name means, either, 'Ra is my Lord' or, more portentously, 'Lord of the Sun'. The appearance of the royal acceptance of the paramountcy of the solar cult was to have long and enduring consequences for Egypt, particularly when it became the dominant cult, particularly identified with the kings of the Fourth Dynasty, who built the great pyramids at Giza and at other sites in northern Upper Egypt.

King Ninetjer

Raneb in turn was succeeded by Ninetjer, who seems to have reigned for a considerable period. He was probably buried in a huge tomb at Saqqara which has been the subject of recent excavations.[23] Rather surprisingly, his name appears in an especially intriguing context, particularly for the secondary theme of this book, the possibility of some sort of contact between Early Dynastic Egypt and Mesopotamia. In eastern Saudi Arabia the remains, sadly depleted, of large tumulus fields near Dhahran, link that part

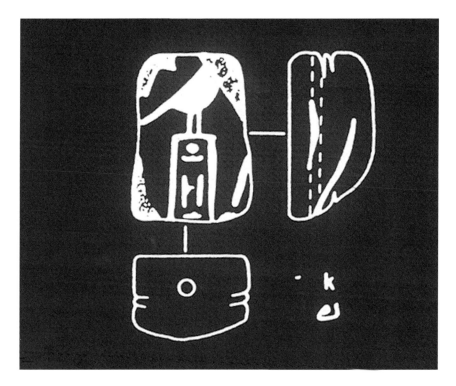

Figure 6.1 The *serekh* of King Ninetjer of the Second Dynasty (*c.*2750 BC) appears on this seal, found in a tumulus near Dhahran in Saudi Arabia. How it came to be placed in a second millennium tomb in eastern Arabia is not known. There is no evidence that it had travelled so far in the king's lifetime; rather it seems likely that it was cached in the Dhahran tomb many centuries after his death.

Sources: J. Zarins *et al.*, 'Excavations at Dhahran South: The Tumuli Field (208-2)', 1983. A Preliminary Report. *ATLAL* 8: 40 (incorrectly attributed in the text); pl. 52 k. National Museum, Riyadh cat. No. 246, B-2.

of the peninsula with the island of Bahrain, which lies in the Gulf some twenty kilometres away, to the east. The predominant culture of the Arabian Gulf, Dilmun, probably had its origins in eastern Arabia. Two quite substantial settlements have been found there, at Abqiaq and Tarut, the latter a notable production centre for finely carved and decorated chlorite vessels.[24] This part of the Arabian coast was included in the polity of Dilmun and even as late as the nineteenth century AD, cartographers included it in the general topographical description, Bahrain.[25]

The Dhahran tumuli are contemporary with and similar in construction to the much larger fields of mounds in Bahrain. In one of the Saudi mounds, designated B.2 by the excavators from the Saudi Arabian Department of Antiquities in 1983,[26] what appears to be a seal bearing the *serekh* of

145

Ninetjer was found. With it were other assorted seals from several periods, some of them much later than the date of the construction of the tumulus itself, which is the second half of the third millennium or even of the regnal dates of Ninetjer which are *c.*2865 BC.

The fact that his seal was found amongst such a collection of others, much later in date, probably precludes it having been taken to Saudi Arabia during the time of his reign or even close to it; little incidentally is known of the events of his kingship. However, B.2 seems to have been chosen, for whatever reason, to hold a cache of seals: nine stamp seals, some with South Arabian inscriptions, one with a possible Aramaic inscription and two which came from levels associated with Neo-Assyrian\New Babylonian ceramics. Several other Egyptian or Egyptianizing seals were found in the same burial mound. The excavators note that a seal with a hieroglyphic inscription was found in a hoard of silver in Bahrain but this dates from the seventh century BC.[27]

In the circumstances the discovery of Ninetjer's seal in B.2 cannot be taken to indicate contact between Egypt and eastern Arabia in the Second Dynasty. It cannot, of course, be entirely ruled out, but its presence with such a medley of seals would suggest that another explanation must be sought. Unlikely though it may seem, perhaps there was a collector of seals resident or travelling in eastern Arabia in the latter half of the first millennium BC (the *terminus post quem* being indicated by the latest of the seals) who, for whatever reason, cached his collection in B.2, but was never able to return to recover it.

Ninetjer is however, to be remembered for another reason: the oldest surviving statue of an enthroned Egyptian king is attributed to him. The execution of the sculpture is fairly crude but the pose adopted was to continue to be used throughout the whole of Egyptian history.[28] His statue predates the more celebrated ones, in a similar pose, of the last of the dynasty, King Khasekhemwy. Ninetjer was buried at Saqqara in a large, subterranean tomb, in land on which the Step Pyramid complex of King Netjerykhet was to be built in the next reign.

Egypt continued to develop her institutions and her rich culture during the reigns of the kings of the Second Dynasty; the evidence, however, is very scanty and the sequence of the kings is only known because the names of the first three appear in order on a statue of a kneeling official, of a slightly later date.[29] After the dominant and forceful sovereigns of the First Dynasty their early Second Dynasty successors seem pale figures by comparison. Indeed, it is difficult to consider those of the Second Dynasty, or at least the early members of the dynasty, as being in the same class of monarch at all. It is possible that they may have been a small local dynasty, of which there must have been many in pre-First Dynasty times, which somehow got itself acknowledged as national rulers.[30] Egypt did not decline in prosperity during the rule of the Second Dynasty. This is very clear from the building of an immense *mastaba* tomb for one of the viziers, Ruaben, at Saqqara where the early kings of the dynasty also chose to be buried, forsaking Abydos.[31]

According to some king-lists Ninetjer was succeeded by Sened, about whom virtually nothing is known. It would have been doubted that he existed at all were it not for an inscription belonging to a Fourth Dynasty priest, Sheri, who was responsible for maintaining Sened's cult at Giza, which thus had survived for at least a hundred years.[32]

As the Second Dynasty unfolded it is evident that some of the ancient influences in the Valley, dormant or repressed during the First Dynasty, began again to stir. Some sort of reaction against the Thinites seems to have occurred and this found its focus evidently in the deep-rooted honours paid by the southern people to the god Set, a southern god, associated with the desert, storm, and violence. He is portrayed as an enigmatic creature, human in body but with a strange, canine and long-muzzled head, with sharply pointed ears. There is little doubt that he is a conflation of a human form with the Egyptian hound, of the same breed as the dog-gods of Egypt, including Anubis and Wepwawet.

Set seems to have been the god of the people of the south, whereas Horus is an aristocratic figure, associated with the princes of This. It might have been expected that the Thinites would have attempted to reconcile the divinity of their house with that of the people on whom their power would ultimately come to rest; there is in fact clear evidence that the early kings reverenced both Horus and Set particularly in the titles of the queens. Nonetheless, the early dynastic conflicts were mythologized as a conflict between Horus and Set, when the two antagonists were locked in a titanic struggle for rule over Egypt after the alleged murder by Set of his brother Osiris, who was, if only in mythological terms, the primeval king.

King Sekhemib-Peribsen

Gradually, the evidence suggests that the supporters of Set gained the ascendancy and, in the latter part of the Second Dynasty King Sekhemib suddenly changed his name to Peribsen, and instead of his name in its monumental *serekh* being surmounted by the victorious falcon he displayed his new name surmounted by the animal of Set, the noble hound whose swiftness was legendary. Clearly, under Peribsen, Set became paramount to the extent that the king felt able to discard the loyalties to Horus for what was perhaps the even older allegiance to Set. In his inscriptions Peribsen declared 'The Ombite (Set was Lord of Ombos) has given the Two Lands to his son Peribsen'.

But the later stages of the Second Dynasty, no matter what were the political realities in the Valley, marked another high point in Egyptian creativity. Large-scale, formal sculpture, often executed in the hardest stones, is one of the glories of Egyptian art and amongst the most splendid legacies to

Figure 6.2 King Sekhemib-Peribsen of the Second Dynasty was unique amongst the kings of Egypt in proclaiming his allegiance to the god Set rather than Horus, and surmounted his *serekh* with the hound associated with Set. His commitment to the god is further confirmed by the presence on the seal of the god Ash, in the form of a canine-headed human.

Source: reproduced from W.M.F. Petrie, *Royal Tombs of the Earliest Dynasties Part II*, pl. XXII no. 179, by courtesy of the Egypt Exploration Society.

be passed by the ancient to the modern world. Here it is possible to detect something like a beginning and then a triumphant progress to the great works of the early Old Kingdom.

The transition between the reigns of Sekhemib-Peribsen and his successor, Khasekhem-Khasekhemwy may have come about as the result of an uprising of the Set peoples against the followers of Horus in the latter years of the Second Dynasty. Sekhemib, coming from the deep south, proclaimed himself Set-King, a title which he alone assumed in the entire sequence of the kings of Egypt; it is possible that he ruled only in the south.[33] To mark his adherence to Set, the ancient patron of his people, he took the name Peribsen, along with his new (or perhaps very ancient) title. So, just as each Horus King was the god incarnate, so he was Set, the personification of the very ancient god of the south.

The Horus and Set Khasekhemwy

Though Peribsen may have been a usurper in the view of the prevailing Horus faction, he may equally have been the scion of a still older line from which the chiefs of Upper Egypt, in times before the kings, descended; at any rate he placed himself in opposition to the Horus Khasekhem who, early

148

in his reign, had gone south to put down a rebellion of the Nubian tribes. This rebellion defeated, Khasekhem returned to the frontiers of Egypt to find Set, in the person of Peribsen, in possession of what he, the Horus, saw as his patrimony. A series of fierce engagements took place, up and down the Valley; the outcome was victory for Khasekhem and defeat for the Set-King. Khasekhem, it is then suggested, assumed a modified throne-name, 'the Horus Khasekhemwy'. This meant 'In him the Two Powers are reconciled', a significant and majestic assertion indeed, in all the circumstances.

This concept of what might have happened in such immensely distant an epoch is merely an attractive thesis, but it provides a plausible reconstruction of events as they may have happened in the Valley so long ago. This version of the conflict of Horus and Set, on which it is based, presented in terms of the rightful (or accepted) claimant (Horus) returning from an excursion beyond the frontiers to find his kingdom usurped (by Set), depends on a long hieroglyphic text inscribed on the walls of the great Horus temple at Edfu,[34] one of the most important religious centres in Old Kingdom Egypt. The version which survives is only derived from Ptolemaic times; it is possible, however, that it preserves much older material.

The text purports to be an *historical* record of the rebellion of Set against Horus and is represented as being declaimed by Imhotep, the chief minister of King Netjerykhet, and the most powerful magus in Egyptian popular legend. He is depicted standing before a nameless king, probably Netjerykhet himself, and recounting the story of the rebellion. Netjerykhet reigned in the early Third Dynasty; he may have been directly descended from Khasekhemwy. The notional Set rebellion would have taken place in the closing period of the Second Dynasty. It is indeed a speculative interpretation but one which has much appeal in explaining what was clearly a crucial and profoundly memorable experience for Egypt in Early Dynastic times.

Whatever else it may do the story of the conflict of Horus and Set confirms the essentially political character of the two protagonists. Peribsen became Set, Khasekhem-Khasekhemwy was Horus and the long saga began. However, it is not without point that Khasekhemwy, the victorious incarnate god, saw his role as conciliator as the most important of his qualities. Like the founder of the dynasty he believed himself to be the reconciler of the opposing factions in the state.

Some of the earliest attempts at royal portraiture in the round, following the single example of Ninetjer come from the end of the Second Dynasty: two statues, one in limestone, the other in schist of King Khasekhem-Khasekhemwy. For works made very nearly five thousand years ago, the statues are remarkable. One, in Cairo,[35] has been oddly bisected: however, its quality is evident. In particular, the carving of the king's cloak, as it stands away from his throat, is masterly. The other, in the Ashmolean Museum,[36] Oxford, is one of the supreme masterpieces of Egyptian art. It shows the

(a)

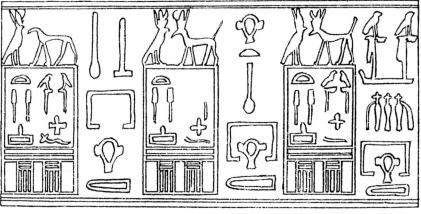

(b)

Figure 6.3 King Khasekhem-Khasekhemwy, (a) the last king of the Second Dynasty, incorporated the symbolic animals of both the god Horus and the god Set on his *serekh* (b), thus ensuring his long-lasting reputation as the reconciler of the opposing factions within the Egyptian state in the formative years of the earliest dynasties.

Sources: (a) As King Khasekhem, reproduced by permission of the Ashmolean Museum, Oxford; (b) Reproduced from W.M.F. Petrie, *Royal Tombs of the Earliest Dynasties Part II* pl. XXIII.197, by courtesy of the Egypt Exploration Society.

Figure 6.4 King Khasekhemwy presided over a period of rapid material advance and achievement in Egypt. This scene, of the king taking part in the ceremony of 'Stretching
the Cord' at the founding of a temple, was part of the door-jamb of his palace at
Hierakonpolis.

Source: photograph John G. Ross.

king seated on his throne, wrapped in his cloak and wearing the White
Crown of the south; beneath his feet the enemies of Egypt are trampled. The
king is tranquil, his eyes placid; already he has assumed his full divinity
and sits enthroned above all creation. The technique of carving is assured
and highly skilled; the sculptor works the stone with absolute mastery and
without any hint of uncertainty.

According to Manetho, the king who corresponds to Khasekhem\
Khasekhemwy in his history was a giant, standing, if it is to be believed,
some eight feet tall. He is said to have ruled Egypt for forty-eight years and
to have been a great military leader; but it is Khasekhemwy's genius as conciliator that is graphically demonstrated, in yet another evidence of the early
Egyptians' genius for synthesizing a whole spectrum of experience in one
brilliant design motif, by the presentation of his royal name, in the *serekh*
enclosure, surmounted by the figures of the two gods, Set standing at peace
with Horus. It is one of the most perceptive pieces of political propaganda
graphics in all history; it is also quite unique in all the long history of the
Egyptian royal formulary.

The tomb of Khasehkemwy at Abydos is an immense, trapezoidal
structure, identified and published more than a century ago.[37] It has been

re-excavated by the German Archaeological Expedition,[38] whose findings have added considerably to the understanding of the importance of this most significant early king of Egypt. One result of these excavations has been the identification of a large number of seal impressions which bear the name of Netjerykhet, of the succeeding Third Dynasty. It appears that Netjerykhet officiated at Khasehkemwy's funeral, the duty of an heir, ideally of a son. From this it has been deduced that Netjerykhet must have followed Khasekhemwy to the throne and that there was no familial break between the two dynasties. Netjerykhet may have been the older king's step-son or his grandson, by Netjerykhet's mother, Nebmaathep. This lady was Khasekhemwy's daughter and may also have been his wife.

Near the tomb of Khasekhemwy American archaeologists have found an extraordinary flotilla of stone ships buried in the desert.[39] The flotilla is still under excavation and it is likely that they will be found to have come from the First Dynasty, their location close to Khasekhemwy's tomb accidental.

A very large enclosure, visible from the air at Saqqara, close to the Step Pyramid's enclosing walls, has long puzzled archaeologists. Known as Gisr el-Mudir it has recently been the subject of remote sensing techniques employed by the National Museum of Scotland's Saqqara survey.[40] Gisr el-Mudir is huge, almost twice the size of Netjerykhet's enclosure, the walls of which run for about a mile and a half. It is not known yet who was responsible for its construction but it has been speculated that it might well be Khasekhemwy.

7

THE THIRD DYNASTY

Innovation

It is difficult to exaggerate the achievements of the Early Dynastic kings of Egypt and their ministers. They were true innovators, creating new forms, processes, techniques, and concepts in virtually every department of life. The extent of what they achieved is not only itself astonishing; apart from the degree of originality required to conceive and set into practice an entire concept of the management of human society, it is bewildering to consider the degree of organization which must have gone into the planning and management of the projects which they achieved. Later on, in the time of the great pyramid builders now approaching, huge projects of design, construction and decoration became almost commonplace. But even in the earliest times the control of the royal enterprises must have been exceptionally complex and, like virtually everything else in Egypt, without obvious precedent, as much as in their use of materials and in the forms which they created.

The reigns of the kings of the Early Dynastic period introduce an entirely new dimension into human experience through the deployment of exceptional creative talent, the management of great and complex resources and an abundance of materials expended on the invention of more and more elaborate funerary monuments. This process culminated in the lifetime of King Netjerykhet (long known by the name Djoser, though it only appears in texts dating from hundreds of years after the king's lifetime) for whom the Step Pyramid complex, that non-pareil of all ancient architecture, was raised at Saqqara.

Without the achievements of this probable first king of the Third Dynasty and the genius of his minister, Imhotep, the triumphs of the kings of the middle centuries of the third millennium in Egypt which are forever commemorated by the towering monuments built on the low sandstone plateau at Giza, would have been impossible. The key to the advances of the Pyramid Age lies in the keeping of the preceding dynasty, the technological strides which were then accomplished bearing comparison only with those of the present day.

The third millennium might better be called the Age of Extravagant and

Complex Funerary Monuments, not a term which rolls lightly off the tongue perhaps, but one which is certainly more pertinent to the character of the time than is a simple identification with metal. If the culmination of this curious obsession with great tombs appears to be represented by the pyramids, they are in fact only one form of monument designed to provide an eternal living place for the great dead.

For reasons which are still very largely obscure peoples with no apparent contact with each other, separated by enormous distances and with totally unrelated cultural traditions began early in the third millennium to build more and more complex structures in which to house the remains of their chiefs and kings and, increasingly, a substantial part of the community's movable wealth. Often these monuments were enclosed in mounds, or were themselves mound-like in structure, though built of stone. In the history of human obsessions the practice represents a curious chapter. From the Orkney islands in the most remote north-west, across Europe, around the Mediterranean through Egypt and Mesopotamia, down the coastlands and islands of the Arabian Gulf, in Oman and away into the Indian subcontinent and beyond, even to China, elaborate tombs of this type were constructed at this time. In the Arabian Gulf, for example, an extraordinary concentration of mound burials is to be found on the principal Bahrain island where it is estimated that some two hundred thousand tumuli were to be seen thirty years ago, the vast majority dating from the late third to the early second millennia.[1] Examples of similar mound fields can be found in eastern Arabia: Oman has its own, even earlier type of mound, constructed often from finely made ashlar blocks of brilliant white limestone.[2] This phenomenon of recurring forms of funerary monument over so widespread a geographical and chronological range is another confirmation of the belief, enunciated particularly by C.G. Jung, that the archetypes repeat themselves in the productions of all peoples, at all times.

THE ACCESSION OF NETJERYKHET

It was not until the beginning of the Third Dynasty, around 2680 BC, that the titanic complex that was intended to preserve for all eternity the body of the first king of the dynasty, the Golden Horus Nejterykhet, was suddenly to appear on the Saqqara escarpment, built entirely of stone, on a scale never before contemplated on the face of the earth. The accession of Netjerykhet to the thrones of Egypt was an event of profound importance; he was the first king to assume that most splendid of all royal titles, 'The Golden Horus'. The Third Dynasty seems to have been connected linearly with the Second; it is generally thought that the great Khasekhemwy left as heiress to his state a daughter or granddaughter. She was the mother of Netjerykhet and was venerated in later times as the ancestress of the Third Dynasty.

For a number of reasons the accession of Netjerykhet marked a new turn in the destiny of Egypt. First, it inaugurated a long sequence of prosperity and tranquillity. Though the reign of Khasekhemwy was recorded as a time of reconciliation and unity it was only in Netjerykhet's time that the resources of the state could be so organized to permit the undertaking of public works of such positively titanic proportions. These great enterprises allowed for the employment of workers and craftsmen on an immense scale. With them came an increasing liberation of the Egyptian creative genius, permitting the thresholds of the arts to be pushed further and further out from their original planes in the centuries which were to follow. Architecture on a monumental scale became a preoccupation of the state which was to endure to the present day; it had its beginnings in Netjerykhet's time.

For the first time, too, individuals other than the kings begin to be identifiable. Imhotep is unquestionably the most notable, the supreme genius of the Egyptian creative experience, but others, though lesser men begin to emerge in all departments of life and activity, to take on clear and often engaging shapes and even make known their names.

Thus as our field of vision of Egypt opens out at this time, around the twenty-seventh century BC, we come to see more clearly the role played by ordinary men and women in the state. The Third Dynasty itself was a relatively brief interlude, seventy years or so in duration; the amazing burst of creative energy which marked Netjerykhet's reign and the genius of Imhotep could hardly be expected to be long sustained at the same level of productivity. However, the arts of sculpture and the making of large-scale statuary developed steadily; technique also advanced, in some cases very remarkably. For example, the manufacture of plywood is first detected in the Third Dynasty, and the means of the cutting of large stone blocks for architectural projects became better understood, leading the way to the building feats of the Fourth Dynasty. The arts of the metal smith and the jeweller also become more and more specialized and refined.

The central and most important feature of the complex of monumental buildings on the escarpment at Saqqara, not far from the mastaba tombs of the great nobles of the First Dynasty, was the ziggurat-like stepped pyramid, six platforms placed one upon the other, making a stairway to the heavens. Beneath this monument the mummy of the king was buried in a deep pink-granite chamber, sunk into the rock. The rooms which abut the actual burial chamber are decorated with tiles of an exquisite blue faience, some showing the king, attended by the canine god Wepwawet, in the celebration of the rituals which by this time hedged the divine sovereign about, determining his every action as much in death as in life. The tiles, in a material whose colour and finish was always to be one of the glories of Egyptian art, show the king as a young and vigorous man running in a ritual race as part of the great cycle of ceremonies associated with the

Heb-Sed festival which itself recalled the events of his coronation; others reproduce, in exquisite detail, the hangings of the palace walls in which he passed his earthly existence.

The Netjerykhet complex is unique. It is effectively without precedent, not merely in Egypt but in the entire world. For centuries its high white limestone curtain walls and the elegant, superbly proportioned kiosks, magazines, and shrines which were built within the walls made it the most remarkable building in the world; perhaps indeed it remains the most remarkable ever built. This mighty structure is constructed with an assurance and a mastery that is breathtaking.

The supreme achievement of the Third Dynasty of Egyptian kings was to preside over the transition from mud-brick architecture to large-scale building in stone. The site at Saqqara has been very extensively restored by the dedicated work of French archaeologists, over the past seventy years.[3] But even the knowledge that most of what is to be seen today, other than the compelling stepped tower of the pyramid itself, is the product of such restoration cannot diminish the grandeur of the concept or the brilliance of its execution.

IMHOTEP

It is not to be wondered at that for thousands of years afterwards the pyramid of Netjerykhet was a place of awe-struck pilgrimage, not only to celebrate the memory of the king for whom it was built but to recall the man who built it, the first universal genius known to history. Imhotep, 'the greatest of magicians' as he was hailed, designed and built Saqqara, not to his own glory but to that of his divine master. But in later centuries Imhotep, too, was worshipped at Saqqara as a benign and kindly divinity, a healer and the god who granted the prayers of the most humble petitioners. Just as the stepped pyramid and its subsidiary buildings together make up the most remarkable single structure constructed up to this point, so the man who designed it must rank amongst the very first of those who by their genius transformed mankind, if what is attributed to him is even partially true. It is entirely possible that no more remarkable creative talent ever lived.

Of the ancestry of Imhotep little is known for certain. By the high titles that he bore, it might be presumed that he was a close connection of the king, possibly even by birth, (it has been speculated that he might have been Netjerykhet's son) whilst some have thought him to have been a commoner who, with the court's recognition of his exceptional genius, rose quickly in the royal service. This was indeed a process frequently encountered in the biographies of successful men in the Third Dynasty, although there is evidence that the old hereditary nobles kept some of their power and influence. Increasingly the administration of the kingdoms was placed in the hands of 'new men', competent and forceful individuals, practical men who served the king well. A later tradition asserted that Imhotep came from Upper Egypt and that his father was Ka-Nefer, the Director of Works,[4] so there may have been a family tradition to account for Imhotep's architectural genius.

Imhotep was the chief minister, advisor, companion, physician, sculptor to the king, a High Priest and a hereditary noble. The recital of his titles and offices is impressive: 'Chancellor of the King of Lower Egypt, First after the King of Upper Egypt, Administrator of the Great Palace, Hereditary Nobleman, High Priest of Heliopolis, Builder, Sculptor and Vase-maker in Chief'.[5] He was the bearer of the king's seal and 'seal-bearer', it will be recalled, signified 'noble'; he is credited with the building of the first temple at Edfu, the repository of much of the early history, or perhaps more accurately, of the legends of origins of the Egyptian people. His most important office was that of High Priest of Heliopolis, which was the ancient centre of Egypt's solar cults. It is possible that Imhotep was responsible for the rise of the cults which celebrated the divinity of the sun which become increasingly apparent during Netjerykhet's reign and in the reigns of his successors, to become dominant in the Fourth Dynasty.

THE CREATIVE SURGE OF THE THIRD DYNASTY

Though Khasekhemwy's legend carries with him a sense of the power of a conciliating and benign monarch and the healing of divisions in the state, Netjerykhet is the archetypal divine King of Egypt. With his reign the centuries of Egypt's splendour began.

There is a notable élan about much of the work of the Third Dynasty which suggests a vigour and a delight in the processes of creation on the part of the artists and craftsmen working at the time. It has been suggested that this characteristic of vigour is 'barbaric', but this is to mistake its character and to ignore the increasing sophistication and cumulative experience of the first two dynasties, a period which in total represented some five hundred years. There is rather a lightness, an elegance of spirit, demonstrated by many of the details of the great complex which Imhotep built to enshrine his divine patron. Even allowing for the extensive reconstruction which has been carried out at Saqqara over the past half century, the quality of the original work can be seen in the carving of small details, in the extremely hard, brilliant white limestone which was employed for some parts of the complex.

From a few tantalizing fragments in the Saqqara complex we know that sculpture in particular advanced rapidly in Netjerykhet's time. Life-size and larger statues flowed from the sculptors' workshops, anticipating the great works of the Fourth Dynasty to come. Statues of private people, including those employed in the intimate service of the king, began to be made. The name and titles of Imhotep himself come from such a discovery. Emery, who worked in Saqqara for many years, would have it that his tomb is nearby, waiting discovery; it is probably as unlikely, alas, as the discovery of Alexander's tomb in Alexandria.[6]

THE STEP PYRAMID

Commissioned by the king to design his burial place Imhotep began, simply enough, by building a substantial version of the *mastaba*-type tomb in which most of Netjerykhet's predecessors had been interred. The *mastaba* was to be a large one and it was to be built in limestone blocks, itself an important innovation. Approximately ten thousand tons of stone needed to be quarried for the *mastaba*, in itself a great quantity. It was, however, to be as nothing when compared with the final extent of the material required for the king's

Figure 7.1 The majestic profile of the Step Pyramid at Saqqara, seen here beyond vegetation which is no longer to be found in its vicinity, was the supreme achievement of the Third Dynasty, though it is possible that another pyramid, even larger than Netjerykhet's was planned. From this brick mountain descended the pyramids of the later kings. That it is a quintessentially Egyptian form and concept is apparent from the stepped mounds which were concealed in the First Dynasty mastabas, centuries before the building of this monument to King Netjerykhet.

Source: photograph John G. Ross.

158

monument. At some point, as this first structure was completed, daring inspiration seems to have seized Imhotep; of course, it could have seized Netjerykhet, but there is no evidence on the point. As a result the resources of Egypt were harnessed to undertake a project the like of which had never before been attempted anywhere.

Though it is difficult to resist drawing a parallel between them because of the Step Pyramid's exterior form, the temptation to link the Sumerian ziggurat directly with the Egyptian pyramid, which bears a superficial resemblance to the Mesopotamian terraced sacred mountain, must be put aside. The origins of the pyramid have been convincingly traced back through the rectangular brick *mastaba* to a sand-piled tumulus mound. The ziggurat emerged as a consequence of a combination of factors, the need to raise sacred buildings above the level of the flood plain, the necessity to repair and rebuild mud-brick structures with frequency, and the predisposition of the Sumerians to regard certain areas as irrevocably sacred, requiring new temples or shrines to be rebuilt directly on the site of their predecessors.

However, a different set of concepts may have underlain Egypt's characteristic monuments. It has been proposed that the inspiration for the terraced structure built to provide eternity for Netjerykhet was a natural phenomenon produced by the differing temperatures of the atmospheric layers over Saqqara which had the effect of making the sun's disc appear as a stepped pyramidal structure. It may be imagined what an impression this would have made on people of the time, given the Egyptians' always powerful response to symbol.[7] A solar stepped pyramid would have been a symbol of immense import to them and not least to Imhotep, with his special relationship to the worship of the sun's disc.

The more familiar, triangular form of the pyramid, which was to be established in the Fourth Dynasty, may well have also been the result of a solar inspiration. This may be confirmed by anyone who has observed what an Egyptian architect with heightened awareness must have seen, towards the time of sunset in the area to the north of Heliopolis, particularly in the winter months, when the rays of the sun break through low cloud and form a perfectly triangular shaft of light over the flat and largely featureless countryside. It is a remarkable sight and one which might well be calculated to inspire an artist contemplating a fitting monument for kings who were beginning to be identified with the sun; few natural events look quite so like the direct and evident intervention of a divinity.

Nonetheless, the fact that this first of all pyramids is stepped or terraced and, moreover, built of rectangular stone blocks reminiscent of the mud bricks of the *mastabas* from which originally it evolved is, in the context of possible Sumerian–Egyptian connections, a coincidence that cannot wholly be disregarded though the stone blocks are much larger than the mud bricks. A further argument against any direct attribution of Sumerian influences in the construction of the Stepped Pyramid must be that no true ziggurats survive from Mesopotamia earlier than those built in the second half of the third millennium, later than Netjerykhet's pyramid by several hundred years. But the real origins of ziggurat building, though not its final form, can probably be traced back to the White Temple at Uruk in the thirty-fourth century BC, which was raised on a series of platforms and, unlike most Sumerian buildings, was built on a limestone base as its foundation.

PYRAMID AND ZIGGURAT

The explanation for such similarities that there are between pyramid and ziggurat may be that they both originated in the same archetype, common to peoples in the Near East five thousand years ago, at an earlier stage of social development. There are many such symbols: the familiar triangular pyramids are clearly a more particularly Egyptian form though even these were to be repeated coincidentally in other cultures, distant in time and clime. Perhaps at the beginning of the third millennium men felt they had, for whatever reasons, to build imitation mountains and to give them a markedly terraced appearance. In Mesopotamia the idea prevailed; in Egypt it did not and the familiar colossal stone triangles evolved.

To the Egyptians, with their belief in the divine order represented by the king, it was a witness to the unique bond which existed between their land and the heavens. Indeed, mysterious and gleaming, it must have seemed like part of the immortal mansions brought down to earth. So the complex seemed to tourists who visited it during the New Kingdom, more than a thousand years after it had been built. The buildings were still then, it seems, intact; visitors left admiring graffiti on the walls which can still be seen, recalling perhaps some second millennium Memphite family's outing to this numinous place.

From time to time, during the early centuries of its existence when it was still a living temple, the sound of chanting and of music, essential components of all rituals in Egypt, would have been heard across the silent spaces between its lonely eminence and the city of Memphis which lay below it. The sounds must have seemed like the echoes of the stars singing as the priests went about their business of perpetuating the life of Egypt through the ceremonies of giving life to Netjerykhet. Its mystery would have been compounded by the fact that all but the king, his courtiers, and the priests would be excluded from the temple precincts.

The achievement represented by the Step Pyramid complex is far greater than that for which the later pyramids, of Khufu, Khafre, and Menkaure stand. They are remarkable, certainly, but they show a clear line of descent from other monuments, including this first pyramid of all at Saqqara. Neither Khufu's pyramid nor those of his successors are *sui generis*; that of

Netjerykhet undoubtedly is. Every element in it is original; it is a compendium of architectural invention. It is also remarkable for what it reveals about the development of large-scale sculpture, a technique which began with the statue of Ninetjer and Khasekhem-Khasekhemwy. Netjerykhet's complex contained evidence of large statues of the king and, no doubt, of the gods. Most of these are lost but one unfinished limestone figure of the king and parts of others survive.

There is however one point of contact between pyramid and ziggurat. Both were obviously forms of the 'sacred mountain', an archetype of the highest antiquity, representing the place on which divinities were accustomed to manifest themselves. It is notable that neither Egypt nor Sumer are really well supplied with anything that could be dignified with the term 'mountain', other than Egypt's Red Sea mountains and the Zagros range to the east of Sumer. It may well be that the reverence with which both peoples regarded the idea of the mountain represents the recollection of a land which had a special significance – it has been suggested that it was their original mutual home – which was itself mountainous; again, the question must remain entirely speculative at this stage. It is interesting nonetheless that the hieroglyph for 'foreign country' is a sign showing mountain peaks.[8]

It is probably unrewarding to seek for other explanations of one of the most perfectly satisfying shapes in relation to its environment that architecture, sacred or profane, has ever evolved. The Greeks, who had a faculty when dealing with the works of foreigners of reacting either with superstitious awe or with startling banality, called the pyramids (in Egyptian, *mer*) 'little cakes', *pyramidoi*, a description of quite overwhelming inappositeness but one which has given them their name today.

CONSTRUCTION

What Imhotep proposed was that the king should occupy for ever a central place in a great rectangular shrine, built of blocks of limestone finely, even exquisitely, worked, which would simulate the land of Egypt. Its centre was to be a great tower (the result of several developments itself) which would rear up, in six stages, each stage stepped up from the one below it, a veritable stairway to the region of the Imperishable Stars, beyond which the king would reign for all eternity. A stellar orientation for buildings, rather than a solar one, is a characteristic of the Third Dynasty and represents the culmination of what may have been one of the most important aspects of aboriginal Egyptian cults, soon to be subsumed into the worship of the sun.

The dimensions and quantities of what Imhotep eventually created for Netjerykhet are immense. The wall which surrounded the stepped pyramid complex measured 536 metres in length by 272 metres in breadth: it is 10.5 metres high, built of fine limestone, one million tons of which were quarried, dressed and laid in courses of spectacular precision.[9] Surrounding the wall was an enormous trench, the purpose of which is unclear. At first Imhotep planned to build a pyramid raised to four steps; then he took the final decision to raise the steps to six. This decision increased the volume of stone from 200,000 tons to 850,000 tons.[10] It should be remembered at this point that we are in Egypt around the year 2650 BC.

Of fine white limestone, brilliantly polished, to cover the outer courses, 70,000 square metres were required. These had to be cut, trimmed exactly, polished, and fitted into place over the monument's entire surface. Within the courtyard Imhotep built dummy buildings, granaries, and store houses, not unlike those on the model estate built during King Aha's reign not far from the Step Pyramid, but infinitely finer in conception and execution and immeasurably greater in scale.

Netjerykhet is thought to have reigned for nineteen years, though this seems little enough time for so much to have been achieved. Assuming that Imhotep began work on the mastaba which was to become a pyramid on the first day of the king's reign, he would have needed to excavate, dress, transport, decorate and place in position one hundred and twenty tons of limestone *every* day for the remainder of the king's lifetime.

Around the colossal central mountain of stone blocks, beneath which the king's body and those of his closest family would lie forever the land of Egypt, north and south, would be laid out, that the king might review it when he chose and, at the same time confer the ineffable benevolence of his presence over the lands for ever. Granaries, storerooms, temples, palaces for 'the Great Ones', stations for the enactment of the sacred dramas were all laid out – and all built in the same glorious, exquisitely worked stone which, in the brilliant sunlight of Egypt, now takes on a wonderful golden hue.

Imhotep, with the confidence of genius, created this unique building in one lifetime on the rocky escarpment which overlooks the ancient capital of Memphis. His confidence was not overreaching. Throughout the complex, one of the largest as well as one of the earliest consciously designed major projects in history, Imhotep was inspired by natural forms: the tall-standing papyrus, the lotus closed or open, the palm trunk. These he modelled in stone with a divine plasticity; nonetheless he was working with materials the properties of which must largely have been unknown to him. What stresses might a stone lintel bear? How to convey the sense of half opened timber door, or a roller blind, pulled down against the sun, in stone.

Imhotep solved virtually all the problems he set himself, brilliantly. Only in one place did his assurance, perhaps, falter. At the single entrance to the whole complex the visitor, even today, passes through a peaceful colonnade, a small hypostyle hall. Imhotep here wished to use columns to support the roof and sought to simulate the bundles of reeds which served the purpose of strengthening walls and doorways in reed or wattle buildings. He built his columns of elegant rose brick, facing them with finely carved skins of lime-stone, imitating reeds. But then – who knew what weight the columns might support? If Imhotep was in touch with colleagues in Mesopotamia he may well have received discouraging reports of the effectiveness of columns in, for example, temple structures which showed a disappointing tendency to fall down, slumping inelegantly into rubble heaps, to the peril of both the users of the buildings and the architects' reputation. Did Imhotep know, perhaps, of the fickleness of columns?

In any event Imhotep supplied his own solution. The columns stand in Netjerykhet's hall to this day, five thousand years later and with some assis-tance from archaeology. They were originally engaged columns, bonded to the walls on either side of the entrance area by solid blocks of limestone: they still endure, if a little apprehensively, clinging to the supporting walls. It is this element of dilemma, even more than the sublimity of the design and the construction of the complex as a whole, which demonstrates both the humanity and the genius of Imhotep.

How did he find craftsmen capable of working the stone, train them, devise tools for them, work out the complexities of the spatial divisions, design all the details (or at least, supervise their design) and be on site every day to see that the huge number of men engaged on the project was properly deployed? The site itself at Saqqara presents one of the anomalies which seem always to attend any consideration of the techniques which went into the construction of the pyramids. The subterranean rock from which the gal-leries were cut linking the various parts of the underground chambers of the tomb itself is so hard that modern investigation of parts of the area has had to be effected by the use of explosives,[11] yet the Egyptians in the first half of the third millennium achieved their excavation, presumably without such assistance. We may ask such questions but we cannot supply the answers.

The boundary wall and South Court

The boundary wall enclosing the complex is itself a remarkable and sophisticated construction. It recalls the great mud-brick walls which enclosed the funerary palaces of the First Dynasty at Abydos except that it consists of exquisitely finished limestone. It has only one real entrance, located in the same place as the entrances to the funerary palace courts Abydos. In addition there are fourteen other dummy gateways. There are one hundred and ninety-six simple bastions decorating the walls; between each bastion are two recessed panels, and two recesses on each side of the bastions. In the courtyard contained by this extravagant surround, as well as all the cultic and ritual buildings, a wild bull's head was found buried in a limestone-lined cist beneath an altar in the South Court.[12] This perhaps pro-vided an echo of the many bulls slaughtered in the First Dynasty so that their horns could decorate the exterior of a Great One's *mastaba,* as happened

Figure 7.2 The long-enduring importance of bulls and the bull cult in Early Dynastic
Egypt was demonstrated by the discovery of a stone-lined chamber under the altar
built in the South Court of the complex, in which a single aurochs skull had been
laid.

Source: from Firth, Quibell and Lauer, *Excavations at Saqqara: The Step Pyramid* (Cairo 1935), pl. 73.

at Queen Herneith's tomb and at that of the Chancellor Nebetka. The presence of the skull of a primigenius bull, like the vastly more ancient burials
at Tushka, demonstrates the immense power that must have been attributed
to the bucranium, which indeed was an ancient talisman for thousands of
years before Netjerykhet's time, that it should lie in the heart of so great a
complex, dedicated to the eternity of a once-living god.

The serdab statue

Within its immense encircling walls the Step Pyramid complex miracu-
lously held one supreme masterpiece surviving, against all the odds, the
depredations of nearly fifty centuries. This is the seated life-size statue of the
King, old and robed for his jubilee, which was found in its little *serdab* or
enclosed chapel set before the northern face of the pyramid and to the east of

the entrance to Netjerykhet's mortuary temple. There Netjerykhet was left to sit, his eyes aligned with a narrow vantage point through which he could observe, for all the eternity he had no doubt confidently expected, the service of perpetual rituals designed to give him life forever and, with that life, prosperity for Egypt.

The serdab statue is one of the world's great masterpieces, a work for all time; in it indeed lies Netjerykhet's immortality. It is carved from a block of limestone: the king sits heavily, for he is old, his head massive under the weight of a great wig and its cover. His cloak is wrapped round him; one arm lies awkwardly across his thighs, the other at his side. His feet are enormous.

Netjerykhet's face, despite the damage which was done to it when his rock crystal eyes were gouged out, is arresting. It corresponds well with the young king shown on the faience tiles but with one notable difference: the young king has an almost Semitic cast of feature, as though somewhere in his ancestry what might in later centuries be called a Bedu strain from the desert people had entered his blood. But with the old king his ancestry is suggested as something more southern; indeed, Netjerykhet's features in old age are distinctly African.

His statue is the most perfect expression of the majesty of an Egyptian god-king to survive. His power is not merely absolute: he is power itself. The nobility of his countenance is supported by the dignity of his body, old though he is. He needs to make no further statement; he can only be approached with awe. Even when viewed from behind, the power that Netjerykhet exudes is still formidable. The great head is like a mountain top; the wig cover making it seem still more immense, adds to the dimension of might and splendour which inhabits.

Not only is the survival of the *serdab* statue miraculous (it was discovered only in the thirties of the last century)[13] and the statue itself a supreme work of art, it is the ancestor of all royal portraits, the archetype of the king enthroned in majesty. It deserves to be recognized as one of the wonders of the world.

THE PRIMEVAL MOUND

The *mastabas* of the early dynasties had within them a development of the primeval mound, the place of original creation in *Zep Tepi*, the First Time, an embryonic stepped structure, concealed inside the internal fabric of the building. It was almost inevitable, therefore, that later generations should express their creative spirit in a shape of pure force, colossal but surging upwards, resting with absolute confidence on the earth, immovable but expressing that reaching out for the firmament – and beyond it, to the realm of the Imperishable Stars – which is so typical of the spirit of early Egypt.

It would have been more extraordinary, perhaps, if the Egyptians had not produced so perfect a shape as the pyramid, at this particular point in their development. That they did so sets the final seal on their achievement; after that expression of creative energy it was only to be expected that decline would inevitably follow. It was not a performance that could ever be repeated, nor one that could even be sustained; indeed, it may be argued that it could not be matched.

The pyramid, the supreme artefact of the age which was now approaching, represented in stone the summation of all that early Egypt was seeking to express. In every aspect of life, particularly those which touched the king in any way, the early builders of the Egyptian state were attempting to reconcile the cosmic with the human, to identify their society with concepts which otherwise defied articulation.

The Egyptians possessed an exceptional ability to synthesize complex propositions and penetrating perceptions in symbol and in expressions of the form and content of buildings. Often such synthesis was occluded. An example, which is pertinent to the origins of the Step Pyramid, is the terraced mound, whose origin lies in the little pile of sand raised above a Badarian grave. The mound signifies the Primeval Hill, the mound of creation on which the creator god settled himself when it first appeared above or out of the waters of the Abyss, on which he performed the first acts which inaugurated the cycle of creation itself.

The most spectacular manifestations of the terraced mound are the Step Pyramid and its companions in other parts of the Valley. The terraced mound would have had a powerful mystical appeal both to Imhotep and to his master. By means of it, Netjerykhet is able to mount to the stars; also it permits the king to fulfil the role of the creator god on *his* mound, in the perpetual renewal of the life of Egypt, which the whole complex at Saqqara encompasses.

The terraced mound evidently meant something of profound importance to the powers of the Third Dynasty and, so far as we can judge, particularly to them. Their successors of the Fourth Dynasty began at once to break away from the stepped form in the experimental structures which King Sneferu developed at Dahshur and Maidum, which achieved their consummation in the pyramids which his successors raised on the plateau at Giza.

There is a still more numinous form of the terraced mound, from much earlier times which is, in a quite literal sense, even more occult. Hidden in the core of the brick-enclosed rubble superstructures of several of the large First Dynasty mastabas at Saqqara is buried, as though waiting for its ultimate liberation or rebirth in the soaring terraces of the Third Dynasty pyramids. The terraced mound is to be found in all periods of Egyptian history, even in the latest, most decadent days. It is one of the most enduring and persistent images developed by the genius of the Egyptian creative spirit.

Some might see elements in the Netjerykhet complex as the last flowering of the 'Mesopotamian connection' in Egypt. The great wall, running for a total length of over one and a half miles, is recessed in a way reminiscent of the recessing of *mastaba* tombs which are in turn derived from Mesopotamian precedents. This similarity with the exterior of a *mastaba* is in line with the monument's rich and complex symbols, and it probably deliberately recalls the earlier structure.

THE 'NEW MEN'

The Third Dynasty is notable for the appearance of 'new men', powerful figures who owed their position less to the status of their birth than to the favour of the king. Imhotep himself may have been one of these; another was Khabausoker, the owner of a handsome mastaba at Saqqara[14] in which he is commemorated with his wife. He is a slightly mysterious figure and was associated with the cult of Anubis; he wears a ceremonial collar which depicts stylized hounds. His association with Anubis led to the fanciful suggestion that he was a sort of 'death priest', who announced to the king the extent of his reign, after which he would be sacrificed.[15] This was at a time when the myth of the ritual death of the king of Egypt gained a degree of acceptance. There is no evidence whatsoever for the practice ever having been current, certainly not in historic times.

Of the works of art of the Third Dynasty, apart from those associated with Netjerykhet himself, those left by another of his contemporaries and high officers, Hesy-re, are amongst the most notable.[16] A series of panels carved in relief in sycamore survive from his tomb at Saqqara. The reliefs have a spare austerity, proportion, and balance which is startling; they forcibly suggest the splendour in which the lives of such officials were passed. Though when they were new they would have been vividly coloured they also suggest dramatically the quality of taste which, even at this early time, marked the perceptions of cultivated Egyptians. Hesy-re's career is of interest in that he is identified as a physician, an honourable vocation in early Egypt, specifically as a dentist. Dentistry was practised extensively by the ancients and evidence from the Arabian Gulf (actually from Bahrain) in the centuries after Hesy-re's time also shows considerable application of dental care, at least to the extent of extracting carious teeth.[17] The extraction was probably effected by the technique of 'elevating' the tooth, working it loose with metal probes. Though the method must have been scarcely agreeable the short-term discomfort would have been well worth enduring for the relief of the toothache.

The Sumerians, with their considerable reliance on the date as an item of diet, suffered piteously from the toothache. In witness of this, they even personified toothache and made it an object of their poetry. Not so the practical

Figure 7.3 The Third Dynasty saw the increasing importance of high officials who were not members of the royal family. One of these 'New Men' was Khabausoker, a contemporary of King Netjerykhet and of Imhotep, the builder of the Step Pyramid. Khabausoker was High Priest of Ptah and holder of various other great offices under the king. He wears a curious collar which appears to be associated with the cult of the canine divinity, Anubis.

Source: M. Murray, *Saqqara Mastabas I* (1905), pl. I. Reproduced by permission of University College London.

Egyptians; their answer to toothache, like that of the Dilmunites of Bahrain, was extraction. In respect of dental care, at least, life in third-millennium Egypt and even in the distant Gulf at the same time must have been preferable to life in late Victorian England where itinerant toothpullers exercised their calling with none of the care or professional concern which the biography of Hesy-re, for one, suggests was demanded in Egypt.

Figure 7.4 Hesy-Re was Vizier to King Netjerykhet and also a renowned physician and
dentist. His tomb was decorated with some exceptionally fine carvings, of which
this portrait of the Minister was part.

Source: The Cairo Museum. Photograph John G. Ross.

KING SEKHEMKHET

A Third Dynasty pyramid which was discovered at Saqqara in the 1950s[18]
was found to be of one of Netjerykhet's successors, the King Sekhemkhet;
his complex is also 536 metres long (presumably there is some significance
in the figure) but only 187 metres wide. When the pyramid, or what
remained of it, was excavated a beautifully made sarcophagus, evidently
unopened, was found in the tomb. The flowers which had been laid on the
stone from which the sarcophagus was carved were still lying there. The
opening to the sarcophagus when it was found, sealed as the priests had left
it, was a curious portcullis type of device; nothing quite like it had been
found before. It may be imagined with what tense anticipation and excite-
ment the opening, and the intact burial evidently contained within it,
excited: alas, for nothing. The sarcophagus was empty. What was more it

had evidently always been empty; no dead man was ever lain to rest within it. The reason why this should have been so is an enigma. Netjerykhet did have two alternative burial places available to him apparently, though both were contained within his great funerary complex. The complex itself was a microcosm of Egypt; it is possible that this is also the explanation for Sekhemkhet's otherwise rather weirdly empty coffin, in an empty pyramid. This enigma is if anything compounded by the possibility that Sekhemkhet's pyramid complex, though uncompleted, may have been designed by Imhotep himself.

THE STEPPED PYRAMID AS ROYAL SYMBOL

The central building in the complex at Saqqara, though it is by far the most majestic and extensive, is not the only stepped pyramid in Egypt. There are several other examples, at Edfu, at Kula near Hierakonpolis, Naqada, Zawyet el-Meiyitin, Abydos and Elephantine,[19] in addition that at Sela, near Fayoum, has been associated with one of Netjerykhet's most distinguished successors, King Sneferu. It is not clear why there should have been this crop of much smaller stepped structures erected at this particular time in Egypt although it has been suggested that they may have been set up in various parts of Egypt as a form of propaganda for the royal power. They tend to be prominently sited in the places where they were built, though not invariably so.[20] It may be that the potent symbolism of the terraced mound was their inspiration, once the monument at Saqqara had come into being.

The pyramid at Kula, north of Hierakonpolis, excited interest when it was first identified because it was oriented in the same directions as were Mesopotamian ziggurats. However, just as the stepped profile of Third Dynasty pyramids, from Netjerykhet's onwards, is the product of a time long *before* the Mesopotamians built ziggurats another explanation than direct influence from Mesopotamia to Egypt must be sought, despite the fact that the great fortress at Hierakonpolis shares the same orientation as Kula. Hierakonpolis reveals many factors which seem to echo or to anticipate Mesopotamian forms. The enigma therefore remains.

The great sunburst of creative genius represented by the erection of the Netjerykhet complex is an extraordinary incident in the life of man. Nothing could have prepared the world for the Step Pyramid; yet those who later followed him on the thrones of Egypt managed to universalize the burial of Egyptian Kings to the extent that they have become a virtual commonplace, familiar to generations who would never see them, as expressions either of the triumph of the human spirit or as monuments to wilful self-aggrandizement.

The soaring terraces of the Step Pyramid represented an apotheosis of the rectangular brick *mastaba* of the early kings. The creation of the true pyramid, the three-dimensional linked triangles, which is so perfect and so satisfying a shape, coincided with the beginnings of the solar cult; as was suggested earlier, the pyramid's shape may well have been inspired by the shafts of sunlight piercing through the winter clouds in the vicinity of Heliopolis, in the startling triangular formation that they sometimes adopt, thrusting downwards from the heavens to the earth. The pyramid reverses the process, reaching up from the earth into the heavens.

8

THE PYRAMID AGE

The splendour of the Old Kingdom

THE FOURTH DYNASTY: KING SNEFERU

The last king of the Third Dynasty was Huni; it is not clear what, if any, relation to him was the next king, Sneferu, who was acknowledged as the founder of the Fourth Dynasty. His mother seems to have been a minor wife of Huni, but we do not know if Sneferu was his son; presumably the annalists did not think so, for otherwise there would not have been a new dynasty commencing with his name. He did, however, marry the Princess Hetepheres, 'the Daughter of the God', who presumably brought him the thrones of Egypt as her marriage portion. He was revered throughout the length of Egyptian history; his reign was always regarded as one of the high points of the Egyptian Golden Age. Virtually uniquely amongst the Kings of Egypt he was remembered by a sobriquet: he was 'the Beneficent King' and his cult was sustained down to Ptolemaic times, more than two thousand years after his death.

His cult was also celebrated as far away as the turquoise mines in Sinai, and as late as the Middle Kingdom a little shrine to his memory was maintained at Dahshur. A simple dish with the charcoal for an offering of incense, was found still on the modest altar which was consecrated there to him.[1]

There are three important monuments which may have been of Sneferu's foundation: the Bent Pyramid at Maidum and two some distance away at Dahshur. It is possible that the one at Maidum, though finished by Sneferu, was begun by Huni; it was certainly attributed to Sneferu in later periods. In the New Kingdom a scribe visited Maidum and recorded that he 'came to see the beautiful temple of Sneferu. He found it as though heaven were within it and the sun rising in it'.[2] The pyramid was restored during the Middle Kingdom, one of the earliest recorded examples of the conservation of an ancient monument. It has been suggested that Sneferu also built the small step pyramid at Seila,[3] one of the series which are believed to be visible expressions of the royal power, set up in a number of places in the Valley.

The founder of the Fourth Dynasty was also a considerable warrior. He

led campaigns both to the south and west to put down troublesome upris-
ings of Nubians and Libyans on the frontiers. He, or one of his officers, left
behind a powerful example of Pharaonic propaganda in the form of a rock
carving showing the king striking down some luckless chieftain in the Sinai
peninsula. Such carvings, the earliest of which date from the First Dynasty,
were displayed on prominent rock faces, no doubt to impress the natives in
perpetuity with the extent and implacable power of the king. The presence
of Egyptian forces in Sinai was occasioned by the need to garrison the mines
of turquoise and the routes to the sources of copper which the king sought
to control.

Sneferu also maintained more peaceful contacts with distant peoples. He
built a series of exceptionally large ships, constructed from cedar wood, and
brought loads of cedar by sea from the great Levantine port of Byblos, with
which Egypt was long to sustain trading relations. Cedar, presumably from
Lebanon, was found in one of the pyramids of his foundation.[4]

QUEEN HETEPHERES

The quality of life for the rulers of Egypt in Sneferu's time can be gauged by
the extraordinarily sumptuous elegance of the furnishings found in the tomb
of his consort, Queen Hetepheres, the mother of Khufu, Sneferu's successor.
Once more it is not only their richness of materials and precision of craftsmanship which amazes: it is, overwhelmingly, the certainty and restraint
with which they are designed.

The hoard of objects from Hetepheres' burial, a fraction of what originally it contained, are amongst the most splendid to survive from the Old
Kingdom, or indeed from any period of Egyptian history.[5] Hetepheres'
tomb was robbed, evidently soon after her death and burial; it appears that
this desecration was discovered and what remained was hastily reburied in a
deeply cut pit. The queen's body however, seems not to have survived. What
did survive however, was a magnificent alabaster sarcophagus, a carrying
chair, exquisitely inlaid with gold, a gold-encased bed and gossamer-fine
canopy, gold implements, and silver bracelets inlaid with butterflies.

Though only a few hundred years separate her time from that when
Egypt was in a state of a preliterate and still experimental society the objects
which were the companions of Hetepheres' living days, are of an austere but
sumptuous splendour, matched with a dignity, restraint, and perfection of
design that is expressed in gold, silver, and rare inlays. The delicate gold
cups, the razors also of gold, golden blades honed to a highly efficient
cutting edge, pottery vases of extraordinary refinement, these, added to the
more familiar furniture including what must surely be one of the most
elegant chairs ever designed, take the breath away.

The products of Egyptian craftsmen at this time ask only to be taken on their own account; it doubtless did occur to those who made them that they also had to please a patron, but that patron was one who shared the ideals and collective understanding of the society from which they came. A portrait of the patron survives, an elegant and handsome lady, seated, holding a life-giving lotus to her fine-boned nose, which, by the accident of slight damage to the surface on which she is portrayed inhaling the scent of a lotus-flower, has a most engaging, retroussé tilt.[6]

The supreme royal substance, in Egypt as elsewhere, was gold and the use of the metal became one of the most frequently encountered witnesses of the sumptuousness and splendour in the Old Kingdom, as in the case of Hetepheres' funerary equipment. It is extraordinary how across the world this yellow metal, which is not in itself so excessively rare (as witness the vast extraction of it over the past five thousand years) has always been associated with kings; they have, it must be said, generally been in a better position to acquire it than most people. In Egypt not even silver, which was considerably rarer than gold, could displace the supreme status which gold occupied in the estimation of ancient peoples: a position which indeed it has never lost, despite the competition of rarer metals and more precious stones.

The advanced standards which even the earliest periods reveal of the Egyptians' technical capabilities is to be found in their mastery of materials, of stone for example, the sculptors and carvers of vessels producing shapes which even today defy easy explanation. Similarly they were exceptionally skilled in the handling of metals, producing fine copper vessels as early as the Second Dynasty. The excavation of an Old Kingdom miners' camp by French archaeologists at Wadi Dara, in the desert east of Dendera,[7] demonstrates the organization involved in the process of extraction and reduction of copper-bearing ores. Five copper reduction ovens were excavated which showed that they had been built on the mountainside and positioned to take advantage of the prevailing winds to provide the draught required to achieve the high temperatures necessary for copper reduction. It would require considerable skill also to control the temperatures which would need to be sustained.

Copper and gold, a sumptuous combination by any standards, encapsulate the epoch much more precisely than bronze: but more immediately still the high culture of the third millennium is represented by the rich funerary cults and the elaborate monuments associated with them. These seem to have been seized on by the creative energies of the peoples of the time, so representing a vast absorption of the wealth of the nations and the labour of uncounted hordes of workers.

KING KHUFU

Khufu, known generally by the Greek version of his name, Cheops, was evidently the undisputed heir to Egypt. He reigned, like his father Sneferu, for some twenty-four years.[8] Though he is reputed to have built the greatest and most enduring monument ever erected by man, there was long thought to be only one surviving portrait of the king. This is a tiny piece in ivory, its very minuteness contrasting ironically with the huge pyramid. The king is shown seated on his throne, wearing the Red Crown of Lower Egypt. In recent years other royal heads have been identified, some tentatively, as portraits of Khufu.[9]

According to Herodotus, he was not remembered warmly by the Egyptians, though there is no reason to suppose that he was a particularly harsh or tyrannical ruler. It has been plausibly suggested that Khufu was trying, in building the Great Pyramid on the scale that he did, to outdo his father, Sneferu. If so, this is to be Oedipal to a titanic degree.

A more kindly aspect of Khufu's character, one which is entirely consistent with the attitudes of Egyptians of the time, is suggested by his evident affection for his dog, Abitiuw.[10] He ordered that a fine tomb, expensively furnished and decorated should be built for Abitiuw, who was one of the king's guard dogs, that, according to the inscription which records the king's command, 'he might be honoured before the great god, Anubis'. The Egyptian affection for their dogs evidently reached the highest levels of the society, with Khufu providing confirmation of the fact, as much as did Queen Herneith of the early First Dynasty.

Further evidence that Khufu may not have been the oppressive tyrant portrayed by Herodotus is indicated by the fact that in the Thirteenth Dynasty, nearly a thousand years after the king's lifetime a priest was serving his cult at Giza. The long-dead Khufu's aid was besought for the continuing welfare of his people.[11]

King Khufu's solar boat

Of all the artefacts to descend from the Fourth Dynasty, with the exception of the pyramids themselves, Khufu's funeral boat is a survival which is little short of miraculous.[12] The boat is a wonderful creation, slender, elegant and beautiful. Even today it is a moving, dramatic, and most precious inheritance, unique, having survived over four and a half thousand years in pristine condition when it was found, even with some of its mooring ropes intact.

The lines of Khufu's boat are exquisite and on the water she must have been a glorious sight. Until the present day no larger boat had sailed the Nile. She has one notable feature which, however tenuously, may link her with more modest sisters in the distant Arabian Gulf: every plank in Khufu's boat is sewn, not nailed or riveted. The technique of sewing craft is immensely ancient; it was still practiced until recent times in the remoter reaches of Oman's coast where it may have possibly originated.[13] As an aside it may be noted that if the boats shown on the rock carvings in the Wadi

Figure 8.1 Arguably the most remarkable survival of an artefact from the Fourth Dynasty is
the solar boat built for Khufu and probably used in his funeral rites. A construction of surpassing beauty the boat has been entirely reassembled, conveying the
exceptional quality of form and design which the finest objects from the Pyramid
Age invariably display.

Source: photograph author.

Hammamat, for example, represent those on which the carriers of Sumerian
or Elamite influences travelled across the Red Sea and were, as is most likely,
sewn, it would be perfectly possible for them to be broken down, carried
overland, even across the desert, to the western Arabian coast, reassembled
and sailed across to Egypt.

An elegance of line and a strict regard for minimal decoration in monumental sculpture and in architecture are amongst the glories of this age.
Throughout the Old Kingdom Egyptian art at its best always demonstrated
these qualities; it was only much later, particularly in the New Kingdom
when alien influences, especially those from northern lands, had penetrated
Egypt, that a more florid, extravagant and luxuriant style of decoration
became predominant. Even then, in some of the finest New Kingdom sculpture for example, it is possible to observe artists striving to return to the
purer style of the earlier periods. In Saite times, much later still, there was a

deliberate archaicizing tendency where pastiches of Old Kingdom forms were conscientiously produced, a rare and remarkable example of the artists of a nation paying deliberate homage to their predecessors of nearly two thousand years earlier.

The Great Pyramid

There is no doubt of the piety which caused such tremendous structures as the pyramids to be erected; the idea of countless slaves dying under the overseer's lash is the product of the perfervid imaginations of nineteenth-century romantics and Hollywood film directors. An example of the Egyptians' power of organization and of the kings' concern for the welfare of their subjects (Egyptian kings, in somewhat later times, liked to think of themselves as the shepherds of their people) is to be found in the corvée system used to mobilize the farmers of Middle Egypt during the inundation when they were unable to work their land. Their attitudes are well expressed by the graffiti scrawled on many of the blocks praising one gang, disparaging another, and generally presenting a remarkable demonstration of cheerful group loyalty, not unlike the supporters of rival football teams, without the hooliganism.

The control of large masses of men engaged in hard, demanding, and often highly skilled work called for organizational procedures of an exceptionally well-developed order. Herodotus maintained that Khufu's Pyramid was built in about twenty years. It contains approximately six million tons of stone, brought from the Mokkatam hills, finely cut and fitted into place course by course. Two and a half million blocks were cut: over twenty years this means manhandling an average of 125,000 blocks each year. Averaged out this means that 300,000 tons of stone had to be excavated, worked transported and put in place, year by year.[14] It is difficult to imagine a modern contractor being prepared to accept such an assignment today, even with a twenty-year completion date for the project.

The architects engaged on these enormous public works seem from the outset to have used the plateaux at Giza and Saqqara as though they were gigantic drawing boards. We must assume that they did produce preliminary drawings, perhaps even scale models on the lines of examples known from later periods, probably adopting the technique of the sand model; however, they seem to have been prepared to change direction in the middle of a huge enterprise or even to introduce entirely new features into it when it was already well advanced.

These changes resulted in an enormous increase in the requirement of stone and, one suspects, in the exasperation of the building supervisors on site. They had themselves to learn techniques for handling these vast quantities. The architect was still prepared to experiment, despite the scale on which he was working. Underlying the pyramid's construction was a profound understanding of mathematics. There are those who have detected the knowledge of the Golden Section φ in the pyramid's internal mathematics.[15]

The adoption of the Golden Section and the Fibonacci series which contains it, would account for the supremely satisfying visual impact which the pyramids, like all structures which employ the proportions of the Golden Section, display. It is not necessary to assume that there are any arcane or occult influences at play here; rather it is the extraordinary 'eye' which Egyptian architects, like their Italian Renaissance successors and the builders of English country houses in the eighteenth century, so evidently shared. It would be unwise to suggest that Egyptian architects worked only by 'eye' and not by the application of some more formal disciplines but the glory of the pyramids as archetypal constructions is that they are essentially human constructs, the expression in massive ranges of stone of human aspirations and the response even to the most extreme technical challenges.

Egyptian mathematics and astronomy

The internal mathematics of pyramid building, especially of the Great Pyramid, are immensely complex: they have been well studied[16] and such studies demonstrate clearly that, despite the improvisatory element in their design, the architects were fully in command and were intensely conscious of the challenge which mass and quantity presented to them. Even if there was a major disaster, as was long suspected to have been the case with the collapse of the Maidum Pyramid, the lessons which it offered were quickly learnt and the architect concerned no doubt went on to build other, more successful monuments. The theory of a major disaster is now somewhat discounted, as a result of the clearance of some of the debris around the pyramid's base.[17]

The sophistication of the building techniques employed in Fourth Dynasty architecture is quite remarkable. To excavate and then pile up the enormous quantities of stone required to produce a pyramid requires careful control and a fine mathematical sense: these the Egyptians presumably acquired empirically, just as they seem to have had a knowledge of the properties of π (or something very close to it) which were obtained from practical experience but which had a profound influence on their ability to design complex structures.[18]

The relieving chambers inside Khufu's Pyramid are rightly celebrated, demonstrating a keen and subtle awareness of the dangers of stress when dealing with such great masses of stone. But more subtle still is the employment of saw-tooth edging to the blocks which go to make up the pyramid, to prevent them splaying out under the tremendous weights pressing down upon them.

It has long been recognized that the siting of Khufu's pyramid and its exceptionally fine precision of alignment to the cardinal points could only have been achieved by observations of the stars. It has been convincingly suggested[19] that the builders established the direction of true north by taking the vertical alignment of two bright stars in the constellation of the Big and Little Dipper, Mizan and Kochab. In about 2500 BC these two were located on opposite sides of the north celestial pole. In 2467 BC an invisible line linking the two passed exactly through the north celestial pole; a plumb line intersecting the stars would point directly to north on the horizon. An observation made after this date would include a systematic error occasioned by the alignment being slightly offset from true north. It is suggested that such astronomical errors are revealed in the orientation of other of the Old Kingdom pyramids, indicating that this system of establishing true north was used by the pyramids' builders.

The extent of the ancient Egyptians knowledge of practical astronomy has been a matter of debate, but this study suggests a high degree of sophisticated observation of the stars and the skilful application of the knowledge so gained. It also suggests that records of the heavenly bodies must have been kept over extended periods of time.

The Pyramids of Giza must have been astonishing sights when they were new. They would have gleamed white as magically as their ancestor at Saqqara a few kilometres away, and have inspired as much wonder and awe. The architect who made the Great Pyramid for Khufu, probably his kinsman and the co-ordinator of the whole colossal enterprise who built a structure which has penetrated the consciousness of succeeding generations like no other, was called Hemiunu. He has about him the look of an assured, decisive man who, given a task, would complete it. He shares some of the manner and authority of Ankhaf who, most likely, built the pyramid for Khufu's eventual successor, Khafre. Ankhaf was probably a son of King Sneferu by one of his minor queens; he was not therefore a contender for the throne and he seems to have served his half-brother loyally. But this was in the future; when Khufu died his death seems to have given rise to dissension in the royal family.[20]

The enigma of the Great Pyramid

Khufu and two of his successors, Khafre and Menkaure, are each the possessor of a name which, of all those people who lived during the third millennium, are known to the greatest number of those who lived after them. As the repetition of a man's name was thought by the Egyptians to be one of the means of ensuring his prosperity in the Afterlife, this must, presumably, be a matter of continuing satisfaction to them. The colossal effort of raising the pyramids at Giza, if they did not in fact ensure the protection of the king's mummified remains (for it must be presumed that they were long ago desecrated and destroyed), at least have kept alive their names, as no one else, living in their time, could possibly imagine.

It must be assumed that the pyramids are gigantic machines designed to subdue eternity: any other explanation seems still more fanciful. Their purpose is to annihilate death. That they failed to achieve at least part of their objective must be presumed by their ruined state, empty interiors, shattered sarcophagi. The immense ingenuity which went into their creation was matched by the cunning of those who penetrated their most secure sanctuaries.

But there always remains that most tantalizing of archaeological possibilities, the offchance that somewhere, deep inside the pyramid or far below its lowest masonry course, its principal inhabitant still lies in secret, surrounded by the treasure of a king of Egypt in his last great ceremony, his gold masked face smiling with the rictus of death and the satisfaction of having outsmarted posterity. It is an intriguing vision.

Over the years during which scientific excavation has been conducted in Egypt there have occasionally been hints that 'hidden chambers' may survive in some of the pyramids. Curious noises, sudden rushes of air or the disappearance of rain-water after a storm have all contributed to the idea that somewhere a chamber may be hidden in which an intact burial might still survive. It is, to say the least, unlikely; but it would be unwise to deny the possibility entirely.

Herodotus relates a curious story about the burial of Khufu at Giza. In Book II he remarks 'the underground chambers which Cheops intended as vaults for his own use: these last were built on a sort of island surrounded by water introduced from the Nile by a canal'.[21] This proposition has been universally discounted by scholars; there is no evidence whatsoever of a subterranean lake and it is generally reckoned that the chambers beneath the pyramid have, like those within its actual fabric, been fully plotted. This is not to say that there can be no other chambers, as yet undiscovered, but there is certainly less evidence to suggest that such might be the case with Khufu than there is in some other pyramids.

There is one later precedent at least for a type of subterranean lake burial that Herodotus seems to be describing; its existence prevents perhaps the absolute dismissal of what might otherwise seem a fairly typical Herodotean canard. In the cenotaph at Abydos of King Seti I, the distinguished father of Rameses II, the sarcophagus was placed on an island with a double stair, which was the hieroglyph for the primeval hill or island on which all creation began.[22] The island was surmounted by a channel filled perpetually with subterranean waters. These were 'the waters of Nun' from which the supreme creator god had first risen. They are the waters of the nether world over which both the sun during the hours of darkness and the dead on their journey to the west had to pass.

It is unlikely that Herodotus had heard of Seti's cenotaph. It is however possible that these subterranean islands, recalling the island of origins, the land of the beginning, did feature in some burial rituals and the priests, who seem to have been Herodotus' principal and often wildly inaccurate source of information, had conflated the practice with the most august sepulchre which they knew. It is notable how often in early antiquity hidden waters beneath the earth are invested with special sanctity and mystery

THE SUCCESSORS OF KING KHUFU

On the death of Khufu he was first succeeded by his son, Djedefre. He was not originally the designated heir; this was Prince Kawab but he died before his father, a common enough occurrence in early Egypt. Some authorities list a shadowy figure, named variously as Bakare, Baufre, Bicheris. He may have been a son of Djedefre or possibly of Khufu himself. He was honoured as the ancestor of the kings of the succeeding Fifth Dynasty and was celebrated in a cult established to his memory.

Whilst it is known that it was Djedefre who completed Khufu's burial and laid down the great ship (or ships, since another awaits excavation) beside his pyramid, there is considerable confusion at this point about the succession of the kings. It appears that factions formed within the royal family, probably the consequence of rival queens backing the competing claims of their respective sons. Whether any of this was apparent to the people of Egypt is unknown; certainly the annalists of the royal house must have been aware of what was going on, for it was their task to record the names of the kings in proper order and to set down the principal events of their reigns.

Djedefre reigned for eight years. He began work on a colossal excavation at Abu Rowash, for what was intended to be his tomb; it would have been immense, had it been completed.[23] A marvellous survival, which indicated perhaps what might have been the quality of any work initiated by the king, is one of the finest portrait heads from the Old Kingdom, in a wonderful violet stone, of the king as a young man.[24] It suggests the splendours which Djedefre's tomb might have contained, had it been realized. He was the first king to adopt the formula *Sa Ra*, 'Son of Ra', which became a permanent part of the royal titulary.

KING KHAFRE

The reigns of the kings of the later Fourth Dynasty, particularly of Khafre, the builder of the second pyramid at Giza highlight another example of the remarkable ability of those Egyptian architects who were responsible for the planning and decoration of the temples or the other immense public

(a)

(b)

(c)

buildings which are amongst the principal achievements of that age. This was the careful siting of statuary within the monumental buildings that contained them and the conditions under which they were displayed for the eyes of the dead king and his companion gods who, theoretically at least, were those for whom their presentation was alone intended.

It may seem that such considerations are relatively slight; it may also appear that to talk of statuary being deliberately sited or of the deliberate presentation of the sculptor's work is fanciful, imputing to the artificers of the past considerations which depend upon the application of the criteria of today to such distant times. Yet such is clearly the case.

There is evidence from Khafre's Valley Temple that the monumental statues of the king were designed to be seen largely in isolation from each other. More than this, special consideration was given to the lighting of the great statues and in the case of those of King Khafre they were top-lit by illumination from clerestories, allowing the sun or the moonlight to move down the line of figures, each set into its niche, in a majestic progression. More subtle still, the statues were also sited so that the light would strike the rose-granite floor at the feet of the great figures and reflect upwards, giving the statues the hues of something like living flesh.

It seems likely that lighting techniques of this order were also employed in Netjerykhet's great mortuary complex at Saqqara; clerestories in the upper reaches of the colonnade which led into the courtyard may have lit statues there. It is testimony once more to the Egyptians' brilliant powers of observation that some phenomenon in nature, light reflected on a pool perhaps or piercing through a breast in the upper levels of a reed structure, was absorbed and transformed into the light pouring down from a clerestory and forming a pool of reflection or from a slit in the upper reaches of a building's walls, which allowed the light to focus on to a particular piece of statuary.

Khafre's portraits, of which there are many, are amongst the most striking from the Fourth Dynasty, a time of the particular advance in portrait

---

Figure 8.2 King Khufu was succeeded on his death by his son, Djedefre, who died after an eight-year reign. Then another son of Khufu became king, Khafre, whom some authorities believed Djedefre had usurped. His pyramid complex as a whole is the most complete surviving from the Fourth Dynasty. In addition to the Great Sphinx, which is attributed to him, his Mortuary Temple survives and, linked with a long causeway to the foot of his pyramid, the Valley Temple (a). This is of a monumental, almost Cyclopaean construction (b) and, with the exception of the so-called Tomb of Osiris at Abydos, is unique in the Egyptian architectural canon. It is significantly anomalous, with massive stone lintels, some weighing upwards of two hundred tons, the manipulation of which represent formidable engineering challenges. The original limestone from which the core structure of the Valley Temple was built and which evidently was severely abraded, has been overlaid by a granite skin (c), the reverse sides of which have been carved to fit over the abraded limestone.

Sources: photographs: author. (a) The Interior of the Valley Temple; (b) 'Cyclopaean' masonry; (c) Overlaying of the granite 'skin' on the abraded limestone.

Figure 8.3 This famous portrait statue of King Khafre is one of the most perfect encapsula-
tions of the idea of the divine kingship. The genius of the sculptor has effected an
astonishingly life-like sense to the immensely hard stone in which the statue is
carved. The figure of the royal god, Horus, rests his wings protectively about the
king's head.

Source: The Cairo Museum. Photograph John G. Ross.

sculpture.[25] The king is depicted with a particularly penetrating, almost
manic gaze, unlike the generally tranquil expression which seems to have
been the accepted mode of royal portraiture. Sometimes his expression is not
a little daunting, at other times peculiarly compelling.

Khafre's Valley Temple

Problems of dating and purpose arise from the Valley Temple which lies
beside the Sphinx and the temple dedicated to the Sphinx itself. The Valley
Temple, linked by a causeway to Khafre's pyramid, is a very strange structure,
cyclopean and stark, with a dominating monumentality. It is one of the most
compelling examples of early architecture in Egypt, indeed in the world; not
the least of its wonders is a polished alabaster floor in the interior of the
temple. The Valley Temple is quite unlike any other Egyptian building, with

the possible exception of the so-called 'Tomb of Osiris' at Abydos which has similarities in the employment of massive blocks in much of its architecture. The building of this temple or shrine at Abydos is traditionally but not wholly convincingly attributed to King Seti I, of the Nineteenth Dynasty.

The Valley Temple's architecture is remarkable for its stark, megalithic simplicity and austerity, qualities which seem at odds with the majesty and splendour of Old Kingdom design generally. It contains exceptionally large lintels, some weighing around two hundred tons; how these were lifted into place in the third millennium is difficult to explain. Nor is the purpose of the temple certain, though it is thought to have been associated with the rites attending the king's mummification.

Apart from the very unusual structure of the Valley Temple, its most perplexing element is that the skin of granite which has been used to face the temple is overlain on apparently earlier, limestone blocks which reveal a similar level of deterioration to that which is apparent in the Sphinx. For the limestone blocks to have deteriorated to the extent that they have suggests a long exposure to very different climatic conditions to those which have prevailed for the four and a half millennia which have elapsed since the conventional dating of the monuments on the plateau at Giza.

The condition of the granite which overlays the limestone core blocks of the Temple is further remarkable for the fact that their surfaces which are laid against the limestone have been shaped to fit snugly against the deteriorated surface of the limestone. It would surely have been far more economical to have smoothed the blocks of the original core to receive the granite facings, which are made of a far harder material, but for some reason this was not done. A further enigma in the construction of the Valley temple is that examination of the fossil assemblages present in the limestone of Giza has not established the source of the Valley Temple's masonry.[26]

The family of King Khafre

Khafre had as wife Meresankh III, the daughter of Crown Prince Kawab who died before King Khufu, of whom he was the designated successor. After the death of Khufu there was some dispute over the succession whereby Djedefre was accepted by part, but not all, of the family. Meresankh's mother backed Djedefre's party but after his death she contrived to marry her daughter to Khafre, who was considered to have restored the rightful line of succession. They had a son, Nebmakhet who died before his father, a frequent occurrence in the lifetime of the dynasty. His tomb provides a pleasing glimpse of the life of the royal family as, according to the inscriptions, it was the gift of a painter, Semer-Ka, whilst Inkaf, a sculptor, supervised its construction and decoration.[27] Khafre's pyramid at Giza, slightly smaller than his father's, is the only one of the three great Pyramids to preserve some of its original limestone casing, on its summit.

The Great Sphinx

The art of the sculptors of Egypt advanced wonderfully during the reigns of Khufu and particularly of Khafre. No work surviving from this period has excited so much speculation, admiration and wonder as the Great Sphinx at Giza, carved from the living rock with the face of a god-king surmounting the body of a colossal lion.

The really remarkable observation about the Great Sphinx, apart from the fact that it is perhaps the most famous piece of sculpture in the world and one of the largest ever made, is that it is virtually unique in the entire canon of Egyptian art. There are sphinxes in abundance, to be sure, particularly those made by the kings of the Middle Kingdom, which are particularly powerful and often rather baleful creations. The type reached a degree of culmination in the Avenue of Sphinxes (though ram- and not human-headed) which still gives an especially operatic look to the approach to the Temple of Karnak. But, singularly, there are virtually no other examples in all the length of Egypt of the sculptural adaptation of boulders, standing rocks, or cliff faces.[28]

Opportunities abounded, after all. To this day many rocks along the river and in the Libyan hills seem to be trying to give birth to a gigantic human or animal shape. The ingenuity of Egyptian engineers would certainly have been equal to the complex tasks involved; they would, one feels, have relished the challenge. The temptation for the living gods who occupied the throne to perpetuate their images amongst the living rock of the Egyptian landscape must have been well-nigh overwhelming. Yet they did not do so.

There must, presumably, have been some constraint, though certainly not self-imposed modesty or diffidence, which prevented them from doing this. Rameses II memorably caused effigies of himself and his consort to be carved in the rock face of their temples at Abu Simbel. Yet this is not quite the same thing as the adaptation of a standing rock outcrop such as a planner of genius in the Fourth Dynasty seized on and in doing so immortalized his king, through its sculpted monumentality. Rameses' work is simple architecture; the creation of the Sphinx on the Giza plateau is art on a heroic scale, involving the adaptation of a landscape. The Great Sphinx is one of a kind; despite the depredations resulting from Turkish artillery practice, his enigmatic smile suggests that his creator knew that he would remain, aloof and unique.

The speculations about the age of the Sphinx have attracted much attention over the past decade. The issue is too complex to be examined here in any depth but the controversy which has arisen around this very singular survival has revealed a number of anomalies which prompt caution in dismissing outright the proposition that there may be more to discover about the Sphinx and its origins than has been suspected hitherto.

The evidence of what appears to be the effects of prolonged periods of rainfall on the rock from which the Sphinx is carved, seems convincing. Whether or not the head of the Sphinx is a portrait of Khafre, as it has traditionally been ascribed, bears little on the question of its origins and their dating. If the head is a portrait of the king (a proposition which is not without its sceptics) this does not necessarily determine when the monument itself was carved; it is perfectly possible that the head was carved or recarved in Khafre's reign, but the ascription to him is unconvincing.

KING MENKAURE

The exceptional ability of Egyptian craftsmen and artists to eliminate inessentials in the reliefs and sculptures which they made, can be seen in works such as the marvellous triad statuary groups made for King Menkaure, the builder of the third pyramid at Giza. The king, now presented not only as the ruler of the gods but as a man of great and vigorous physical beauty, is shown as it were coming out of the stone itself, supported by two divine companions. The king is depicted as smiling, almost as if welcoming the observer, his head lifted confidently, assured both of his divinity and his beauty. The distinctly African cast of the king's features, like those of Khufu in the tiny ivory piece which was found at Abydos and of Netjerykhet in his *serdab* statue, prompts the speculation whether the pyramid builders were not, after all, black Africans or that at least there was a strong African strain in their ancestry. This question has often been put, and as quickly suppressed, except by African historians who have perhaps been too enthusiastic in their espousing of this possibility. But the Giza kings of the Fourth Dynasty do share a notably African cast of feature.

A pleasing anecdote is told of Menkaure which, like that of King Khufu and his dog, suggests a more human dimension to the builders of the pyramids. During the building of his pyramid, when he visited the site to view its construction, he gave orders that a band of the workers engaged on it should be detailed to build a tomb for one of his friends, a noble named Debhen. The king's generosity was considerable. Debhen's tomb was lined with stone, the first example of such a feature. It also contained an exceptionally early landscape scene, of men climbing a ramp to burn incense at a shrine at its summit.[29]

Gradually, as the generations passed, the plateau around Giza filled up with its royal dead and their extraordinary monuments. Every part of the great buildings was covered with polished stone; the temples, built in darker stones, contrasted with the pyramids, which towered above the other burial places which clustered round them, their occupants hoping thereby to draw to themselves some part of the vicarious immortality which proximity to the mountains of stone of the kings' tombs promised for them. Laid in rows the *mastabas* of the courtiers and the small pyramids of the queens and the royal children have a forlorn and touching quality, even now. They must then have constituted a well-planned, orderly city of the princely dead.

When it was completed the complex of monuments at Giza, polished in the perfection of an ideal form, must have been an astonishing sight. From every face of the pyramid, through the night as much as in the day, light must have been thrown back into the immensity of space as from a colossal jewel.

KING SHEPSESKAF

The Sun God and his devotees had been making significant advances of position throughout the Fourth Dynasty. Khufu's name was compounded with that of Khnum, a ram-headed creator god from the Aswan region; most of his successors took names compounded with that of Re, the sun god, ruling in Heliopolis. The priests were gaining power and asserting themselves at the expense of the king's divine absolutism.

The last king of the Fourth Dynasty gives some evidence of what might well be interpreted as an attempt to reject the domination of Re and his cult. His name was Shepseskaf; he seems only to have reigned for four years. He rejected, too, the idea of the pyramidal funerary monument and instead reverted to something like the earlier form. He built a great low-lying rectangular structure with a rounded top and sharply angled ends which gave it the shape of a gigantic sarcophagus. This is the Mastabat Faraon which, though it is badly ruined, may still be seen at Saqqara.

It is only a matter of speculation whether Shepseskaf's reign was curtailed by the intervention of the priests, fearful of the possibility of his limiting their power. There is one rather touching piece of evidence which suggests that his qualities as a man were as notable as his acts as a king, concerned to restore the power of his house. His queen was called Bu-nefer; it was she who conducted the ceremonies at Shepseskaf's funeral, a responsibility usually carried out by a brother or a son. It must be presumed that she loved him.

Throughout his life the king was surrounded by ritual and richly symbolic ceremony. The degree to which this formality must have dominated the king's life and the lives of those who were closest to him must have been immense. The ceremony will have had a practical value however. If the king was incompetent or idle the round of ceremonies could be intensified to occupy his time, leaving the running of the state to more able or committed officials. Such is only speculation but it would be wholly within the Egyptian perspective to have invented this device of political management, along with all the others which they clearly did initiate.

What life must have been like in the days of the earlier kings, for example in the time of Netjerykhet or Khufu, can only be imagined. But the loneliness of the king's office is recalled in the sad advice, given to a later occupant of the throne: 'fill not thy heart with a brother: know not a friend'.

9

THE OLD KINGDOM

Fulfilment and decline

A consequence of the immense organization needed to build the pyramids, and the recruitment and training of the hosts of artists and craftsmen necessary to work on all the various divisions of the project, was that in the later decades of the Old Kingdom, when the king no longer absorbed most of the available labour and talent in the construction of his pyramid, a pool of highly skilled workers and craftsmen existed on which the nobles and indeed even the merely prosperous could draw to build and decorate monuments for themselves. This aspect of life in the Old Kingdom is reflected in the apparent 'democratization' of Egyptian religion, a phenomenon which has often been commented upon. The argument proceeds that first the king alone was guaranteed immortality; then his attendants, family, and most intimate courtiers were brought in the scope of the Afterlife by being buried close to him. It may seem a naïve view for a sophisticated people, but there is little doubt that the fact that a minor self-made official or tradesman could afford to commission a handsome tomb led quite quickly to the insistence that such a tomb was worth commissioning and that the individual concerned could expect to enjoy an eternity once reserved exclusively for his betters. This was to lead ultimately to a sort of democratization of death and the loss of the primordial Egyptian attitude to the world beyond death. Later in the Old Kingdom we see the king himself acknowledging the change and giving his favoured courtiers 'houses of millions of years', tombs which were intended to serve as estates for eternity, comparable with the lands, herds and servants with which he would reward those who served him in their lifetimes.

THE OPERATIONS OF GOVERNMENT

There is little enough known of the ways in which the royal government of Egypt worked, how decisions were taken, to what extent projects were planned before being started, or how instructions were transmitted from the source to the place where the action was. It is evident that there must have

been an orderly process for the consideration of affairs of state, for the recording of decisions and for the inspection and reporting of progress and results.
No doubt some element of royal (or divine) whim played its part in advancing a particular idea or project, but generally speaking the quality of work
which has survived from Old Kingdom Egypt is so exceptional that neither
its planning nor its execution could have been left to chance. The Egyptian
respect for order, for the interconnections which they saw existing between
all things, animate and inanimate, would have tended towards seeking an
assured structure lying beneath the projects which they undertook.

Many of the titles of senior officials of the earliest periods have been
recorded. They suggest the complexity of a developed bureaucracy, the long
usage of title which had become florid and orotund, and a clear recognition
of how enthusiastically all officials (and no doubt others) respond to titles of
honour.[1] Thus there was 'The Controller of the Two Thrones', 'He who is at
the Head of the King', 'the Master of the Secrets of the Royal Decrees', 'He
of the Curtain', (a title which suggests an early form of intelligence gather-
ing, or perhaps simple eavesdropping) in addition to the less specific 'Sole
Companion to the King' and other marks of distinction which were evidence
of the royal favour. There were offices called 'The House of the Master of
Largesse', the base from which the royal bounty was distributed to those in
need or to those whom the king wished to reward. There was even an 'Overseer of the Foreign Country'. 'Hereditary Prince' was an important and
ancient rank. It had its origins, rather surprisingly, in a term which meant
'Mouth of the People'.

The collection and husbanding of the royal revenues by means of taxes
levied on provinces, towns, individual landowners, and farmers was the
responsibility of the Treasurers, of whom there were two, one for each
kingdom. They worked from the White House in the case of the southern
kingdom and from the Red House for the northern. Even in so practical a
task as the control of the exchequer, the characteristic duality of Egypt was
still maintained.

One of the sources of Egypt's strength in remote antiquity was undoubtedly the king's ability to identify able newcomers in his entourage, even in
its humblest ranks and, even further, to encourage his nobles to watch out
for exceptionally talented youngsters who, early on in their lives, could be
singled out for the state's service. The rewards were great for such men. In
the Old Kingdom there existed an elaborate system of social dependency
ranging from the king downwards. Officials and members of the great
households were rewarded with gifts of jewellery and furniture, clothing,
metal ware, vases, pottery, and land: first these descended from the King,
then the recipients would be expected to pass on some part of their benefits
to their dependants in turn. A similar process may be seen at work in
Middle Eastern monarchies today.

Later in the Old Kingdom princes of the royal line do not seem generally to have occupied the highest offices. Presumably they represented a danger to the succession, as appears to have been demonstrated in the Fourth Dynasty; like the Tudors, the kings of Egypt tended to seek out and promote their own men who thus would look to them only as the source of favour and fortune.

THE KING AS SOLE PRIEST

Very large numbers of both educated and uneducated Egyptians were employed in the service of the many temples across the land. Their service demanded a great congress of grand and lesser priests, acolytes, tradesmen, labourers and workers of all sorts on the estates which supported them. In the rituals and rites of the temples and the service of the gods the king was, theoretically at least, alone in his relationship with the divine. In theory, therefore, the king, as principal immanent divinity, conducted every ritual in every temple throughout Egypt: the officiating priest was merely his surrogate. In reality, however, the companies of priests attached to the great temples were powerful, sometimes even representing a degree of opposition to the royal authority.

The power of the temples was exercised by these professional priests who lived in them and on their endowments, which could be very considerable. Their duties were various. First and foremost they were responsible for the sacrifices, for maintaining the proper honours appropriate to the god-king. They might be attached to a temple or to a tomb, endowed to keep alive the *ka* of the dead king: they might conduct the huge and colourful ceremonies which took place in the great temples, year in and year out.

One of the most agreeable characteristics of early Egyptian society is that, whilst intensely autocratic in character, it was nonetheless flexible, permitting men of talent, no matter what their racial or social origins, to move into the highest reaches of the administration. When the king is god, differences in degree amongst his subjects are of relatively minor significance. The selection and training of artists, however, demands a more subtle system, a more precise schedule than the recruitment of officials to administer the royal estates or to officer the levies.

THE ORGANIZATION OF MANUFACTURE

The degree of organization required to maintain the equipment of the temples and the royal courts must have been prodigious. The scale on which the pottery, stone-carving, and copper-casting industries were organized was considerable; when the demands of monumental and funerary architecture are added, the extent of the need for experienced craftsmen in all these fields is obviously formidable. The number of workers in what might be called 'craft industries' must, on the evidence of their surviving products, presumably only a fraction of their real output, have been very high, as significant a percentage of the Egyptian population as that, say, employed on the land.

It is rare (though not entirely unknown) to encounter a badly made stone vessel or wasted pot; quality-control standards in early Egypt were exceptionally high, befitting the technical ability of the craftsmen. Standards, by and large, were maintained over hundreds of years and the ability to do that was itself remarkable.

It is intriguing to speculate what sort of administration existed to ensure that the remarkable consistency of design was maintained. We know that royal officials were given, nominally at least, responsibility for the supervision of the making of royal statues, or for the architecture of the royal tomb. However, it is difficult to believe that these great officials, often with many appointments to discharge, were more than the presiding figures over groups of less exalted executives who actually co-ordinated and supervised the work.

It is impossible, however, not to wonder how the Egyptian artificers managed even to meet the demands of their royal clients. In Netjerykhet's time, for example, tens of thousands of jars, plates, vases, and vessels of every conceivable shape and size were placed in the king's tomb with lavish prodigality. Presumably some, if not all, of these objects had been used in the palaces of the king; it is possible, however that many were made for funerary purposes alone. To have produced this quantity of stone vases an immense industry must have existed, yet so far little trace of extensive industrial workings has been discovered. This is the more surprising when it is considered that there must have been manufacturing centres or, at the very least, collection points where the products of what must have been an army of outworkers were assembled. Once again the logistics baffle and respect for the organizational powers of the ancient Egyptians soars.

An antiquarian note is struck, incidentally, by the contents of Netjerykhet's tomb. The names of virtually every king who preceded him on the Two Thrones is found inscribed on the stone vessels, which were piled up in his tomb in such enormous quantity, filling the subterranean magazines. When assembling this collection of vessels Netjerykhet especially honoured a sculptor, Ptahpehen, who held the title 'Maker of Vases'.[2] This perhaps meant more than its apparent modesty suggests, since Imhotep also bore it. Ptahpehen received what must have been the signal privilege of having vases inscribed with his name included amongst the royal cache.

The products of different craftsmen, perhaps of particular workshops or studios, can be detected in different parts of Egypt; there seems, therefore, to have been some sort of national distribution system for the products of workshops to use. This is particularly true of pottery products, where it is also easier to detect. In the case of stoneware however, there is a notable consistency over the years and over the whole land between the various types of vessel manufactured. There is, of course, an amazing medley of forms and sizes: the much vaunted Egyptian conservatism in art (a conservatism which in fact is more apparent than real) did not prevent them from adding new shapes to the catalogue of vessels which they produced. But once a shape or form became accepted it was adopted apparently over many hundreds of square miles, sometimes over the whole country.

If the temples, particularly those consecrated to Ptah, were the repositories of the corpus of approved designs and forms of products manufactured either for the royal service or for the rituals of the temples (a considerable assumption but certainly not entirely insupportable), there must have been some system of information exchange or flow from the temple to the many different and widespread workshops which would have carried out their manufacture. It may have been simply a matter of handing on the techniques from generation to generation, from father to son. Those lines in the normal course of nature must sometimes have been interrupted, yet the forms often survived over very long periods. The traditions of the craftsmen's work seem to have been living traditions, not merely the work of copyists. Nothing has survived to indicate how the central authority passed on its design instructions: the medium may have been entirely perishable, of course, but some such system must surely have existed.

The principles that apply to the making of stone vases apply equally to most objects of Egyptian manufacture. In the Old Kingdom the walls of tombs and their associated buildings belonging to the royal family and distinguished nobles were customarily decorated with scenes of daily life in Egypt, in the palaces, and in the countryside. Many variations exist and certainly it is often possible to detect the hand of a master in one set of carvings and a more provincial, less talented hand in another. But the designs are broadly consistent and the conventions employed by the artists, the curious distorted frontality, for example, which is so odd a feature of Egyptian portraiture of humans when compared with the absolute literalism often employed for animals, is consistent everywhere in Egypt from the Fourth Dynasty onwards, when seemingly someone had determined that this was how it was to be done.

The ability of Egyptian artists to handle frontality with perfect assurance is demonstrated by their development of stone sculpture in the round. This was a slightly later form in its development than the making of stoneware vessels; for example, predynastic artists rarely seem to have attempted monumental statuary on any real scale, contenting themselves with enchanting miniatures which, nonetheless, are often the ancestors of the later, greater forms. There is some evidence that in the early days they worked in wood for the large-scale statues which adorned the temples.

In late predynastic times ivory was frequently carved in formal, rather rigid shapes. Generally these objects are modestly domestic: combs, ladles, and spoons for example; some of which are already of a formidable elegance.

The Egyptians were always enthusiastic board-game players, and developed a variety of games with counters in the form of animals; some of these, the lions and dogs for example, are especially fine and seem to have within them already the promise of the towering monumental forms to which in the distant future they will be expanded. These will eventually become the adornment of the temple colonnades of massive sphinxes with which later, more pretentious ages loved to ornament the land of Egypt.

Pottery figurines, as well as those carved in ivory, were made in large quantities in early times. Some were clearly votive objects: others are less clear in their purpose but they want nothing in appeal. It may be, however, that the apparently less durable substance of fired clay was not considered so significant by whatever authorities actually determined the form that more significant objects were to take, for there seems to be more random variety in the early decades in the objects made from clay. However, pottery once it is fired has an unequalled capacity to survive and in consequence a wealth of pottery objects has come down to the present time.

THE RISE OF MEMPHIS AND THE POWER OF PTAH

The key to this examination of the organization and direction of manufacturing procedures in early Egypt lies in the shadowed interiors of the great temples dedicated to the supreme craftsman-god, Ptah of Memphis. Of all the great Egyptian divinities Ptah is in many ways the most mysterious. Yet he was to survive throughout Egyptian history, from the earliest times to the latest, a powerful influence in the creative life of the country.

Although he was one of the supreme national divinities, Ptah was particularly identified with the city of Memphis. There, the centre of the royal administration was firmly fixed at the apex of the Delta, where Upper and Lower Egypt meet, south of Cairo. 'Memphis' is anachronistic, being a Greek form of the name of the pyramid of Pepi II, which was not built until quite late in the Sixth Dynasty. In earlier times the city was called Ity-tawy; Pepi's pyramid was called Men-nefer and the Greek corruption of this praise-name produced 'Memphis'.

Memphis was not only the royal capital; it was also the centre for the cults of the artificer god, the supreme creator god. Ptah was particularly associated with the creator kings of Egypt, those who laid down her foundations so securely in the First Dynasty and, to a lesser degree, in the Second. In the Second Dynasty however, the cult of the sun begins to edge its way into official religion; the names of several of the early kings of the dynasty bear names which are compounded with that of Re, the personification of the sun-in-splendour. Re's main cult centre was at Iwun, now Heliopolis (the city of the sun, like 'Memphis' another Graecism, though a more acceptable one), today a suburb of Cairo.

According to the myths, Memphis was founded by the legendary Unifier, Menes, who is perhaps to be identified with Narmer or Aha. However, archaeology has indicated that there are predynastic levels at Memphis, which show that a settlement of some sort existed there before it was chosen – as indeed seems to have been the case – to become the royal capital.[3] The decision to build a city which symbolized the integration of the two domains, was a brilliant and inspired political decision. The fact that, alone of all Egypt's major settlements, Memphis survived throughout the Dual Kingdom's history, is yet another proof of the remarkable sense of the techniques of state-building which the founders of the kingship possessed.

Ptah's origins are obscure. He seems to have been associated with the kings of the First Dynasty; whether this means that he too originated in This (somewhere in the region of Abydos) or in Hierakonpolis is not known. It does appear, however, assuming the legend to be correct, that when the royal capital was established at Memphis Ptah was swiftly recognized as the city's presiding divinity and the earliest temple in his name was established there.

The High Priest of Ptah at Memphis was one of the greatest of the Great Ones of Egypt, an immensely powerful member of the ruling elite and a close confidant of the king. His was the supreme directing intelligence of the armies of sculptors, potters, craftsmen in jewels, copper, gold, silver, and wood; he, no doubt, was close by whenever a decision affecting the royal tomb or the creation of a great temple was required in the innermost councils of the king. Through the undying traditions of Ptah's priests the survival of Egyptian forms in architecture and manufacture were doubtless realized.

THE CRAFTSMAN AND THE PROLONGATION
OF LIFE

Above all other considerations the Egyptians were obsessed with the prolongation of life and with enabling the king to maintain the life and prosperity of Egypt. Much Old Kingdom statuary, for example, was astonishingly lifelike: no subsequent culture, nor even the Greeks at their best, achieved quite the perfect simulacra of living beings that the Egyptians brought off so completely in the early centuries of their history.

The Egyptians believed that life could be prolonged beyond death by a mixture of magical incantations, spoken or carved on the tomb's walls, the provision of food and the appurtenances of living, either real or simulated, and by the careful preservation of the body and of the body's appearance, the last being effected by the making of statues. The immense quantity of statues which survive from the Old Kingdom make it clear that they are, or are certainly intended to be, portraits of the subject represented. They may

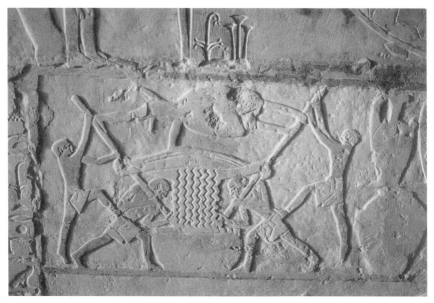

(a)

(b)

be idealized, to the extent that most subjects chose to have themselves represented as younger, rather than older. To this rule the great seated statue of Netjerykhet is a majestic exception and there were others who did not decline to have themselves represented as old, fat (a witness of prosperity) or even crippled.

Egyptian sculptors brought to the making of statues the same genius for observation which they deployed in their delighted recording of the ways of animals and of the countryside. There is no mistaking an Old Kingdom statue for one from a later period. Old Kingdom figures stand or sit four-square; the planes of their faces tend to be broader than those of their successors, their eyes fixed on eternity. The sculptors of the Old Kingdom devised the 'archaic smile', later to be identified so firmly with Greek *Kouroi*, two thousand years before those statues were made, celebrating the sometimes ambiguous beauties of young Hellenes. But whereas the Greek smile frequently hovers on the edge of a simper, the Egyptian model is exalted, essentially anticipatory, as at the approach of a vision of glory.

The production of statuary was extensive and the workshops which produced them must have been large and busy institutions. Not all the statues made at this time are of the finest quality; some are distinctly provincial whilst others, though they have come from securely documented excavations, are sometimes bizarre or simply incompetent to the extent that were they to appear on the antiquities market in Cairo they would be dismissed as counterfeit. But these lapses from a vigorously controlled production quality are comparatively rare.

The finest Old Kingdom statuary was, so far as we know, produced with the simplest tools, though often the sculptors chose to work with the hardest and most intractable stones. Pounding, abrading, and cutting with copper bits and stone tools produced some of the greatest works of art ever made, fashioned with a quality of detail and finish which is so often miraculous.

Closely allied to the Old Kingdom genius in sculpture is that of carving in relief. The ability of such artists of this period is quite uncanny; on the one hand they could sustain a dense and complex sequence of images, of

---

Figure 9.1 The tomb of Nefer and his father Ka-Hay, who were with various of their relatives at Saqqara, provides an opportunity to observe the quality of life of a high official of the late Old Kingdom and also to reflect upon the good fortune which in Old Kingdom Egypt in particular often attended able men from outside the royal or noble lineages to rise high in the service of the king. Nefer's tomb is a joyful compendium of the highly civilized pleasures of life at the court and in the countryside in the twenty-fifth century BC. It also contains one of the earliest and best preserved mummies, which demonstrates how the art of mummification declined in later periods.

Sources: (a) The Nefers' pet baboon assists in the Wine Harvest. Photograph E.L.B. Terrace; (b) The Mummy of Waty. Photograph Author.

scenes from daily life for example, over an extensive surface, without ever losing the coherence and vitality of the whole, whilst on the other they could produce an immediacy of impression which can really only be compared with drawing in stone, with the assurance of the placing of a line around the jaw or the suggestion of the fullness of a cheek which would hardly be approached by an Italian master.

To judge by later evidence reliefs on this scale were produced on a sort of production line procedure. The area to be covered would be marked out first of all with a grid of squares so that the design, of which a miniature version or a drawing would first be prepared, could be worked out on the grid, in an enlarged format. The master would direct the drawing. At successive stages craftsmen would incise, cut, polish, and colour the relief, all under the master's supervision and that of his closest assistants. The technique would have been familiar to Leonardo or Michelangelo in their creation of a mural or a complex piece of statuary.

THE FIFTH DYNASTY – LIFE IN THE VALLEY

The scenes depicted on the walls of tombs throughout Egypt, but especially the later Old Kingdom period, particularly at Saqqara in the shadow of the royal monuments, are vibrant with life. This indeed is their purpose: they are part of the supreme third-millennium national industry of Egypt, the celebration of life and its prolongation into eternity.

No aspect of life is overlooked. Work in the fields, counting the cattle, entertainment in the family, pastimes of all sorts, the arts, building, cultivation of the vine, fishing, building boats, harvest time, all manner of work and involvement is represented. The trades are represented, as are some of the learned professions: the scribe, the doctor. Not much is shown, at this period, of ritual and the worship of the gods: this is still principally a matter for the King, the great priests, and their immediate entourages. Their practices might ensure the ever repeated rounds of birth and plenty but they seem distant from the preoccupations of ordinary men. The well-founded Egyptian was master of his own world and could conceive of no more perfect existence. All was for the best, indeed, in the best (or in a sense perhaps the only) of all possible worlds – always excepting, of course, the transfigured world of the gods, but even that was only Egypt existing in the celestial dimension.

The immense document which is represented by the tomb reliefs is often punctuated by captions, by the words of the participants in the activities which the reliefs depict. Egyptian was a language rich in metaphor and in cheerful insult: the language of the ordinary people recorded on the walls is earthy, uninhibited. It is also joyous: the fisherman, wading into the water, politely says 'Good Morning' to the different types of fish swimming at his feet.

THE RISE OF SOLAR CULTS

The gradual intrusion of the ordinary people into the world of the Great Ones begins, tentatively, in the Fourth Dynasty, increases in the Fifth, and becomes characteristic of the Sixth. It coincides with other, perhaps more significant, and doubtless related, changes in the nature of Egyptian beliefs, in the monarchy, and in monumental architecture.

Some authorities have proposed that the early royal religion in Egypt, up to and including the Third Dynasty, was linked with the stars.[4] The evidence, either way, is slender but certainly the Pyramid Texts, assuming these to be more ancient than the time in which they were first inscribed on the walls of the Sixth Dynasty pyramids, seem to identify the divine king as a star and it is amongst the stars, or even beyond them, that he seeks his eternal habitation.

The stars are valuable instruments for measurement and the Egyptian engineers and architects of even the earliest periods seem to have been capable of making complex and sophisticated empirical observations which they used to align their buildings. The precision with which the monumental buildings of the Early Dynastic period and the early Old Kingdom are aligned is legendary; that precision was achieved by careful alignments on selected stars and the skillful use of water channels, the consequence of the careful observation of the behaviour and properties of water which large-scale irrigation projects and techniques had made familiar. With the advent of the Fourth Dynasty, however, the sun cult, the prerogative of the hierophants of Heliopolis, began to rise above the other cults of national or royal status. As a general principle gods and their adherents dislike, and energetically resist, change: sensibly so, since an enthusiasm for change amongst their followers seldom bodes well for divinities. Similarly, the priesthoods which purport to serve the gods represent a substantial investment, often built up over many generations. They always formed one of the most powerful corporations in ancient society, hierarchic and carefully institutionalized. They were ready to use every device to maintain their power and influence.

They were not always successful, however. In Sumer the temple corporations were evidently the repositories of state and economic power in the late fourth and early third millennia. Their influence was reduced and, in part at least, replaced by the secular power of the war-band leaders who gradually institutionalized their positions and eventually became kings. The royal power, and the court which surrounded the kings was more open, more accessible to ambitious outsiders than the temple priesthoods which were, by definition, arcane and exclusive.

In Egypt the neat equation of king and god relieved much of this potential area of antagonism. Even so it is possible to detect, in the early centuries, several shifts in the nature of the cults which were practiced in the Valley and in their relative influence. Once the unification was adopted as state policy, national cults began to emerge, gradually to rise above the local cults which had kept the loyalty of the ordinary folk over the millennia. The decline in the star cults associated with the king, the reduction in the status of Ptah, the corresponding rise of Re in Heliopolis, and the inversion of the role of Set with his consequent presentation as a malignant influence, who once was the god of a large proportion of the Valley dwellers, all demonstrate the way that, even in Egypt, the political influence of temple cults was employed to satisfy the need for power.

After the death of the last ruler of the Fourth Dynasty, King Shepseskaf, the dynasty changed again, though there was still probably some familial connection with the previous line. Now, however, the cult of Re emerged supreme: the king is hailed as 'son of Re'; whereas he was the great god immanent, he is now merely a divine son, content to carry out quite menial tasks in the service of his father, who sails supreme above the Egyptians' world.

The king whose name heads the Fifth Dynasty is Userkaf; it is probable that he married a senior royal daughter, perhaps the sister of Shepseskaf. Userkaf may also have been a member of a branch of the royal family, though not the ruling one; there was a story that the dynasty descended from the daughter of King Djedefre[5] or from the mysterious Bafre. He was followed by Sahure and Neferirkare. Their commitment to the sun cult was strong; according to legend all three were brothers, all fathered on their mother by Re. The influence of the priests of the sun cult, centred at Heliopolis, now became dominant; their propaganda becomes pervasive and very effective.

The Fifth Dynasty, like those that had gone before it, had a distinctive style of royal funerary monument: the sun temple, built close to the Nile and notable for a proud-standing obelisk in the temple court which was part of the complex. Beside the temple, in several cases, a stone solar barque was built, recalling the boats which had been lain beside the dead king, in various forms, since the First Dynasty. International contact was now widespread. Even distant islands in the Aegean such as Cythera received evidence of the Egyptian king's existence, in this case a small marble cup inscribed with the name of Userkaf's temple.[6]

KING SAHURE

Sahure built the royal cemetery at Abusir, from whose ruins much of the evidence for the character of life in Egypt and the royal courts in the Fifth Dynasty has been recovered. From the reliefs of the Sahure sun temples it is clear that Asiatics to the east of Egypt, the Badu of the Arabo-Palestinian deserts and their cousins inhabiting the eastern Egyptian desert, were now becoming increasingly troublesome. It was necessary for the king to take punitive action against them. But he also traded with the easterners, sending ships to Byblos and to the mysterious land of Punt.

One of the finest artefacts from Sahure's reign, which shows the quality of work which could be produced almost as a matter of routine in the later Old Kingdom, is a group portraying the king in the company of a nome god, now in the Metropolitan Museum, New York. This has been described as provincial work, lacking the highest qualities. If this is so, it is a tribute to the master craftsmen of the Egyptian provinces: in fact, it is the equal of the very finest work which survives; only in Egyptian art criticism could the term 'provincial' be used pejoratively. Its massive quality is particularly notable, imparting a remarkable sense of strength and power to it. Several of the kings of the dynasty were to compound their names with the word 'Nefer' which means, variously, 'good', 'vital', 'perfect', as well as with the name of the sun god. From this time most of the names of Egyptian Kings are praise names of each king's particular dynastic or personal divinity.

THE RECORDS OF LIVES FULFILLED: OFFICIALS, SCRIBES, ARTISTS, MUSICIANS, DOCTORS

The Egyptians, especially those living during the Old Kingdom, had a particular concern for the recording of a man's career in the formal security of his tomb, which thus presented a sort of petrified obituary. There was a multiplicity of such appointments with which an ambitious official might be favoured during his lifetime: directorships of the royal administration, supervisory functions, inspectorates of outlying posts in the bureaucracy, temple ranks, and appointments at the court. Some of the most exalted appointments, those which were particularly identified with or brought the holder into personal contact with the king, tended to be honorific and ceremonial and were reserved largely for the high nobility. A king's descendants would, in succeeding generations, tend to move down through the upper reaches of the bureaucracy as new generations, closer to each new monarch, filled the highest places. There must have been considerable sources of power in the awarding of office and its emoluments.

The special glory of the Fifth Dynasty must be the reliefs and the portraits of the kings, nobles, high officials and their families that the sculptors produced. Both these categories of works of art show subtle but distinct variations with the forms that preceded them. The reliefs are more intimate in the scenes which they depict, frequently humorous and often with elements of stylization and formality which are remarkable. This may be demonstrated by, for example, the papyrus screen which is laid down on some of the stone-cut reliefs of hunting in the marshes – a favourite subject which suggests that the Delta in northern Egypt was becoming a more familiar place for the nobility and king to visit, a consequence, in all probability, of an increasing ability to drain the marshes which would otherwise have been too water-logged to allow for much settlement or penetration. These reliefs have something of the elegance and formality of Chinese painting.

The records of the careers of the quite ordinary men who achieved success in the service of the kings survive from this time. In several cases it is possible to trace a line of such successful men, forming a small dynasty of builders and architects, civil servants or the priests of a royal temple foundation. Many of the recitals of their services and the appreciation which they were accorded by the king reflect that complacency (some might say smugness) which seems to be fairly typical of the prosperous Egyptian of this period.

From the earliest days of the First Dynasty and from the first attempts at writing and the keeping of records the names and titles of officials and other, lesser folk have been preserved. The great offices of state, those associated with the king directly had their own considerable authority and antiquity reaching back, in all probability, to predynastic times. But even in these early days we read of specialization, of trades, the arts, medicine and the first appearance of professions, in the sense of avocations followed through a lifetime after some form of training or apprenticeship. That these were related either to the membership of the retinue of a king or great noble did not diminish the growing importance which the role of the artist, craftsman or artisan was acquiring.

In the First Dynasty, in the melancholy rolls of the sacrificed dead who were sent to accompany their masters (or mistresses) into the Afterlife, we learn of carpenters, sailors, shipwrights, musicians, hairdressers. In the later dynasties such people lived out their normal span and were to discharge their skills over a lifetime. This may have had a salutary consequence for in the Old Kingdom it is clear that many professions, crafts and trades were practiced in families, father to son, often over extended generations.

The profession of scribe was regarded most highly, not least by the scribes themselves. It seems likely that all the male members of the elite families were literate and in many cases the women were too. Literacy was a prerequisite in the royal service, the upper levels of the priesthood and in the government service. A boy who could read the hieroglyphs and write them skilfully – no mean task – could anticipate a lifetime's employment and its rewards, not the least of which would be the respect, even the envy, of his fellows. The upper levels of the government service and the priesthood could be very valuable situations for individuals of application and enterprise. To be reasonably well placed meant that an office-holder man could benefit family and native village, all very properly.

Artists in every discipline – sculpture, painting, the carving of reliefs – were amongst the most favoured who particularly encouraged the retention of their practices in family groups. We know the names of many of them. Thus one Inkaf was the sculptor who worked on the tomb of the important

Fourth Dynasty queen, Meresankh III, the wife of King Khafre.[7] Another Inkaf, a generation or so later, may have been the son or nephew of the elder Inkaf.[8] A much valued artist was Niankhptah who worked for the great noble Ptahhotep in the Fifth Dynasty.[9] Most unusually, Niankhptah was allowed to 'sign' the reliefs which he designed and of which he no doubt supervised the carving, in Ptahhotep's handsome mastaba at Saqqara, which so vividly pictures life on a great estate at the height of the Old Kingdom's prosperity. The reliefs include a self-portrait of Niankhptah accepting a drink from a boy attendant.

A very confident painter, Seni, was employed by the ruler of the ninth Upper Egyptian nome, the Panopolite, the capital of which was at Akhmim. He claimed that he himself had undertaken the decoration of at least two of the tombs cut into the rocks of a mountain at Hawawish, in which the princes of the nome were buried.[10]

Architects and those who were described by titles such as 'Chief of All the Works of the King' were, not surprisingly, highly regarded. In early times they were often the close relatives of the king himself but later men of a less exalted status who also undertook the supervision of the building of monuments, the building and restoration of temples and, a thriving industry, the building and decoration of the tombs of the great and of lesser dignitaries. One of the finest Old Kingdom statues, now in the Egyptian Museum, Cairo,[11] is of Ti, a high priest in the reign of King Niuserre. He was an important landowner and included the supervision of the funerary complexes devoted to the cults of dead kings. He was evidently able to command the service of the talents of the most skilled artists of the day, for his tomb is brilliantly decorated and he himself is immortalized in one of the most imposing statues surviving in Egypt from any period.

Nekhebu was such an architect who left an autobiographical inscription in which he emphasized his humble beginnings on the pathway to eventual eminence. The impression which he gives of a simple country boy made good is somewhat reduced by the knowledge that his father and grandfather were both Viziers, hence the most powerful men in the Dual Kingdom at the time.[12] Nekhebu's son was also a distinguished public servant. Altogether the family was an example of the dynasties of officials active over several generations.

A feature of life in Old Kingdom Egypt must have been the great festivals and public ceremonies involving the participation of the king. Many of these were extremely elaborate and required very considerable organization and the marshalling of large forces, of singers, musicians and dancers, in addition to the priests and officials who took part. Sneferunefer in the Fifth Dynasty was a professional musician from a family of musicians and he was responsible for the mounting of royal entertainments.[13]

Ka-Hay was a singer in the household of King Neferirkare in the Fifth Dynasty.[14] The story of his son, which is recorded in considerable detail in their family tomb, will serve as an example of how a man of relatively modest origins who lived to become one of the 'Great Ones' (or very nearly) of Egypt in the Old Kingdom. Ka-Hay was a member of a family which had long provided musicians to the court to play and sing in the constant round of ceremonies and for the solace or delight of the king and his companions. Ka-Hay was evidently exceptionally gifted musically and his voice attracted the king's notice. He became something of an intimate of the king and, to show him particular favour, the sovereign gave the order that Ka-Hay's son should be educated with the royal children. For an Egyptian of modest origins this was roughly equivalent to his son being given a place at Eton, with the promise of a fellowship at a senior Oxford college, followed by entry into the upper ranks of the Treasury, the certainty of a peerage, and the affectionate familiarity of the royal family. Fortunate was the boy to whom such a prospect opened; the boy in this case, Ka-Hay's son, was called Nefer.

The one essential element to Nefer's success was that he should become the intimate friend of the king-to-be, the heir to the throne of Egypt, the prince, who in all probability was to reign as Niuserre. All was well; eventually Nefer was named Sole Companion to the king and was the perpetual recipient of his bounty. He progressed in the administration, becoming, eventually Overseer of the Court. It is estimated that he died around the year 2400 BC.

His tomb is a joyous celebration of his life and good fortune. Nefer did not forget his family in the days of his prosperity: when the king gave him his tomb, 'the house of millions of years', so that, as the inscriptions charmingly declare, 'he might grow very beautifully old',[15] Nefer brought his family with him. Numerous adults were buried there, his wife and his father and mother, most of whom seem to have been singers. One of them was even a prophet of the goddess who had charge of ritual music.

The wall reliefs are still gaily painted, rich in colour. They are less sophisticated than the finest work of the time, a shade provincial, it must be admitted, but their charm is in no way diminished by their naïveté. They show life continuing for ever on Nefer's estates in Lower Egypt where the grape harvest is underway and a family pet, a handsome and vigorous cynocephalus baboon, himself helps the workers turn the wine press.[16] In another scene the same baboon stands proudly on the prow of one of Nefer's ships, which is being loaded for the journey to his estates in Upper Egypt, and directs the sailors loading the ship with imperious gestures, a magisterial *baton de commandment* gripped in his paw.[17] We even see carpenters preparing Nefer's sarcophagus, a handsome coffin made in the time-honoured style of a palatial building with recessed walls, a concept which had thus endured for the best part of a thousand years. Nowhere, in the whole of Egyptian art is the delight in life celebrated so joyfully as in Nefer's tomb; nowhere, too is the humour of the Egyptians, a kindly and generous-hearted humour, so well recorded. An engaging feature of Nefer's eternal mansion is that the workers on his estate, the fishermen, sailors, gardeners, and household servants are all named, so that they may share in their master's immortality.

Nefer, his wife Khensuw, and their dog – one of the breed of prick-eared hunting hounds – watch all the activity with evident satisfaction.[18] As is fitting for someone who, despite his eminence, was the scion of a family of musicians, Nefer has a small orchestra included amongst the amenities that he took with him into the tomb.[19] All in all, his tomb portrays a late Old Kingdom idyll.

A greatly respected profession was that of medicine. Many doctors are known from the records of the Old Kingdom and it is remarkable that almost half the names of all doctors known from Ancient Egypt come the Old Kingdom period.[20] This has to be regarded as a tribute to the quality of life in the early centuries of Egypt's existence and it was one that was not to be replicated in other cultures for millennia to come. Not only was medical practice widespread it was also diverse and highly specialized. Every great household had its resident physician; in the royal households there are the names and descriptions of doctors who were apparently specialized in a variety of conditions which would be recognized today: Iny of the Fourth Dynasty, the Chief of Court Physicians, was a specialist in conditions of the abdomen and bowels and in the treatment of body fluids. He was honoured with burial at Giza, near the kings who were his patients.[21] Other specialisms included ophthalmology, gastroenterolgy and proctology.[22]

Niankhsekhmet[23] was favoured by his patient, King Sahure, who, at his request, gave him an inscribed 'false door' for his tomb. The king himself oversaw the carving of the inscription; it was painted blue. Niankhre,[24] also of the Fifth Dynasty, was also Court Physician. He specialized in the treatment of scorpion stings, doubtless a skill which was frequently called upon.

The animals were also cared for in Old Kingdom Egypt and there was a recognized category of practitioners who were veterinarians. At a different level Peseshet was 'Director of Female Physicians',[25] suggesting that there were specialists in gynaecological and related conditions and that there were women who were qualified to practice as doctors.

The work of medical specialists doubtless benefited from the work of the temple staff who specialized in mummification. This involved the complex dissection of the cadaver and much must have been learned about anatomy in the process. It is a remarkable fact that the processes of mummification in the Old Kingdom were much more successful than those of later periods.

An extraordinary survival of what is probably the finest mummy known from Egypt lies deep in a recess of a rock-cut shaft in the tomb of Nefer and Ka-Hay, described earlier. It is the mummy of a man, one of the very few known from the early period: it seems not to be the remains of Nefer, however, since a wooden box laid close to the body bears the name 'Waty'. He lies on his back as though asleep, a sleek and well-fed gentleman, naked, lying as though taking his siesta.[26] His body is perfect. Even the soft tissues of eyelids, lips, and genitals, for example, remain intact and unblemished. He has a small moustache; the outline of his mouth is full and firm. The body seems to have been wrapped in gossamer-fine linens, every part of it, and then bathed in some fine plaster-bearing liquid which when dry, shrank very slightly to provide a perfect outline for the body which was within it. The effect is miraculous.

One of the delights which most ancient Egypt can deliver to its devotees is that the lives of countless Egyptians, of all ranks and none, have been preserved and made available to subsequent generations. The Egyptians were concerned, as are all writers of autobiography, to give a good account of themselves and of the time in which they lived. As a result it is possible for someone living in the modern world to imagine with what confidence, with what certainty indeed, an Egyptian gentleman, a landowner perhaps or a high official of noble rank of the Fifth or Sixth Dynasties, looking out across his estate as evening came on, must have faced life. Order prevailed, the Two Lands were in equilibrium, and the king was secure at the centre of the universe. Not even the assurance of a landed gentleman in nineteenth-century England could quite have equalled it. The tranquillity and order of life in the Valley is demonstrated by the way in which the ordinary daily concerns of the people, the great ones as well as the simple, begin to predominate on the walls of the tombs.

THE HUNT

Amongst the events recorded in the tombs, to ensure their perpetuation in eternity, were the sports of various kinds practiced by the Egyptians, who clearly enjoyed both participating in them and watching them on high days and festivals. Water sports were common, but seem to have been reserved for the lower orders; indeed, to call them 'sports' at all may be overstating what seems, often, to have been little more than good-natured competitions between rival groups of boatmen to see who might throw the opposing crew into the river. Hunting in the marshes was clearly felt to be a more appropriate pastime for a gentleman and many are the representations of Old Kingdom nobles, their families, retainers, and, not infrequently, their pet animals, hunting with spear or throwing-stick the fish and birds with which the Delta teemed. The kings and the great princes hunted the large animals – lion, giraffe, hippopotamus. These occasions were evidently attended by as much protocol and ritual as a hunting excursion by Louis XIV; they were probably as carefully stage-managed and no doubt the king returned to his palace after a hunting trip with a gratifying 'bag'.

There are many scenes in late Old Kingdom *mastabas* of the great nobles and landowners hunting on their estates. The favoured form of the hunt seems to have been the driving of the quarry – gazelle, ibex, hare, sometimes wild cattle – onto corrals; the huntsmen then proceed to slaughter the animals wholesale.

In all the scenes depicting the hunt the *tjesm*, the slender hunting hound, is present, enthusiastically assisting the hunters. The hounds were trained to pursue and harry the prey, wearing them down and remaining with them until the huntsmen arrived to dispatch them. In the later years of the Old Kingdom some nobles chose to decorate their tombs with scenes of sports and recreation. One of the favoured motifs was to show sets of naked boys dancing, flinging themselves about in an acrobatic and energetic program. These, the original gymnopaedie, are matched by other groups of youths wrestling, running races, or leaping over poles held by their companions.[27]

THE EROSION OF THE KINGSHIP

The round of ceremonies in the temples of the Dual Kingdom, the never-ending rituals of the worship of the high gods, were intended to keep in constant equilibrium the security of Egypt and to effect the service of the divinities who determined its life and prosperity. The most essential purpose of the temple rites was to provide the king with his proper context as the incarnation on earth of the divine Horus. Only when Egypt was first in decline after the disintegration of the Old Kingdom, did the king begin more and more to be recognized as mortal. Then his attributions of divinity become largely conventional, the expression of what once had been, rather that the extraordinary phantasm which the combined genius of the propagandists, artists, priests and the king himself contrived to create in the early centuries of dynastic rule.

The rise of the powerful court and official families, to be matched in the next dynasty by the increasing power of the provincial nobles and their consequent detachment from the centre of royal power, contributed to the gradual erosion of the position of the king. It may well be that originally the rise of ordinary men to positions of power was the consequence of a calculated decision by the kings to try to limit the influence of the great nobles. In the Fourth Dynasty most of the power and the significant offices of state had been concentrated in members of the king's close family, a return to the nepotism which prevailed in the Early Dynastic period. These circles increased as the generations went by, and as the bureaucracy became more complex requiring more officials to manage it, the king was obliged to relinquish, little by little, his absolute control of the state machine. No doubt the rise of the priesthoods and the extent to which the temples acquired the revenues of the land, by endowment and by the sort of pious coercion which religious communities have always exercised on the credulous, also contributed to the shift of power away from the king, making it more difficult for him to balance one interest against the other and so allow the royal or state interest to ride supreme over the rest.

Whether the administrators of the Dual Kingdom fully apprehended the decline which the central authority was experiencing and its implications for the future, is not clear. That at least one of the kings understood the necessity of reform is clear from the reign of Djedkare, one of the kings of the later Fifth Dynasty, who ruled for nearly fifty years. He was long remembered as a wise and prudent sovereign who sought to reorganize the central administration and to restore a greater degree of royal control, implying that he recognized that it had been damagingly diminished. He strengthened in particular the administration of Upper Egypt, establishing a headquarters for the purpose in Abydos. But in the end, the pressures of history, the misjudgements of some of his predecessors, the gradual decline of the economy and the rise of the provincial nobles, weighed against the kingship.

KING WENIS – THE PYRAMID TEXTS

Despite the gradual curtailment of the royal status the Fifth Dynasty ended on another note of high achievement. The last king of the dynasty was the Horus Wadjtawy Wenis, whose name is sometimes rendered 'Unas'; he is commemorated by portrait statues of large scale and high quality of production, some of which are only now emerging from the enfolding sands. But the supreme inheritance from Wenis reign is contained in the subterranean chambers of his pyramid at Saqqara, a relatively modest one when compared with the great prototypes at Giza, were found inscribed on the walls, in finely cut hieroglyphs, decorated with a blue paint whose brilliance matches that of medieval heraldry or the illustrations in one of the better Books of Hours, the texts of spells, incantations, and all manner of sacred mutterings which were designed to facilitate the king's journey from this life to his perpetual life beyond the ever-circling stars.

The Pyramid Texts, as they have come to be known, are unique: no other ancient culture has anything even remotely like them.[28] They are presented in the form of 'Utterances', declarations either in the voice of the king or of the gods and spirits who attend him. Many are obviously of considerable antiquity, descending from predynastic times. The chieftains of the predynastic people may also have been regarded as magicians; the Pyramid Texts are full to bursting point of magic.

Many of the texts are written in the form of dialogue, antiphonal exchanges between two or more participants in the great ceremonies, the language of which they record. This again suggests the importance which the Egyptians attributed to dramatic utterance and to play-acting; the Pyramid Texts are a performing script for the king and his attendants on his last great journey to the stars.

The complexity of the language of the texts is multiplied by the Egyptians' enthusiasm for punning. This punning is achieved not only verbally, by using words of similar sound or meaning in differing or related contexts, but also visually by the use of hieroglyphs which convey a meaning by their pictorial form as well. For this reason, quite apart from the immense distance of time over which they have reached us, the Pyramid Texts are literally (and in a special sense, visually) untranslatable.

It is not known when they were collected in the form in which they appear in Wenis' pyramid; certainly it must have been long before his lifetime. They survived throughout Egyptian history, one of the people's most important pieces of cultural impedimenta. In the Middle Kingdom they were inscribed on the interiors of the decorated coffins which replaced the more monumental enclosures for the dead which the Old Kingdom so prodigally employed. In later times still they formed the basis, though often corrupted, of the various forms of what is generally called the Book of the Dead. This took the form of papyrus scrolls buried with the dead, inscriptions in the tombs, and extracts painted onto sarcophagi and mummy wrappings. In their original context, in the pyramid of Wenis, the texts have another dimension: they form a sort of continuous hymn through all the rooms of the pyramid on the walls of which they are engraved, so that the reader (or the spirit of the dead king) moves through them adding the dimension of space to the others in which the texts exist.

The Pyramid Texts are amongst the most complex and certainly the most arcane of the survivals of the minds of the men who lived in Egypt at this time. They are largely impenetrable to the contemporary mind: were they fully comprehensible they would tell more about the Egyptians of the early dynasties than any of the material remains of their time.

Throughout the dynasty it is possible to see a continuous increase in the number of inscriptions and written records with which the kings set down the principal events or preoccupations of their reigns. So extraordinary is the legacy of the visual arts which the Egyptians of the Old Kingdom have left that their literary output can easily be overlooked. It is, however, a remarkable production and is as much a manifestation of the Egyptian spirit's search for expression and fulfilment as is the other artists' work in stone or metal. From this time onwards writing, one of the noblest of the Egyptian arts, may also be recognized as one of the most rewarding to study.

The Egyptians developed to a unique degree the art of both visual and verbal punning: they delighted in the games which words and characters can be encouraged to play with each other. For such games hieroglyphs are exceptionally well suited; because the characters represent actual objects as well as suggesting concepts they are many-levelled and the inscriptions which they make are, in consequence, exceptionally rich and complex. They often, too, sustain a particularly close, sometimes almost a mystical relationship with other aspects of the society from which they sprang, notably belief and custom. In this way the written language becomes another means to perpetuate the life of the society and make it accessible visually, interacting with, for example, the architectural detail of a pyramid or the expression of the ceremonies attending the appearance of the king.

This Egyptian genius for graphic synthesis is shown to special advantage in the variations that they developed in the hieroglyphs which expressed concepts relating to horizon, mountains, and sunrise. The hieroglyph ⊔[29] denotes a mountain, covered with sand; it means 'mountain'. With the addition of another peak it signifies 'foreign land' ⊔⊔.[30] The horizon, 'the place where the sun rises' is represented by the same ideogram, with the addition of the sun's disk rising between the two peaks of the mountain ⊙.[31] A further variation shows the hill lit with rays of the rising sun ⊖.[32] This is the 'hill of the sunrise'; and like the others is an early hieroglyph recorded in the Pyramid Texts. In a stroke of creative genius and by the addition of another element, the hill of sunrise, now suffused with sunlight, becomes an ideogram meaning 'to appear in glory' and is used to mark the appearance of the king, the son of the sun from the Fourth Dynasty onwards, on occasions of high state.

THE SIXTH DYNASTY

King Teti

Again the dynasty changed after Wenis died, presumably fortified for his journey by the efficacy of the texts; once again in all probability, continuity of the line and the blood was ensured by a princess, perhaps Wenis' daughter, who married Teti, the first king of the Sixth Dynasty. If the annals are to be believed, women had ensured the continuity of the royal line since the end of the First Dynasty had been preserved; setting aside the possibility of a *mésalliance* or unlicensed dalliance by one or more of the royal mothers of the kings, the genes of Narmer and his bloodline may still have been handed on to the new dynasty, almost a thousand years after his lifetime – or such at least was the royal fiction.

It was a very different Egypt to which Teti succeeded from that which Narmer knew. Now Egypt was unquestionably the greatest power on earth and seemingly immutable in its institutions and the way of life of its people. Since Netjerykhet's time, over three hundred years earlier, king after king had created superb monuments, cased them in glittering white limestone or other brilliant stone, and laid them about with temples and pavilions, pools and gardens. Everywhere the ordinary Egyptian cast his eyes he would have seen wonders, the whole a concentration of material splendour unexampled in human experience and probably never to be repeated in quite this prodigality and density. For a man born in Wenis' reign and living on into the early years of King Pepi II, seventy years or so later, Egypt must have seemed as eternal and unchanging as she had done since King Khasekhemwy finally achieved the reconciliation of the Two Powers and made order supreme. But in fact the end was approaching.

King Pepi I

There was still much grandeur left, still great works to be done and marvels achieved. The most energetic of the early kings of the dynasty seems to have been Pepi I, who reigned long and built extensively. He was a vigorous administrator and a skillful politician who allied himself in marriage with some of the great provincial dynasts, hoping perhaps that by doing so he could restore the loyalty to the throne of that caste. The erosion of the nobles' support of the throne had come about, ironically, as a result of earlier kings' over-generous grants of land and power to the provincial magnates. Now there was simply little left to give them.

The most remarkable survival from Pepi's reign is a large, standing copper figure of himself, supported by a smaller figure of his son, probably his successor Merenre. The statues are made by beating sheets of copper over a wooden core, a technique pioneered in Sumer, many hundreds of years earlier; the two statues, of father and son, have been restored in recent years. They come from Hierakonpolis, which demonstrates that the ancient Falcon city of predynastic times was still honoured, long after it had ceased to be the focus of the cults which had initiated the drive to unite the Two Lands.

King Pepi II

Merenre did not long succeed his father; there is some evidence that he was in his teens when he died. He was succeeded by the remarkable Pepi II who, according to the annals, came to the throne when he was six years old and reigned for ninety-four years, dying as a centenarian. Though ninety-four years sounds improbable, in the opinion of most authorities the weight of evidence suggests that Pepi's was in fact the longest reign of any king known to history and that there is nothing inherently implausible in the figures attributed to his life span. What is quite certain is that his long life marked the effective end of the Old Kingdom and hence of that great experiment which had been begun so long before by the Thinite kings.

In all probability Pepi was the child of his father's old age; his reign began well. The well-known record of young Pepi's delight at the impending arrival at his court of a dancing dwarf brought to him from Nubia by Harkhuf,[33] the governor of Elephantine, is charming and shows that Egyptian kings were engagingly mortal when they chose to be. Indeed, mortality, or perhaps the want of it, was the principal problem of Pepi's interminable reign.

Stories about Pepi abounded. He is said to have pursued amorously one of his generals, Sasenet, to whose house he was observed creeping after nightfall.[34] He also seems to have been especially attached to one of his high officials, who was known by the affectionate nick-name Hekaib, conferred on him by the king. He was, unusually for a non-royal person, proclaimed a god, his cult surviving for several hundred years at Elephantine, of which he had also been nomarch, though long after Harkhuf.[35]

Pepi must have outlived all of his contemporaries and most of their children. The state atrophied; the power of the magnates grew. The king was still powerful enough to cause a splendid pyramid to be built as his tomb with its attendant magnificent monuments; he was able also to commission appropriate burial places for his wives and family. Pepi seems to have tried to contain the power of the great nobles, which was increasing rapidly throughout the Sixth Dynasty. But the corruption was already too deep; the spark was burned out. Egypt was exhausted and at Pepi's death two centuries of uncertainty and the disruption of its institutions began to descend on Egypt.

10

THE END OF THE OLD KINGDOM

The fundamental dynamic of the society which rose in Egypt in the third millennium was both theocratic and theocentric in a quite literal sense. The prosperity and survival of Egypt was the dominant concern of the Egyptian state; indeed the king, who brought together in his own person all the diverse elements of the natural world, humanity and divinity, was acknowledged as a god precisely because only thus could he, with absolute assurance, determine the fates and ensure that the Egyptian state was protected from all harm. There is thus really no such construct as 'Egyptian religion', as later ages would understand the term: to an Egyptian of the early third millennium the concept of *religion* would be meaningless. The integration of identity, survival, the state, and the rituals recognizing the gods' (or perhaps a sole divinity's) concern for Egypt was absolute. The most disastrous consequence of the approaching crisis at the end of the Old Kingdom, when in some cases even the shrines of the gods and the supposedly eternal mansions of the kings were ruthlessly destroyed by the mob, was the separation of religion into a discrete function.

The rulers of the Middle Kingdom, who reimposed order on Egypt were, it might be said, gods only by courtesy. The priesthood, already emerging as a power in the state in the middle of the third millennium, grew more powerful still and contributed in large part to the collapse of the Old Kingdom. The priests emerged at last with a significance almost equal to the king's power. Gradually religion (as the modern world might understand the term) became separated from its exclusive relationship with the kingship and became something to whose benefits all men might individually aspire. By the time of the New Kingdom, in the second half of the second millennium, the essential Egyptian ethos, as promulgated during the thousand years to the end of the Old Kingdom, was hopelessly and irrevocably corrupt.

The Fifth and Sixth Dynasties represented the culmination of the long sequence which started with the little communities which began to cling to the Valley in the sixth and fifth millennia. The supreme elegance and confidence of Fifth and Sixth Dynasty art is the most emphatic statement of this final triumph of the Egyptian spirit. Paradoxically – and Egypt is ever the land of paradox – the seeds of change, even of destruction, were already germinating, soon to flower and smother the true, native spirit.

However it was achieved, the absolute role of the king was diminished. From being something very like the immanent manifestation of the supreme divinity, he became merely one of many gods; he was content to row in the barque of Re or to act as his scribe, a far cry from his earlier unique divinity. As the king's power declined and that of the temples' rose, the great nobles were not slow to assert their interest and that of their families.

THE RISE OF THE MAGNATES

The king needed allies: the reign of Shepseskaf suggests that the advance of the priests was occasionally resisted. There is evidence that more and more the king rewarded his courtiers and officers with grants of land, drawn from what must at the outset have seemed an inexhaustible bank, from the royal domains. But as the prosperity of the magnates increased, so did their arrogance; over the generations they lost their loyalty to the crowns, other than in the increasingly merely formal recognition of the king's sovereignty. The position was still more acute in the case of the nomarchs, the governors of the provinces into which Egypt was immemorially divided: there were generally forty-two of them. In the later Old Kingdom these governorships, once the gift of the king conferred on those servants on whose service he could rely, became more and more frequently regarded as hereditary fiefs, descending from father to son with only a passing nod to the royal prerogatives. The nomarchs, 'great overlords' as they were called, became, in effect, independent princes, ruling their districts with little concern either for the central authority or, it may in general be suspected, for the welfare of their subjects who, in earlier times, always had recourse to the justice of the king if ever they had cause to show oppression or exploitation either by their masters, if they were workers on the land, or by the officials of the state.

As the pride of the provincial nobles increased, the state which they maintained becoming more and more superb at the expense of the dues which should have been applied to the royal and central government, another force began to emerge which likewise demanded recognition and reward. This was the class of 'new men'; artisans, craftsmen, and specialists whose particular skills, practiced in a trade or a vocation, brought them prosperity and the desire for advancement for themselves and their families.

All of these influences, wholly alien to the original social structure of the unified kingdom which the Thinite princes had made, began to wear away the foundations of the state. Though this must be speculation further down the scale still, it is not unreasonable to suspect that similar pressures for advancement (in the next world as much as in this one, for this was, after all, Egypt) began to affect even the lowly amongst the population; it may be speculated that the most potent of political motivations, envy, was already manifesting itself. It would be contained for long centuries because of the nature of Egyptian society but beneath the surface it must have been suppurating ripely.

The diminishing of the royal authority and its decline from the status of absolute divinity must have allowed these influences to grow and to gain a hold from which they could not be uprooted. The king might for the while attempt to limit the power of the priests as Shepseskaf evidently did: the incitement of the pious mob and some effective religious sleight of hand would soon set the balance in the temples' favour once again. Similarly Pepi II, whilst still in command of his powers, would try to hold back the arrogance of the nobles, but to no avail. They could continue to assert themselves and to ride roughshod over every interest but their own, no doubt excepting the interests of the priesthoods, for those of a recalcitrant nobility and an avaricious clergy have always found common cause.

But there was a still greater menace facing Egypt, from beyond the hitherto secure frontiers with which she had surrounded herself. The phenomenon which now bore down in Egypt was one which had been piling up, like a dense and threatening storm cloud on the horizon, and which had already brought destruction and black ruin to other lands around.

INCURSIONS FROM THE DESERT

The changes which overcame Old Kingdom Egypt were similar to those experienced by other Near Eastern societies in the late third millennium. The dangers which now beset the Valley, and in doing so unleashed all the tensions and dissensions which were ready to tear the fabric of Egypt asunder, emerged from the desert. The menace was represented in real terms by the tribes and savage hordes which had always lived in the heartlands of the deserts, alternately looking with envy and contempt (to judge at least by later, similar cases) at the mighty civilization which they now saw lying open and vulnerable to them.

The way of life of the desert peoples was markedly different from those of the Sumerians and the Egyptians. They eschewed the cities which were so typical of Sumerian society, and they did not attempt to create the highly centralized nation-state which was Egypt's particular and unique contribution to the history of politics. Some had, of course, come to settle around the coasts and in the oases but many were in all probability nomadic though closely linked by the complex but enduring network of familial and clan ties which have always bound the desert peoples together. To the Sumerians the majority of the desert people were those 'who know not grain', just as to the

Egyptians they were 'the sand-dwellers' and were accorded other, less restrained, sobriquets.

The desert people had long standing and mutually supportive relationships with the settled people. The nomads, to use a term which is probably anachronistic in that they did not necessarily display the cohesion and accepted customs of those to whom the term may be applied today, were important in the exchange systems on which so much ancient trade depended and for the provision of livestock from the herds which they managed. However, towards the last quarter of the third millennium this relationship began to change and the desert dwellers began to scent the prospect of political power and, hence, access to the wealth and sophistication of the Valley peoples.

SARGON THE GREAT

It would be remarkable if one man could intervene in the processes of history and effect such a degree of total change as now ensued throughout what once was called 'the Fertile Crescent'; nonetheless, an official in the court of the King of Kish called Sharrukhin, and known more familiarly as Sargon, now emerged as a leader of exceptional authority and charisma. He swept to power over the fragmented and divided city states of Sumer which after more than a thousand years of brilliant flowering were now showing signs of exhaustion and incipient collapse.[1]

Sargon now established a glittering capital at Agade (whose whereabouts is still unknown) and a dynasty which endured for more than a hundred years – a creditable duration for any political construct in Sumer. He absorbed most of the culture of Sumer, only pausing to semiticize the names of the gods, and to adapt the Akkadian language to Sumerian cuneiform, to which in fact it was particularly ill-suited. He, or his grandson and most important successor Naram-Sin, is said to have fought a battle against and defeated a king called Manium. It was once believed, before the dating of the Akkadians was brought down to the period that it occupies today, that Manium was Menes, the mythical founder of the First Dynasty of Egypt; by accepted chronologies today this is impossible.

It is, however, possible that Sargon and his Egyptian contemporaries Wenis, Teti, and Pepi I may have known of each other's existence. From the Fourth Dynasty Egypt traded with Ebla[2] (Tell Mardikh), a great emporium in northern Syria, which also maintained relations with Dilmun in the Arabian Gulf.[3] Doubtless too Sargon's claim[4] that his empire ran from the Lower Sea (the Arabian Gulf) to the Upper Sea (the Mediterranean) would have meant that the Levantine cities where his agents and armies were active would have made his name known to the Egyptians. Sargon's empire even penetrated to the Holy Land of Dilmun in the Bitter Sea (another name for the Arabian Gulf), but whether the Egyptians either knew of this or cared if they did, is not known.

Region-wide collapse

Within a century or so of Sargon's reign and during the lifetimes of his immediate heirs, Egypt experienced a collapse which must have made the fall of even the more populous Sumerian cities seem trivial events in comparison. The last quarter of the third millennium was as decisive in the course of history as was the last quarter of the fourth. Whereas, however, the earlier period had seen the introduction of a time of exceptional creativity and achievement the end of the third marked the appearance of darker influences, of flames flickering at the edges of the glorious cultures which were swiftly consumed.

THE LOW NILES

It is really not at all clear why this cataclysm should have hit so extended a region as it did, embracing Egypt and much of Iraq, and reverberating up the eastern Mediterranean coast. It is likely that it was provoked not only by those influences which came out of the desert but also by another of those relatively minor climatic changes which it is now recognized have had a profound an effect on man's social progress so frequently. As far as Egypt was concerned, it is known that there was a series of low Nile floods,[5] of failures in the inundation, towards the end of the Old Kingdom. In normal circumstances the Nile served its children well but occasionally an exceptionally high or an exceptionally low Nile could bring, on the one hand, devastating floods, on the other unassuageable drought; in either event, it meant tragedy on an immense scale to the people of the Valley.

As the Sixth Dynasty moved towards its end, the political uncertainties rising from the decline of the royal authority and the increasing fragmentation of the administration coincided with a dramatic change in Egypt's environment. The millennium which had seen the phenomenal development of Egyptian society and culture had enjoyed a period of relatively benign climatic conditions in which agriculture and animal husbandry flourished. The era of poor Niles heralded the onset of a marked aridity when the summer temperature soared; the climate which now characterized Egypt was to remain largely unchanged until the present day.

The low Niles at the end of the Old Kingdom and the hardship which they would have produced amongst the whole population of Egypt which depended upon assured production from the fields, would have been the cause of unrest throughout the Dual Kingdom. The extortions of the feudal nobility (which are clear, if only from the occasional inscription of one who recorded the fact that he stored grain and resources to be distributed to his people, contrasting this with what otherwise might be considered the customary depredations of those of his rank) would have added to the unrest. The king's power was reduced; the army was probably disaffected and the temples were no doubt extracting whatever advantage they could. The Asiatics and other barbarian tribes sensed the time was right and with devastating effect they fell on Egypt.

The causes of the decline and disintegration of the order established by the kings and which had endured from the time of Aha to the reign of Pepi II, were a combination of what has become a familiar phenomenon in the history of nations. Climate change, gradual in operation but insidious in outcome, adversely affected the social economy of Egypt. Short term political decisions, designed to relieve the problems of the moment with little concern for the longer term, the over-rewarding of powerful elements in the state eroded the central authority whilst advancing the power of the magnates, who were not slow to take advantage of conditions which were so much to their interest. Perhaps for the first time but certainly not for the last, a breakdown of the dominant political structure occurred in the wake of economic crisis and the rise of too powerful subjects, a combination of pressures which an ancient governmental system could not withstand.

The most remarkable conclusion about the decline of the Old Kingdom, despite the trauma attending the end of her most fertile period of the highest achievement, was that Egypt still had two thousand years of history, much of it glorious, still to enjoy. The ancient kings could at least have that satisfaction, from their home beyond the Imperishable Stars.

There are several of what purport to be eye-witness accounts of the calamities which now befell Egypt; one of these survives in the form of a text which has come to be known as 'the Admonitions of Ipuwer'.[6] In this long, mutilated poem, one of the treasures of Egyptian literature and amongst the oldest known surviving texts, Ipuwer, a wise man, laments that the king is old, secure in his palace, unaware of Egypt's sufferings which are kept from him by venal courtiers. The catastrophes which have struck Egypt are twofold: the incursion of foreigners who have flooded into the Valley unchecked and the total reversal of the established social order. This aspect of the disaster, the envy and rancour of the lesser people in the society, is indeed the most complained of: servant girls can usurp the places of their mistresses, officials are forced to do the bidding of uncouth men and the children of princes are dashed against the wall, all inversions of the order of nature profoundly shocking to the observer who records the events of this melancholy and unprecedented time. It is not, however, certain that the 'Admonitions' are quite what they seem to be. It may be that they are an example of a favourite Egyptian literary device, the scribal exercise, in this case probably written well after the events which it claims to describe.[7] Nonetheless the 'Admonitions' do express vividly what must have been the dismay of those to whom the disintegration of the established order was catastrophic.

There is little doubt that a large part of the destruction of royal and noble tombs (other than the apparently wholesale destructions at the end of the First Dynasty) occurred during this time. Admittedly it was nothing new; tombs were always there to be pillaged not only by robbers seeking their precious contents but also by architects and master builders seeking readily available supplies of cut stone. But the First Intermediate Period undoubtedly witnessed the destruction of much of what had survived from the brilliant centuries of the Old Kingdom. The wonder is that so much still remained for later generations to speculate with awe on what splendours must have attended the lives of kings and nobles alike.

That the Egyptians of later centuries were not entirely indifferent to the depredations that successive destroyers of the ancient tombs, who included kings as well as less exalted robbers, is shown by the efforts of the eldest son of King Ramesses II, Prince Khaemwaset of the Nineteenth Dynasty. He was the High Priest of Ptah and set out on a deliberate policy of identifying, recording and restoring the monuments of those who had preceded his family on the thrones of Egypt. He was his father's Crown Prince; sadly, he died before the immensely long-lived Ramesses and Egypt lost one who would probably have been a worthy and enlightened king.

The Egyptians themselves looked back to the third millennium as a Golden Age, where there was believed to have been a harmony amongst all things. They identified it with the rule of the great god Re, identified in turn with the sun by the theology of Heliopolis, with Saturn in other philosophies. Re however grew old: the poet described his bones becoming silver, his flesh gold, his hair and beard lapis lazuli. Even in describing the decline of an age the Egyptians could not disavow poetic imagery which recalled their predilection for sumptuous and costly materials, brought to them from distant lands with arduous toil.

THE FIRST INTERMEDIATE PERIOD

There is a small but telling irony in the collapse of the Old Kingdom and of all that it represented, which reveals itself now when considering the direction from which came the final impetus which toppled the established structure of the state. At the end of the fourth millennium influences from Sumer or Elam (and perhaps from the Gulf) reached Egypt and seem to have acted as wholly benign stimuli, contributing to the acceleration of the rate of growth of the embryonic Pharaonic state prodigiously. A thousand years later it was once again influences from the east which entered the Valley but this time, to destroy and not to build.

Certainly, after the end of the third millennium matters in Egypt were never wholly the same again. The upheavals of this time continued for more than a century; it was remarkable enough that anything at all survived. This time of trouble is known to Egyptologists as the First Intermediate Period; during it there is evidence of increased contact with eastern lands, not all of it the consequence of conflict. Trade obviously continued with some vigour and perhaps surprisingly the times produced some of the finest literature to survive from Egypt, of which the Admonitions of Ipuwer is an example but by no means the only one.[8]

After Pepi II's death he was succeeded by the son of his old age, Merenre II, who seems to have reigned only for a year when he in turn was succeeded by a queen, Nitocris (Nitiqret).[9] At this point history slides into legend: Nitqret is said to have wrought vengeance on the mob which had murdered Merenre her brother and then herself committed suicide.

STABILITY VERSUS DECLINE

Manetho, the historian of Ptolemaic times, dramatically categorized the ephemeral Seventh Dynasty as 'Seventy kings in Seventy days'. The Eighth Dynasty, ruling from Memphis and probably related to the kings of the Sixth Dynasty, managed to maintain some sort of order in the region of the ancient capital, but with little influence elsewhere. One of these kings, Hakare Ibi, contrived to build a pyramid at Saqqara which contained a recension of the Pyramid Texts.[10] Another, Neferkahor, held on to the throne for four years, during which time he issued decrees, even directing the Governor of Upper Egypt on what offerings should be made in the temples on the occasion of his accession.[11]

Occasionally there are glimpses of what were obviously attempts to maintain some sort of order in the Dual Kingdom, or in what then remained of it. Iuu was Vizier during the Eighth Dynasty;[12] he was a devotee of Anubis and was buried at Abydos. Conditions were not so far gone that he was prepared to forgo the sacred unguents which he was entitled to have buried with him. Far away from Memphis it was evidently easier to maintain something like the customary life of a prosperous individual; thus Merery was a priest in the temple of Hathor at Denderah.[13] He assumed an impressive repertoire of titles and describes himself as the successor of the nomarch of the Sixth Upper Egyptian nome, of which Denderah was the capital. The last king of this shadowy dynasty was Demedjibtowy,[14] who was overthrown by a powerful contender for the kingship from a family of princes whose seat was at Heracleopolis.

That there was unrest in parts of the country is indicated in some of the funerary inscriptions of the time. Thus Rehu, an official residing at Akhmim, the capital of the Ninth Upper Egyptian nome records fighting between rival forces from the north and south of the country during the transition between the Eighth and Ninth Dynasties.[15] Akhmim was on the frontier between the two rival forces, in a confrontation which the kings in Memphis evidently lost. Rehu was however still able to commission an attractively decorated tomb though the work is not as fine as the best of the Old Kingdom. He also records bull-fights, a popular spectator sport of the region which evidently continued to be held and which Rehu evidently very much enjoyed. That standards were not wholly lost is also indicated by the tomb of Setka at Elephantine which again is far from the centre of affairs where such disputes as there were seem principally to have been located.[16]

The rise of the Heracleopolitans

The Heracleopolitan rulers who provided the Ninth and Tenth Dynasties gradually extended the area over which they had control and by the time the Tenth Dynasty was established they were in command of much of Lower Egypt and the south to the borders of the lands controlled by the princes of Thebes. The Heracleopolitan dynasty was to survive for about a hundred years. Its founder was one Akhtoy, nomarch of the Twentieth nome of Upper Egypt.[17] Exasperated by the dismal vacillations of the kings in Memphis he seized control of Middle Egypt and proclaimed himself king. He imposed a greater degree of control on the nomarchs (of whose number he had recently been one) which was generally unwelcome; he had a posthumous reputation for rapacity and cruelty which may have been the revenge of the nomarchs whom he sought to circumscribe. According to Manetho he went mad and was killed by a crocodile, an end which several kings of Egypt seem to have encountered, a fact which makes its probability questionable. He was regarded as the legitimate king by much of the country and his dynasty regarded themselves as the true successors of the Sixth Dynasty kings.

Wahkare Akhtoy and Ankhtifi

Wahkare Akhtoy III was a long-reigning monarch, holding the throne for about fifty years.[18] He was supported by one of the few great princes of the time, Ankhtifi, the nomarch of Edfu and Heliopolis. As a counterbalance to Ipuwer the autobiography of Ankhtifi is revealing.[19] Ankhtifi was not inclined to underrate his own achievements, describing himself as 'the beginning and the end of mankind, such a man as had never before been seen, whose equal would never again appear'. Despite this generous assessment of his own significance enough is known of his history to suggest that he did attempt to provide some aid to the people of his province, indicating both that their hardship was real and that some sort of relatively benign authority was not wholly lost. Ankhtifi's tomb at Mo'alla is very prettily decorated and indicates that not all sense of quality and the ability to achieve it were lost at this time.

Ankhtifi was also a partisan of Neferkare, one of the more successful rulers of the Tenth Dynasty who managed to extend his control over much of the north of Egypt as well as parts of the south.[20] Nubian mercenaries were recruited by the Heracleopolitans; one of these was Seni who lived and was buried at Gebelein.[21] His stela shows him with his wife, his sons, servants and two alert, well behaved hounds, who sit obediently before him.

Several dynasties of local princes are known from this time. A succession of rulers with the name Djehuynakht maintained some state at Hermopolis (ancient Khmun); the family is known from the Eighth Dynasty.[22] One of the Djehutynakhts skilfully allied himself with the victorious founder of the Eleventh Dynasty, King Nebhetepre Montuhotep II (2061–2010 BC); another was ruling until the Twelfth, during the reign of the great King Senwosret III (1878–1814 BC), suggesting that the family had a notable ability to survive. Their rule embraced the Thirteenth, Fifteenth and Sixteenth nomes.

The rise of Thebes

Meanwhile the star of the princes of Thebes was rising. For much of the time that the two families ruled their respective domains they maintained relations which, in diplomatic parlance, were 'proper'. Gradually however the Theban house, whose rise to fortune has been promoted by a noble ancestor, Inyotef who had proclaimed himself King of Upper and Lower Egypt[23] increased their influence at the expense of their contemporaries in Heracleopolis, further to the north. His pretensions to the sovereignty were not generally accepted however, though later he was awarded the posthumous status of the founder of the Eleventh Dynasty. Eventually his great-grandson, Nebhetepre Montuhotep II was to reunite the Valley under his rule and he became undisputed king; this did not happen until many years into his long reign however. The opposition of the Heracleopolitans and their allies required Nebhetepre Montuhotep to fight many demanding campaigns before he could savour the fruits of being the Dual King in truth. Thus began the Middle Kingdom.

The First Intermediate Period was notable for the importation into Egypt of many new influences from abroad. Trade, after a decline in the early years, flourished and Egypt shared in the general prosperity which the Near and Middle East as a whole enjoyed in the decades on either side of the start of the second millennium BC.

One small but significant aspect of Egyptian life received a substantial advance during this time. Dogs had always been valued and respected members of the great households, as hunters, guards and companions. This last aspect of the long-standing relationship between dogs and humans, which the Egyptians were the first to institutionalize and to integrate the dog firmly into their society, now took on a new, extended dimension and the dog became a beloved companion, honoured in life and mourned in death. Although, as we have seen dogs were the favoured companions of the Great Ones from the earliest days of the kingship, their acceptance generally in the society seems to take on a new character in the First Intermediate Period and extends into the coming Middle Kingdom when the dog becomes a familiar component of every Egyptian family of substance. The dog which principally was to enjoy this privileged position was the *tjesm,* the ancient, ubiquitous, prick-eared Egyptian hunting hound.[24]

The scarab

It is during this period that the Egyptians began to make in notable quantity one of their most typical products, the scarab seal. In the same late third and early second millennia the Arabian Gulf traders also developed a highly distinctive form of seal (as distinctive indeed as the scarab was to be), a circular domed stamp, its reverse often quartered and pierced with one or more dotted circles with the designs, often of exceptional liveliness, being incised on the face or obverse.[25] Very occasionally seals in the form of scarabs are found in one site in the Gulf at this time, Failaka in the Bay of Kuwait, suggesting direct contact with Egypt.[26] It is fair to speculate, in view of their often remarkable similarities of design, which one came first and whether the Egyptians adapted the circular Gulf seals (which seem to have originated in Bahrain), adapted them to the not dissimilar form of the scarab beetle and, typically, turned them into something completely Egyptian. Occasionally there are other suggestive correspondences between the design of the Gulf seals and Egyptian forms which cannot altogether be explained by chance or the common response to similar needs or occasions. Contact and familiarity through trade are the most probable explanations.

A CHANGED WORLD

But if trade continued between the centres of power in Egypt, however much these had changed as had the world outside, the soul of Egypt, if a nation may be said to possess so intangible a faculty, was changed still more. When stability was restored the forms and eternal marks of Egyptian society survived virtually intact, but its essential god-ordained nature was never more quite to be recalled, as it had been during the first glorious millennium when Egypt was young. The process of growth was complete: Egypt was now mature, a vehicle as every individual and every state must be, for influence and stimulus from outside.

The individual in the state now began to assert himself, just as the state began to assert itself as an individual entity. The corporate nature of the Egyptian state, unified under the immanent divine ruler, shattered, and the interests of the individual rose supreme. The fierce characteristic and individuality of the desert people may have been responsible, at least in part, for this transformation in the nature of Egypt. The idea of the society being devoted wholly to the promotion of the divine now began to fade; though other peoples would proclaim themselves 'chosen' or suggest that their society's rulers were determined solely by reference to the divine, no society after the collapse of the Old Kingdom in Egypt ever approximated to its unity of the human and divine, or demonstrated so absolutely the indivisibility of the two.

The world beyond Egypt's borders was stirring into life; the course of the next four thousand years was beginning to be set. The states which were emerging belonged, more evidently than ever Egypt did, to the world of modern man. Old Kingdom Egypt really was the ultimate sophistication of the late Neolithic society, raised to the dimension of a nation-state, written not only large but in hieroglyphs. The identity between man and god which was one of the essential elements in early Egyptian belief was swept away by the changes which supervened in the aftermath of the Old Kingdom's decline. When the king was recognized as the god he drew all humanity into himself; through him it was renewed and perpetuated. But now man and god were separated, forever.

At the same time, from the same sources, another terrible uncertainty began to manifest itself. In the semitic mind there was no certainty of the survival of the individual after death; indeed, most semites who had considered the question at all clearly believed that at death the individual was extinguished. This concept, of course, struck at all the accepted canons of Egyptian belief; if, at one time, the King alone had been certain of immortality, for hundreds of years all Egyptians above the humblest levels of society had believed in the prospect of a well-endowed and agreeable existence in a sort of eternalized Nile Valley, where the crops grew more lushly even than they did in the Valley itself. Egypt clung to the outward form of her rituals and observances but increasingly the centre of her belief was hollow. The glory, quite literally, had departed. The institutions of Egypt were restored by the kings of the Middle Kingdom; like the unification more than a thousand years earlier this reconsolidation of the Two Lands was achieved by a southern family. They were princes of the region around Thebes which for the first time now comes to prominence.[27] Successive Amenemhats and Montuhoteps vied with one another in the complexity of their throne names and in their dedication to the restoration of the unity and grandeur of Egypt.

The Twelfth Dynasty which followed was one of the high points of the Egyptian experience; it will also serve as the witness of the change which had come over the Two Lands. One of its greatest sovereigns was Senwosret III who reigned at the beginning of the second millennium BC. He was a remarkable ruler, wise, compassionate and brave; he was long remembered.

He caused himself to be represented in a series of portraits which are quite unique in the Egyptian canon. Though he was indisputably still the most august sovereign in the world of the time, Senwosret chose to have himself represented naturalistically, often without the trappings of divine authority with which it had hitherto been considered appropriate to invest a royal portrait in Egypt. But by his time, the gods had gone from Egypt. Whereas Menkaure could face the world smiling with divine assurance, attended by divinities, Senwosret shows himself as a man full of years, weary and haggard with the awareness of the responsibilities of rule. His face is drawn, careworn but sensitive, almost suffering; it is the portrait of an incarnate god who has looked into the innermost sanctuary and found it an empty room.

11

EASTWARDS FROM EGYPT

The north eastern quadrant of Africa has a long coastline due west of the Arabian peninsula; Egypt and Arabia share much of the Red Sea. As a consequence of Egypt's geographical location, lying at the precise point where influences from north and south, east and west tend to converge the Valley was, particularly in historic times, a sort of cultural sump into which these many diverse influences flowed. That the Egyptian personality remained pristine and distinct in its earliest manifestations despite these infusions was a tribute to the sturdy roots put down by the earliest immigrants.

Underlying much of what has gone before in this study is the recognition that many scholars of an earlier generation believed that Egypt and Sumer had a common ancestry, whilst others attributed the impetus for the later phases of Egypt's civilization to the efforts of Sumerian colonists. Some have believed in a 'dynastic race',[1] representing them as invaders following the standards of Horus, who came into the Valley as conquerors. Similarly, the primacy of Egypt, as the heartland of the sun Kingdoms, began to be argued forcefully by the diffusionists, who saw all the great historic cultures of the ancient Near East, South America and ultimately of Europe, having their common origins in Egypt. Neither of these theories has much support today.

In more recent years scholars have been guarded in accepting the direct involvement of the Sumerians in Egypt because of the formidable barrier of the great deserts which lie between Mesopotamia and Egypt and the equally formidable distance represented by the sea route, which is the only alternative access to the Nile Valley; nor has there been any archaeological evidence of a Mesopotamian presence in Egypt, with the exception of the occasional find of small, generally disassociated objects. Three factors in particular have begun to qualify this opinion: first, the recognition of the significance of such material evidence of Mesopotamian motifs and iconography which have been found in the context of late predynastic and Early Dynastic Egypt; second, the undoubted similarities between Mesopotamian beliefs, rituals and cults especially those which became associated with the Egyptian kingship and, third; the most recent developments in the study of the archaeology of Arabia.

The Arabian peninsula was virtually virgin territory, archaeologically speaking, until a generation ago; it is vast, a small continent with a wide variety of different environments and societies within its borders. Those borders are the natural ones of sea, mountain and desert, and whilst much of its land surface is harsh and inhospitable, around the edges of the deserts, on the coasts, and in the great oases, life has flourished, in all probability for as long as man has been a bipedal hominid. As befits so large an expanse of territory, approximately the size of the whole of Western Europe, Arabia contains many disparate traditions and many differing archaeological regions. Each part of Arabia reveals a past which is distinct, the product of climate, topography and the influence of other cultures.

Far more archaeological research has been carried out in eastern Arabia and on the islands and the western coastal states of the Arabian Gulf than in other regions of Arabia. This work has centred on successive seasons of survey and excavation carried out by Danish teams, working there since the early 1950s. The results of this work have often been dramatic and far reaching.[2] First came the wholly unexpected discovery of Ubaid period artefacts which were identified in a number of sites in north-eastern Saudi Arabia.[3] The majority of the pottery found was Ubaid III, dated to c. 3800 BC, hence equivalent to the early Naqada I period in Egyptian prehistory. Subsequently Ubaid evidences have been found on sites all down the Arabian coast and on several of the islands.

A particularly important series of excavations revealed a considerable culture flourishing in eastern Arabia and the Gulf from the early third millennium BC. The most extensive evidence of this culture has come from Bahrain, which was its centre from c. 2200 BC. Bahrain is now generally identified with Dilmun, the Sumerian archetypal Holy Land, the home of the gods and a place of primeval innocence. Dilmun was also the centre of a wide-ranging and long-lasting mercantile tradition, which is extensively documented in Sumerian sources and in the records of their successors, the Akkadians and the Old Babylonians.[4]

Whilst several of the surviving references to Dilmun celebrate its island character it appears that the centre of Dilmun shifted over the centuries from what may have been its earlier location in eastern Arabia, with important settlements on the island of Tarut and inland near Abqaiq; only later, it appears, did it come to mean mainly the principal Bahrain island. There a settlement was established on the northern shore late in the third millennium, which was continuously occupied and rebuilt down to post-Alexandrian times and beyond. A monumental temple site, also on the north of the island near the village of Barbar, was rebuilt three times between 2200 BC and 1700 BC approximately.[5] This appears to have been consecrated to a divinity associated with water, probably Enki, the Sumerian god of the sweet waters under the earth, the Lord of the Abyss, though a possibility remains that Ninhursaq, the Sumerian mother goddess, Enshag (the son of

(a)

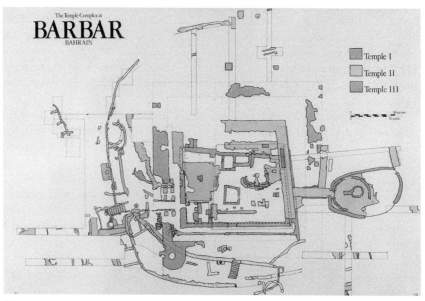

The Temple Complex at
BARBAR
BAHRAIN

Temple I
Temple II
Temple III

(b)

Enki), or Šamaš/Utu the sun god, may also be commemorated there. In the vicinity of the Barbar temple site and indeed in much of the northern reaches of the island are extensive and so far largely unexcavated remains, many of which are probably temples or cult structures. Dilmun was exceptional in its reputation for sanctity and there is little doubt that many great divinities were honoured there.[6]

Bahrain is remarkable for the extraordinary density of its fields of grave mounds. Approximately two hundred thousand very well constructed mounds have been recorded in Bahrain, the majority dating from the late third/early second millennia and thus matching the time of Dilmun's special importance to the people of the Mesopotamian cities who traded with the islands.[7] This time coincided with the latter part of the Old Kingdom, the period of decentralization in Egypt known as the First Intermediate Period and most of the Middle Kingdom, thus representing the Fifth to the Twelfth Dynasties.

Dilmun acted as the entrepôt for the business conducted by Mesopotamian merchants and their counterparts from the great, bleak, brick-built cities of the Indus Valley, like Moenjodaro and Harappa. Dilmun's trade routes also encompassed the hinterland of Arabia, Iran, Afghanistan, Anatolia, and most important, the major resource of copper located in what is today the Sultanate of Oman.

The dominant concern of the Gulf's trade in the mid third-millennium and later was the movement of copper, from the rich mines of Oman to the Sumerian cities, which were almost entirely without natural resources. Ancient mine workings dating from the third millennium are to be found in northern Oman and communities concerned with copper's extraction, smelting, and distribution, were established along the coast of what is today the United Arab Emirates, particularly at Umm an-Nar, a small island just off the shore of the modern state of Abu Dhabi at Hili, a settlement in the great Buraimi oasis, at Dalma, an island lying off Abu Dhabi and at Bat and Ibri in the Sultanate.[8]

The Dilmunites, whose far-ranging exploits took them not only to the Indus Valley but northwards, deep into Syria and Anatolia and, in all

---

Figure 11.1 At Barbar, a village in the north of Bahrain in the Arabian Gulf, a large late-third/early-second millennium temple was built on the north shore in three stages, the first of which coincided approximately with the closing years of the Old Kingdom. The temple itself is a handsome construction (a) but its most notable feature is the presence of a Temple Oval, a mound of pure white sand held in place by a revetment the plan of which (b) recalls the oval structure at Hierakonpolis of nearly a thousand years earlier and the other examples known from sites in Mesopotamia, including Khafaje in northern Sumer (see pl. 10b).

Sources: Illustrations: (a) Author; (b) Plan of the temple structure. From M. Rice, *The Temple Complex at Barbar, Bahrain*, Manama, 1983: 29.

probability, to the Levantine coast, were intrepid seamen and adventurous in the search for new markets. They were undeterred by distance; like those of their Mesopotamian contemporaries their ships were versatile, seaworthy vessels. A discovery at a site on the Bay of Kuwait of the model of a sailing craft has been dated to *c.*4000 BC.[9] The people of the ancient Gulf were, indeed, the first to devise sailing craft capable of cutting across the ocean.

The archaeology of Dilmun and of the island of Bahrain in particular, though it is yet relatively little known, in fact has a history extending over more than one hundred years. The first report on the antiquities of Bahrain was the work of Captain E.L. Durand, a British civil servant employed by the Viceroy's office in Calcutta, who visited the islands in 1878–9. His subsequent report on his visit 'On the Antiquity of the Bahrain Islands' was published in two versions,[10] one for the Viceroy's Office, the other for The Royal Society for Asian Affairs.[11] He addressed a meeting of the Society in 1880 which prompted the first scholarly analysis of ancient Dilmun in modern times. This was the work of the Society's director, Sir Henry Creswick Rawlinson, a leading scholar of the day, who commented with great erudition on Durand's text in his commentary on Durand's report.[12] Rawlinson observed that 'Dilmun' might convey the meaning 'The Blessed Isle'.[13] This attribution of holiness to Dilmun is crucial to an understanding of its character. It was the primeval, archetypal Holy Land to the Sumerians and, it may be suspected, perhaps to other still earlier peoples who may have lived in the Gulf and eastern Arabia.

Durand was followed to Bahrain by two well-known nineteenth-century travellers, Theodore Bent and his wife, in the late 1880s. Bent presented a report on his visit to the Royal Geographical Society[14] and in the discussion which followed Cecil H. Smith of the British Museum toyed with the idea that Bahrain might have had some special significance to the Egyptians. Smith suggested that 'To Nefer', accepted as one of the Egyptian names for the land of Punt, one of the most frequent loci cited in later times as the home of the gods, might in fact mean 'the Holy Island' and refer to the island of Bahrain.[15] Then in 1906 Colonel F.B. Prideaux conducted the first scientific excavation of Bahrain's most notable antiquities, the grave mounds, particularly a group at Aali, which had also attracted Durand's interest.[16] Subsequently these structures, many of which are very large, became known as the Royal Tombs, the putative burial places of the ancient kings of Dilmun, dating from the late third millennium BC.

It was probably Prideaux' report which came to the notice of one of the age's outstanding scholars, William Matthew Flinders Petrie, who throughout his immensely long life was deeply concerned with the origins of Dynastic Egypt. Writing in the magazine *Ancient Egypt*, which he founded to popularize the study of the Nile Valley civilization, he identified the alien, non-Egyptian influences which he, like others, felt could be detected in the late predynastic cultures.

The strong Mesopotamian suggestions of the design have, as we noted before, no exact parallel in the East. They seem rather to belong to a people of Elamite or Tigran origin and ideas who had progressed on their own lines. The presence of shipping as an important factor would be against their having come to Egypt across the Arabian desert. The probability seems that they branched off to some settlement in the Persian Gulf (such as the Bahreyn Islands) or on the South Arabian coast and from their second home had brought its style and ideas into Egypt.[17]

In another article, charmingly called 'The Geography of the Gods', in which he examines the geographical origins and associations of the principal divinities of Egypt, he writes:

The general diffusion of the worship of Hathor and her identification with many other deities or genii points to her belonging to the Dynastic people, as already stated. The movement of the dynastic people appears to have been by sea round from the Persian Gulf and up the Red Sea into Egypt.[18]

Later, in one of his works of popularization *The Making of Egypt*, he returned to the same theme. Speaking of the 'Falcon tribe' which he believed had conquered Egypt prior to the beginning of the First Dynasty, Petrie says:

This Falcon tribe had certainly originated in Elam, as indicated by the hero and lions on the 'Araq knife handle. They went down the Persian Gulf and settled in 'the horn of Africa'. There they named the 'Land of Punt', sacred to later Egyptians as the source of the race. The Pun people founded the island fortress of Ha-fun which commands the whole of that coast, and hence came the Punic or Phenic peoples of classic antiquity.

Those who went up the Red Sea formed the dynastic invaders of Egypt entering by the Qoceir-Koptos road. Others went on to Syria and founded Tyre, Sidon and Aradus, named after their home islands in the Persian Gulf.[19]

Petrie speaks of the prospect of Arabian Gulf as well as Elamite influences being present in predynastic Egypt with an assurance which might be taken for an expression almost of certainty. It is not clear why he considered that the Gulf islands were involved at all for, as will be seen, there is no evidence of significant, settled human occupation of the Bahrain islands until well into the third millennium. But Petrie kept Bahrain and the Gulf in his mind for many decades. He even contemplated that he might 'dig in the

Bahrein (sic) islands'[20] in the early part of his career, but nothing came of the idea.

Nineteenth-century commentators seem often to have believed that the Egyptians and the Sumerians had either a common origin or were influenced in their formative periods by some other, third party. Evidently Petrie saw the people of the Gulf islands fulfilling this role; perhaps he took his Herodotus more seriously than other scholars have done.

In Sumerian texts which celebrate Dilmun various epithets are customarily attached to it, by which it is represented as a paradisial place where the gods dwelt and in which numerous acts of creation took place. It is called the Land of Crossing, the Land where the Sun Rises (for the Land is situated in the Sea of the Rising Sun) and throughout its literature particular emphasis is placed on Dilmun's purity:

> The Land Dilmun is a pure place, the Land Dilmun is a clean place,
> That place is clean, that place is bright.[21]

Thus, above all else, Dilmun is a pure place, perhaps even *the* pure place. Dilmun was *Meskillag*, 'the land of pure decrees', and one of its tutelary goddesses was named *Ninsikilla*, the Lady of Pure Decrees.

From the earliest times the Egyptians seem to have maintained the idea that many of the beliefs and events which characterized their 'culture' – to employ a term which, of course, they would not have recognized – had their origins in a far distant island. The evidence for this belief is contained in various collections of texts and inscriptions. These notably include the Pyramid Texts, some of which certainly descend from predynastic times and the inscriptions of the Horus Temple at Edfu, which, though Ptolemaic in date, incorporate much evidently older material; Edfu was an important cult centre from early times. Inscriptions from the Thoth Temple at Hermopolis,[22] may also contain recollections derived from the predynastic communities and, like the Edfu texts, describe the Egyptian peoples' ideas of their origins. It would appear from these texts that the Egyptians preserved, however faintly, memories of an island, far distant towards the east, on the edge of the world, where the first and most crucial acts of creation occurred and where the first and second generation of gods had their home. The evidence is extensive and dense; the amount of references to islands, surrounded by water and sometimes by the sea, is suggestive and compelling. The references which follow unless otherwise stated, have been taken from studies of the Edfu and Hermopolis inscriptions.[23]

It is surely significant that the Egyptians, a people whose predominant environment was desert bisected by a river, were intensely conscious of the character and generally numinous quality of islands. In two great sources of mythology, specifically dealing with the origins of their society, islands appear constantly under various poetic if frequently mysterious names. The frequency of the island image is remarkable; it is difficult to accept that the islands to which these references point were the little mounds of silt exposed as the annual inundation of the Nile waters withdrew, yet this is the conventional explanation. With the Egyptians of antiquity it is a good general rule to accept that what they say is what they mean.

One of the most frequent symbols for the first land to emerge at the creation is the Primeval Hill or Mound. Its location is sometimes explicitly marine in character: thus in the Pyramid Texts, Utterance 484 speaks of 'the Primeval Hill in the midst of the sea'.[24] The land here is specifically a sea-girt island and not a hillock of mud revealed by the withdrawal of the waters of the inundation which has so often been described as the first land to appear at the Creation.

The Island of Peace was associated with the rising sun; then it became 'the Island of Flame'. It was the Divine Emerging Island which appeared from the Abyss of primeval waters, personified as *Nun*, the oldest of the gods according to some theogonies. In this context the Primeval Hill sometimes was called Ta-Tanen; Tanen was the Lord of Creation, the god of the Primeval Mound in Memphite theology and a precursor of Ptah. He was also regarded, like his Sumerian counterpart, Enki, as a god of the depths. From the Island of Flame (or Fire) came, in the very beginning, *Hike'*, the personification of the vital essence which to Egyptians was the basis of life. The island was a magical place, far distant to the east, beyond the limits of the world, a place of everlasting light where the gods were born. As the king declares in one of the Pyramid Text Utterances, 'I go up this eastern side of the sky where the gods were born'.[25] In the great incantation which forms Utterances 273/4 of the Pyramid Texts, in which the deified king leaps into the Heavens and consumes the other gods in a celestial cannibal rite, the text proclaims the magical nature of the Island of Fire:

> The King is the Bull of the Sky,
> who conquers at will,
> who lives on the being of every god,
> who eats their entrails,
> Even of those who come with their bodies full
> of magic,
> From the Island of Fire.[26]

The gods are said 'to give an island' to the justified Osiris and Egyptian legend spoke of 'Middle Island', an unknown, distant locality which was reached by the boat of Anty, the ferryman, who carried passengers to the island like Sursunabi,[27] the ferryman of Ziusudra the Faraway, who carried Gilgamesh to seek the Ancient who had been translated to Dilmun by the gods after the Flood.[28] There were many ferrymen who feature in the Pyramid Texts; several of them are associated with regions to the east. Thus

Utterance 359 observes: 'O Re, commend me to the ferryman of the Winding Waterway, so that he may bring me his ferryboat ... in which he ferries the gods ... to the eastern side of the sky'.[28] One of Horus's titles is 'Horus of the Land of Sunrise'. He is often saluted as Horus of the Horizon (Harakhte) in which the horizon signifies the land of light, the mountains to the east of Egypt, at the eastern edge of the earth.

The island was repeatedly identified as a place of reeds; the land there was marshy. One of its names, as we learn from the Book of the Dead, was the 'Field of Reeds of the Blessed'. This, too, is said to be located on the eastern edge of the world. Both the Egyptians and the Sumerians sustained the most affectionate memories of their earliest shrines or temples which were built of reeds. Thus the Edfu temple in its innermost recesses reproduces the archetypal reed shrine in stone; the Sumerians, on the other hand, immortalized in their poetry Ziusudra's reed hut, to the walls of which Enki whispered the warnings of the Deluge to come.

At the creation, according to the Edfu inscriptions, the creator spirits brought into existence a number of sacred places of which the first two were the Mound of the Radiant One' and 'the Island of Re'. Others included the High Hill, the Oil-Tree, and the Place of Ghosts. The land contiguous to the original island was called Wetjeset-Neter. Other names by which the island was known in the beginning, as well as the Island of Peace, were the 'Island of Trampling' and the 'Island of Combat'. The island first lay in darkness surrounded by the primeval waters called *Wa'ret*. Its original inhabitants and sovereigns were falcons. Horus, who was hailed as Lord of the Land of Sunrise, was represented as a divine falcon. Adjacent to the Wa'ret were several sacred places: the *pay-lands*.[29] These included the 'Island of Fury'. The island was the site of the archetypal temple and is to be recognized as the 'Homeland of the Early Primeval Ones'.

According to the Hermopolitan myths the sun god himself was born in a pool which existed on the Primeval Island. In the Edfu texts the island itself is called the 'Pool which came into existence at the Beginning'. The island was the nucleus of the world. The gods who emerged in this period were the 'Most Aged Ones of the Primeval Time'. The pool stood on the edge of the island; it was surrounded by reeds. The island was known to be the realm of the falcons. It was associated with the idea of the death of an early generation or company of gods; the gods were killed, it appears, in some form of battle; the island may have become their tomb. The falcons who were the island's original rulers became associated with its funerary customs, thus recalling the early generation of gods who met their deaths there.

The lands in the vicinity of the island were known, as we have seen, as *pay-lands*. The creator brought them into existence by drying up the water around the place of origins and so exposing the land; this could be very fair, if poetic, description of the origin of the *sabkha*, the dried up salt pans which are to be found in many Gulf coastal sites. He went on to create the world.

Then the creator, who is now revealed as Tanen and his companion, the Falcon, seem to have made a journey through the Wa'ret which took in some of the *pay-lands*. They appear to have set out on their journey from the island. There is no indication at this point that the Falcon is divine; it seems that he assumes or is granted divinity at a somewhat later stage. Tanen, however, is a god. The island is the 'Place of the Ancestors'.

In the Edfu tradition the ancestors came from places far distant from Edfu itself, which is concerned to present itself as the home of the Egyptian people. Indeed, the assumption of such ancestor gods as their own was part of the Edfu's campaign in asserting its claim to be recognized as the Egyptian homeland. The first temple of the Falcon originated in the 'Blessed Island of the Child'. The temple itself is identified with the 'Primeval Mound, the Divine Emerging Island'. The Primeval Mound is identical with the Pure Land, one of the most frequently employed epithets of Dilmun and a description fitting for an archetypal Holy Land anywhere.

There is a curious epigraphic parallel here, relating to the idea of purity. A frequently repeated glyph in the iconography of the stamp seals which are perhaps the best known artefacts to survive from the Gulf settlements of the late third/early second millennium BC, is the foot or footprint, a symbol which indeed also appears in Mesopotamia in the earliest times. In Egypt, by contrast with Mesopotamia and the Gulf, the hieroglyph which represents the foot is shown in profile; it means 'place' or 'position' and also represents the consonant 'b'.[30] However, there is a special usage of the hieroglyph in the Pyramid Texts, though employed very rarely, where it appears as a compound. The compound consists of the foot with a jar from which water is pouring. The meaning here is 'Pure', 'Clean', ⨅ as in Utterance 513 from the Pyramid Texts: 'Be pure: occupy your seat in the Bark of Re: row over the sky and mount up to the distant ones: row with the imperishable stars, navigate with the Unwearying Stars'.[31]

There is, at present, no archaeological evidence whatsoever to support the idea of direct contact between the Gulf people and the early Egyptians before the end of the third millennium. But if there were to be a common denominator between the Sumerians and the Egyptians it could prove to be the ancestors of the people who ultimately became the Dilmunites. It is possible that the texts' concern with the *pay-lands*, the process of their drying up, the wanderings of Tanen and the Falcon, and the repetition of the island motif might represent the memory of a disturbed and precarious period in the people's history, when they were living in the Arabian peninsula, near the Gulf, perhaps around the perimeter of the al-Rub al-Khali or in its vicinity. Late Neolithic populations, who were very skilled workers in stone, flourished there and lacustrine conditions persisted well into late prehistoric times around the edges of what is now the Empty Quarter. The shores of the lakes and the sea were densely covered with mangrove, which would be a reasonable origin for the idea that they were edged with reeds.

We know that there is no evidence for an invasion of Egypt or anything like it in the period immediately before the unification. In the light of later history it seems more likely that what Mesopotamian influences there are in Egypt and, perhaps, what recollections there may be of the Primeval Island in the Egyptian consciousness, were implanted by relatively small bands of men, traders perhaps or refugees from a dying environment. It probably only needed one of them to be an exceptionally accomplished and persuasive raconteur for his stories of life in the far distant Land of the Sunrise to make a profound, even a lasting impression, on his hearers, particularly if his audience comprised the able chief of a lively congeries of clans and his close associates.

The mention of the power of story-telling prompts the recollection of the Enchanted Island, of which the Shipwrecked Sailor told so marvellous a tale.[32] He had been voyaging to the mines (where were those mines located, one would wish to ask, that he had to sail so far to reach them?) when a storm destroyed his ship and, alone of all his companions, he was cast up on the shores of a lonely island. There he was most graciously received by the island's divinity, a human-headed serpent of a notably kindly disposition, who was bedecked in gold and lapis lazuli. The serpent-king introduced himself as one of the rulers of Punt; this appears to be the only occasion when Punt is identified as an island. The serpent-king courteously declined the offer of the sacrifices of asses, which, rather surprisingly, the sailor proposed to him. Well he might refuse it, if Punt proved to be located in or adjacent to east Arabia, for the asses of the Hasa province have long been famous.

When the sailor eventually left the island he was loaded with treasures by the generous serpent. To anyone acquainted with the customary merchandise of Dilmun's traders the gifts make familiar reading for they are all products for which the island's trade was later celebrated: perfumes, ivory, rare woods, and, very strikingly, baboons, though what an Egyptian was to do with such animals in which his own land abounded is not clear. The sailor was also presented with hunting dogs. This too is remarkable in that Anubis, who, in certain of his manifestations was undoubtedly the prick-eared, fleet Egyptian hound, is proclaimed as 'Anubis who presided over the Pure Land'.[33] Since, in several of his forms, Anubis is a god of the dead, this utterance seems to link a funerary divinity with the Pure Land of myth. The serpent-king returned the sailor safely to the residence of the King of Egypt, which he reached after a sea-voyage of two months. Even in the Middle Kingdom, when this engaging story was first written down, magical islands in far-away seas still exercised a fascination for the Egyptians.

It would be foolish indeed to assert that *all* references to islands in Egyptian religious or mythological texts must refer to the memory of a land which is Dilmun; it may well be that none refers specifically to it, though other possible candidates do not spring as readily to mind. Even such references as there are, are certainly not precise; the island probably existed in the dimension of myth more often than being fixed anywhere on the earth's surface. But it is not impossible that the recollection of a sacred island, which may have become Dilmun, was a direct inheritance or was handed on to the Egyptians by a third party; perhaps one of the eastern groups which comprised the early migrants into the Nile Valley in the sixth and fifth millennia bore the memory with them. Then it was conflated with the perhaps understandable response of a riverine people to think in terms of the great waters of their river withdrawing to reveal an island at the beginning of the sequence of creation.

It is, however, difficult to identify any island with a reputation for special sanctity, of great significance as a burial place, lying far away to the east of Egypt which so precisely matches the required topography as does Bahrain. If Bahrain is Dilmun, the Sacred Pure Land of later Sumerian myth, then Bahrain's topography, its central mountain, a large natural pool, reed- (or mangrove-) lined shores, and its proximity to Arabia's *sabkha* may be something more than merely suggestive in the context of the emergence of one of the founder stocks of the earliest Egyptian community, and its ideas of its origins. But there is one serious reservation which must be made about any claims that Bahrain might have to be 'To Nefer', the Egyptians' land of origins. This has to do with the chronology of Arabian Gulf archaeology.

Dilmun, the Sumerian land of primeval innocence and abundance and the focus of much of the cities' overseas marketing campaigns, features in Sumerian records as early as the latter part of the Uruk and the Jemdet Nasr periods. The earliest textual references to Dilmun occur in tablets from Uruk, dated to *c.*3000 BC.[34] These are the oldest written records in the world; they list the names of countries, including Dilmun, in the order of their distance from the city. However, it seems likely that at this time Dilmun really meant eastern Arabia, which was often embraced within Dilmun's dominion in later times. Thus far at least no unequivocal fourth- or early-third-millennium material has been excavated from Bahraini sites. One Jemdet Nasr seal was recorded from a grave at Al Hajjar, an important burial site in Bahrain, but it seems likely that this was some sort of heirloom or talisman; it had been re-cut since its original making.[35] Early-third-millennium material has been recovered in considerable quantities from east Arabia, and numerous Ubaid sites, dating back into the fifth millennium, are well known there and in Bahrain.

There seems to have been an important early settlement near Abqaiq in eastern Arabia and another on the island of Tarut; the settlement of islands is one of the most characteristic models of early habitation in the Arabian Gulf. Tarut has not yet been excavated extensively, but the Danish expeditions which first visited the sites there in the 1950s and 1960s reported significant evidence of early periods on the upper levels of the principal mound in Tarut itself, suggesting a long history of occupation.[36]

Later, without doubt, Bahrain was Dilmun and was celebrated through-out Sumer for its sanctity and for its numinous character. By then, of course, the time of the foundation of Egypt had long passed and it may be that the earliest recollection of the Egyptian people was of an otherwise undifferenti-ated island in that distant, eastern sea.

All of this, of course, does nothing to explain the mechanism by which the several and in so many ways crucially important influences from Mesopotamia actually reached Egypt. The rich repertory of designs featuring high-prowed Mesopotamian-style boats were obviously very significant to the people who were active in recording their preoccupations at the end of the predynastic, in which influences from Mesopotamia came into the Valley.

The Mesopotamians, Sumerians and Gulf people alike, were adventurous and far-ranging seamen. The Egyptians were not, sensibly preferring to stay in their well-favoured Valley. Trade never achieved the sophistication or the extent in Egypt that it did in eastern lands; so much was easily to hand in Egypt anyway that there was no need to explore unknown regions in search of metals, stone, or other materials, other than, to a degree, timber for their larger vessels and the fine woods which were used in the decoration of their mansions, of daily living as much as of eternity.

The crucial question is whether the products of the east reached Egypt by a sea route, or over land. The sea route, though the run from the head of the Gulf to the central Red Sea looks formidable, but is entirely feasible. Sailing south from the headlands of the Gulf the prevailing winds would carry the craft, which were quite substantial and capable of bearing up to twenty tons of merchandise, down to Bahrain, on to the northern Oman coast, round the towering headland of Ras Musandam, down the Omani coast, and out into the Arabian Sea. The currents prevailing in the northern Indian Ocean would now take over and carry the craft along the southern Arabian coast to the Bab al-Mandab, at the entrance to the Red Sea. Here the temptation must have been strong to leave the open sea and beat up the enclosed waters of the Red Sea, heading north. The eastern shore (the west coast of what is now Saudi Arabia) must have been less favoured than the western or Egypt-ian littoral though the fact that the 'western Arabians' portrayed in the Jubba-style rock carvings found near the west coast, at Bi'r Hima[37] north of Jiddah carry weapons which are not only like those of their Egyptian contemporaries suggests that contact of some sort had long existed. Whilst archaeological survey and excavation has not been exhaustive in south-west Saudi Arabia, nor in the adjacent highlands and coastal regions of Yemen, some evidence of contact across the Red Sea have been found at Sihi, in south-west Arabia.[38]

Though the sea route appears the easier, in fact a land route across Arabia, from east to west, is just as feasible, given the circumstances of the late fourth millennium and even into the third millennium, as one by sea skirting the coast. It would also be a good deal shorter. Nor is it necessary to think exclusively in terms of a route which would run across the northern Arabian deserts, from the headlands of the Gulf or from the extreme southern Mesopotamian cities towards Gaza, then permitting the traveller to drop down through Palestine and enter Egypt from Sinai and the northern gates of the Two Lands.

This entirely hypothetical sequence would have come about in the last centuries of the fourth millennium, when Mesopotamian influences are at their most considerable. But there may have been an even earlier phase of the contact between proto-Egyptians and proto-Mesopotamians during the time, two millennia earlier when the great migrations of peoples in the Near East began to transform the demographic composition of what were to become the principal centres of population of the Old World.

It is clear that there was considerable contact between predynastic Egypt and Palestine. Pottery from the latter source is frequently found not only in such Delta sites as Buto, where it is common, but further south also, including as part of the contents of royal graves, no doubt as a result of trading. It is also clear that in the late predynastic\Early Dynastic times there was contact overland from Egypt with the coastal sites of the Levant. In particular timber such as cedar was imported for use in the emerging royal 'courts' in the Nile Valley, shipped from Levantine ports to the Delta and then down the river. It is certainly possible, even likely, that if this contact were effected by Mesopotamian travellers, who knew the cities of the Levantine coast and possibly even the nearer Mediterranean islands, particularly Cyprus, some would have encountered Egyptians and from them learned of the riches of Upper Egypt, especially the gold-bearing regions.

Some of the Mesopotamians would probably not have resisted the impulse to see for themselves and would have travelled, however apprehensively, southwards. There they would have encountered the cities which were moving ineluctably towards the dynastic age. In the sixth and fifth millennia BC and perhaps from much earlier still there was a significant population in eastern Arabia and particularly in the south-eastern quadrant of the peninsula.[39] Then lakes and substantial marine transgressions, running inland from the Gulf, allowed a larger faunal population, including man, to flourish. It has been suggested that the people of this region were ancestral to the people who made Ubaid pottery in Mesopotamian centres like Ur, called, for convenience, the Ubaidans; they may have been ancestral to the Sumerians.

The early inhabitants of the Gulf were in all probability well established around the periphery of ar-Rub al-Khali and especially in what is now northern Oman. But gradually, in addition to the desiccation which the Arabian peninsula was undergoing from c. 5000 BC, other factors, perhaps excessive hunting, perhaps through the destruction of trees by the domesticated goat or by human agency or a combination of these, the climate began to deteriorate and the desert, represented in Egyptian mythology by Set, the god of confusion and Lord of the East, began to move in towards the areas which previously had been able to support a population of men and animals. It probably happened quite quickly and in its happening is an object lesson for the present day. In a generation or two, certainly well within the memory of men who could recall the stories of their grandfathers, it is possible that the people were forced to move, some eastwards and then north, others westwards along the edges of the dying lakes. These would reach the Red Sea; then the journey to Egypt would once more face the people of south-eastern Arabia as it had perhaps already faced some who had gone on the long sea route.

In addition to whatever significance the islands of the Gulf may have had to the proto-Egyptians and their Ubaidian contemporaries it is possible that Oman was an important location for them both. The funerary architecture of Oman is the most developed at this date of any comparable culture in the Gulf. Seals of Mesopotamian provenance and attributable to the Jemdet Nasr period at the end of the fourth millennium and others with an Elamite provenance, of similar date, have long been known in Egypt and are no doubt also to be associated with the presence of traders.

The scarab seal, though it is known during the Old Kingdom, really only came into its own after the Old Kingdom's collapse and appears in quantity during the First Intermediate Period towards the end of the third millennium. During this time there were considerable incursions into the Valley from the east and Asiatics, including no doubt people from the fringes of the Arabian peninsula, began to enter Egypt. This is the time of the greatest mercantile activity by the Dilmun merchants and the Mesopotamian and Indus Valley traders based on the Bahrain Islands. The seals from Kuwait indicate clearly there was some contact through the medium of the merchants with Egypt at this time at least.[40]

Whether such contact represented the continuation of a longer two-way trading relationship is unclear, however. There is as yet no certain evidence of Egyptian artefacts or influence in Sumer or the Gulf at the time when the eastern lands were evidently making so profound a contribution to Egypt. This negative evidence may in fact support the idea that the Mesopotamians' principal route was by sea; the prevailing currents would carry ships westwards along the Arabian coast but the return journey, if it were attempted, would be hazardous and very difficult.

The early traders of Mesopotamia, India-Pakistan, Anatolia and the Levant were quite prepared to found small colonies, perhaps little more than ethnic or linguistic ghettos, in the cities with which they traded. There seems to have been a long-lasting tradition of the merchant houses establishing branches in foreign cities, which acted both as buying and selling agencies and as bankers, providing facilities, for example, for the bearers of letters of credit from the head office.

There is no definite evidence of such a practice in Egypt; trade was never the consuming interest to the Egyptians that it was to their more commercially-minded contemporaries. There is no reason to doubt that Mesopotamian traders or their agents reached Egypt, or that, equally likely, they established permanent or semi-permanent bases in the Valley. Egypt must have seemed an exceptionally favoured region of the world to people accustomed to the much less well-endowed lands of Sumer and the east.

If, as seems most like, there were Mesopotamian traders who knew the southern Nile Valley, they will have brought the news of their discoveries back to their homeland and in telling of its rich resources and amiable environment have encouraged the younger sons of rulers, the sons of early 'Great Men', or the hierarchs of the temples, to venture out in search of adventure and profit. Once again this is sheer speculation, yet something like it must have happened, for how else did these influences reach the Valley and become so deeply embedded in the dawning Egyptian consciousness? What is certain is that if such influences did penetrate the Valley in this or in some other way, they rapidly became Egyptianized.

Close contact with Mesopotamia did not last long; it may have been spasmodic during Naqada I and more frequent and extensive during Naqada II. In the decades immediately around the traditional date of the unification of the Two Lands, in the thirty-second century BC, these contacts seem to have reached their climax, then diminished, ultimately ceasing entirely in the middle of the First Dynasty. It will already have been seen that the trade in lapis may be the benchmark for the contact and its absence for its cessation. Lapis does not appear again in Egyptian contexts comparatively late in the Old Kingdom.

Much of the evidence for contact with western Asiatic ideas that does exist is visual and is connected with the kingship. It must at least be possible that the princes who created the unified kingdom Egypt were supported by migrants from Sumer. Amongst the more prominent of the bearers of Sumerian ideas into the Valley must have been at least one with a notable architectural bent, for he was able to persuade the kings to adopt a Jemdet Nasr fortified palace facade as their badge and to introduce a very un-Egyptian style of recessed buttresses and panelling on their most important buildings, palaces, and tombs. These elements are the most extraordinary of all the assimilations by Egypt of Sumerian forms, suggesting a really profound degree of influence by the easterners.

The practice of the ritual holocausts of attendants at the burials of the kings has already been noted as fundamentally un-Egyptian. They cannot however be attributed to eastern influences, in the present state of knowledge. The practice is known from Sumer, where the death pits of Ur and Kish contained rich burials of royal or sacred personages attended by dozens of retainers, guards, and courtiers. But the Sumerian examples are from a

time long after the custom had died out in Egypt. The Ur burials are dated
*c.*2500 BC by which time the humane and life-rejoicing Old Kingdom was in
full and splendid swing.

There is evidence from the Epic of Gilgamesh, that towering monument
of Sumerian literary genius, of the practice existing in still earlier times in
Sumer, for the death of Gilgamesh, King of Uruk, in the twenty-seventh
century BC seems to have been the occasion, at least as it is recorded in verse,
for the sacrifice of many of his intimates. The possibility cannot be dismissed that the custom had far earlier antecedents still in Sumer, reaching
back into the fourth millennium, but that the evidence has disappeared, has
simply not been found or that the practice originated in some other location,
knowledge of which was common to both peoples, before they assumed their
historic identities.

A further enigma remains to be resolved at Barbar, on the site of the
triple-layered temple remains. The most important features of the site
throughout its long history, extending over six to seven hundred years, seem
to have been the various holy wells which were sunk there and which evidently formed one of the principal elements both in the site's architecture
and in the rituals which were practiced there.

The well of the Second Temple is the best preserved on the site today,
though that of Temple III has not yet been excavated. The well of Temple II
is a handsome square chamber, built of finely cut limestone blocks, none of
which is particularly large. It opens to a flight of processional stairs leading
up to the main terrace of the temple, from the waters which rise from a perpetual spring in the chamber's floor; the spring is still active today. The
limestone blocks of which the chamber is constructed are quite untypical of
the architecture of Dilmun-Bahrain at the time, to the extent at least that it
is known. It is equally quite unlike the construction of buildings in Sumer,
at this period late in the third millennium. Sumerian architects in the third
millennium tended always to work in brick and rarely in stone; the same
small well-cut blocks can be seen at Barbar in the revetted oval retaining
wall which supports the platform on which the temples were built.

It can only be a matter of speculation as to the origins of the men who
built the Barbar temple. It is tempting, however, to see in them men who
shared the same tradition as those who built the great, eccentrically shaped
tomb for Khasekhemwy at Abydos,[41] where the stone courses of the tomb
chamber look remarkably like those at Barbar. But again chronology suggests a hiatus of nearly a thousand years between the two structures.

Most remarkable of all is the fact that at Barbar a mound of pure sand,
contained by an oval, masonry revetment, lies at the heart of the temple
structures, just as it does at Hierakonpolis and in Sumerian sites such as
Khafajeh, Al-Ubaid, Tepe Gawra and Tel Brak.[42] If the implications to be
drawn from these apparent coincidences in form could be substantiated, they
would be quite staggering. The problem of chronology in the case of Barbar

remains, but the similarity in the architectural technique in the walling of the Barbar chamber and Khasekhemwy's tomb, the oval mounds at Barbar and Hierakonpolis, and the 'anchors', begins to present a formidable case for the presence in Bahrain of builders who shared their traditions with Egypt.

Yet for the Egyptians there does seem to be the memory of a distant land, an island on the edge of the world, God's land, the Land of Sunrise where, in the mist-enshrouded days of fable and folklore memorable events occurred which, with their repetition over generation by generation, acquired the characteristic of the marvellous and the mysterious. The recollection spills out from that deep well of the human psyche, the unconscious, at its most potent and enduring when it encounters events or individuals who contribute to its own archetypes. Such may have been the case in the days when men were still in a highly experimental stage of societal living and, in Egypt and Sumer, harnessing what they identified as powers of limitless potency.

There may be another explanation for these puzzling correspondences. Early cultures, particularly those which were, or which were set to be, complex societies, show many symptoms of inspiration and organization. As we have noted islands were always mysterious and beckoning, though elusive. The Mesopotamians had a mysterious island in the midst of the sea; perhaps the Egyptians only dreamed of one. We are dealing, after all, as both peoples testified, with that time before time, the time of the gods.

12

C.G. JUNG AND ANCIENT EGYPT[1]

The formative dynamic which led to the origins of the ancient Egyptian state can be illuminated by a consideration of some of the perceptions adumbrated by Carl Gustav Jung in his work on the human psyche and, by accepting some of the insights advanced by him, to understand how Egypt appeared to emerge from a condition not greatly different from that of other late Neolithic societies to a highly sophisticated and complex nation-state in a very short space of time. His work can also contribute to an explanation as to why Egypt has continued to evoke so powerful and immediate a response in the minds of countless individuals over the past five thousand years of human history, especially in relation to the formation of what was to become the Western world. A consideration of the relevance of Jung's postulates to the development of the archetypal, pristine state which emerged in Egypt at the end of the fourth millennium BC will demand a review of such issues as the nature of the individual, of individual consciousness and of what may seem the still mistier regions of the collective unconscious as they were relevant to, and affected the lives and attainments of, the early inhabitants of the Nile Valley.

Though such concepts are now part of the familiar jargon of many studies related to man as a social animal, they have not been applied so widely to the study of societies themselves. Yet there is no doubt that the psychoanalytical principles articulated by Jung when applied to the individual can, with qualifications as to scale and the influences of social environment, be applied also to the study of those groups which make up societies and thus to the societies themselves.

The psychological paradigms which contribute most to an understanding of the mechanisms which drive human groups and determine their behaviour, are expressed in Jung's voluminous writings, explaining his concepts of analytical psychology. This is less dogmatic than the discipline formulated by Freud and his followers; it is more concerned with the effects on the individual psyche of those psychological drives which are common to all humanity at all times and which are universal in their application. Jung sought to identify the common psychic inheritance of mankind and to explain human behaviour in terms of, and as a consequence of, that inheritance.

At various times during his long and remarkably creative life C.G. Jung seems to have felt himself strongly drawn to Egypt. As a boy he had ideas of becoming an archaeologist and developed a precocious interest in Assyriology and Egyptology.[2] There was no faculty at that time for the study of archaeology in his local university of Basle and so he turned to one of the two professions which had always engaged his family, medicine; the other was the Church and hence, perhaps, his lifelong concern with the religious motivation. It is difficult to imagine that Jung would have made so universal a contribution to the understanding of the nature of man, had he become an archaeologist rather than a doctor, one who turned his attention early in his career to the yet infant study of the human psyche. To this study he was to give a particular direction, specifically in the field which has become generally known as 'analytical psychology'.

Jung's contribution to the development of a science of human nature was many-levelled. In particular he identified and defined the role of the collective unconscious, the common psychological inheritance of all living humans shared with all humans of the past. He was profoundly aware of the importance of dreaming but he saw the dream as a repository of the unconscious heritage; he was as strongly moved by the repetition of identical or directly related symbols in different ages and cultures.

Although he came under Freud's influence early on in his career as an alienist, he broke with him over the older man's insistence on the paramountcy of sexuality in determining psychological characteristics or disturbance. Jung did not undervalue the importance of sexuality but preferred to relate it to the whole persona, seeing it as a part, not as the whole. Throughout his career he explored regions of human experience which he believed came out of the unconscious. To the Freudian and the rationalist many of these seemed arcane, even bizarre: alchemy, astrology, the foreshadowing of the future by events or dreams, even the phenomenon of unidentified flying objects, all came under Jung's serene but penetrating and inspired scrutiny. But Jung's use of such material did not necessarily imply either his acceptance or even his belief in it.

Much more directly than Freud Jung seems to have understood that there was a deep and very special stratum of experience underlying the familiar stereotype of 'ancient Egypt'. Even in the early years of the century this stereotype was already well formed and it tended to prejudice an understanding of the unique nature of the Egyptian experience, certainly of the experience of the earliest periods. To Freud, responding naturally to his own Jewish cultural heritage, Akhenaten and Moses were the most arresting figures of pre-exilic times;[3] he considered, as others have done, that Akhenaten was the initiator of the concept of monotheism, which seemed, in the intellectual judgment of the time, both to anticipate and to find its fullest flowering in the Old Testament version of the intervention of the divine in human affairs; this view is not unreservedly supported today. Jung on the other hand saw ancient Egypt as providing a unique set of examples of the universality of psychological paradigms. He considered Akhenaten as creative and mystical, whilst Freud saw him also as a vindication of his concept of the Oedipus complex, witnessed by the desecration of his father's monuments.[4]

Descended from solid Swiss Protestant stock Jung was not so God-driven as his Viennese colleague and his recognition of the deep levels of the human consciousness and, in particular, of the collective unconscious drew him on to speculate about pre-conscious levels and the nature of the 'primitive'. This was a word which Jung employs perhaps a little too freely for today's taste when speaking of societies which had still, in his time, escaped the full consequence of western cultural expansionism. However that may be, Jung came closer to apprehending the nature of pristine societies than any observer before him. Not only did he appreciate the quality of such societies and of the people who comprised them, but he also appreciated, with exceptional insight, the significance which the understanding of such societies had for the world of his own day.

JUNG IN EGYPT

Jung visited Egypt on two occasions, first in 1925 and then again in 1932. The 1925 experience seems to have been the more influential and came towards the end of his journey to Africa, an experience which was evidently of great importance to him, undergone at a time of his life when he was under great stress and in need of psychic renewal. The impact of Africa on him was evidently profound, though he does not seem to have written of his Egyptian visit, other than in letters to some of his correspondents, until *Memories, Dreams and Recollections* was published in 1959.

He was a creature of his time and of his own cultural heritage, which inevitably influenced, though did not imprison, him. One consequence, however, of the attitude which characterized African society as 'primitive' was to think of the experience of the Africans whom he met (as well, evidently, as the Arabs) as being on a level of cultural development less advanced than that of his own European background. In setting out for Africa, he recalled, 'The desire then grew in me to carry the historical comparison still further by descending to a still lower cultural level'.[5] This was to be sought in 'Africa where one meets men of other epochs'.[6] Jung's recognition of the deeper levels of human consciousness and, in particular, of the collective unconscious, drew him on to speculate about preconscious levels and what he tends to describe as the nature of the 'primitive'.

The approach from the south

When he actually set off for Egypt he came to the country from the south, travelling up from east Africa, observing that he wished:

> to approach this cultural realm not from the West, from the direction of Europe and Greece but from the South, from the sources of the Nile. I was less interested in the complex Asiatic elements in Egyptian culture than in the Hamitic contribution.[7]

Jung's remarkable perception of the essentially African character of Egypt is clearly demonstrated by this observation, but he does not appear to have written further about his actual experience of Egypt during his journey there.

THE 'SELF AND INDIVIDUAL OF THE PEOPLE'

He continued to meditate on Egypt and on the particular nature of the Egyptian psyche. The most extended consideration is recorded in the *Collected Letters*, in which many of his references to Egypt are contained; in a letter to Frau Johanna Michaelis which deals with the special nature of Egyptian psychology in high antiquity he wrote:

> Your questions are not easy to answer. Your conjecture that Ancient Egyptian psychology was somehow fundamentally different from ours is probably right. Those millennia had indeed different problems. On one side a torpid impersonal unconsciousness reigned, on the other a revealed consciousness, or a consciousness inspired from within and hence derived directly from the Gods, personified in Pharaoh. He was the self and individual of the people. The spirit came from above. The tension between above and below was undoubtedly extreme, hence the opposite could be held together by means of equally rigid forms. The duality of the ruler is based on the primitive belief that the placenta is the brother of the new born child which as such often accompanies him throughout life in ghostly fashion, since it dies early and is ceremonially buried. (C/f Levi Strauss, *Primitives and the Supernatural*). The Ka is probably a descendant of the placenta. White and red are sacred colours in India too, for instance the temple walls are painted with white and red stripes. What they mean is not clear to me. Your interpretation as light and blood is extremely probable but one should have historical proofs. The tension between above and below in ancient Egypt is in my opinion the real source of the Near Eastern saviour figures,

whose patriarch is Osiris. He is also the source of the idea of an individual (immortal) soul. The purpose of nearly all rebirth rites is to unite the above with the below.[8]

This letter is central to Jung's view of Egypt. The idea that the king represented 'the self and individual of the (Egyptian) people' is especially telling, and it is an idea to which Jung returns frequently. So too is Jung's awareness of the balance of opposites which was always one of the most important marks of the Egyptian psyche manifested in social organization, religious belief and art. The suggestion that the placenta represents the king's twin provides, as we have seen, the explanation for its place in the line of royal standards borne before the Early Dynastic kings in procession; indeed, it is the only convincing explanation for the appearance of the placenta in Early Dynastic rituals.

Jung overestimates here, as he does in other contexts, the role of Osiris; far from being the 'patriarch' of 'Near Eastern saviour figures', Osiris is a relative latecomer, for whose cult on any extensive or national scale there is little evidence until late in Old Kingdom times. Atum, Geb, or even Ptah and Re would be more convincing candidates in Egypt, whilst there are more formidable contenders still, if one is looking for early patriarchal figures, in Sumerian myth.

Jung was much impressed by the figure of Osiris as the dying god, reborn in his son; he saw him as the father god who brings into being his own son and successor. The king of Egypt was not identified with Osiris until after death and then only from late Old Kingdom times. Jung justified his belief in the influence of Osiris by attributing the origins of his cult to approximately 4000 BC. In this he was out by some two thousand years, the consequence of relying on the very high chronologies popular in his younger days. In another context he gives the same date for the beginning of writing.

The power of paired opposites

In his letter to Frau Michaelis Jung makes reference to her views on the significance of red and white. These colours were of profound importance in Egypt. Red was the colour associated with the north, whilst white was the colour of the south. The two were always maintained in opposition and always paired: the red and white crowns, the red and white houses for their respective centres of government. Jung may not have appreciated fully the potent symbolism that red and white would have conveyed to an Egyptian but it is very much to be doubted if that symbolism would have encompassed light and blood. On another occasion Jung was to come nearer to the Egyptian idea of the two colours when he referred to the alchemical notion of red and white as 'the Royal Pair', opposites perpetually destined to unite.

THE LIGHT ON THE EASTERN HORIZON

One result of his African journey was the observation that the cult of Horus was that of the 'newly risen divine light',[9] the first light at dawn, the glimmer on the eastern horizon. This is the worship of Horus in the Horizon, Harakhte, though its significance in Egypt was probably greater in later times than it had been earlier. In the New Kingdom, for example, it was believed that the Sphinx represented Harmachis, another manifestation of Horus in the Horizon, and it was worshipped as such. Jung observed the remarkable phenomenon of the Nile baboons which seem to wait for the first rays of the sun and then rise and greet its glory. This moment is brilliantly captured in the great temple of Abu Simbel where a line of cynocephalus baboons is depicted on a frieze at the top of the temple's facade. The baboons sit on their haunches, their paws raised, applauding the sun's rays as they strike them when the temple is bathed in the first light of dawn. The allegorical significance of the baboons' action is not in the least diminished by the knowledge that their response is primarily physiological, for the animals are in fact wakening themselves and boosting their circulation, torpid after the night's sleep. Jung identified the phenomenon with the worship of Horus, an entirely accurate observation.

The moment when the dawn spreads up the eastern sky is a magical one in Egypt, to this day. The whole world falls silent, all created things seem poised and motionless, the very air, no matter how balmy, is palpable. The light on the eastern horizon is strange, milky white, tinged with saffron and pale violet, spreading its radiance rapidly, intensifying in colour as it does so. Then, with the impact of a shout breaking the silence, the sun surges up from the horizon, swinging rapidly into the sky to begin his progress in daily triumph. It is a moment which Nielsen brilliantly captures in his 'Helios' overture, though his sun is Aegean.

The sensitivity of the Egyptians to the world around them and their capacity for synthesizing disparate phenomena into a single poetic image are nowhere better demonstrated than in this celebration of the sun returning to the world. The Egyptians were fascinated by the band of light which appears on the eastern horizon to herald the reappearance of the sun each day. They expressed this moment as the god returning after surviving the perils of the night, when he travelled in his divine bark through the underworld. It was remarkably acute of Jung to have realized how significant a moment this was.

JUNG AND THE PRECESSION OF THE EQUINOXES

The moment immediately before the dawn was of special importance in many of the rituals which were associated with the 'heliacal' rising of the great constellations. As the light on the horizon intensifies a constellation can be seen for a few moments, before it disappears in the light of the newly risen sun. To the ancients this was an especially charged event. The constellations which appeared in this way included Sirius, the most important of all the heavenly bodies to the Egyptians for it was associated by them with the renewal of the year, and those other constellations which were identified as heliacally dominant in the cycle of the Precession of the Equinoxes.

Like many others who came before and after him, Jung was inclined to regard the divinities of ancient Egypt as representations of celestial or astronomical phenomena. In this he was perhaps more liberal than most in his acceptance of what have come to be regarded as the more speculative, even arcane areas of scholarship. He was much interested in the greatest demonstration of celestial mechanics, the Precession of the Equinoxes, revealed by the appearance of one of the twelve Zodiacal constellations on the eastern horizon immediately before the sun's appearance at dawn.[10]

Jung was convinced of the influence of the Precession on the course of human affairs, a view which is coming increasingly, if still guardedly, to be accepted by some historians of science.[11] The entire cycle of the Precession is said to represent a Great, or Platonic, year. This is an idea which seems to have had a special meaning and significance to him for he returns to it on several occasions. In speaking of the uncertainties of his own day he often attributes real or anticipated calamities to the fact that the world was passing from the sign of Pisces to that of Aquarius, a transition bringing changes which he considered as calamitous as those which heralded the transition from Taurus to Aries, sometime around 2000 BC, after the Old Kingdom ended.[12] Jung saw these periods, when the universe is conceived as moving from one sign to another in the Universal Zodiac (just as the solar zodiac moves from one 'house' to the next) at intervals of approximately 2,160 years, as times of particular distress and melancholy, when cataclysmic events are likely to beset mankind. Jung described these periods as 'transitions between the aeons'.[13]

It is generally agreed by historians who have considered the question that knowledge of the Precession does not extend back into the third millennium, but was first defined in Hellenistic times by Hipparchus of Bithynia. Hipparchus drew on somewhat earlier records, compiled a century and a half before his lifetime. But this may not be the full extent of the matter for it is clear that empirical observation of celestial phenomena can predict the Precession over a more limited time-scale than its 25,920 year sequence would appear to require. The observable constellations appear to retrogress by one degree of arc in seventy-two years; thus in only two or three lifetimes, or with longer recorded observations retained for example by a temple community, a discernible shift of a constellation or star marked against a natural feature, such as a hilltop or a stand of trees, would become evident. The quality of ancient Egyptian observation of natural phenomena is unquestionable and the deduction of the effects of the Precession would have been well within their capabilities. It should be remembered that travellers to Egypt in the later centuries of her history frequently recorded the pride of the temple communities in the integrity of the records which they kept, expressly from ancient times.

THE POWER OF CELESTIAL SYMBOLISM

To Jung the recurrence of symbols associated with certain of the constellations in the several epochs of human history, during which the great civilizations of antiquity emerged and first flourished, was compelling. This recurrence indicated that the choice of a given image as the archetype of the aeon which was identified as the dominating constellation in the dawn sky and which was reflected in the art, architecture and cults of the period, is not merely accidental or the outpouring of excited imaginations. The Twins, the Bull, the Ram, the Fish all figure in the catalogue of ancient symbolism during the epochs conventionally attributed to them, extending roughly from the seventh millennium to the end of antiquity (and, in the case of Pisces, on to the present epoch); all were important to Jung and indicative of their choice as significant forms amongst the societies which were directly ancestral to our own. Each of the constellations with which they were identified rose heliacally in the dawn light, at the vernal equinox, at approximately two thousand year intervals from c.6500 BC to the end of the ancient world.

The evidence that the most refined astronomical observation was practiced in Egypt in the mid-third millennium BC (and probably even before that) is clear from the precision with which the pyramids at Giza are aligned to the cardinal points, a precision which could only have been achieved by their alignment to the stars[14] and, as was demonstrated earlier, has an immensely long history in Egypt. This fact alone makes Jung's belief in the Egyptians' knowledge of the Precession a good deal less speculative than it once might have seemed.

THE STATE, KINGSHIP AND INDIVIDUATION

Jung's understanding of the most important single aspect of the culture which arose in the Nile Valley, the kingship, led him to view the development of early Egypt as being determined by those profound levels of consciousness to which the individual psyche may have access but is probably itself unable to recognize or define. The exceptional quality of the Egyptian psychic experience, the rapid development of its institutions, rituals, hierarchies and canons of belief and organization which is a consequence of the outflowing of the archetypes, makes it possible to identify something very like an emerging 'self', in archaic Egyptian society.

To compare the processes at work in the earliest phases of the Egyptian state which were manifested in the arts and social forms that flourished there, with the condition that Jung defined as 'individuation' will demonstrate this point.[15] Egypt's development as a complex society is analogous to the experience of the individual growing to self-awareness and the emergence of what was to become the first fully articulated nation-state in human history, for the state, like the king, may be considered to be the 'self' of the extended group. It is precisely this moving towards a fully realized apprehension of statehood that allows the comparison to be made with the progression of the self to the realization of its own discrete identity.

The concept of individuation describes the progress towards maturity experienced by the self, in the course of which the self acquires awareness of its own individuality, its own separate existence, distinct from its fellows. This process is clearly comparable with the transition to self-awareness which the Nile Valley culture seems to have undergone, particularly in the period from the end of the fourth millennium to the last part of the third.

In this one instance Jung's concept of individuation would seem to be specially pertinent to the study of the emergence of a society as highly individual as Egypt in its first flowering. Though it can only be expressed through analogy it is nonetheless revealing; it must however be emphasized that nothing in his writings explicitly permits the extension of Jung's theories relating to the individual psyche to the emergence of a state organization, whether Egypt's or any other. Nonetheless, the exceptional quality of the Egyptian experience, which he himself recognized, the rapid development of sophisticated institutions, rituals, hierarchies, and canons of belief, supported by the outflowing of a stream of what can only be recognized as classic Jungian archetypes make it possible to identify something very like an emerging 'self' in late predynastic and Early Dynastic Egypt. In considering Jung's response to Egypt it is illuminating to examine the nature of early Egyptian society in terms of some of the postulates of analytical psychology, which he defined.

It is possible in these terms to speculate about the dynamics which lie below Egypt's early flowering of art and the creation of the first fully realized artistic tradition allied to emergent nationhood. In doing so it will be well to acknowledge the problems attendant on any attempt to relate the findings of one discipline to the study of another, a procedure which often results in something like an attempt to count apples with pears. In this case, however, it is tempting (and more, it is revealing) to draw a comparison between what appear to be the processes at work in the earliest appearance of the Egyptian state together with the arts which flourished there, and the experience of individuation. It is possible to do this because so much of the actual procedures of development can be traced in early Egypt. It is also a witness to the truth that states, even those which manifest such extra-ordinary characteristics as Egypt in its early centuries, are essentially human constructions.

'Individuation' is described by Jung as the maturation process of person ality induced by the analysis of the unconscious, is the process whereby the psyche becomes aware of its discrete existence and its relationship to other individuals and entities with which it is required to deal. It describes the progress towards maturity experienced by the self. Individuation makes pos-sible the transition from the collective experience and from the pervasive influence of the collective unconscious to the identification by the individual of distinct and specific responses to his or her environment at all levels. This procedure is comparable with the transition to self-awareness which the population of the Nile Valley underwent, particularly in the period from the middle of the fourth millennium to the last centuries of the third.

The acceptance of these three concepts depends upon the understanding that *all* humans, of all periods and backgrounds, share a common psychic inheritance. This inheritance will be conditioned by particular circum-stances, of environment, education, social pressures and the inculcation of specific systems of belief. Nonetheless, in essence the inheritance of our human past, and that of the period which preceded the attainment of our present state of 'modern' humanity, is common to us all no matter in what age we live or where we may pass our lives.

THE HUMAN PSYCHE: THE UNCONSCIOUS

Jung's contribution to the uncovering of the deeper levels of the human psyche focused in particular on definitions of the collective unconscious, the concept of the archetypes and of individuation. Each of these needs to be examined in an attempt to establish its relevance to what was occurring in late predynastic Egypt, though to attempt to do so briefly (or even suc-cinctly) runs the risk of dealing inadequately with what are extremely complex and many levelled propositions. The definitions proposed by Jung himself provide a starting point: he was aware of the difficulties in gaining acceptance for his propositions. Thus, 'The hypothesis of a collective uncon-scious belongs to the class of ideas that people at first find strange but soon come to possess and to use as familiar conceptions'.[16]

This has been the case with the concept of the unconscious in general. The philosophical idea of the unconscious, in the form chiefly presented by Carus and von Hartmann, had gone down under the overwhelming wave of materialism and empiricism, leaving hardly a ripple behind it, until gradu-ally it reappeared in the domain of medical psychology.

At first the concept of the unconscious was limited to denoting the state of repressed or forgotten concepts:

A more or less superficial layer of the unconscious is undoubtedly personal. I call it the *personal unconscious*. But this personal unconscious rests upon a deeper layer, which does not derive from personal experience and is not a personal acquisition but is unborn. This deeper layer I call the *collective unconscious*. I have chosen the term 'collective' because this part of the unconscious is not individual but universal: in contrast to the personal psyche, it has contents and modes of behaviour that are more or less the same everywhere and in all individuals. It is, in other words, identical in all men and thus constitutes a common psychic substrate of a suprapersonal nature which is present in everyone of us.[17]

THE COLLECTIVE UNCONSCIOUS

Individuation marks the transition from the collective experience and from the pervasive influence of the collective unconscious to the identification by the individual of specific and distinct responses to his environment, at all levels. The collective unconscious is, according to Jung, to be found at work in all societies and at all ages; its identification was amongst the most profound insights of the century which, as shown in the extract quoted above, Jung saw as constituting 'a common psychic substrate of a suprapersonal nature which is present in every one of us'.

...AND THE 'GREAT IDEA'

The progress of the early rulers towards the concept of the unification of the Valley is thus directly analogous to the process undergone by the psyche when it is moving towards its own individuation. The definition which expresses the acquisition by the individual of the awareness of its own discrete existence and its interaction with the world around it, is precisely mirrored in the unfolding of the campaigns of the early rulers of the southern Valley to achieve the unification of the whole, itself an expression of individual identity.

The unification of the Valley was the 'Great Idea' which the early kings of Egypt pursued with remarkable determination culminating in its ultimate formulation into a politically unitary state. This was a very singular concept in that, as is the case with so many Egyptian innovations, it was entirely without precedent. No other people had ever attempted to produce a nation (the very concept was otherwise unknown) out of an extended region with a diversity of traditions and social organization.

Jung demonstrated that the recognition of the role of the collective unconscious casts light on many of the less rational or otherwise inexplicable apprehensions and motivations of the human psyche at its most profound level. In a pristine society such as Egypt's it can be observed at work in a way quite different from the experience of later cultures. The collective unconscious is the fountain from which the archetypes flow, that concept so close to the Platonic vision of the *eidos*. The collective unconscious in Egypt would, in this view, be especially powerful and as pristine a phenomenon as the society itself.

To apply the idea of individuation to Egypt in the earliest centuries of its corporate existence is not, of course, to deny the role of the individual, nor the variety and diversity of the specific experiences undergone by all the individuals then living in the Valley. But in the collective phase of their experience may be found an explanation for the swift and apparently ready acceptance of forms, customs, beliefs, and social organization over extended distances and time-scales, which are evident at this time and which are otherwise difficult to explain. It is even possible that the Egyptians had some sense, in this early phase, of the psychological implications of the transition from the collective unconsciousness to the individual; this would account for their personification of the strange, indeterminate, bisexual divinity called Atum, who is sometimes spoken of as the 'Undifferentiated One'.

DUALISM

A telling parallel between the experience of individuation at the level of the individual self and what was happening collectively in Egypt at this time is demonstrated by the appearance of the almost obsessional pairing (which was earlier described), the constant linking of apparent opposites in everything concerned with the emergent Egyptian state. As Jung observed;

> It is a psychological fact that as soon as we touch on these identifications we enter the realm of the syzygies, the paired opposites, where the One is never separated from the Other, its antithesis. It is a field of personal experience which leads directly to the experience of individuation, the attainment of the self. . . . In this matter words and ideas count for little. This realm is so entirely one of immediate experience that it cannot be captured by any formula but can only be hinted at, to one who already knows.[18]

Jung also called individuation a 'mysterious conjunction, the self being experienced as a nuptial union of opposite halves'.[19] It is to this phase of the experience that the widespread idea of the special significance of the Twins belong: the pair of something more than mortal beings, like Gilgamesh and Enkidu (the most potent example of the type), who encapsulate different, often opposing characteristics but yet are ineluctably bound together, two halves, almost, of some more total being. To the same idea belongs Plato's charming fairy tale of the Golden Age when the human race consisted of dual beings who, their felicity incurring the always spiteful jealousy of the gods, were divided by them and now roam the world, each looking for his (or her) pair. In the remarkable Egyptian preoccupation with dualism, the conviction was implicit that everything has its counterpart or opposite; even the king himself was conceived as a twin. In the ancient world twins were always regarded as uncanny, the possessors of unusual powers and distinctly odd. The Egyptians believed that at the time of the fashioning of the king prior to his birth, a task discharged by the ram-headed god Khnum who had charge of such matters, his twin was created and translated at once to the Beyond, where he existed in a sort of parallel existence to the king's. It should be noted that the royal twin is not the same as the *Ka*, an etheric double possessed by everyone. The idea of the twin as the eternal counterpart of the living king is probably an African concept. The king's placenta is regarded as a twin existing in a celestial dimension.

Another striking demonstration of this idea of the dual identity of the king is provided by his invocation as the 'two-dwellers-in-the-palace; that is Horus and Set'. Here the king seems to be accepted as the personification of the two eternal opposites, the two perpetually warring ancient divinities who are only reconciled in his person. The queen was 'she who looks on Horus and Set'; the great Khasekhemwy ('the Two Powers are Reconciled') proclaimed the resolution of this duality of personality in his throne name. By proclaiming it in the *serekh*, the ancient heraldic device which contained the king's most sacred name, surmounted by both the falcon of Horus and hound of Set, he revealed the twinship of the two gods, though not in terms of their notional kinship, for Horus was Set's nephew, at least in the explanation provided by Memphite theologians.

In Egypt this need to reconcile apparent opposites is one of the most explicit elements in the formulation of the early state. The Dual Kingdom; the union of Upper and Lower Egypt; the Horus of the north and the Horus of the south; the two contenders Horus and Set; the pairs of gods and goddesses at their creation; the Lions of Yesterday and Tomorrow; the shrines of Upper and Lower Egypt; the Two Ladies (one of the royal titles referring to the tutelary goddesses of the kingdoms); the Two Crowns; even the remarkable repetition of red and white symbolism in the crowns, palaces, and the lands themselves, all conspire to emphasize the duality of existence, as much as the fundamental duality which was so important a dynamic for the state which was evolving on the Nile's banks. As we have seen, at the king's coronation pairs of individuals representing the crafts which powered the economic life of Egypt appeared before him: milkmaids, butchers, and cabinet makers, for example, two by two like characters in a nursery rhyme.

THE ARCHETYPES

> The term 'archetype' ... designates only those psychic contents which have not yet been submitted to conscious elaboration and are therefore an immediate datum of psychic experience ... The archetype is essentially an unconscious content that is altered by becoming conscious and by being perceived, and it takes its colour from the individual consciousness in which it happens to appear.[20]

With individuation manifested in the formation of a nation-state came a streaming out of the archetypes, which is a phenomenon of the condition for, as Jung states, 'in this still very obscure field of psychological experience, where we are in direct contact, so to speak, with the archetype, its psychic power is felt in full force'.[21] In early Egypt many of the archetypes are already apparent in the art of the time; they are already dominant and immensely powerful, having their origins in a past far removed from the time even of the unification. Jung defined the archetypes, in the context of the collective unconscious, as 'archaic or – I would say – primordial types, with universal images which have existed since the remotest times'.[22]

The greatest and most enduring of all the archetypes which Egypt released was undoubtedly the king himself. The king was the centre of the universe; sometimes indeed he was simply titled 'Lord of All', an honorific otherwise held by the great and exalted god Ptah. In early times one of the royal titles was *ity* which seems to be associated with the idea of fatherhood; the king was father of his people, just as he was their shepherd and, occasionally, their herdsman. This last idea is obviously connected with the cattle cults of the peoples of the remoter reaches of the Nile Valley who represented so important a component in the founder stocks of the Egyptian people, from whom the dynastic Egyptians were in large part descended.

THE DIVINE KINGSHIP

The Egyptians were a logical and pragmatic people, though some of their processes of thought may seem obscure to the present day. Having conceived of the kingship as the linchpin of the unitary state which was emerging along the Nile's banks, it was by an entirely consistent intellectual synthesis that they should combine the fact of the mortal kingship with undying divinity. Thus the king and his office were perfectly reconciled; though the holder of the office might die and so be recalled to his other realm beyond the stars, the Divine Kingship continued unchanging. The king was the Good God; he was also the Wise Ruler and also the Prince, in the sense of being the First or Great Individual.

The king is seated on a throne with seven steps. He wears a crown, a ritual costume and carries objects associated with his office, such as the flail and the crook, sometimes a mace, the first two of which emphasizes Egypt's nature as an agrarian society whilst the mace indicates the king's role as a warrior. He is attended by deferential followers, courtiers who are designated to discharge responsibilities related to his person or his dress and sometimes by a retinue of gods. He has the power of life and death and destroys Egypt's enemies. In all of these acts the king discharges an archetypal role.

The 'Great Individual'

The king of Egypt was the first example in recorded history of the archetype identified in psychological parlance as 'The Great Individual'.[23] This long-enduring figure is often encountered in epic and mythological contexts. He is heroic in scale and action; Gilgamesh and, on the mythical plane, Herakles are good examples of the type, so too, though on a different scale, is Alexander the Great.

The Great Individual is an agent of profound change, by his actions or example releasing great charges of psychic energy into the society or community with which he is engaged. He is, in the generally employed sense of the word, 'charismatic'. In addition to his heroic qualities he may also be a sacrificial figure who suffers or dies for his followers. The hosts of dying gods belong to this category.

According to the Pyramid Texts, the most venerable series of sacred writings in the world, which emphasize the unique nature of the king and are designed to ensure his survival after death, the king existed before the creation of the world.[24] In the way of the Great Individual he will eventually decline from his position of primacy, to assume something more like a mediatory role, a process which the Egyptian kingship precisely experienced, when the glory in which the Early Dynastic and early Old Kingdom kings reigned was replaced by the still-powerful but more circumscribed state of the kings of the Middle and subsequent kingdoms. Eventually, the figure of the Great Individual will disintegrate, a process which is often also the fate of the society of which he was once the prime mover. This disintegration may actually be mirrored in the Great Individual's physical dismemberment, as was mythically expressed in the death of Osiris. This was eventually to be Egypt's destiny.

Egypt was unique – and uniquely fortunate – in having at its disposal not merely one but a number of Great Individuals amongst the kings of the earliest dynasties. Their powerful influences, which effected such dramatic developments in the early centuries, continued to resonate throughout the Valley for many hundreds of years after their lifetimes. Whilst they lived their unique status was preserved and identified by their being represented on a superhuman scale, or raised high above their followers, whenever it was necessary actually to represent them. Thus they were preserved for ever in their archetypal roles.

The festival of renewal

When considering the ceremonies which attended the king in his archetypal function Jung was much taken by what he saw as the special importance to the Egyptians, corporately, of the Heb-Sed festival. This was the elaborate series of ritual enactments which the king underwent at certain points in his reign. Its purpose was to renew his psychic forces, effectively to bring him to rebirth. The Heb-Sed was particularly important in the case of a long-reigning king; its usual first occasion was on the thirtieth anniversary of his coronation, though this could be varied.

The king seems to have experienced a symbolic burial and resurrection, on which he again took possession of the lands of Egypt. He mounted his throne in the company of the gods and great priests of Egypt and signified his possession of the four quarters of the world. Jung suggested that the king's acts on this occasion and his assumption of the crown, robes, insignia and regalia of the kingship proclaimed him the *Anthropos*, the archetypal universal man.[25]

THE GODS

The relationship between the Egyptians of the early periods and the gods ('Divine Powers' is perhaps a better term to apply to these ambiguous entities) was essentially a collective one. There is no sense of a direct or personal connection between the individual and the gods, other than through the mediation of the king and his worship as one of the company of divinities of whom he was both the peer and, occasionally, the ruler. As expressions of the inexpressible the divine powers of Egypt have never been surpassed; their extraordinary power is the product of their origins in Egypt in its pristine form, at the point where the society's progress towards the manifestations of its own individuality demanded the definition of its particular dynamic characteristics and those less material but still profound influences which the people recognized around them. It is entirely to be expected that, in the collective state of mind represented by the inhabitants of the Nile Valley in the fourth millennium even before the advent of the kingship, the archetypes should come into existence themselves in a form in which they could be recognized when the collective unconscious demanded that they should be manifest. They were personified as entities or powers beyond nature, as they assuredly were, given the manner in which they were conceived. The Egyptian word for them is *netjer,* which is inadequately represented by the word 'god'.

THE DIVINE ANIMALS

In the company of the divine entities the king is attended by the flock of Egyptian animal archetypes, each displaying not only his own potent nature, but also symbolic of some larger dimension. The tremendous bull; the majestic lion, both early symbols of the king; the swift hound; Horus the soaring falcon, the exemplar of kingship itself; Wepwawet, the alert and watchful dog; the baboon; an entire menagerie of zoomorphs surged out of the subconscious of the emerging Egyptian personality. As Jung again observed, 'The archetypes are the imperishable elements of the unconscious but they change their shape continuously'.[26] The Egyptians were not, of course, the first to employ animal forms to express ideas so profound that they were beyond words, even beyond abstract symbols, but they fixed them so completely that no mythology could ever equal either their endurance or their penetration.

The perception which Jung so frequently displayed when considering the nature of myth and the outpouring of the archetypes in antiquity is nowhere more acutely expressed than in his observation of the nature of the divine animal:

> Zarathustra is an archetype and therefore has the divine quality, and that is *always based on the animal*. Therefore the gods are symbolized as animals; even the holy ghost is a bird, all the antique gods, and the exotic gods are animals at the same time. *The old wise man is a big ape really*, which explains his peculiar fascination.[27]

This is a quite remarkable insight into the process of god-making, when the gods are realized in animal form. It was the special genius of the Egyptians first to recognize the nature of the archetypes and, in so doing, to conceal their nature in animal forms when they manifest themselves. The majority of the high gods of Egypt have an animal persona; only Ptah, who is one of the greatest of the divine powers, is invariably shown in human form though even he can also be manifested in the bulls – Apis, Mnevis, Buchoris – which are sacred to him; however, in this case the bull is Ptah, not Ptah the bull. The Egyptians went still further in interpreting the animal forms in which the gods appear as archetypes by merging their physical presence with human forms: the gods are animal-headed when they appear in the rituals and when they are attendant upon the king.

It is surely significant that theriomorphs, the conflation of animals and humans, play little part in the symbolism of the Old Kingdom, in comparison with their proliferation in the later periods of Egyptian history. In the third millennium, all was assured and determined, the Valley was secure and the gods, principally because they are remote from the affairs of humans, do not represent menace.

Very frequently in myths which arise from archetypal sources the animals are helpful to men, aiding them in trials or rescuing them from danger. The 'helpful animal' is an archetype recognized by Jung and Egypt provides examples of the intervention of the helpful animal in human affairs. The story of the Shipwrecked Sailor from the Middle Kingdom is one of these.

The Egyptian attitude to animals probably explains the generally friendly nature of the theriomorphic and zoomorphic divinities: animals were part of the natural world which they shared. As such, they were worthy of respect, even of veneration in later times. Jung was responding to his own unconscious when he remarked, in the extract quoted earlier, that 'the old wise man is a big ape really'. The Egyptians were in advance of him in this perception for Thoth, the god of wisdom is very frequently represented as a baboon. The cynocephalus, the same species that so impressed Jung when its members seemed to be greeting the sunrise, was sacred to Thoth and one of the most ancient animal deities, known in the First Dynasty, was a baboon, 'The Great White'.

The people of ancient Egypt and Carl Gustav Jung alike recognized the archetypal significance of the ape, a remarkable instance of correspondence over a great tract of time. The acknowledgement of the primate nature of modern humans is fundamental to an understanding of what happened in Egypt in the early centuries of its corporate existence. There were two special qualities which determined the nature of the archaic Egyptian society: it is hierarchic and it is pristine. Egypt is the first, most perfectly realized complex society because it is organized on firmly hierarchic principles. Man belongs to the order 'Primate'; whilst he is a particularly developed form of primate, with special skills and qualities none of these obscures his essentially primatial nature.

Most primates, and certainly all the higher primates, the great apes and the chimpanzees for example, live in structured bands most, though not all, under the leadership of a dominant or alpha male. The alpha male will be attended by (and eventually will have to compete with) a group of lesser-ranking males.

Thus, dominance over the group by an individual is an inheritance which is drawn from the most distant frontiers of our species. By an extraordinary insight the Egyptians clearly apprehended the nature of the dominant leader of the group, the primatial 'Great Individual', the 'big ape' as hierarch. The leap from this relatively simple concept to the idea of the kingship, with all its attendant ceremony and ritual with the overlay of divinity, is immense but wholly logical. In conceiving the kingship the Egyptians acknowledged the primatial nature of human society and by its creation, wittingly or not, maintained a connection between the impending complex societies into which humankind was evolving and the small bands which, for all of mankind's previous history, as primate and as modern human, had provided the hierarchic structure which made the group viable. It was as if the

Egyptians of late predynastic times and the early centuries of dynastic rule attempted to reconcile the condition of humans who had chosen to live in groups which were so vastly greater in number than anything that primates could endure. That they ultimately failed does not diminish the nobility of the attempt to restore the human condition to its primatial matrix.

SYMBOLISM IN EARLY EGYPT

Underlying much of the ancient Egyptian perception of the visible world is another world of symbols and symbolism. The subtle psychology of the Egyptians of the early centuries of the existence of the Dual Kingdom often led them deliberately to represent one object or concept by another. The capacity to do this permeated their works and is fundamental to an understanding of their world.

An important event in the development of the corporate Egyptian psyche, which exercised a profound influence on later events, was the shift in the middle of the third millennium from predominantly stellar cults to those which took their inspiration from the sun and which, from the Fourth Dynasty onwards, dominated the royal cults. Stellar cults have stronger Mesopotamian affinities than do those which acknowledged the sun as supreme; it may be that the observance of the stars was a vestige of the ancient Western Asiatic influences which percolated into the Valley to such notable effect in the late predynastic period. As such, they were perhaps considered inappropriate for a belief system which was based on the idea of the supreme divinity of the king, a concept which could obviously be more easily accommodated in the apparently unique nature of the sun, compared with the myriads of stars visible from the Egyptian deserts. The significance of stellar cults was not forgotten however, as witnessed by the constant identification of the king as a star in the Pyramid Texts.

If something of this sort happened, just as the Fourth Dynasty came to power, it would account for its expression in architectural form by changing the shape, though not the essential nature, of the pyramid tomb. The Step Pyramid is demonstrably a staircase to the heavens, a concept echoed by the stepped platform on which the king's throne stood. The true pyramid represents the rays of the sun petrified and made eternal, to protect the body of the king for ever; it took its canonical shape early in the Fourth Dynasty during the lifetime of the remarkable King Sneferu. It then assumed its place as one of the great archetypes, standing in majesty on the plateau at Giza. The pyramid is the archetypal Egyptian symbol. Four thousand five hundred years later it evokes instant recognition; it has probably been reproduced more frequently in more media than any other human artefact.

The final seal of Egypt's progress to statehood and the full achievement of her historic personality was the creation of the Pyramids during the Third and Fourth Dynasties. The Pyramid is the supreme artefact linking earth and heaven, land and sky, the mortal and the divine, and the most powerful assimilation of light then possible to technology. As we have seen, the Pyramids came out of the deep levels of the unconscious of the Egyptian people and of the state in its first supreme manifestation. With their erupting into three-dimensional form Egypt was in effect, fully mature, its historic destiny achieved: all afterwards was, inevitably, decline.

There is another symbolic form, associated with the pyramid shape, which lay even deeper in the Egyptian unconscious. This was the frequently depicted line of triangular hills which appears on the pottery of Naqada II, several hundred years before the pyramids appear. The Nile Valley is not generously supplied with sharply peaked hills; the limestone and sandstone hills which it does possess are usually not isolated in such a way as to emphasize a triangular shape. It may be that the triangular hill was locked in the collective unconscious of the Egyptians, whose basal population were immigrants into the Valley and who may have retained some recollection of a mountainous or at least a hilly landscape, with which they were once identified. The hieroglyph for 'foreign land'[28] is the same three hills, a similarity which might be thought to support such an association. More likely still is that the Naqada hills and the pyramid are expressions of the same archetype. The three-dimensional triangle is a peculiarly satisfying shape and one which is replicated in many forms, in many different contexts throughout history.

THE SYMBOLISM OF THE TOMB

Although the final, accepted shape of the pyramid arose both from the promptings of the unconscious and by the happy chance of a natural phenomenon inspiring an artist of genius, the pyramid has in fact a long evolution before its shape becomes determined. The evolution of the pyramid as tomb can be traced back to the shallow graves of the Badarians, the first identifiable culture in southern Egypt, who raised a little mound of earth over the burial to mark it. By late predynastic times, as for example at Hierakonpolis, graves were marked by a lightweight superstructure, a canopy raised over the grave which might contain the burials of cattle and dogs as well as humans. At much the same time, more substantial tombs were being erected in Abydos and Naqada for high status individuals who, it has been suggested, may have been the rulers of important reaches of the Valley, before the arrival of the kingship. Similarly at Hierakonpolis, the famous painted Tomb 100 marks the appearance of a high status burial with painted decoration on the interior walls, which is the ancestor of the countless mastaba tombs of the Old Kingdom which are alive with scenes of life in Egypt carved on the walls. Later, the practice of painting the interiors of tombs would be resumed, with magnificent effect in Middle Kingdom, in the richly decorated coffins associated with that period and particularly in New Kingdom burials.

As with everything else in Egypt, élite burial practices were transformed with the coming of the kingship at the end of the fourth millennium. The burials of the First Dynasty kings in their funerary palaces at Abydos have already been described, as have the mastabas of the great nobles at Saqqara and other sites. In this present context however, all the early tombs have a common feature: in the centre of the tomb, over the actual burial, was placed a little mound, sometimes of sand alone, sometimes contained within a brickwork structure. In some cases the brickwork enclosing the mound is stepped.

It is the latter feature which gives the clue to the connection between the relatively simple predynastic graves and the later immense tombs which were built for the kings and their ministers. The internal mound becomes more important as the First Dynasty progresses, seeming to grow in importance. The mound which descends from the little piles of sand atop the Badarian burials finally erupts, first in the triumphantly powerful expression of the Step Pyramid complex and then in the huge monuments of the Giza plateau. This extraordinary 'growth' of the internal mound from the earth in which it has been germinating, to its final eruption fully realized in the form of the pyramid, is a very exact metaphor for the emergence of the nation-state, also apparently fully realized, from the land of Egypt and from the collective unconscious of its people.

THE EVOLUTION OF BURIAL CUSTOMS

The collective character of the society can also be seen in the customs attending the burial of the king. As a consequence of some extraordinary persuasion by the royal propagandists or by the evidently overwhelmingly charismatic figure of the king himself, the society was apparently prepared to accept the idea that only the king might, by right, avoid the dismal experience of death, and, as the supreme divinity, go on to an eternal existence beyond the stars.

All other creatures were evidently fated only to continue to exist through him and through his survival; only by ensuring his continued existence could the future of the whole land of Egypt be preserved. The individual was nothing; Egypt, in the person of the king, subsuming all others to himself, was all. It is in this sense, particularly in the earliest years of the kingship, that the king is Egypt's self.

This belief had in it the seeds of its own decay. The idea that the people survived through the survival of the king led in time to the belief that the retainers sacrificed at the king's death (and also at the deaths of the very greatest nobles) would continue to serve, and then that proximity to the royal burial could ensure their immortality with the king's family and his ministers.

Gradually the nobles and high officers of the Dual Kingdom, particularly in the later centuries of the Old Kingdom, began to adopt the forms of what had been the royal prerogatives of burial. Eventually, in the late period every man was his own Osiris, when that god, originally an alien in the Valley, became the symbol of regeneration and the focus of the hopes of eternal life by even the most humble servitor or tiller of the land.

The change which overcame the Egyptian view of the ceremonies appropriate after the death of the individual may also reveal an awareness of the transition from the collective to that of the individual consciousness. In the earliest times the death of the individual may not have been considered as especially significant to the community. The community, particularly in the person of its leader and personification, continued undying. As the process of individuation wore away the old communal and collective spirit of the society and the individual psyche began to flourish and to demand its own recognition, so the needs of the individual even after death began to be apprehended and all the complex industry associated with the care of the individual's immortality was brought into being.

The Egyptians have been described as a people inordinately preoccupied with death. Such an attitude misunderstands them: the Egyptians were wholly preoccupied with life and with its prolongation. Death was an incident in man's experience of life; in the case of the king, death was attended by the most elaborate ritual. For all, death marked a transition from one state of being to another.

The considerable activity which was directed towards ensuring survival after death, first of the king, later of his closest assistants, and ultimately of all, had the effect no doubt of concentrating the Egyptians' minds on an acceptance of the inevitability of death. More than most people, therefore, their lives represented a preparation for the experience of dying. In thus preparing themselves they proceeded further along the path to a still more fully realized individuation. Jung recognized the importance of accepting the inevitability of death as an aspect of life, though he did not link this perception directly with the Egyptian experience.[30]

Because they manifest a collective persona the Egyptians of this early period are, or at least seem to be, different from most people who have lived in the world after them; Jung, in the extracts quoted earlier, clearly apprehended this essential fact. Their genius is particularly expressed in the making of artefacts, from the relatively humble pottery vessel to the pyramid or the most majestic image of the Divine King; the most sublime artefact they made was Egypt itself, splendid, beautiful and richly complex. Whilst the underlying, seemingly eternal principles of Egyptian art and design are the products of the peculiarly Egyptian collective unconscious, there is another specific manifestation of this collective stream, that body of spells, incantations, the mutterings of priests, and the first recorded inspired literary expression of the striving after the Divine, known as the Pyramid Texts.[31]

THE TEMPLE AS ARCHETYPE

Similar powerful forces were at work in the evolution of the temple, another archetypal Egyptian artefact. The oldest representations of cult buildings show them to have been animal in shape and made from reeds. Once again, the manifestation of divinity in animal form is demonstrated in the shape of the shrine. As Egypt's temples became ever larger and more complex, the archetypal little reed shrine is still retained in the heart of the temple, enclosed in darkness.

The temple is a microcosm of the world, its roof the sky. The forest of columns which supports the roof are both the pillars which in Egyptian belief support the sky and the primeval grove of trees or the banks of reeds and mangrove in the primeval island from which began the gods' original journey to found the Dual Kingdom. In the Jungian canon the forest is also a synonym for the unconscious, a quality which is also shared by the temple.[31] Within the temple, as in the depths of the unconscious, lie the most obscure but at the same time the most potent symbols. The mystical nature of the temple is revealed by the forest of columns which at once conceals its interior and also draws the hierophant deep into its further recesses, where the most sacred part of the temple is located, the place of the living presence of the god. The officiant, priest or king, goes further and further into the darkening interior as if he were pursuing some ideal form, as it might be of an animal barely glimpsed, into the heart of the temple-forest.

Little is known of the rituals conducted in the temples of the early dynasties but their symbolic character will have been fully apprehended by those who had access to their interiors. In later times, initiations in the higher ranks of the priesthoods were carried out there and their identification with the unconscious and the revelations which it can provide will have been explicit. The Egyptian temple fulfils an archetypal function of much complexity and the fact of its doing so accounts for much of its mysterious and numinous quality.

The original and formative Egyptian experience had been that of the extended group, leavened with the occasional brilliant flash of individual genius. The images which are the common currency of Egyptian art and architecture are archetypes, products of the collective unconscious. The falcon perched on the *serekh* as the eponym of the royal clan for example, the everlasting symbolism of the crowns, a poetic image such as the two lions joined back to back signifying Yesterday and Tomorrow, are all examples of this phenomenon. Such archetypes are all products of the early Egyptian collective unconscious; it is this which gives them their often mystical, faintly uncanny but hauntingly familiar character.

Egypt's decline, her gradual descent from the unimaginable heights of the third-millennium experience to the haunted shells of the temples of later times, parallels the individual's progress towards maturity and beyond. Once maturity was reached the experience comparable with that of individuation was realized. Egypt's coherence and the integrity of her pristine personality began to fragment, never to be wholly rejoined.

In the time of the early Middle Kingdom kings, whilst the earlier periods were still, as it were, in sight, the principal elements of immemorial Egypt were retained. But soon alien influences virtually swamped the Valley, corrupting for ever the unique experience that was Egypt in its first flowering.

THE ANCIENT EGYPTIAN PSYCHE

Expressing a profound insight, Thomas Mann, a creative genius who himself consciously explored the process of creation throughout his artistic life, observed that 'the Ego of antiquity and its consciousness of itself was different from our own, less exclusive, less sharply defined'.[32] Mann was writing in the context of the work of Sigmund Freud whose theories of psychoanalysis have only a limited relevance to the understanding of the psychology of high antiquity when compared with those of C.G. Jung. But the truth which Mann expressed is fundamental to an understanding of the processes which were at work in the creative output of the men of the earliest high cultures. In particular the lack of exclusiveness of the Ego of which he writes is markedly true of the Egyptian personality in Early Dynastic times. The Egyptian of the early periods is simply less individualized than has come to be expected from someone living in a highly cultured, well structured, and organizationally advanced society. The Egyptian experience of the time is still closer to the collective experience, the experience of the group, almost (though this is patently an overstatement) the experience of the species. Parallel with this collective experience, manifested also by an intense sense of 'belonging' and, perhaps paradoxically, of an identity specifically as part of the group, was the developing awareness of the individual and the capability of the individual to express a separate identity. Initially such individuality was yet another prerogative of the king and his closest companions, though doubtless it was not acknowledged in such specific terms. Throughout the later phases of the Old Kingdom, as demonstrated by the increasingly naturalistic art of the tomb reliefs for example, the emergence of the individual was evidently one of the factors which marked the most notable change in the society and which ultimately weakened the fabric of the state.

The momentous events of the last quarter of the fourth millennium when the progress towards the combination of the little principalities which it is presumed then comprised the polity of the Valley really began, led the Egyptians to undertake the creation of a complex political system and to extend it over a large and extended area, embracing several local cultures. The Egyptian collective unconscious must have been dramatically activated by this process, releasing a variety of archetypes even as it released creative initiatives triggered by them. In a small and closely knit community, with fairly immediate communications by means of the river, these could be apprehended rapidly from one end of the Valley to the other. It is a further tribute to the early kings that they realized this to be the case and pursued the unification of Egypt relentlessly, ultimately to achieve it despite many setbacks and frequent disappointments.

Innocence and a sense of collective election are fundamental elements in the ethos of the Egyptians who founded and sustained the Egyptian state in its early centuries. There is thus no sense of sin or guilt in early times, to be experienced by the individual. Such concepts, too, came later, again perhaps creeping in from the desert wastes, to temper the original innocence of the people of the Valley. The power of the original creation may be gauged by the consideration that the history of Egypt after the Pyramid Age is a history of decline. From its highest point, so quickly achieved and main-tained with such assurance, Egypt gradually declined, though many of the outward forms remained.

To apply the concept of individuation to the progress of a community, from its earliest expressions of self-awareness to the full engagement of all the complex elements of state politics and management, can provide a frame into which otherwise disparate and apparently inconsequential factors can be associated and made coherent. The concept works precisely because the indi-vidual in the society is not yet a personality fully differentiated from his fellows. The beginnings of specific distinctions can however be traced: the emergence of trades and even the specializations of function within the state, though these will operate still to a very limited degree.

The phenomenon of the Divine Kingship itself, the most profound of all Egyptian inspirations, grew out of the same pristine and uncontaminated state which allowed the free flow of so many of those elements which have come to be associated with the process of individuation and which appear in such abundance in the late predynastic and Early Dynastic periods, in the reaches of southern Egypt.

The Divine King is the supreme Egyptian political concept and the product of the unique Egyptian-African psyche. The idea of the Divine King emerged precisely at the point when the society over which he was to be raised was beginning its progress towards the attainment of its own distinct and individual identity. But the king, once he is recognized as such, is fully individuated in name, in function, and in the numinous quality with which he and his office are already invested.

It is in this context, too, that the monumental public works which are so much a feature of the early centuries of the Egyptian state's existence must be considered. As the process of individuation advanced, and as the king assumed an ever more exalted position, the essential Egyptian spirit began to find expression in massive works which engaged the whole society and absorbed much of its resources. Such resources were not wasted, nor deployed extravagantly; their employment was the inescapable consequence of the burgeoning of the individuality of the Egyptian state. The monuments were, initially, the product of the need to protect and nourish the king's individuality. Later, as the individual Egyptian begins to take on a more precise outline, the role of the king diminishes, first to that of a god among gods, later still to something like the mediator between gods and men, with what amounts to little more than a sort of honorary divinity. Once again, the decline of Egypt from its pristine greatness can then be seen as part of the process of the state's realization of its own individuation.

THE PYRAMID TEXTS AS PSYCHOANALYTICAL PRIMERS

The Pyramid Texts, whose importance and significance can hardly be exaggerated, enshrine collective memories of the people who gave them life. These memories are the products of the earliest aspirations of the Egyptians as a group, when they were first experiencing that sense of election which led to nationhood. Some of the texts are in the form of dialogues, demonstrating how ancient is the form of antiphonal exchange, sometimes between spirits, sometimes focusing on the king as the principal actor in the drama, sometimes in the form of exchanges between priests officiating in a complex ritual.

The Pyramid Texts are known from a series of 'editions' carved on the walls of royal tombs of the late Fifth Dynasty and the Sixth Dynasty. This was the high point of the Old Kingdom community's coherence and assurance; society then was in balance with nature and it must have seemed to be unthreatened, unchanging, and eternal. The texts do not display notable tensions such as, for example, those which the near-contemporary late Sumerian or Akkadian texts often reveal; the Egyptians' characteristic state of tranquil complacency seems unimpaired until it is finally blown away with all the rest of the mooring posts of the Old Kingdom world.

The Texts are still little understood. The obscurity of their language and the strange images which they evoke are difficult, if not impossible, to comprehend. There is no evidence that Jung was conscious of their significance in any detail, though he knew of their existence. During his lifetime a version of the texts was translated by the great German Egyptologist Kurt Sethe who, though some of his interpretations have been questioned by more recent authorities, was the first to make them generally accessible to a modern audience. The most celebrated version of the Texts is that carved in exquisite hieroglyphs on the subterranean walls of Wenis' pyramid at Saqqara and originally infilled with a brilliant blue paste.[33] The Wenis texts, like the others which succeeded them, are a compendium of the most profound expressions of the ancient Egyptian spirit.

C.G. JUNG AND ANCIENT EGYPT

Jung's response to Egypt seems largely to have been stimulated by random factors of sudden insight rather than systematic study. However, in his attitude to his journey down the Nile in 1925 he seems to have come very close to penetrating the essential nature of Egypt's aboriginal and essentially African culture. It is the more surprising that he seems not to have written more extensively about his journey, though he always acknowledged the deep level of significance that he felt towards Africa. It was Egypt's African roots to which Jung most readily responded. It was precisely in those roots that the 'soul' of Egypt will be found and which provide the most productive sources of analysis. Africans seem always to have recognized the essential duality of man's nature.

Predictably, Jung was much taken with what he recognized as the complex Egyptian concepts of the psychic elements in man. The Egyptians recognized several distinct entities as different aspects of man's spiritual essence, or perhaps even as different essences. The *ba* corresponded to the idea of the enduring, incorporeal spirit possessed by everyone which would, in the later Osirian cults at least, be judged according to the individual's behaviour in life. The *ka* was the essential self created at the time of the individual's conception and coexisting in a non-material order of existence; Jung's perception of the king, in his role as the 'self of the people', as the community's *ka*, is very apt. The *akh* was the transfigured spirit, living in the realms of light, or in terms of a later eschatology, among the blest; the *akh* was a force which could be invoked to assist the deceased in the journey to the Afterlife. The king, as described earlier, seems in addition to have had a double, a twin, who existed independently of the king's earthly life and who was identified with the royal placenta. The double kept, as it were, the king's place in the region beyond the Imperishable Stars, to which the king would be translated after death.

Jung thought long and deeply about that aspect of the psyche which reveals itself in dreams or in circumstances of profound trauma, and which seems to exist independently of space and time. In doing so he came close to that analysis, or probing of the self, which the Egyptian division of the psyche into the several parts or distinct 'selves' implies. His equation of the king with Egypt's 'self' was itself a profound insight; he clearly recognized

that both the person of the king and the office of the kingship were fundamental to the understanding of the origins of the Egyptian state and the
ethos which underlay it.

Though Jung has been portrayed, as much by his admirers as by his
critics, as a mystic, almost a magus (a persona which he clearly was not at all
averse to assuming, for the occasion) he considered himself, first and foremost, to be a healer. In this, though he may not have been immediately
aware of it himself, he comes very close indeed to one of the most singular
aspects of the history of the earliest kings of Egypt.

Most peoples, whether ancient or of more modern times, have tended
always to celebrate their heroes as great warriors, preferably as conquerors.
The Egyptians too, were not wholly without such pretensions, but they were
outweighed by another, perhaps more ennobling trait. They admired
amongst their earliest heroic figures especially kings who were healers or
who achieved their reputation by the reconciling of opposite or conflicting
elements in the society over which they reigned so majestically.

Jung was aware of the power of the opposites in the structure of the
Egyptian state, particularly in its formative phases. As a doctor and as a
pioneer psychologist he, too, was a healer and a reconciler of opposites,
expressed in the conflicting elements of his patients' personalities. He
would, it is surely not too fanciful to suggest, have found much in common
with the great if mysterious figures who occupied the throne of Egypt in the
first brilliant centuries of its existence.

It must be said that Jung himself never devoted as much attention to the
application of his theories to the emergence of complex societies as has been
argued here. That he was interested in the psychological dynamics of past
societies is clear, especially from his correspondence and he was firm in his
belief of the universal application of such concepts as the collective unconscious and the influence of the archetypes.

In the decades which have passed since Jung's death in 1961 his work and
his influence have both been the subjects of scrutiny, by those who are alien-
ated by what they see as the streak of mysticism and what has come to be
called 'New Age' pseudo-science, as by those who see him as one of the most
original and important minds of the past century. Because Jung possessed
one of those towering intellects which encompasses a vast range of interests,
enthusiasms and areas of study and because he was a man who was never
afraid of speculation, who wrote ceaselessly, lectured, corresponded and was
subject to the excited pursuit of media and the channels of communication
which became so readily accessible during his lifetime, his work provides a
rich field for the proving of almost any theory, supportive or derogatory,
which may be advanced by his protagonists or his detractors.

Like other great figures of the recent past he has been exposed to the
mandatory process of revisionism, the reassessment of his theories and the
significance of his life. The disparagement which has already been focused on

some what appear to be his more arcane beliefs has been observed; to his admirers, these are sometimes mildly embarrassing but in the main they reflect simply the preoccupations of the society in which the commentator lives. So universal was Jung's range of reference and interest that he could hardly have resisted commenting on the issues of his own day, even those which were relatively ephemeral. Many of these issues touched on the stuff of one of his own principal fields of interest, myth, of which indeed he was a connoisseur. Given the extent of Jung's own exposure of his beliefs and praxis it is inevitable that some of his more quaint views should demand revision or, perhaps more charitably, setting them into the context of their time and of Jung's own life experience.

Another phase of Jung's involvement with the society of which he was a powerful, even an oracular voice, touches the application of his work in the political dimension and his own commitment, such as it was, to contemporary political postures. This aspect of the process of revision has focused particularly on Jung's attitude to Nazi ideology and the issue as to whether he can be classed as manifesting symptoms of the condition customarily described as 'anti-semitism'. He has also been accused, fancifully, as promoting himself as the focus of a new, non-Christian religion.[34]

Jung was a product of late nineteenth century Protestant German Switzerland; he was thus born as it were with an inbuilt programme of definite preconceptions, a situation little different from most people. He was intensely conservative in his social attitudes; he was not especially interested in politics, believing that the unconscious, his particular domain, was largely indifferent to, if not entirely unaware of political events. He exhibited a dislike of the modern world, thus evincing an attitude which many of his generation who lived through a period of marked social disintegration, shared with him.

His dislike of the present and his belief in the universality of the workings of the unconscious as common to all humans, inclined Jung to be suspicious of 'the new'. He saw the unconscious as working at a succession of ever deeper levels, the family, the larger society, even ultimately the animal. Jung was a committed anti-communist and distrusted profoundly all populist movements. He believed in the nowadays deeply unfashionable idea of government by the élite. The presence of this highly equivocal attitude has obviously disturbed some of the commentators on his life.[35]

However, Jung could not entirely avoid contact with some of the currents which ran through the society of his time. His most notable – and in many ways his most extraordinary – encounter with the shadows of the political life came in the aftermath of the First World War, a time of extreme political upheaval in Central Europe, when he detected the stirrings of 'the beautiful blond beast, beyond good and evil', in his analyses of a number of his German patients.[36] This was further reinforced by his recognition of the Wotan archetype, when he saw the return of the wild, irrational berserker god in the German unconscious.

These experiences led him to anticipate, with some apprehension, an upsurge in the psychic energy of the 'volk', which clearly was to find expression in the acceptance by the majority of the German people of the ideology of the National Socialist Party. He recognized the coming of the Nazi Party, supported by the appearance of the 'blond beast' and the return of Wotan, as evidence of the power of myth when it collided with the realities of politics.[37]

Jung's attitude to the Jews has been questioned. Fundamental to this question is the extent and character of his relationship with Freud, profoundly emotional as it was, almost to a neurotic degree. Jung distrusted the idea, propounded by some of Freud's disciples that there was a 'Jewish psychology'. He regarded Jews as possessing distinct characteristics as a group,[38] a view which would hardly be supported today and, like many others of the time, distrusted some aspects of what was seen to be their influence on the contemporary society. He was, however, never 'anti-Jewish'; to accuse him of 'anti-semitism' reveals the poverty of language of those who use the term, since 'semitic' and its cognates can only be applied in a linguistic sense, for that is the only meaning which the word possesses. 'Anti-semitism', if it means anything at all can only mean an antagonism to or antipathy for speakers of semitic languages: in the contemporary world the only native speakers of a semitic language are the Arabs.

Jung's views of the politics of his time do not have any significant bearing on his primary insights into the workings of the human psyche. Like every other man who has expressed himself about fundamental questions and attempted to provide answers to them, he would no doubt have expressed himself differently if he had lived in an age when such matters are approached, on the one hand with scepticism and on the other with a set of entrenched political attitudes which, during his lifetime would have been anathema to him.

Jung's attitudes to the society in which he lived were, to a remarkable degree, consistent with those views which he expressed about the Egyptian state. As was discussed above, his most pertinent insight here was his recognition of the personality and office of the king. The presence of 'the Great Individual' in so decisive a period as the formation of the Egyptian state, supported by a dedicated, highly talented élite impressed him deeply, as did the nature of the society which, in its early centuries at least, must have corresponded closely with his own projections of the ideal.

CHRONOLOGICAL TABLE

BC	EGYPT			MESOPOTAMIA	THE ARABIAN GULF
2000	Seventh to Tenth Dynasties	The Middle Kingdom Senwosret III Nebhetepre Montuhotep II		End of Neo-Sumerian Empire Ibbi-Sin Shulgi	Dilmun flourishes Copper shipped from Oman to Bahrain Qala'at al-Bahrain City II Barbar Temples I, II Royal tombs at Aali
2200	The Sixth Dynasty	Pepi II Pepi I Teti Wenis	The Pyramid Texts	Gudea of Lagash Naram-Sin Sargon of Akkad The Akkadian Empire	Qala'at al-Bahrain City I Sargon claims sovereignty over Gulf
2400	The Fifth Dynasty	Niuserre Sahure Userkaf			
	The Fourth Dynasty	Shepsekaf Menkaure Khafre Djedefre Khufu Sneferu	The Pyramid Age		Dilmun in Eastern Arabia Beehive tombs in Oman
2600	The Third Dynasty	Huni Khaba Sekhemkhet Netjerykhet	The Step Pyramid	Early Dynastic III Early Dynastic II	Settlement on Tarut Island

THE OLD KINGDOM (spanning the Fifth, Fourth and Third Dynasties)

Period	Date / NAQADA	Dynasty	Rulers / Sites	Sites	Phase		Notes
EARLY DYNASTIC PERIOD	2800	The Second Dynasty	Khasekemwy Peribsen-Sekhemib Ninetjer Raneb Hotepsekhemwy				
	3000 NAQADA III	The First Dynasty	Qa'a Semerkhet Den Djet Aha	Royal Tombs at Abydos Nobles' tombs at Saqqara Sacrifice of retainers	Early Dynastic I		
	3200 NAQADA II	Dynasty 'O'	Narmer Scorpion II Scorpion I Iry-Hor Ro	Adaïma Hierakonpolis			
PRE-DYNASTIC	3400 NAQADA II		Buto, Ma'adi				
	3600 BADARIAN CULTURE			Merimde Bani Salame			Evidence of fishing and seasonal settlements
	4500				Ubaid IV Ubaid III Ubaid II		
	5000	First settlements in the Nile Valley			Ubaid I		

NOTES

INTRODUCTION TO THE NEW EDITION

1 Atlal, *The Journal of Saudi Arabian Archaeology*, published by the Department of Antiquities and Museums, Riyadh, and *The Journal of Oman Studies*, published by the Ministry of National Heritage, The Sultanate of Oman.

2 The Department of Antiquities, the Sultanate of Oman, the Department of Antiquities and Museums, the Kingdom of Saudi Arabia.

3 The first Bahrain National Museum; the Qatar National Museum; The Oman Museum; The Museum of Archaeology and Ethnography, Riyadh; The Museum of the King Abdul Aziz Military Academy, Riyadh; The Museum of the Sultan's Armed Forces, Bait al-Falaj, Sultanate of Oman; six regional museums in Saudi Arabia, at Najran, Jizan, Al-Ula, Taima, Jawf and Hofuf; Qasr al-Masmak, Riyadh; a study of the captioning of the collections in the Egyptian Museum, Cairo.

4 An entire bibliography has erupted over the issues outlined here in recent years. The seminal work was Bauval and Gilbert (1994), followed by Bauval and Hancock (1996) and Bauval, R. (1999) *Secret Chamber: The Quest for the Hall of Records*, London. An attempt to counter the arguments advanced in these and similar works was produced by Lawton, I. and Ogilvie-Herald, C. (1999), *Giza The Truth. The People, Politics and History behind the World's Most Famous Archaeological Site*, London. See also Picknett and Prince (1999) *The Stargate Conspiracy*, London, for a similar demolition, supported by an alternative theory.

5 Bauval and Hancock, 1996: passim, but particularly 117–28, 298–304, 305–8.

6 Gauri, K.L. (1984) 'Geological Study of the Sphinx', *Newsletter ARCE 127* 24–43, cited in Reader op. cit. (n.25).

7 Lehner op. cit.: 67. Gantenbrink, R. 'Videoscopische Untersuchung der sog. Luftcanaql der Cheops pyramide' (presented to the German Archaeological Institute, Cairo, dated March 4 1997).

8 The non-alignment of Mintaka with the third of the three main pyramids at Giza (that associated with Menkaure) has been reviewed convincingly in the two works cited in n.4 above.

9 See Ch. 1, n.10.

10 Hahn, J. (1971) 'La Statuete masculine de la grotte du Hohenlenstein – Stadel (Wurtemburg)', *L'Anthropologie* 75: 233–44.

PREFACE TO THE ORIGINAL EDITION

1 The text has been lightly edited, principally to revise comments which later research has judged no longer to be valid.

1 THE LAND OF EGYPT

1 The term 'Early Dynastic Period' is preferred today rather than 'Archaic Period' which was in general usage in the past but is now regarded as expressing a subjective or qualitative judgement.

2 Manetho, *The Aegyptiaca*, trans. W.G. Waddell (1940) Cambridge, Mass. and London; Verbrugghe G.P. and Wickersham, J.M. (1996) *Berossos and Manetho, Introduced and Translated: Native Traditions in Ancient Mesopotamia and Egypt*, Michigan.

3 For an overview of the early kingship see Wilkinson (1999) and Baines, J. (1991) 'Origins of the Egyptian Kingship', in O'Connor, D. and Silverman, D. (eds) *Ancient Egyptian Kingship*: 95–156.

4 Mellaart (1967) *Catalhüyük: A Neolithic Town in Anatolia*, London.

5 Kenyon (1957) *Digging up Jericho,* London; (1979) *Archaeology in the Holy Land* (fourth edition).

6 Midant-Reynes, 1992/2000: 69–72, 146–52.

7 Muzzolini, A. (1992) 'Dating Earliest Central Saharan Art: Archaeological and Linguistic Data' in Friedman and Adams (1992): 147–54.

8 Vance Heynes, C. (1990) 'Geological Evidence of Pluvial Climates in the Nabta Area of the Western Desert, Egypt' in Wendorf and Schild (1990): 355–71.

9 Dakhla Oasis Project 1982–6, *JSSEA*. McKim Malville, J. *et al.* 'Megaliths and Neolithic Astronomy in Southern Egypt', *Nature,* vol. 392: 488–90.

10 Bell, B. (1970) 'The Oldest Records of the Nile Floods', *Geographical Journal* 136: 569–73; Butzer, K.W., 'Nile Flooding History' in Bard (1998): 568–70.

11 Potts, 1990: 12–22. Also Rice, 1994: 65–77, for discussion and references, principally in relation to Eastern Arabia and the Gulf.

12 Kassler, P. (1973) The Structures and Geomorphic Evolution of the Persian Gulf', in B.H. Purser (ed.) *The Persian Gulf*, Berlin.

13 Roaf, M. (1970) 'Excavations at Al-Markh, Bahrain: a Fish Midden of the Mid-fourth Millennium', *Paléorient* 2.

14 Zarins (1982) 'Early Rock Art of Saudi Arabia', *Archaeology*, 35: 20–7; Khan, M. (1991) 'Recent Rock Art and Epigraphic Inscriptions in Saudi Arabia, PSAS: 21: 113–22.

15 McClure, H.A. (1971) *The Arabian Peninsula and Prehistoric Populations*, Miami.

16 For an attractive review of Petrie's career see Drower, M.S. (1985) *Flinders Petrie: a Life in Archaeology*, London.

17 Emery, 1949–58; 1961.

18 Quibell, J.E. (1913) *Excavations at Saqqara (1911–1914): The Tomb of Hesy*, Cairo; (1923) *Excavations at Saqqara (1912–1914): Archaic Mastabas*, Cairo.

19 Firth and Quibell with lower, 1935 *Excavations at Saqqara: The Step Pyramid*, Cairo.

20 Petrie 1900, 1901a.

21 Emery 1949, 1954, 1958.

22 See Comparative Chronology Table.

23 Petrie 1953.

24 Quibell 1900; Quibell and Green 1902.

25 Adams, B. (1974) *Ancient Hierakonpolis: Supplement.* Warminster; (1995) *Ancient Nekhen: Garstang in the City of Hierakonpolis*, New Malden.

26 Reisner, 1942, 1955.

27 Lauer, J.-P. (1962) *Histoire Monumentale des Pyramides d'Égypte: Les Pyramides à Degrés (111ᵉ Dynastie)* Le Caire; (1976) *Saqqara: The Royal Cemetery of Memphis: Excavations and Discoveries since 1850*, London.

2 THE ROOTS OF THE EGYPTIAN STATE

1 The king of Egypt's most frequently employed title was *nebty-tawy*, which is transliterated 'he of the sedge (of Upper Egypt) and the bee (of Lower Egypt)', sometimes conflated as 'Lord of the Two Lands'. Nowadays the more concise term 'Dual King' is increasingly preferred, perpetuating the Egyptian preoccupation with dualism.
2 See below n.23 below on the excavations at Buto, conducted since 1983 by the German Archaeological Institute, Cairo.
3 McKim Malville *et al.*, 1998.
4 See Spence, K., Ch. 8, n.19.
5 McKim Malville *et al.* op. cit.
6 Kuper, 2002 in Friedman (ed.): 5.
7 Wendorf and Schild, 1984: 9–18, 49–72.
8 Ibid.: 71.
9 *EA* 2: 13.
10 Vermeersch, P. *et al.* (1984) 'Une miniére de silex et un squelette du Paléolithique supérieur ancien à Nazlet Khater, Haute-Egypte', *L'Anthropologie* 88: 231–44.
11 Idem (1998) 'A Middle Palaeolithic burial of a modern human at Taramsa Hill, Egypt', *Antiquity* 72: 475–84.
12 Weigall, 1909: pls. XXIX, XXX, for an early recorded example.
13 The bull-cult in Egypt was of profound importance, all-pervasive and long sustained. See Rice, 1998: Chapter 10, 'The Royal and Divine Bull in Egypt'.
14 Mellaart, 1965: passim.
15 Mellaart, J. (1975) *The Neolithic of the Near East*, London: 15.
16 Zeuner, 1963: 221–8; Trigger *et al.*, 1983: 20, 29, 119.
17 Rice, 1998: principally Ch. 10.
18 A Naqada I pottery dish, originally in the Golenishchef collection in Moscow, illustrated in A. Scharf (1928) 'Some prehistoric vases in the British Museum and remarks on Egyptian prehistory', *JEA* 14: 261–76.
19 Osborn, D.J. with Osbornová (1998) *The Mammals of Egypt:* 57–68, Warminster.
20 An interesting but controversial view of the longevity of the human–canine relationship is considered in Vila *et al.* (1997) 'Multiple and Ancient Origins of the Domestic Dog', *Science* 276: 1687–9.
21 Junker, H. (1929–40) Vorläufiger Bericht über die Grabung der Akademie der Wissenschäften in Wein, auf der neolithischen Siedlung von Meimde Beni Safame (West delta). *Anzeigen der Alcademie der Wissenschaften in Wien. Philosophisch-historische Klasse* 1929, 1930, 1932, 1934, 1940.
22 De Bono, F. and Mortensen, B. (1990) *El Omari: a Neolithic settlement and other sites in the vicinity of Wadi Hof*, Helwan: 81, pl. 28.1.
23 von Der Way, T., in Bard, 1999: 180–4.
24 Faltings, D. 'Canaanites at Buto in the early fourth millennium', *EA* 13: 29–32.
25 Clay 'cones', often with decorated heads, were inserted in the walls and columns of early Sumerian monumental buildings. In the case of those used to decorate free-standing columns the technique sometimes had the effect of weakening them, resulting in their collapse.
26 Friedman, R. (2000) 'Ceramic Nails' in *Nekhen News* 12: 13.
27 Illustrated in Scamuzzi, E. (n.d.) *Egyptian Art in the Egyptian Museum of Turin*, New York: pls. I–V, especially pl. V.
28 Baumgartel, 1947: Figs 13, 19, 36, 37, 38, 39, 43, 44, 45, 46, 48, 49, 50.
29 Ny Carlsberg Glyptotek Æ IN 1722. Acquired in Cairo by Fr. W. von Bissing, taken into the Ny Carlsberg Glyptotek in 1934.
30 Petrie, W.M.F. (1900): 32; pl. VI, Ashmolean Museum 1896. 1908. E3202.
31 Wilkinson, 1999: 35, 41–2, 43; J. Seeher in Bard, 1999: 91–3.
32 Kuhrt, 1998: vol. 1: 70–1.

3 THE PURSUIT OF THE DIVINE

1 Lhote, H. (1958) *A la Découverte du Fresques du Tasil*, Paris (trans. as *The Search for the Tassili Frescoes* (1959)) London, introduced many of the rock paintings of the Western and Central Sahara to an international audience. The author appears to have been responsible for the suggestion that some of the paintings showed 'Egyptian influence'; see especially pls. 26, 30, 33, 35, 36, 38, 39, 48, 51, 52–3, 60.

2 Weigall, 1909: pls. XXIX, XXX, XXXVI.

3 Winkler, H., 1938–9: passim but especially 1938: XXXIV, XXXV, XXXVI.

4 Dunbar, J.H. (1940) *The Rock Drawings of Lower Nubia*, Cairo.

5 Ibid.: 46.

6 Fuchs, G. (1989) 'Rock Engravings in the Wadi Barramiya, Eastern Desert of Egypt', *The African Archaeological Review* 7: 122–54.

7 Ibid.: Fig. 4.

8 Rohl, D. (ed.) (2000) *The Followers of Horus: Eastern Desert Survey Report Vol. 1*, Basingstoke.

9 Ibid.: pls. 82.10, 83.12.

10 Ibid.: pls. 38.5–6, 39.6.

11 Zarins *et al.*, 1981: pl. 34 A, B.

12 Rijksmuseum van Leiden, Netherlands, 3.1.6.

13 Emery, 1958: pl. 103a.

14 Safar, F. *et al.* (1982) *Eridu*: pl. 111, Baghdad.

15 Carter, R. and Crawford, H. (2002) 'The Kuwait-British Archaeological Expedition to as-Sabiyah; Report on the third season's work' *Iraq LXIV*: 1–14. Carter, R. (2002) 'As-as-Sasbiyah: excavations by the British Archaeological Expedition to Kuwait' *PSAS* 32: 13–30.

16 Emery, 1954: 138, pl. XLV.

17 Musée de Lyon 1598.

18 JE 34210 = CG 64868. Saleh and Sourouzian, 1987: no. 52.

19 CGJCW9ii § 42.

20 Kjaerum, P., *Failaka/Dilmun: The Second Millennium Settlements. Vol. 1:1: The Stamp and Cylinder Seals*: pl. 262.

21 Gardiner, 1969: sign R8.

22 Petrie, 1953: A2 (The Manchester Museum).

23 Vandier, J. *et al.* (1973) *L'Egypte avant les Pyramides* (exhibition catalogue): 16–17, pl. 3.

24 Lewis Williams, J.D. (1991) 'Wrestling with Analogy: A Methodological Dilemma in Upper Palaeolithic Art Research', *PPS* (57.1): 151.

25 Lewis Williams, J.D. and Dowson, T.A. (1988) 'The Signs of all Times: Entoptic Phenomena in Upper Palaeolithic Art' *Current Anthropology* 24: 201–45.

26 Ibid. (1989) *Images of Power: Understanding Bushman Rock Art*, Johannesburg.

27 Zarins, 1986: op. cit.

28 Te Velde, H., 1977: 25–6.

29 Ibid. 141–51.

30 Ibid. 63ff.

31 Ibid. 129–33.

32 Gwyn Griffiths, J. (1960) *The Origins of Osiris*, Munich, reviews the various suggestions made by scholars of earlier generations who sought to identify the Egyptian god Osiris with a Mesopotamian prototype. He quotes S. Mercer, *The Religion of Ancient Egypt*, who identified Osiris with Asar, a title of the Babylonian god Marduk, citing many correspondences between them. Despite the fact that the Egyptian name of Osiris is Asar, it is unlikely that such speculations would attract much support today, but Osiris' origins remain obscure.

33 Frankfort, 1948: 83–4.

34 Burstein, S.M. (1978) *The Babyloniaca of Berossus*, Malibu. Also Verbrugghe and Wicker-sham, 1996; Chs. 1, 2, 3.
35 Frankfort, 1948: 352, Ch. 2, n.5.
36 Gardiner, 1969: sign C 10.
37 Heinrich, E. (1936) *Kleinfunde aus den Archaischen Tempelschichten aus Uruk*, Berlin. Nissen, H.J. (1988) *The Early History of the Ancient near East (9000–2000 BC)* (trans. E. Lutzeier with K.J. Northcutt), Chicago: 190.
38 Rundle-Clark, R.T. (1959) *Myth and Symbol in Ancient Egypt*: 216, London.
39 Lloyd, S. and Müller, H.W. (1980) *Ancient Architecture*: pl. 18, London.
40 Amiet (1980) *Glyptique Mésopotamienne Archäique*: pls. 12.204, 16.272, 44.641, 46.656, 120, 1606, 1607.
41 George, A. (1999) trans. *The Epic of Gilgamesh: A New Translation. Tablet XI The Standard Version: XI8–XI31*, London.
42 Dryer, G., 1992: 293–9: 1993a: 23–46: 'A Hundred Years at Abydos' *EA 3*: 10–12.
43 Arnett, W.S. (1982) *The Prehistoric Origins of Egyptian Hieroglyphs. Evidence of the Development of Rudimentary Forms of Hieroglyphs in Upper Egypt in the Fourth Millennium*, Washington: pls. 5; ii. 2a 1 and 2 (after Petrie and Quibell, 1895): 12; pl. XXXIV.
44 Meltzer, 1970: 193–4.
45 Mellaart, 1965: 220.
46 Wilkinson, T.A.H. (2002) 'Uruk into Egypt' in *Artifacts of Complexity: Tracking the Uruk in the Near East*, Warminster: 241–3.
47 Gardiner, 1969: sign S20.
48 Ibid.
49 Roth, M., 1993: 77–9.
50 Ibid.: 77. The author cites H. Frankfort (1949) as linking the attributes of the two divinities.
51 Ibid.: 78.
52 Ibid.: 77. However, the author puts the suggestion that, as the representations of the ceremony have a greater antiquity in Egypt than in Sumer, it was Egypt which in this case influenced her eastern contemporary.

4 THE ROYAL POWER CENTRES

 1 Adams, R. McC. (1965) *Land Behind Baghdad: A History of Settlement on the Diyala Plains*, Chicago: (1972) 'Patterns of urbanisation in early southern Mesopotamia' in Ucko, P.J. *et al.* (eds) *Man, Settlement and Urbanism*, London.
 2 Williams, 1986.
 3 Dryer, 1992: 295.
 4 Ibid. *EA 3*: pl. p.11.
 5 Dyer op. cit. pls. 6.1–4; 1993: pl. 7 c-j.
 6 Dyer, G., in Baird, 1999: 110.
 7 Weeks, 1972.
 8 Crowfoot Payne, J. (1993) *Catalogue of the Predynastic Egyptian Collection in the Ashmolean Museum*: 3, Oxford.
 9 Emberling, G. and McDonald, H. (2001) 'Excavations at Tel Brak 2000: Preliminary Report', *Iraq LXIII*: 21–54; Figs 7, 12.
10 Andersen, H. (1986) 'The Barbar Temple: Stratigraphy, Architecture and Interpretation' in Khalifa and Rice: 170–2; Doe, D.B. (1986) 'The Barbar Temple: the Masonry' in Khalifa and Rice: 188–90; pls. 52, 53.
11 Quibell and Green, 1902: 3–6; pls. LXV, LXXII, LXXIII.
12 Friedman, R., 2000. See Ch. 2, n.18.
13 *EA 18*: 32.

14 Adams (1974) *Ancient Hierakonpolis*: 59–60; pls. XV, XVI, Warminster.
15 Kjaerum, 1983: 59, 60, 63, 67, 76, 88, 90, 177, 183, 204, 209, 224, 229, 234, 236, 357. Alsindi, K.M. (1999) *Dilmun Seals, Bahrain*: 196–203.
16 Compare Adams, 1974: pl. 38. 324 with Zarins, 1978: pls. 68, 69.
17 Zarins op. cit.: 157, pls. 67.58; 545, pl. 68.
18 Quibell, 1900: pl. XV 1, 2, 4.
19 Hoffman, 1980: 119–37.
20 Davies, V. and Friedman, R. (1998) *Egypt*: 25–7.
21 Ibid.: 27.
22 Hoffman (1980) *JNES* 39: 119–37.
23 Adams, B. (1998) 'Something Very Special down in the Elite Cemetery', *Nekhen News* 10: 2–3.
24 Ibid.
25 Adams (1999) *EA* 15: 29–31.
26 Ibid.: 30 (illustrated 31).
27 Adams, B. (2000) 'Some Problems Solved in the Locality 6 Cemetery', *Nekhen News* 12: 4–5; colour illustration: 16.
28 Hoffman [with Lupton and Adams], 1982: 38–9; 59–60.
29 Maish, A. (1998) 'Trauma at HK43', *Nekhen News* 10: 6–7.
30 Ibid. illustration: 7.
31 Hoffman *et al.*, 1982: 56.
32 Ibid. (Berger, M.): 61–2; fig. 1.18.
33 Quibell and Green, 1901: 28–30.
34 Kemp, 1973: 36–43. Ibid.: 43–5.
35 Midant-Reynes, B. *et al.* (1996) 'The Predynastic Site of Adaïma', *EA* 9:13–15.
36 Ibid.: ill. p.15.
37 Ibid.: pl. p. 14.
38 *EA* 18: 32.
39 Crowfoot Payne, J. (1968): 'Lapis Lazuli in Early Egypt', *Iraq* XXX: 58–61.
40 Wilkinson, 1999: 163.
41 Porada, E. (1980) 'A Lapis Lazuli Figurine from Hierakonpolis in Egypt', *Iranica Antiqua* vol. XV: 175–80; pl. 1.
42 Rice, 1994: pl. 8.6.

5 THE DUAL KINGS

1 The latter part of which is frequently designated 'Dynasty 0'.
2 This text survives from the reign of King Senwosret I (Frankfort [1948] Ch. 2, from Sethe, K. (1928) *Dramatische Texte zu altägyptischen Mysterienspielen Untersuchungen zur Geschichte und Altertumskunde Ägyptens, Vol X*, Leipzig).
3 CAH 1.2: 36.
4 Gardiner, 1969: sign N 28.
5 Ibid.: sign O41.
6 From the 'Main Deposit', Hierakonpolis; Ashmolean Museum, Oxford.
7 Wilkinson, 1999: 39, 51.
8 Petrie, 1953: pl. 13.
9 Ibid.: F15–16.
10 Ibid.: pl. J25 (reverse); K 26 (obverse).
11 *Mesopotamia*: Amiet (1980): pls. 26. 424; *Susa*: Amiet (1966): 34B, 35 (compare Narmer Palette Petrie [1953]: K36). See also the extensive review of foreign (Mesopotamian and Elamite) iconography in late predynastic Egypt in Smith, 1992, in Friedman and Adams (eds), 1992: 235–46.

12 Zarins, 1982: 68.545.
13 Ashmolean Museum, Oxford: Grave 1610. 1895: 795.
14 Amiet, 1966: pl. 42A.
15 Asselburghs, 1961: pls. XL, XLI.
16 Lurker, M. (1974) *The Gods and Symbols of Ancient Egypt*: 91 (as 'Onouris').
17 Petrie, 1953: E14 'Two Gazelle Palette' obverse.
18 Wilkinson (1993) 'The Identification of Tomb B1 at Abydos: Refuting the Existence of a King *Ro*Iry-Hor', *JEA* 79: 241–3.
19 Dryer, G. (1992) 'Horus Krokodil, ein Gegen könig der Dynastie 'O'', in Friedman and Adams: 259–63.
20 Dryer, see Ch. 5, n.7.
21 Asselburghs (1961): 309, pl. XXIII; Spencer (1993): 73, pl. 52.
22 Petrie, W.M.F. (1915) *Ancient Egypt*: 168, 172; View 4; Page, A. (1976) *Egyptian Sculpture: Archaic to Saite. From the Petrie Collection*: pl. 1. London.
23 Petrie, 1900, 1901a.
24 Emery, 1949, 1954, 1958.
25 Emery (1938) *Excavations at Saqqara: The Tomb of Hemaka*, Cairo.
26 Emery, 1949: Tomb 3357.
27 Dryer, G. (1987) 'Ein Sigel der frühzeitlichen Königsnekropole von Abydos', *MDAIK* 43: 33–43.
28 Dryer, G. *et al.* (1996) 'Umm el-Qaab. Nachunterschungen in Frühzeitlichen Königsfriedhof. 7/8 Vorbericht', *MDAIK* 52: 11–81.
29 Dryer, G., see Ch. 5, n.7 and Ch. 6, n.20.
30 *EA* 14:31.
31 Emery, 1954: Tomb S3357.
32 Friedman, R. (2001) 'The Archaeology of Vanity', in *Nekhen News* vol. 13: 12, ill. p. 19.
33 Emery, 1961: 59; fig. 21.
34 Reymond, E.A.E. (1962) 'The Primeval Djeba', *JEA* 48: 81–8: (1963) 'The Origins of the Spear I' *JEA* 49: 140–6: (1964) 'The Origins of the Spear II' *JEA* 50: 133–8: (1965) 'The Cult of the Spear in the Temple of Edfu', *JEA* 51: 144–8.
35 Petrie, 1901: 16–17; Frontispiece.
36 Petrie (1925) *Tombs of the Courtiers and Oxyrhynkos*: 4, 5; III, IV.
37 Ibid. pls. XII, XIII (especially no. 537).
38 Emery, 1949: S 3471 13–69.
39 Emery, 1954: S3503: pls. VIb, VIIa, VIIb.
40 Rice, 1998: Ch. 10.
41 Petrie, 1953: pl. G17.
42 Mellaart, 1965: 65, 111, 118; pl. IV, figs 11–16, 22, 23, 64.
43 Rice, 1998: 178–81, 267.
44 Musée du Louvre E 11007.
45 Emery (1959) 139–58.
46 Emery, 1938: 29; Frontispiece, pl. 12e, cat. No. 307.
47 BM EA 55586.
48 Emery, 1949: op. cit.
49 Emery, 1958: 73–97; pls. 85, 86, 87, 90.
50 Ibid.: 76; pl. 91b.
51 Emery, 1949 (as 'Enezib'): 82–94; pls. 20–35, especially 24.
52 Ibid. pl. 27b.
53 Petrie, 1900: 13; pl. LX.
54 Emery, 1949: 116, 123; 1958: 33, 97, 109.
55 Wilkinson, 1999: 82.

6 THE LEGACY OF THE FOUNDER KINGS

1 Frankfort, 1948: 47, n.49, quoting Gardiner 'The Autobiography of Rekhmire'.
2 Midant-Reynes *et al.*, 1996: 13–15.
3 Saad, 1947, 1951.
4 Noted by D. Jeffreys in Bard, 1999: 367–8.
5 See n.3.
6 Midant-Reynes, 1992/2000: 82–3, 124.
7 Wood, 1987: 67, 69.
8 Ibid.: 64.
9 Petrie Museum of Egyptology UC. 28614B.
10 Kohler, E.C. (1998) 'Excavations at Helwan – New Insights into Early Dynastic Stone Masonry' *BACE* 9: 65–72.
11 Reade, C. (2002) 'Giza Before the Fourth Dynasty', *The Journal of the Ancient Chronology Forum*, vol. 9: 5–21.
12 Firth, C.M. (1927) *The Archaeological Survey of Nubia. Report for 1901–1911*: 204–7, Cairo.
13 Williams, 1986: passim.
14 Ibid.: 109–12; pls. 34, 38.
15 Seidelmeier, S. (1996) 'Town and State in the Early Old Kingdom. A View from Elephantine' in Spencer, 1996: 108–27.
16 Ibid.: 111.
17 Zarins, J. and Zahrani, A. (1985) 'Archaeological Investigations in the Tihama Plain', *Atlal* 10: 48–9. Newton, L.S. and Zarins, J. (2000) 'Aspects of Bronze Age art of Southern Arabia: The Pictorial Landscape and its Relation to Economic and Socio-Political Status', *AAE Vol. 11*, no. 2: 155.
18 Obverse of the Narmer Palette, bottom register right.
19 Strouhal, E. (1992) *Life in Ancient Egypt*: 134–5, Cambridge.
20 Wilkinson, 1999: 82.
21 Ibid.: 240–1.
22 Ibid.: 83.
23 Excavations of the University of Hanover; *EA2* (1992): 13.
24 Bibby, 1973: 28–36. Zarins, 1978: op. cit.; Potts, 1990: 178–81.
25 Prideaux, Col. F.B. (1912) 'The Sepulchral Tumuli of Bahrain', *Archaeological Society of India Annual Report 1908–9*: 62–3 (quoting Yaqut), Calcutta.
26 Zarins, J. *et al.* (1983) 'Excavations at Dhahran South – the Tumuli Field. A Preliminary Report', *Atlal* 8: 25–54.
27 Kraus, R. *et al.* (1989) 'The Silver Hoard from City IV Qala'at al-Bahrain', in Potts (ed.) *BBVO* 2: 161–8.
28 Simpson, W.K. (1956) 'A Statuette of King Nineter', *JEA* 42: 45–9; Wilkinson, 1999: 85–6, pl. 3.2.
29 Statue of Hotepdief, EMC JE34557 (=CG1); Saleh and Sourouzian no. 22.
30 Wilkinson, 1999: 89–91.
31 Reisner, 1936:138; fig. 60 (after Quibell *Archaic Mastabas* pl. XXX).
32 CAH 1.2: 20, 31, 35; Wilkinson, 1999: 89–91.
33 Ibid.: 89.
34 Blackman, A.M. and Fairman, H.W. (1942) 'The Myth of Horus at Edfu', *JEA* 28: 32–8; (1943) *JEA* 29: 2–36; (1944) *JEA* 30: 5–22.
35 Egyptian Museum Cairo: JE 32161.
36 Ashmolean Museum E517.
37 Petrie, 1901: pl. LXIII; Wilkinson, 1999: 91–4.
38 Dryer, G. (1991) 'Zur Rekonstruktion der Oberbauten der Königsgraber der I. Dynastie in Abydos', *MDAIKI* 47: 43–7.

39 O'Connor, D. (1989) 'Boat Graves and Pyramid Origins: New Discoveries at Abydos, Egypt', *Expedition* 33: 5–17: 'The Earliest Royal Boat Graves', *EA* 6: 3–7.
40 Emery, 1949: S 3471 13–69. Mathieson, I. *et al.* (1995) 'Sensing the Past', *EA*: 26–7.

7 THE THIRD DYNASTY: VISIONS OF ETERNITY

1 Potts, 1990: 208–15.
2 Ibid.: 237–43.
3 Firth and Quibell (1935); J.-P. Lauer (1976) *Saqqara, The Royal City of Memphis: Excavations and Discoveries since 1850*, London.
4 Hurry, J.B. (1928) *Imhotep. The Vizier and Physician of King Zoser and Afterwards the Egyptian God of Medicine*: 5; Appendix C, The Pedigree of Imhotep, Oxford.
5 Lauer op. cit.: 92.
6 Lauer (1997) 'Recent Discoveries Made During the Search for Imhotep's Tomb': 217–44.
7 Verner, M. (1997/2001) quoting architect Ladislav Køivsky; no further bibliographic information provided.
8 Gardiner, 1969: sign N25.
9 Lehner, 1997: 84 and plan; 87 profile.
10 Lehner op. cit.: 84–93.
11 This interesting observation is contained in Verner, 2002: 116, citing 'the Czech astronomer Ladislav Køivsky' but without further bibliographical information.
12 Firth and Quibell, op. cit. vol. 1, 70, 116; vol. 2, pl. 73.
13 *Illustrated London News*, Feb. 28 1925; Firth and Quibell op. cit. vol. 2: pls. 24b, 28a, b; 29. 1–4; 30.
14 Murray, M.A. (1904) *Saqqarah Mastabas*, vol. 1: 3; pls. 1–2; vol. 2: 1–12, pl. 1; Stevenson Smith (1958/1981): 61–7; ills. 49, 50. Egyptian Museum, Cairo CG 1385.
15 An interpretation of a relief of King Niuserre of the Fifth Dynasty 'receiving seven lives from Anubis the death-god', inspired by Dr Murray's theories of Egyptian royal death-cults, was developed by G.A. Wainwright (1938) in *The Sky Religion in Egypt, Oxford*.
16 Quibell, J.E. (1913) *The Tomb of Hesy: Excavations at Saqqarah*, Cairo. Terrace and Fischer, 1970: no. 4, 33–6; W. Wood (1978) 'A Reconstruction of the Reliefs of Hesy-Re', *JARCE* 15: 9–24; Egyptian Museum Cairo 1426.
17 Højgaard, K. (1986) 'Dental Anthrological Investigations on Bahrain', Khalifa and Rice: 164–72.
18 Goneim, Z. and Lauer, J-P. (1956) 'Découverte du tombeau sud de l'Horus Sekhem-khet dans son complexe funéraire à Saqqarah', *RdE* 20: 97–101; Edwards, 1996: 62.
19 Verner op. cit.: 140.
20 Seidelmayer, 1996: 122; fig. 3.

8 THE PYRAMID AGE: THE SPLENDOUR OF THE OLD KINGDOM

1 Fakhry, A. (1959–61) *The Monuments of Sneferu at Dahshur, 2 vols*, Cairo.
2 Edwards, 1993: 78.
3 Lesko, L., 1988; Seila, 1981, *JARCE* 25: 216–35.
4 Lehner, 1997: 103.
5 Reisner and Smith (1955): pls. 5, 6, 7, 8, 9, 12, 15abc, 16, 26–7, 28, 29, 37a, 39a, 40abc, 49.
6 Ibid. fig. 30.
7 Castel, G. *et al.* (1992) 'Les mines de cuivre du Ouadi Dara. Rapport préliminaire sur les travaux de la saison 1991', *BIFAO* 92: 51–65. Grimal, N. (1993) 'Travaux du l'Institut Français d'Archéologie Orientale en 1992–1993', *BIFAO* 93: 425–519; idem (1996) 'Travaux de l'IFAO en 1995–1996', *BIFAO* 96: 489–617.

8 The length of the reigns of Fourth Dynasty kings may have been underestimated. Sneferu, for example, may have reigned for a considerably longer period than the twenty-four years attributed to him.

9 *L'Art égyptien au temps des pyramides*. Exhibition catalogue Paris 1999: pls. 31, 32.

10 Reisner, G.A. (1936) *MFA Bulletin* XXXIV no. 206: 97.

11 Memi, in Hodjash S. and Berlev, O. (1982) *The Egyptian Reliefs and Stelae in the Pushkin Museum of Fine Art, Moscow*: no. 42, 93–5.

12 Nour, M.Z. (1960) *The Cheops Boats Pt. 1.*, Cairo.

13 Ministry of Information and Culture (1979) *Oman, A Seafaring Nation*: 107–12, 154, Muscat.

14 Lehner (1997) provides metric computations and notes the exceptional accuracy of the Pyramid's orientation and the precision of its measurements, a consideration noted by many commentators.

15 Tomkins, 1973: Ch. XV, 189–200.

16 Stecchini, L.C. (1992), in Tomkins op. cit.: 287–382.

17 Lehner, op. cit.: 97–100.

18 Stecchini, op. cit.: 377.

19 Spence, K. (2000) 'Ancient Egyptian Chronology and the Astronomical Orientation of Pyramids', *Nature* vol. 408 16 November 2000: 320–4; with a commentary by O. Gingerich, on which the observations here are based.

20 Grimal (1988/1992): 72.

21 Herodotus Book 11.125.

22 Reeves and Wilkinson, 1996: 137–9, particularly 139.

23 Lehner, 1997: 120–1; Chassinat, E., 1901: CRAIB 617–9; Grimal, N. 'Traveaux de l'IFAO en 1994–5 à Abou Rowash', *BIFAO* 95: 545–51.

24 Musée du Louvre F 12626. *L'Art égyptien au temps des pyramides*. Catalogue no. 57.

25 Ibid. Catalogue nos. 59–66 (Chéphren/Khafre).

26 Noted by C. Reader, op. cit., quoting work by T. Aigner: 16.

27 Stevenson Smith (1946/1949) 351–2, 352i, figs 232–3.

28 But see Donohue, V.A. (1992) 'The Goddess of the Theban Mountain', *Antiquity Vol. 66*, no. 253: 871–5, for an interesting survey of the possible exploitation of natural rock formations, hitherto unrecognized, including some ascribed to predynastic times.

29 Breasted, J.E. (1906) *Ancient Records of Egypt*, vol. I: §§ 210–12. Reisner, G.A. (1942) *Giza Necropolis*: 221, 310, 358–9.

9 THE OLD KINGDOM: FULFILMENT AND DECLINE

1 A more detailed review of Early Dynastic officials' titles will be found in Wilkinson, 1999: 135–9.

2 Lacau, E. and Lauer, J.-P. (1959) 'La Pyramide à Degrés IV: Inscriptions graves sur les vases': 65ff. pl. 25. *BIFAO* 1981 'Bol de Ptahpehen', cat. no. 9, Musée du Louvre E11016.

3 Jeffrey, D. and Tavares, A. (1994) 'The Historic Landscape of Early Dynastic Memphis', *MDAIK* 50: 143–73. Jeffreys, D. (2001) 'High and Dry? Survey of the Memphis escarpment', *EA* 19: 15–16. Wilkinson, 1999: 357–62.

4 Lehner, 1997: 212–15.

5 Dodson, A. (1995) *Monarchs of the Nile*: 34. London.

6 Evans, A.J. (1897) *Journal of Hellenic Studies* 17: 349; figs 23, 24.

7 Reisner and Stevenson Smith, 1955: 5; Dunham, D. and Simpson, W.K. (1971) *The Mastaba of Queen Meresankh III*. Giza Mastabas Vol. 1, Boston, Mass.

8 Stevenson Smith, 1946/9: 351–2, 353; figs 232, 233.

9 Paget, R.F.E. and Pine, A.A. (1898) *The Tomb of Ptah-Hetep*: 29 (ref. 'Ankh-en-Ptah') pl. XXXII. Stevenson Smith op. cit.: 354, 360.

10 Kanawati, N. (1980–2) *The Rock Tombs of el-Hawawish: The Cemetery of Akhmim*. 10 vols, Sydney.

11 Steindorf, G., 1913; see Ch. 9, n.16.

12 Wilson, 1951: 89–90; Durham, D. 1938: *JEA* 24: 1ff.

13 Manniche, L. (1991) *Music and Musicians in Ancient Egypt*: 121–2, London.

14 Moussa and Altenmüller (1971). Mainz.

15 Ibid.: 10.

16 Ibid.: pl. 12.

17 Ibid.: pl. 23.

18 Ibid.: pl. 2.

19 Ibid.: pl. 27.

20 Nunn, 1996: 11.

21 Junker, H. (1928) 'Der Stele des Hofarztes "Iry" ', *ZÄS* 63: 53–70.

22 Nunn, op. cit., 118–19.

23 Breasted 1: §§ 237–40 (as 'Nenekhsekhmet').

24 Junker, H. (1929–55) *Giza I-XII*, Vienna and Leipzig. Nunn op. cit.: 99–100. Egyptian Museum, Cairo 6138.

25 Nunn, op. cit.: 124–5.

26 Mussa and Altenmüller, op. cit. ('Shaft 8') pl. 40a.

27 Smith, 1949: 210–11; figs 81abc, 82, 83.

28 Faulkner (1969/1998): the Ancient Egyptian Pyramid Texts, Oxford.

29 Gardiner, 1969: sign N26.

30 Ibid.: sign N25.

31 Ibid.: sign N27.

32 Ibid.: sign N28.

33 Goedicke, H. (1981) 'Harkuf's Travels' *JNES* 40: 1–20; Lichtheim 1: 23–7.

34 Parkinson, R.B. (1991) *Voices from Ancient Egypt*: 54–6. London.

35 Habachi, L. (1985) 'The Sanctuary of Heqaib' AV 33.

10 THE END OF THE OLD KINGDOM

1 Kurht, 1995: vol. 1: 48–55.

2 Loprieno, A. in Bard, 1999: 40.

3 Pettinato, G. (1983) 'Dilmun nella documentazione epigrafica di Ebla', *BBVO* 2: 75–82.

4 Pritchard J.B. (ed.) (1955) *Ancient Near Eastern Texts Relating to the Old Testament*: 267–8 (trans. A.L. Oppenheim), Princeton.

5 Butzer, K.W. in Bard, 1999: 570.

6 Lichtheim 1: 149–62.

7 Ibid.: 149–50.

8 Ibid.: 83–97.

9 Grimal, N. (1988/1992): 89, 93, 128 (trans. I Shaw).

10 Jequier, J. (1935) *Fouilles à Saqqarah: La Pyramide d'Abu*, Cairo.

11 Hayes (1953/1990): 137; fig. 80. Metropolitan Museum of Art 14.7.11.

12 Hodjash and Barlev, 1982: no. 20, 57.

13 Hayes, op. cit.: 138–9, fig. 81. Metropolitan Museum of Art 98.4.2.

14 CAH 1.2: 198.

15 Kanawati, N. (1980).

16 Baines and Málek, 1980: 72; Edel, E. (1967) *Die Felsgräber der Qubbet el-Hawa bei Assuan*, Wiesbaden.

17 Waddell, W.G., 1948: 61, 63; Hayes, op. cit.: 143–4.

18 CAH 1.2:470–1; Lichtheim op. cit.: 97–104.
19 Lichtheim, op. cit.: 85–7.
20 CAH 1.2:464, 474.
21 Fischer, H.G. (1961) 'The Nubian Mercenaries of Gebelein during the First Intermediate Period', *Kush* 9: 44–80.
22 CAH 1.2:470–1; Grimal, 1992: 144.
23 Newberry, P.E. (1936) 'On the Parentage of the Intef kings of the Eleventh Dynasty', *ZÄS* 72:118–20; Winlock, 1947: 5, 6.
24 Osborn with Osbornová: 57–66.
25 Kjaerum (1983); passim. For Gulf trade generally, see Alsendi, K.M. (1999) *Dilmun Seals*, Bahrain, and Crawford, H. (2000) *Early Dilmun Seals from Saar: Art and Commerce in Bronze Age Bahrain*, London.
26 Kjaerum, op. cit.: nos. 315, 316.
27 Winlock (1947); Grimal, op. cit.: 155–81.

11 EASTWARDS FROM EGYPT

1 Of these, Petrie was probably the most distinguished, Elliot Smith the most misguided, who believed that all aspects of civilization diffused from Egypt. Emery also accepted the idea of an alien incursion into Egypt in the late predynastic period.
2 A series of Danish Archaeological Expeditions worked, first in Bahrain and later in other Gulf states, from the mid-1950s to the 1980s. Their work was recorded in *KUML*, the journal of the Jutland Archaeological Society and in occasional publications: of these, the series *Failaka/Dilmun: the Second Millennium Settlement,* reporting on their work on the island in the Bay of Kuwait are at present the most comprehensive; similar volumes are in preparation on the Bahraini sites. Reviews of the principal features of the work in Bahrain will be found in Khalifa and Rice (1986).
3 Ubaid sherds were first reported from eastern Arabian surface sites by two amateur archaeologists, G. Burkholder and M. Golding. They were followed by a professional survey and series of excavations carried out by A.H. Masry and subsequently published (Masry, 1974). In later years Ubaid pottery has been found on many sites throughout the Gulf; reported in *AAE*. Most recently an important Ubaid site, with surviving settlement levels, has been identified at es-Sabiyah in the Bay of Kuwait.
4 Leemans, W.F. (1959) *The Old Babylonian Merchant*, Leiden;.
(1960) 'The Trade relations of Babylonia and the question of relations with Egypt in the Old Babylonian period', *Studia et Documenta ad Iura Orientis Antiqui Pertinentia 6,* Leiden.
5 Rice (1983) *The Temple Complex at Barbar, Bahrain*, Manama. See also Andersen, Doe, Mortensen in Khalifa and Rice (1986).
6 Bibby, G. (1986) 'The Land of Dilmun is Holy', in Khalifa and Rice op. cit. Nashef, K. 'The Deities of Dilmun' in Khalifa and Rice.
7 Potts, 1990, vol. I: 173–8, 208–15.
8 Frifelt, K. (1991) *The Island of Umm an-Nar: the Third Millennium Graves*, Aarhus. Ibid. (1995) *Umm an-Nar The Third Millennium Settlement*, Aarhus.
9 See Ch. 3, n.15.
10 Durand, Capt. E.L. (1879) *Notes on the Islands of Bahrain and Antiquities as Submitted from the Political Resident, Persian Gulf to the Foreign Department*, Calcutta: 1–13.
11 Ibid. (1880) 'The Islands and Antiquities of Bahrain', *JRAS* n.s. 12 pt. 2.
12 Rawlinson, Major-General Sir H. (1880) 'Notes on Captain Durand's Report on the Islands of Bahrain', *JRAS* n.s. 12, pt. 2.
13 Ibid.
14 Bent, J.T. (1890) 'The Bahrain Islands in the Persian Gulf', *Proceedings of the Royal Geographical Society* 12: 1–19.

15 Smith, C.H., in discussion following Bent's paper.
16 Prideaux, Col. F.B. (1912) 'The Sepulchral Tumuli of Bahrain', *Archaeological Survey of India. Annual Report 1908–9*: 62–4.
17 Petrie, W.M.F. (1917) *Ancient Egypt Pt. IV*: 34, 36.
18 Ibid. (1917) *Ancient Egypt Pt. III*: 119; for 'Pun' (sic), see Drower, 1985: 213.
19 Ibid. (1939) *The Making of Egypt*: 77, London.
20 Drower, M.S. 1985: 196.
21 A slightly different translation is provided in Jacobsen, T. *The Harps the Once . . . Sumerian Poetry in Translation*: 184, Yale. George, A. (1999)*The Epic of Gilgamesh: A New Translation*. The Standard Version (Old Babylonian): Tablet X 150–80.
22 Cauville, S. (1987) *Essai sur la théologie du temple d'Horus à Edfou*, Cairo.
23 The following references to the myth of origins from inscriptions at Edfu and Hermopolis are drawn, unless otherwise stated, from Reymond, E.A.E. (1969) *The Mythical Origins of the Egyptian Temple*, Manchester and New York; see also bibliography therein.
24 Faulkner (1969/1998) U. 484. The same expression 'in the midst of the sea', is used to describe a king of Dilmun (then 'Tilmun') by the king of Assyria in the seventh century BC.
25 Ibid. U473.
26 Ibid. U273/4.
27 *Urshanabi* in the Old Babylonian Standard Version.
28 E.g. Lichtheim I: 48 U517; Faulkner, op. cit. U359.
29 Land contiguous to the Falcon's primeval domain. Reymond, op. cit.: passim especially 137–9.
30 Gardiner, 1969: sign D60.
31 Faulkner, op. cit.: U513.
32 Lichtheim, I: 211–14.
33 Faulkner, op. cit.: § 805.
34 Englund, R. 'Dilmun in the Archaic Corpus', in Potts (ed.) 1983; Nissen, H.J. 'The Occurrence of Dilmun in the oldest texts of Mesopotamia', in Al-Khalifa and Rice (eds) 1986.
35 Rice, M. (1972/1988) 'Al-Hajjar revisited: the grave complex at Al-Hajjar, Bahrain (revised, with photographs)', *PSAS* 18: 79–94; pl. III.
36 Bibby, 1973: 28–35.
37 Zarins, 1982: Bir Hima.
38 Zarins, J. and Badr, H. (1986) 'Archaeological Investigations in the Tihama Plain II', *Atlal* 10: 48–9.
39 McClure, 1971.
40 Kjaerum, 1983: pl. 2. 315, 316.
41 Petrie, 1901: pls. LVII 4–6i.
42 Rice, 1994: 156–63; figs 7.2, 7.3ab, 73c, 7.4.

12 C.G. JUNG AND ANCIENT EGYPT

1 This chapter has been revised extensively incorporating material introduced from Rice, M. (1997) *Egypt's Legacy: The Archetypes of Western Civilization 3000–300 BC*, Chapter 2.
2 Jung, C.G. (1961) *Memories, Dreams, Reflections*, London. Recorded and edited by Aniela Jaffe. Originally published (1959) as *Erinhungen, Träume, Gedanken*. Translated by Richard and Clara Winston. Hereafter 'MDR': 90, 158.
3 Freud, S. (1990) *Moses and Monotheism. Three Essays*, London.
4 Montserrat, D. (2000) *Akhenaten: History, Fantasy and Ancient Egypt*, London: 95–6, 105 ff.
5 MDR 256.

6 Interview with George Dupuis in *Gazette de Lausanne* republished as a pamphlet 1958. Published (1980) in McGuire, W. and Hill, R.F.C. (eds) *C.J. Jung Speaking*: 374, London.
7 MDR: 256.
8 CGJCL 1: 259–61.
9 MDR 251–2; CGJCL I: 44.
10 CGJCW: 9ii §§ 136, 148, 150.
11 de Santillana, G. and von Dechend, H. (1969) *Hamlet's Mill*, London, though sometimes seemingly wilfully obscure, is a work of considerable perception and influence.
12 CGJCL 2: 225.
13 Ibid.: 229.
14 Lehner (1997): 18, 212.
15 CGJCW 9i: §§ 489–524, 525–626; 7: 266–406.
16 CGJCW 9i: § 1.
17 Ibid.: § 3.
18 CGJCW 9i: § 195.
19 CGJCW 9ii: § 117.
20 CGJCW 9i: § 6.
21 Ibid.: § 5.
22 Ibid.: § 6.
23 Neumann, E. (1954) *The Origin and History of Consciousness*: 211, 357–9. Appendix I 'The Group and the Great Individual': 421–35.
24 Frankfort op.cit: Divinity of King 33–7, 56–7, as creator 150.
25 CGJCW 9ii: §§ 309–10.
26 CGJCWgj: S301.
27 CGJ. Seminar on Nietzsche's Zanathustria, ed. James L. Jarrett, Princeton, 1998.
28 Gardiner, 1969: sign N25.
29 CGJCW 13: § 231.
30 Faulkner (1969/1998).
31 CGJCW 8: § 790; 16: § 469 (as archetype); 10: § 695.
32 Mann, Thomas (1936) 'Freud and the Future', in *Life and Letters Vol. 15* no. 5: 90–1.
33 Piankoff, A. (1968) *Egyptian Religious Texts and Representations, Vol. 5: The Pyramid of Unas*; trans. with Commentary. Princeton.
34 This topic has been extensively explored, most recently by Noll, R. (1996) *The Jung Cult* and (1997) *The Aryan Christ*.
35 Noll has been answered by Ellwood, R. (1999) 'Carl Gustav Jung and Wotan's Return', in *The Politics of Myth: a Study of C.G. Jung, Mircea Eliade and Joseph Campbell*: Chapter 2, n.36, New York.
36 CGJCW 10: § 6: 433; § 10: 17, 447, 458.
37 CGJCW 10: §§ 371–99.

ABBREVIATIONS

AAE	*Arabian Archaeology and Epigraphy.*
AAR	*African Archaeological Review.*
Afr. Hist. Stud.	*African Historical Studies,* Boston.
Atlal	*The Journal of Saudi Arabian Archaeology*, Riyadh.
BBVO	*Berliner Beiträge zum Vorderen Orient, Berlin.*
BIFAO	*Bulletin du l'Institut Français Archéologique Orientale.*
Cd'É	*Chronique d'Égypte*, Brussels.
CRAIB	*Comptes Rendus de l'Académie des Inscriptions et Belles Lettres*, Paris.
CG	Catalogue Général, Egyptian Museum, Cairo.
CGJCW	C.G. Jung, *Collected Works* (followed by volume number).
CGJCL	C.G. Jung, *Collected Letters* vols 1 and 2.
EA	*Egyptian Archaeology.*
EWns	*East–West* new series.
JAOS	*Journal of the American Orientale Society*, New Haven, CT.
JARCE	*Journal of the American Research Center*, Cairo.
JE	*Journal d'Entrées*, Egyptian Museum, Cairo.
JEA	*Journal of Egyptian Archaeology.*
J. Econ. Social Hist. Orient	*Journal of the Economic and Social History of the Orient.*
JNES	*Journal of Near Eastern Studies.*
JOS	*Journal of Oman Studies.*
JRAS ns	*Journal of the Royal Asiatic Society* new series.
JSSEA	*Journal of the Society for the Study of Egyptian Antiquities.*
Khalifa and Rice	Al-Khalifa, H.A. and Rice, M. (eds) *Bahrain Through the Ages: The Archaeology* (Proceedings of the Bahrain Archaeological Conference 1983).
MDAIK	*Mitteilungen des Deutschen Archäologischen Instituts*, Cairo.
MDR	C.G. Jung, *Memories, Dreams, Reflections.*
News. Soc.	*Newsletter of the Society for the Study of Egyptian*

Stud. Egypt. Ant.	*Antiquities*, Ontario.
PSAS	*Proceedings of the Seminar for Arabian Studies*, London.
ZÄS	*Zeitschrift fur Ägyptische Sprache und Altertumskunde*, Leipzig and Berlin.

BIBLIOGRAPHY

Adams, B. (1974) *Ancient Hierakonpolis*, with supplement, Warminster.

—— (1988) *The Fort Cemetery at Hierakonpolis (excavated by John Garstang)*, London.

Adams, R.McC. (1965) *Land Behind Baghdad: A History of Settlement on the Diyala Plains*, Chicago.

—— (1972) 'Patterns of Urbanization in Early Southern Mesopotamia', in P.J. Ucko *et al.* (eds) *Man, Settlement and Urbanism*, London.

Adams, R.McC. *et al.* (1977) *Saudi Arabian Archaeological Reconnaissance, 1976, Preliminary Report on the First Phase of the Comprehensive Survey Program – Eastern Province, Atlal*, vol. 1.

Adams, W.Y. (1977) *Nubia: Corridor to Africa*, London.

Alster, B. (1983) 'Dilmun, Bahrain, and the Alleged Paradise in Sumerian Myth and Literature', in D. Potts (ed.) *Dilmun: New Studies in the Archaeology and Early History of Bahrain, BBVO* 2.

Amiet, P. (1966) *Elam*, Paris.

—— (1980) *La Glyptique Mésopotamienne Archäique*, Paris.

—— (1986) 'Susa and the Dilmun culture', in Khalifa and Rice.

Anderson, H.H. (1986) 'The Barbar Temple: Stratigraphy, Architecture and Interpretation', in Khalifa and Rice.

Asselberghs, H. (1961) *Chaos en Behersing*, Leiden.

Baines, J. and Málek, J.(1982) *Atlas of Ancient Egypt*, London.

Bard, K.A. (ed.) (1999) *Encyclopedia of the Archaeology of Ancient Egypt*, London.

Baumgartel, E.J. (1955) *The Cultures of Prehistoric Egypt*, 2nd edn, vol. 1, Oxford.

—— (1960) *The Cultures of Prehistoric Egypt*, vol. 2, Oxford.

—— (1970b) *Petrie's Naqada Excavation: A Supplement*, London.

Bauval, R. and Gilbert, A. (1994) *The Orion Mystery: Unlocking the Secrets of the Pyramid*.

Bauval, R. and Hancock, G. (1996) *Keeper of Genesis: A Quest for the Hidden Legacy of Mankind*, London.

Bent, J.T. (1880) 'The Bahrain Islands in the Persian Gulf', *Proceedings of the Royal Geographical Society* 12: 1–19.

Bibby, T.G. (1973) *Preliminary Survey in East Arabia 1968*, Aarhus.

—— (1986a) 'The Land of Dilmun is Holy', in Khalifa and Rice.

—— (1986b) 'The Origins of the Dilmun Civilization', in Khalifa and Rice.

Boussian, J. (1981) *Pottery from the Nile Valley*, Cambridge.

Brunton, G. and Caton Thomson, G. (1928) *The Badarian Civilisation*, London.

Burstein, S.M. (1978) *The Babyloniaca of Berossus*, Malibu.

Butzer, K.W. (1975) 'Patterns of Environmental Change in the Near East During Late Pleistocene and Early Holocene Times', in F. Wendorf and A.E. Marks (eds) *Problems in Prehistory: North Africa and the Levant*, Dallas.

Butzer, K.W. (1976) *Early Hydraulic Civilization in Egypt: A Study in Cultural Ecology*, Chicago.

Cialowicz, K.M. (1992) 'Problème de l'interpretation du relief Predynastique tardif. Motif du palmier et des giraffes', *Zeszyty Nankowe Universyteu Jagiellonski MLXVII Prace Archneologiczne 53*.

Coldstream, J.N. and Huxley, G.L. (eds) (1972) *Kythera: Excavations and Studies Conducted by the University of Pennsylvania Museum and the British School at Athens*, London.

Cornwall, P.B. (1943) 'Dilmun: the History of the Bahrain Islands Before Cyprus', unpublished PhD thesis, Harvard University.

Cornell, J. (1981) *The First Stargazers. An Introduction to the Origins of Astronomy*, London.

Crowfoot Payne, J. (1968) 'Lapis Lazuli in Early Egypt', *Iraq* 30 (1).

Doe, D.B. (1984) 'The Barbar Temple Site in Bahrain: Conservation and Presentation', in Khalifa and Rice.

—— (1986) 'The Barbar Temple: the Masonry', in Khalifa and Rice.

Drower, M.S. (1985) *Flinders Petrie: A Life in Archaeology*, London.

Dryer, G. (1992) 'Recent Discoveries at Abydos Cemetery U' in van den Brink (ed.) *The Nile Delta in Transition 4th–3rd Millennium BC: 293–9*, Proceedings of the Seminar held in Cairo 21–24 October 1990, at the Netherlands Institute of Archaeology and Asiatic Studies, Tel Aviv.

—— (1993a) 'Umm al Qa'ab. Nachuntersuchungen in früzeitlichen königsfriedhof, 5/6 Vorbericht', *MDAIK* 49: 23–46.

—— (1993b) 'A Hundred Years at Abydos', 3:10–12.

Dunbar, J.H. (1941) *The Rock Pictures of Lower Nubia*, Cairo.

Dunham, D. (1978) *Zawiyet el-Aryan*, Boston.

Editions des musées nationaux (1973) 'L'Egypte avant les Pyramides', Paris.

Edwards, I.E.S. (1993) *The Pyramids of Egypt*, 5th edn, London.

Emery, W.B. (1949–58) *Great Tombs of the First Dynasty*, vol. 1 (1949) Cairo; vol. 2 (1954), vol. 3 (1958) London.

—— (1961) *Archaic Egypt*, Harmondsworth.

Englund, R. (1983) 'Dilmun in the Archaic Uruk Corpus', in Potts (ed.) *BBVO 2*.

Fairservis, W.A. Jr *et al.* (1971–72) 'Preliminary Report on the First Two Seasons at Hierakonpolis', *JARCE* 9: 7–68.

Fakhry, A. (1959) *The Monuments of Sneferu at Dahshur*, vol. 1: *The Bent Pyramid*, Cairo.

—— (1961) *The Monuments of Sneferu at Dahshur*, vol. 2: *The Valley Temple*, 2 pts, Cairo.

Faulkner, R.O. (1969/1998) *The Ancient Egyptian Pyramid Texts*, Oxford.

Firth, C.M. *et al.* (1935) *Excavations at Saqqara: The Step Pyramid*. 2 vols. Cairo.

Frankfort, H. (1948) *Kingship and the Gods*, Chicago.

—— (1956) *The Birth of Civilization in the Near East*, London.

Frankfort, H. *et al.* (1949) *Before Philosophy*, Harmondsworth.

Friedman, R. and Adams, B. (eds) (1992) *The Followers of Horus*, Oxford.

Frifelt, K. (1975a) 'A Possible Link Between the Jemdet Nasr and the Urum an-Nar Graves of Oman', *JOS* 1: 57–80.

—— (1975b) 'On Prehistoric Settlement and Chronology of the Oman Peninsula', EWns 25 (3–4): 359–424.

Gardiner, A. (1969) *Egyptian Grammar*, Oxford.

Garstang, J. (1902) *Mahâsna and Bêt Khallaf*, London.

—— (1904) *Tombs of the Third Egyptian Dynasty at Reqaqnah and Bet Khallaf*, London.

Goettler, G.W. *et al.* (1976) 'A Preliminary Discussion of Ancient Mining in the Sultanate of Oman', *JOS* 2.

Goneim, M.Z. (1956) *The Buried Pyramid*, London.

—— (1957) *Horus Sekhem Khet*, vol. 1, Cairo.

Griffiths, J.G. (1960) *The Conflict of Horus and Seth*, Liverpool.

—— (1966) '*The Origins of Osiris*', Munchner Agyptologische Studien 9.

Grimal, N. (1992) *A History of Ancient Egypt*, trans. Ian Shaw, London.

Hassan, F.A. (1980) 'Radiocarbon Chronology of Archaic Egypt', *JNES* 39: 203–7.

Hayes, W.C. (1953) *The Scepter of Egypt*, vol. 1, Cambridge, Mass.

—— (1990) *The Scepter of Egypt*, Fifth printing, revised with accession numbers for all objects illustrated, Cambridge, Mass.

—— (1984) *Most Ancient Egypt*, Chicago.

Hays, T.R. (1975) 'Neolithic Settlement of the Sahara as it Relates to the Nile Valley', in F. Wendorf and A.E. Marks (eds) *Problems in Prehistory: North Africa and the Levant*, Dallas.

Helck, H.W. (1970) 'Zwei Einzelprobleme der thinitischen Chronologie', *MDAIK* 26: 83–5.

Hendrickx, S. (1999) Review of Wilkinson, T.A.H. State Formation in Egypt: Chronology and Society, *JEA 85 241–5*.

Hennessy, J.B. (1967) *The Foreign Relations of Palestine During the Early Bronze Age*, London.

Hepper, N. (1969) 'Arabian and African Frankincense Trees', *JEA* 55: 66–72.

Herrman, G. (1968) 'Lapis Lazuli: the Early Phases of its Trade', *Iraq* 30 (1).

Heyerdahl, T. (1980) *The Tigris Expedition*, London.

Hoffman, M.A. (1979) *Egypt Before the Pharaohs: The Prehistoric Foundations of Egyptian Civilization*, New York.

—— (1980) 'A Rectangular Amratian House from Hierakonpolis', *JNES* 39: 119–37.

—— (1982) *The Predynastic of Hierakonpolis – An Interim Report*, Cairo.

Højgaard, K. (1986) 'Dental Anthropological Investigations on Bahrain', in Khalifa and Rice.

Hornung, E. (1971–83) *Conceptions of God in Ancient Egypt*, trans. J. Baines, London.

IFAO (1981) *Un Siécle de Fouilles Françaises en Égypte 1880–1980*, Paris.

Jenkins N. and Ross, J. (1980) *The Boat Beneath the Pyramid*, London.

Jung, C.G., *Collected Works* vols 5, 9 Pt. 1, 9 Pt. 2, 10, 14.

—— (1973, 1976) *Collected Letters*, 2 vols., London.

—— (1963) *Memories, Dreams, Reflections*, recorded and edited by Aniela Jaffe, London and Glasgow. (Originally published as *Erinnerungen, Träume, Gedanken*).

Kanawati, N. (1977) *The Egyptian Administration in the Old Kingdom*, Warminster.

Kantor, H.J. (1944) 'The Final Phase of Predynastic Culture: Gerzean or Semainean?' *JNES* 3: 110–36.

—— (1952) 'Further Evidence for Early Mesopotamian Relations with Egypt', *JNES* 11: 239–50.

—— (1965) 'The Relative Chronology of Egypt and its Foreign Correlations Before the Late Bronze Age', in R.W. Ehrich (ed.) *Chronologies in Old World Archaeology*, Chicago.

Kees, H. (1961) *Ancient Egypt: A Cultural Topography*, ed. T.G.H. James, trans. T.F.D. Morrow, London and Chicago.

Kemp, B.J. (1966) 'Abydos and the Royal Tombs of the First Dynasty', *JEA* 52: 13–22.

—— (1967) 'The Egyptian First Dynasty Royal Cemetery', *Antiquity* 41: 22–32.

—— (1973) 'Photographs of the Decorated Tomb at Hierakonpolis', *JEA* 59: 36–43.

—— (1982) 'Automatic Analysis of Predynastic Cemeteries: a New Method for an Old Problem', *JEA* 68: 5–15.

Al Khalifa, H.A. and Rice, M. (eds) (1986) *Bahrain Through the Ages: The Archaeology* (Proceedings of the Bahrain Historical Conference 1983), London.

El Khouli, A. (1978) *Egyptian Stone Vessels*, 3 vols, Mainz-am-Rhein.

Kjaerum, P. (1983) *Failaka/Dilmun: The Second Millennium Settlements*, vol. 2: *The Stamp and Cylinder Seals*, Aarhus.

—— (1986) 'The Dilmun Seals as Testimony of Long-distance Relations in the Early Second Millennium', in Khalifa and Rice.

Krzyzaniak, L. (1977) *Early Farming Cultures on the Lower Nile: The Predynastic Period in Egypt*, Warsaw.

—— (1979) 'Trends in the Socio-economic Development of Egyptian Predynastic Societies', *Acts of the First International Congress of Egyptologists*, Cairo.

Kuchman, L. (1977) 'The Titles of Queenship: part I, the Evidence from the Old Kingdom', *News Soc. Stud. Egypt. Ant.* 9–12.

Kuhrt (1995) *The Ancient Near East, c. 3000–330 BC, Vol. 1.* 2 vols., London.

Landstrom, B. (1970) *Ships of the Pharaohs*, London.

Larsen, C.E. (1983a) *Life and Land Use in the Bahrain Islands: The Geoarchaeology of an Ancient Society*, Chicago.

—— (1983b) 'The Early Environment and Hydrology of Ancient Bahrain', in Potts (ed.) *Dilmun, BBVO* 2.

Lauer, J.P. (1973) 'Remarques sur la plannification de la construction de la grande pyramide', *BIFAO* 73: 127–42.

—— (1974) *Le mystère des pyramides*, Paris.

—— (1976) 'A propos du prétendu désastre de la pyramide de Meidoum', *C d'E* 51: 72–89.

Lehner, M. (1997) *The Complete Pyramids*, London.

Lichtheim, M. (1975) *Ancient Egyptian Literature: A Book of Readings. 1 The Old and Middle Kingdoms*, Berkeley, California.

Lucas, A. and Harris, J.R. (1962) *Ancient Materials and Industries*, 4th edn, London.

Lupton, C. (1981) 'The Other Egypt. In Search of the Lost Pharaohs', *Lore* 31 (3): 2–21.

McClure, H.A. (1971) *The Arabian Peninsula and Prehistoric Populations*, Miami.

Mackay, E. *et al.* (1929) *Bahrein and Hemamieh,* Publications of the British School of Archaeology in Egypt, vol. 47, London.

Masry, A.H. (1974) *Prehistory in Northern Arabia: the Problem of Interregional Interaction*, Miami.

Matheson, I. *et al.* (1997) The National Museums of Scotland Saqqara Survey Project 1993–1995: Gisr el-Mudir, *JEA* 83: 17–54.

Mellaart, J. (1965) *Çatal Hüyük: A Neolithic Town in Anatolia*, London.

Meltzer, E.S. (1970) 'An Observation on the Hieroglyph *mr*', *JEA* 56.

Mercer, S. (1959) *Earliest Intellectual Man's Idea of the Cosmos*, London.

Michalowski, K. (1969) *The Art of Ancient Egypt*, London.

Midant-Reynes, B. (1992/2000) *The Predynastic of Egypt: From the First Egyptians to the First Pharaohs*, trans. I. Shaw, London.

Midant-Reynes, B. *et al.* (1996) 'The Predynastic Site of Adäima', *EA* 9.

Mond, Sir Robert, and Myers, O.H. (1937) *Cemeteries of Armant*, 2 vols, London.

Moorey, P.R.S. (1983) 'From Gulf to Delta in the Fourth Millennium BCE: the Syrian Connection', in *Ancient Egypt*, Oxford.

Morgan, J. de (1903) *Fouilles à Dahchour en 1894–1895*, Vienna.

—— (1925–27) *Prehistoire Oriental*, 3 vols, Paris.

Mortensen, P. (1971) 'On the Date of the Barbar Temple in Bahrain', *Artibus Asiae* 33.

—— (1984) 'The Bahrain Temple: its Chronology and Foreign Relations Reconsidered', in Khalifa and Rice.

Moussa, A.M. and Altenmuller, H. (1971) *The Tomb of Nefer and Ka-Hay*, Mainz-am-Rhein.

Newberry, P.E. (1922) 'The Set Rebellion of the IInd Dynasty', *Ancient Egypt*, 1922, pt 2.

Nibbi, A. (1981) *Ancient Egypt and some Eastern Neighbours*, New Jersey.

Nissen, H.J. (1986) 'The Occurrence of Dilmun in the Oldest Texts of Mesopotamia', in Khalifa and Rice.

Nordstrom, H.A. (1972) *Neolithic and A-group Sites*, Uppsala.

Nunn, J.F. (1996) *Ancient Egyptian Medicine*, London.

Oates, J. (1986) 'The Gulf in Prehistory', in Khalifa and Rice.

O'Connor, D.B. (1971) 'Ancient Egypt and Black Africa – Early Contacts', *Expedition* 14: 638–47.

—— (1974) 'Political Systems and Archaeological Data in Egypt: 2600–1780 BC', *World Archaeology* 6: 15–38.

—— (1993) *Ancient Nubia: Egypt's Rival in Africa*, Pennsylvania.

Oppenheim, A.L. (1954) 'The Seafaring Merchants of Ur', *JAOS* 74.

Petrie, W.M.F. (1896) *Naqada and Ballas*, London.

—— (1900) *The Royal Tombs of the First Dynasty*, pt I: *Egypt Exploration Fund Memoir*, 18, London.

—— (1901a) *The Royal Tombs of the Earliest Dynasties*, pt II: *Egypt Exploration Fund Memoir*, 21, London.

—— (1901b) *Diospolis Parva, Egypt Exploration Fund Memoir*, 20, London.

—— (1902) *Abydos*, pt I: *Egypt Exploration Fund Memoir*, 22, London.

—— (1903) *Abydos*, pt II: *Egypt Exploration Fund Memoir*, 24, London.

—— (1921) *Prehistoric Egypt*, Corpus, London.

—— (1939) *The Making of Egypt*, London.

—— (1953) *Ceremonial Slate Palettes: Corpus of Proto-Dynastic Pottery*, London.

Petrie, W.M.F. and Quibell, J.E. (1895) *Naqada and Ballas*, London.

Piankoff, A. (1968) *The Pyramid of Unas*, Princeton.

Porada, E. (1980) 'A Lapis Lazuli Figurine from Hierakonpolis in Egypt', *Iranica Antiqua* 15.

Porter, B. and Moss, R.L.B. (1927–51) *Topographical Bibliography of Ancient Egyptian Hieroglyphic Texts, Reliefs and Paintings*, 1st edn, 7 vols, Oxford.

—— (1972) *Topographical Bibliography of Ancient Egyptian Hieroglyphic Texts, Reliefs and Paintings*, 2nd edn, vol. 2.

Potts, D. (1983) 'Barbar miscellanies', in D. Potts (ed.) *Dilmun: New Studies in the Early History of Bahrain, BBVO* Band 2.

—— (1984) 'The Chronology of the Archaeological Assemblages from the Head of the Arabian Gulf to the Arabian Sea (8000–1750 BC)', in R.W. Ehrich (ed.) *Chronologies in Old World Archaeology*, 3rd edn, Chicago.

—— (1990) *The Arabian Gulf in Antiquity. Vol.1: From Prehistory to the Fall of the Achamenid Empire*, Oxford.

Quibell, J.E. (1898) *El Kab*, London.

—— (1900) *Hierakonpolis*, pt 1, London.

—— (1907) *Excavations at Saqqara (1905–6)*, Cairo.

Quibell J.E. and Green F.W. (1902) *Hierakonpolis*, pt 2, London.

Reader, C. (2000) 'Giza Before the Fourth Dynasty', *The Journal of the Ancient Chronology Forum*, vol. 9: 5–21.

Reisner, G.A. (1923) *Excavations at Kerma*, pts 1–5, Cambridge, Mass.

—— (1931) *Mycerinus: The Temples of the Third Pyramid at Giza*, Cambridge, Mass.

—— (1936) *The Development of the Egyptian Tomb down to the Accession of Cheops*, Cambridge, Mass. and London.

Reisner, G.A. and Smith, W.S. (1955) *A History of the Giza Necropolis*, vol. 2: *The Tomb of Hetep-heres the Mother of Cheops*, Cambridge, Mass.

Réunion des Musées Nationaux (1999) *L'art égyptien au temps des pyramides*, Paris.

Reymond, E.A.E. (1969) *The Mythical Origin of the Egyptian Temple*, Manchester.

Rice, M. (1983) *The Barbar Temple Site, Bahrain*, Bahrain.

—— (1984b) 'The Island on the Edge of the World', in Khalifa and Rice.

—— (1994) *The Archaeology of the Arabian Gulf: An Introduction*, London.

—— (1990) *Egypt's Making: The Origins of the Egyptian State 5000–2000 BC*, London.

—— (1997) *Egypt's Legacy: The Archetypes of Western Civilization 3000–300 BC*, London.

—— (1998) *The Power of the Bull*, London.

—— (1999) *Who's Who in Ancient Egypt*, London.

Roth, A.M. (1993) 'Opening of the Mouth', *JEA* 79: 57–79.

Rundle Clark, R.T. (1969) *Myth and Symbol in Ancient Egypt,* Manchester.

Saad, Z.Y. (1947) *Royal Excavations at Saqqara and Helwan* 1941–45, Cairo.

—— (1969) The *Excavations at Helwan: Art and Civilization in the First and Second Egyptian Dynasties*, Oklahoma.

Saleh, A. and Sounouzian, H. (1987) *The Egyptian Museum, Cairo: The Official Catalogue*, Mainz.

Sanlaville, P.J. (1986) 'Shoreline Changes in Bahrain since the Beginning of Human Occupation', in Khalifa and Rice.

Scamuzzi, E. (n.d.) *Egyptian Art in the Egyptian Museum of Turin*, New York.

Sellers, J.B. (1992) *The Death of Gods in Ancient Egypt*, London.

Seidelmayer, S.J. (1996) 'Town and State in the Early Old Kingdom: a View from Elephantine' in Spencer, J. (ed.) *Aspects of Early Egypt*, London.

Shaw, I. (ed.) (1999) *The Oxford History of Ancient Egypt*, Oxford.

Simpson, W.K. (ed.) (1973) *The Literature of Ancient Egypt; an Anthology of Stories, Instructions and Poetry*, with translations by R.O. Faulkner, E.F. Wente Jr, and W.K. Simpson, New Haven, Conn. and London.

Smith, C.H. (1890) 'The Bahrain Islands in the Persian Gulf', *Proceedings of the Royal Geographical Society* 12.

Smith, H.S. (1964) 'Egypt and C14 dating', *Antiquity* 38: 32–7.

—— (1966) 'The Nubian B-group', *Kush* 14: 69–124.

—— 'The Making of Egypt: A Review of the Influence of Susa and Sumer on Upper Egypt and Lower Nubia in the Fourth Millennium BC', in Friedman and Adams (eds) *The Followers of Horus*, Oxford.

Smith, P.E.L. (1968) 'Problems and Possibilities of the Prehistoric Rock Art of Northern Africa', *Afr. Hist. Stud.* 1: 1–39.

Smith, W.S. (1946) *A History of Egyptian Sculpture and Painting in the Old Kingdom,* Boston and London.

—— (1958) *The Art and Architecture of Ancient Egypt*, London.

Spencer, A.J. (1993) *Early Egypt: The Rise of Civilization in the Nile Valley*, London.

Spencer, J. (ed.) (1996) *Aspects of Early Egypt*, London.

Steindorf, G. (1913) *Der Gräb des Ti*, Leipzig.

Stevenson Smith (1946–49) *A History of Egyptian Sculpture and Painting in the Old Kingdom*, Oxford.

Strouhal, E. (1989–92) *Life in Ancient Egypt*, Cambridge.

Tompkins, P. (1972) *Secrets of the Great Pyramid*, London.

Trigger, B.G. (1965) *History and Settlement in Lower Nubia*, New Haven, Conn.

—— (1968) *Beyond History: The Methods of Prehistory*, New York.

—— (1976) *Nubia under the Pharaohs*, London.

Trigger, B.G. *et al.* (1983) *Ancient Egypt, A Social History*, Cambridge.

Ucko, P.J. (1968) 'Anthropomorphic Figurines of Predynastic Egypt and Neolithic Crete', *Occasional Papers of the Royal Anthropological Institute*, 24.

—— (1976) 'The Predynastic Cemetery N 7000 at Naga-ed-Der', *C d'E* 42: 345–53.

Vandier, J. (1936) *La famine dans l'Egypte ancienne*, Cairo.

—— (1952) *Manuel d'archéologie égyptienne*, vol. 1, Paris.

—— (1958) *Manuel d'archéologie égyptienne*, vol. 3: *Les grandes époques, la statuaire*, Paris.

Velde, H. te (1967) *Seth, God of Confusion: a Study of His Role in Egyptian Mythology and Religion*, Leiden.

Verner, M. (1994) *Forgotten Pharaohs, Lost Pyramids*, Prague.

—— (2002) *The Pyramids: Their Archaeology and History*, London.

Waddell, W.G. (1940) *Manetho*, Cambridge, Mass. and London.

Ward, W.A. (1964) 'Relations Between Egypt and Mesopotamia from Prehistoric Times to the End of the Middle Kingdom', *J. Econ. Social Hist. Orient* 7: 1–45 and 121–35.

—— (1970) 'The Origin of Egyptian Design-amulets ("Button Seals")', *JEA* 56: 65–80.

—— (1971) *Egypt and the East Mediterranean World 2200–1900 BC*, Beirut.

Way, T. von der (1992) 'Excavations at Tell el-Fara'in/Buto in 1987–1989' in E.C.M. van den Brink (ed.) *The Nile Delta in Transition 4th–3rd Millennium BC* 1–10, Tel Aviv.

—— (1996) 'Early Dynastic Architecture at Tell el-Fara'in/Buto', in M. Bietak (ed.) *Haus und Palast in alten Ägypten/House and Palace in Ancient Egypt*, Vienna.

Weeks, K. (1972) 'The Niched Gateway at Hierakonpolis', *JARCE* 9.

—— (ed.) (1979) *Egyptology and the Social Sciences, Five Studies*, Cairo.

Weigall, A.E.P. (1907) *A Report on the Antiquities of Lower Nubia*, Cairo.

—— (1909) *Travels in the Upper Egyptian Desert*, London and Edinburgh.

Weil T.R. (1961) *Recherches sur la 1ere Dynastie et Les Temps Prepharaoniques*, 2 vols, Cairo.

Weisgerber, G. (1978) 'Evidence of Ancient Mining Sites in Oman: a Preliminary Report', *JOS* 4.

Wendorf, F. (ed.) (1968) *The Prehistory of Nubia*, 2 vols, Dallas.

Wendorf, F. and Schild, R. (1980) *Prehistory of the Eastern Sahara*, New York.

Wendorf, F. *et al.* (1970) 'Egyptian Prehistory: Some New Concepts', *Science* 169: 1161–71.

Wilkinson, T.A.H. (1995) 'A New King in the Western Desert', *JEA* 81: 205–9.

—— (1999a) *Early Dynastic Egypt*, London.

—— (1999b) 'State Formation in Egypt', JEA 85:

—— (2000) 'What King is this: Narmer and the Concept of the Ruler', *JEA* 86: 23–32.

Williams, B. (1980) 'The Lost Pharaohs of Nubia', *Archaeology* 33: 12–21.

—— (1986) *Excavations between Abu Simbel and the Sudan Frontier Vol. III. The A-Group Royal Cemetery at Qustul. Cemetery L*, Chicago.

Wilson, J.A. (1951) *The Burden of Egypt: An Interpretation of Ancient Egyptian Culture*, Chicago. (Reprinted as *The Culture of Ancient Egypt*).

Winkler, H.A. (1938–89) *Rock Drawings of Southern Upper Egypt*, 2 vols, London.

Winlock, H.E. (1947) *The Rise and Fall of the Middle Kingdom in Thebes*, New York.

Wood, W. (1987) 'The Archaic Stone Tombs at Helwan', *JEA* 73: 59–70.

Zarins, J. (1978) 'Steatite Vessels in the Riyadh Museum', *Atlal* 2.

—— (1982) 'Early Rock Art of Saudi Arabia', *Archaeology* 35.

Zarins, J. *et al.* (1980) 'Preliminary Report on the Central and Southwestern Provinces Survey', *Atlal* 4.

Zeuner, F.E. (1963) *A History of Domesticated Animals*, London.

INDEX

eBooks – at www.eBookstore.tandf.co.uk

A library at your fingertips!

eBooks are electronic versions of printed books. You can store them on your PC/laptop or browse them online.

They have advantages for anyone needing rapid access to a wide variety of published, copyright information.

eBooks can help your research by enabling you to bookmark chapters, annotate text and use instant searches to find specific words or phrases. Several eBook files would fit on even a small laptop or PDA.

NEW: Save money by eSubscribing: cheap, online access to any eBook for as long as you need it.

Annual subscription packages

We now offer special low-cost bulk subscriptions to packages of eBooks in certain subject areas. These are available to libraries or to individuals.

For more information please contact webmaster.ebooks@tandf.co.uk

We're continually developing the eBook concept, so keep up to date by visiting the website.

www.eBookstore.tandf.co.uk

932 R497a

Rice, Michael, 1928-

Egypt's making